CAMBRIDGE

Official Cambridge Exam Preparation

Be Curious

Teacher's Book 2

Stephanie Dimond-Bayir

With Caroline Nixon and Michael Tomlinson

Map of the book

	Vocabulary	Grammar	Cross-curricular	Literature	Assessment
Hello Page 4	Main character names Numbers Colours	**Greetings and introductions** *What's your name?* *I'm Henrietta.* *How old are you?* *I'm three.*			
1 Our new school Mission: Make our classroom English Page 6	Classroom objects and people Extension of classroom objects Sounds and spelling: *p*, *b*	***Where …?*** **Prepositions *in*, *on*, *under*, *next to*** *Where's the crayon?* *It's on the desk.* **Singular and plural nouns** ***this/these*** *What's this?* *It's a window.* *What are these?* *They're windows.*	***Be kind at school*** Learn about being kind to classmates	***The first day*** A play script Social and emotional skill: Helping others	Pre A1 Starters Reading and Writing Part 1 Speaking Parts 1 and 2
2 All about us Mission: Make an *All about me* book Page 18	Family Parts of the body Sounds and spelling: *th*, *t*	***is/are*** *Who is she?* *She's Jenny. She's a girl.* *Who is he?* *He's Jim. He's a boy.* ***have/haven't got*** *I've got brown hair.* *They haven't got green eyes.* *Have you got red hair?* *Yes, I have. / No, I haven't.*	***Using our senses*** Learn about the five senses and sense organs	***Sara's favourite game*** A real-life story Social and emotional skill: Showing concern for others	Pre A1 Starters Reading and Writing Part 2 Speaking Part 2
3 Fun on the farm Mission: Make a farm Page 30	Farm animals Adjectives Sounds and spelling: *c*, *k*, *ck*	***is/are* + adjective** **adjective + noun** *He's a nice cat.* *They aren't old chickens.* ***has/hasn't got*** *It's got long ears.* *It hasn't got small feet.* *Has it got a long face?* *Yes, it has. / No, it hasn't.*	***What do animals give us?*** Learn about animal products	***How cows got their spots*** A fantasy story Social and emotional skill: Identifying the feelings of others	Pre A1 Starters Reading and Writing Part 3 Speaking Part 3
	Review units 1–3				
4 Food with friends Mission: Organise a picnic Page 44	Food and drink Extension of food and drink Sounds and spelling: *a*	***like/don't like*** *I like chocolate.* *Harry doesn't like chocolate.* *Do you like chocolate?* *Yes, I do. / No, I don't.* **Making requests and offers** *Can I have some chocolate, please?* *Here you are.* *Would you like some ice cream?* *Yes, please. / No, thank you.*	***Making a recipe*** Learn about ingredients and methods of cooking	***A picnic with friends*** A real-life story Social and emotional skill: Sharing	Pre A1 Starters Listening Part 3 Speaking Part 4

	Vocabulary	Grammar	Cross-curricular	Literature	Assessment
5 Happy birthday! Mission: Have a present-giving party Page 56	Toys Extension of toys Sounds and spelling: *h*	***whose …?*** **Possessive *'s*** **Possessive adjectives *my, your, his, her, our, their*** *Whose bike is this?* *It's Jim's bike. His bike's orange.* ***want/wants*** *Does he want a teddy?* *Yes, he does. / No, he doesn't.* *What does he want? He wants a helicopter.*	***Shapes around us*** Learn about shapes	***The twins and their robots*** A real-life story Social and emotional skill: Saying sorry	Pre A1 Starters Listening Part 2 Speaking Part 4
6 A day out Mission: Plan a wildlife tour Page 68	Vehicles and places Zoo animals Sounds and spelling: *ai, a–e*	***there is/are*** *There's a car.* *There aren't any shops.* *Are there any animals?* *Yes, there are. / No, there aren't.* ***let's …*** *Let's play a game.* *That's a good idea.*	***Animals in the wild*** Learn about animal habitats	***When we go to the zoo*** A poem Social and emotional skill: Understanding and expressing feelings	Pre A1 Starters Reading and Writing Part 4 Speaking Parts 1 and 2
	Review units 4–6				
7 Let's play! Mission: Plan a sports day Page 82	Sports and hobbies Sports verbs and extension of sports Sounds and spelling: *s*	**Present continuous** *What are you doing?* *I'm riding a horse.* *What's she doing?* *She's swimming.* *Are they cleaning the car?* *Yes, they are. / No, they're not.* ***can* for permission** *Can we play tennis?* *Yes, you can, but you can't play here.*	***Look after your body!*** Learn about how we can keep our bodies strong	***A good friend*** A real-life story Social and emotional skill: Identifying ways of being a good friend	Pre A1 Starters Listening Part 1 Speaking Part 3
8 At home Mission: Invite a friend to my house Page 94	Rooms and objects in the house Extension of objects in the house Sounds and spelling: *i*	***can* for ability** *I can swim.* *He can't sing.* *Can you ride a horse?* *Yes, I can. / No, I can't.* **Prepositions *in front of, between, behind*** *There's a small rug in front of the armchair.*	***Houses around the world*** Learn about different kinds of houses around the world	***The clock on the wall*** A poem Social and emotional skill: Comforting others	Pre A1 Starters Listening Part 4 Speaking Part 4
9 Happy holidays Mission: Go on holiday Page 106	Clothes At the beach Sounds and spelling: *j, h*	**Imperatives** *Look at this T-shirt.* *Clean those shoes.* ***like/enjoy* + gerund** ***me too / so do I*** *I like flying my kite.* *So do I.* *I enjoy taking photos.* *Me too.*	***What can we see on holiday?*** Learn about features of natural landscapes	***The monkey and the shark*** A traditional story Social and emotional skill: Identifying friends	Pre A1 Starters Reading and Writing Part 5 Speaking Parts 3 and 4
	Review units 7–9				

Checklist for Pre A1 Starters preparation

Paper	Part	Task	Practice
Listening 20 minutes	1	Draw lines between names and people inside a picture.	*Preparation*: Pupil's Book Unit 7 Page 92 *Practice*: Activity Book Unit 7 Page 92, Test Generator Unit 1 Starters Progress Test
	2	Write numbers and spellings of names	*Preparation*: Pupil's Book Unit 5 Page 66 *Practice*: Activity Book Unit 5 Page 66, Test Generator Unit 6 Starters Progress Test
	3	Multiple choice. Tick the correct picture.	*Preparation*: Pupil's Book Unit 4 Page 54 *Practice*: Activity Book Unit 4 Page 54, Test Generator Unit 4 Starters Progress Test
	4	Follow instructions and colour parts of a picture.	*Preparation*: Pupil's Book Unit 8 Page 104 *Practice*: Activity Book Unit 8 Page 104, Test Generator Unit 8 Starters Progress Test
Reading and Writing 20 minutes	1	Put a tick or cross to show whether the sentence is correct or not for a picture.	*Preparation*: Pupil's Book Unit 1 Page 16 *Practice*: Activity Book Unit 1 Page 16, Test Generator Unit 1 Starters Progress Test
	2	Write yes or no to show whether a sentence about a picture is true or false.	*Preparation*: Pupil's Book Unit 2 Page 28 *Practice*: Activity Book Unit 2 Page 28, Test Generator Unit 2 Starters Progress Test
	3	Write words, using given jumbled letters, next to a picture.	*Preparation*: Pupil's Book Unit 3 Page 40 *Practice*: Activity Book Unit 3 Page 40, Test Generator Unit 3 Starters Progress Test
	4	Gap fill about an illustrated subject. Write one noun in each gap.	*Preparation*: Pupil's Book Unit 6 Page 78 *Practice*: Activity Book Unit 6 Page 78, Test Generator Unit 6 Starters Progress Test
	5	Write one-word answers to questions about three scene pictures.	*Preparation*: Pupil's Book Unit 9 Page 116 *Practice*: Activity Book Unit 9 Page 116, Test Generator Unit 9 Starters Progress Test
Speaking 3–5 minutes	1	Point to parts of the picture and place object cards in the correct place.	*Preparation*: Activity Book Unit 1 Page 15, Activity Book Unit 6 Page 77 *Practice*: Test Generator Starters Practice Test
	2	Answer questions about the picture.	*Preparation*: Activity Book Unit 6 Page 77 *Practice*: Test Generator Starters Practice Test
	3	Answer questions about the remaining object cards.	*Preparation*: Activity Book Unit 9 Page 115 *Practice*: Test Generator Starters Practice Test
	4	Answer personal questions.	*Preparation*: Pupil's Book All Units Pages 15, 27, 39, 53, 65, 77, 91, 103 and 115 *Practice*: Test Generator Starters Practice Test

About Be Curious

Be Curious

What is Be Curious?

Be Curious is an engaging and effective approach to learning which uses:

- Lively activities with clear objectives
- Age-appropriate, engaging topics which support learner progress and collaborative learning
- Real-world contexts and language
- Development of life competencies and test skills
- Scaffolded tasks which support learners of all abilities
- A unifying learner-centred methodology which supports life-long learning.

Be Curious provides both general English and comprehensive preparation for Cambridge English Qualifications, jointly published with Cambridge Assessment English. Student-centred learning is a core part of the course, with ongoing unit tasks giving ample opportunity for collaborative learning.

Be Curious rigorously introduces and practices all of the language required by YLE/Key exams, and is informed by research in second language acquisition and learner language.

Key features of Be Curious

Activities are based on **real-world skills and situations** that learners find engaging and fun. All four skills – reading, writing, listening and speaking – are used to explore interesting topics. The activities scaffold the learning to support both stronger and weaker learners. Grammar and vocabulary are developed through communicative activities which have a clear purpose and encourage learners to use language naturally. All new language is heard, read, written and spoken as learners acquire it and the language is then consolidated throughout, building as the units progress.

Be Curious and the Key Competencies

Key Competencies are a combination of knowledge, skills and attitudes designed to help learners develop tools which they can use both academically and in a wider social context. As an aid to lifelong learning they lay the foundations for the future when they move on to higher level studies and the working adult world.

School subjects in primary education should all contribute to the development of the eight different competencies established by the new LOMLOE law in Spain. English language, of course, has a direct connection to the competence of linguistic communication. *Be Curious*, however, offers numerous opportunities for the development of all the eight competencies throughout the course and also includes Emotional competence, which while not being part of the official curriculum, is frequently identified as having equal importance.

The official competencies are mapped in the Teacher's Book with icons to help you identify them:

	C1 Competence in linguistic communication
	C2 Multilingual competence
	C3 Mathematics, science and technology competence
	C4 Digital competence
	C5 Personal, social and learning to learn competence
	C6 Citizenship competence
	C7 Entrepreneurship competence
	C8 Competence in cultural awareness and expression

Be Curious and the Cambridge Life Competencies Framework

There have been many initiatives over the years to address the skills and competencies our students need for the 21st century and for the jobs of the future we cannot even anticipate yet. At Cambridge, we have developed a way to evaluate life competencies in the context of English language programmes: **The Cambridge Life Competencies Framework.** Competencies are a combination of knowledge, skill and attitude:

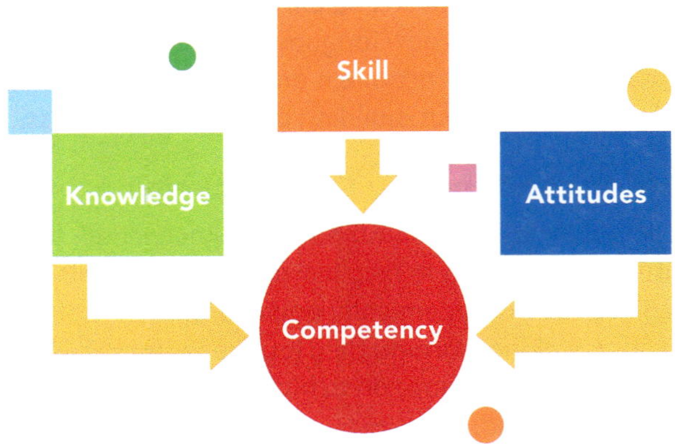

The Cambridge Life Competencies Framework groups competencies into six core areas: Creative Thinking, Critical Thinking, Learning to Learn, Communication, Collaboration and Social Responsibilities. There are three foundational layers that span the six core areas: Emotional Development, Digital Literacy and Discipline Knowledge. The six core areas and three foundational layers correlate to the key competencies set out by the LOMLOE law in Spain:

The Cambridge Life Competencies	LOMLOE Key Competencies
CREATIVE THINKING	C7
CRITICAL THINKING	C3 C7
LEARNING TO LEARN	C3 C5
COMMUNICATION	C1 C2
COLLABORATION	C5 C6 C7
SOCIAL RESPONSIBILITIES	C5 C6 C8
Emotional Development	C5
Digital Literacy	C4
Discipline Knowledge	C3

Each unit of *Be Curious* maps to skills within the Cambridge Life Competencies Framework. This provides opportunities for formative assessment and assessment through competencies to gain a broad view of each learner's development. The backbone to this approach is through a series of **Learning Situations** or projects called Missions.

Missions

The Life Competencies Framework is a key feature of the unit Missions, and the enquiry-led approach builds on creativity, critical thinking, problem solving and decision making.

Each unit is structured around a 'Mission' which helps learners to set objectives at the beginning and understand their end goal and learning outcomes. Outcomes are also clearly stated at the beginning of each lesson so that learners can understand and think about them. The teacher's notes suggest creative ways to share these with the learners.

Missions are based on real-world **learning situations** with a focus on real English. They give learners the opportunity to build up a portfolio of their work as evidence of their learning and help them to reflect and evaluate their own learning even at a young age. As part of this approach, there are frequent opportunities for learners to reflect on what they have learnt and help them plan for the next stage of learning, with practical tips on how teachers can help learners to do this.

In addition, there is a bank of **Key Competence Activities** at the back of the Pupil's Book related to each unit topic and the eight Key Competencies. These can be used to build around the Missions, or simply reinforce the competencies through class and home activities.

Cross-curricular learning

The **cross-curricular** sections also develop life competencies through critical thinking and wider discipline knowledge. Content learning is developed through the second language vice versa. Cross-curricular learning supports linguistic diversity and is a powerful tool that can have a strong impact on language learning.

Why cross-curricular learning is important for language learning

Research on second language acquisition has shown that exposure to naturally occurring language is necessary to achieve a good level of competence in the language. Acquiring a second language is a long and natural process. Learners need to have access to spontaneous speech in an interactive context and the cross-curricular lessons in *Be Curious* provide learners with this access. Learners have to expand their linguistic resources in order to deal with the demands of content learning. Using a second language to grasp non-language content requires a depth of processing which leads to improved language acquisition. Learning is a problem-solving activity and cross-curricular learning requires learners to solve problems through a second language.

The benefits of using cross-curricular learning in the classroom

- Cross-curricular learning relies on intrinsic motivation, that is, the learners are involved in interesting and meaningful activities while using the language. Lessons provide opportunities for incidental language learning. Incidental learning has been shown to be effective and long lasting.
- Through exposure to interesting and authentic content, cross-curricular learning leads to greater involvement and helps increase learner motivation.
- Through the interactive and co-operational nature of the tasks, cross-curricular learning helps boost self-esteem, raise self-confidence, build learner independence and teach learner organisational skills.
- Through the integration of language and content, cross-curricular learning encourages creative thinking.
- Cross-curricular learning fosters learning to learn through the use of learning strategies and study skills.

Cross-curricular learning in Be Curious level 2

Every age has its own characteristics. In this level, learners require longer input to be able to show production. The acquisition of the second language has to grow to allow them to understand and repeat the content. This can be achieved by following a communicative approach. In level 2 we therefore mostly focus on oral skills in cross-curricular lessons in order to produce accurate reading and writing skills in the future. The topics covered in the cross-curricular lessons have been chosen to make the learners feel secure with the content in each lesson and to motivate them to use the English language.

Preparation for Cambridge Pre A1 Starters in Be Curious 2

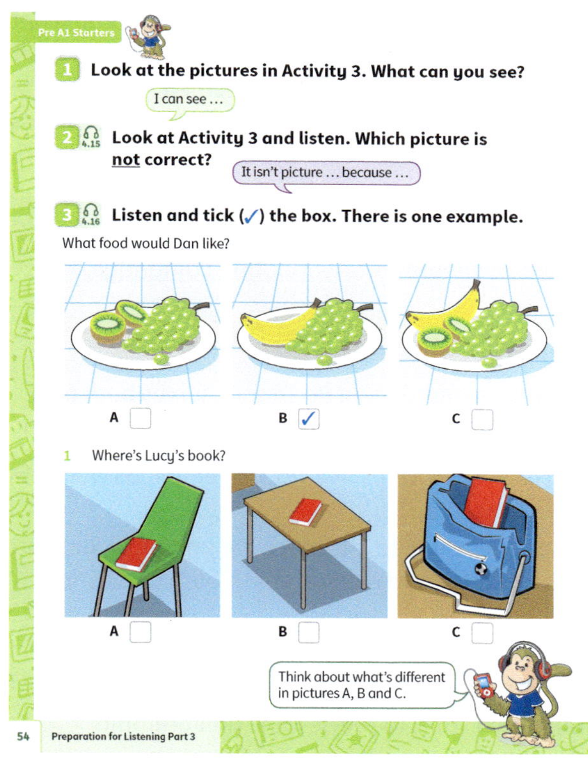

Through the unique partnership of Cambridge University Press & Assessment, *Be Curious* is the first course to naturally integrate test preparation and formative assessment in a fun and effective English course. This well-rounded formula equips learners with the skills and abilities to approach Cambridge English tests with real confidence.

Be Curious contains a motivating 'test builder' stage in each unit which develops the skills needed for test success and test strategies for younger learners. It familiarises learners with Cambridge test formats in a positive context which prioritises progress in learning and develops confidence. Learners are fully prepared for Pre A1 Starters by the end of level 2 of *Be Curious*.

Throughout each unit, learners are gently introduced to Cambridge exam-style tasks, identified with the YLE monkey. This starts to familiarise learners with Pre A1 Starters activity structures and task types.

In each unit of level 2, the Pupil's Book Exam preparation page focusses on one part of the Pre A1 Starters test. It breaks down the task and focusses on the skills needed to complete it step-by-step. The lesson trains learners and provides tips and insights into what learners can do to achieve their best.

The Activity Book follows on by giving learners an opportunity to practice the task in full, building on what they have learnt in the Pupil's Book.

As a final step, the *Be Curious Test Generator* includes full Pre A1 Starters practice tests.

This fully-scaffolded approach prepares learners and gives them confidence. It trains them to be adaptable and think actively. It supports teachers with real exam training and it gives you an invaluable measurement of your learners' progress. This approach also gives *Be Curious* its OFFICIAL badge.

A full set of flashcards and colouring in sheets, which can be integrated into lessons for all the new vocabulary items in the 2018 spec is available here: worldoffun.cambridge.es

Audio visual material

The audio visual material in *Be Curious* serves both as a learning aid and as a tool to increase learner motivation.

Be Curious level 2 features five videos per unit as well as video in each review section:

- A unit opener video to introduce the unit topic, activate prior knowledge and help establish both class and individual learning objectives
- An animated chant to consolidate the first set of unit vocabulary
- An animated story to preview the unit grammar
- An animated song, with optional karaoke, to consolidate the second set of unit vocabulary
- A presenter led documentary to facilitate cross-curricular learning
- There are also interactive review quizzes in our three review sections.

Components

Pupil's components

Pupil's Book with eBook

Activity Book with Home Booklet and Digital Pack

Teacher's components

Teacher's Book with Digital Pack which includes:

- Teacher's Resources
- Test Generator
- Presentation Plus (IWB component)
- Access to Pupil's digital Practice Extra
- Access to Pupil's eBook
- Wordcards (online)
- Print Flashcards and Posters also available

Visit ***cambridge.org/becurious*** **&** ***cambridge.es/becurious*** to find all the information you need on the wide variety of components of *Be Curious* and how they can be combined to meet your needs.

The Pupil's Book

The Pupil's Book features:

- an introductory unit, 'Hello'
- nine core units with audio and audio visual content
- sticker activities for each unit
- three Review units
- a sixteen page Key Competencies Activity Bank (two pages of activities per Key Competence)

Pupil's Book unit walk-through

Be Curious level 2 is based around life on a farm where the Friendly family live alongside the farm animals. Grandma and Grandpa Friendly live in an older house there, and Mr and Mrs Friendly and their children Jim and Jenny live in a modern house. The family have a cat called Cameron and many farm animals who are friends.

Be Curious level 2 begins with a two-page introductory unit which introduces the Friendly family and the animals on their farm. It also presents/reviews basic greetings, numbers and colours.

This is followed by nine core units, each with 12 lessons. The Teacher's Book contains a 'Warm-up' and an 'Ending the lesson' activity for each of the 12 lessons and the Review units. The 'Warm-up' is designed to prepare learners for the lesson and engage them fully. The 'Ending the lesson' activity is designed to consolidate what they have learnt in the lesson. The Review sections appear after every three units.

The 12 lessons in each core unit are:

- Lesson 1 Unit opener and Mission set up
- Lesson 2 Vocabulary 1 presentation
- Lesson 3 Story with new language presented in context
- Lesson 4 Language Practice 1 and Mission Stage 1
- Lesson 5 Vocabulary 2 presentation and song
- Lesson 6 Language Practice 2 and Mission Stage 2
- Lesson 7 Cross-curricular presentation
- Lesson 8 Cross-curricular consolidation and Mission Stage 3
- Lesson 9 Literature – story focus
- Lesson 10 Literature – response to story and social and emotional skills
- Lesson 11 Pre A1 Starters skills builder
- Lesson 12 Unit review and Mission in action

Lesson 1

Unit opener and Mission set up

Lesson 1 opens the unit with a colourful illustrated page which sets up the context for the unit and introduces some of the core language that follows.

SA Learners are introduced to their first self-assessment in a self-assessment spot. They are invited to think about how much they can do at this stage of learning. This will allow them to see how much progress they have made by the end of the unit. At this stage:

- learners have a chance to think about the topic and what they already know about it
- they are asked to assess which language they know and what they can't say yet.

- Learners then complete a simple drawing or writing task to encourage them to think about what will follow in the rest of the unit. This task also personalises the learning and makes it relevant to their lives.
- The unit Mission is then set up. Three stages and a Mission completion activity are clearly outlined. The Activity Book contains a corresponding Mission statement page which helps learners to understand the stages of the Mission and is then revisited as the learners progress through the Mission.

Lesson 2

Vocabulary 1 presentation

The first focus on vocabulary is presented and practised in Lesson 2 based on the topic of the unit and with a colourful cartoon illustration to contextualise the language. This shows the Friendly family and their friends and animals in typical real-world situations, and contextualises the vocabulary to present meaning.

- The learners see and hear the new language first of all and are required to give a simple response, e.g. pointing, colouring or numbering as they recognise the vocabulary.
- The learners are then encouraged to produce the language accurately in an engaging chant.
- This is followed by a consolidation task, usually requiring learners to respond to questions using the new vocabulary.
- SA Learners are then asked to self-assess their progress with the new language.

Lesson 3

Story with new language presented in context

Lesson 3 provides a song – the Friendly Farm – which is repeated in each unit so that learners can join in. The song is followed by a story or 'sketch' which practises the new vocabulary and introduces the grammar point to follow.

- Learners listen and read the language using the pictures to help them understand.
- The Teacher's Book provides comprehension checks for the teacher to use to support and check understanding.
- At this stage the learners are only exposed to new language. The sketch and pictures help to establish the meaning.

Lesson 4

Language Practice 1 and Mission Stage 1

In Lesson 4, the new grammar point is practised and Mission Stage 1 is completed.

- Gracie's Grammar box highlights the target language which learners have heard in the sketch, and gives learners a chance to say and hear the language. It highlights key features of the language form in a simple, age-appropriate way. Pronunciation can also be corrected at this point.
- This is followed by a sticker activity using a picture. The picture helps the learners to understand the language through context. Learners listen to the language and give a response by choosing the correct stickers to add to the picture.
- The sticker activity is usually followed by a task requiring the learners to read and write using the new language.
- Learners then complete Mission Stage 1 using the language they have learnt so far in the unit. The Mission Stage 1 activities usually involve listening and speaking collaboratively to complete a topic-focused task. It requires learners to make decisions and be creative in order to complete the task.
- SA Once Mission Stage 1 is completed, learners are directed to complete a reflection and self-assessment from the Mission statement page in the Activity Book.

Lesson 5

Vocabulary 2 and song

This lesson uses a song to develop the topic and introduce further new vocabulary.

- Learners listen to the song and complete simple tasks such as numbering, colouring, drawing or doing actions.
- Learners then sing the song with actions to consolidate the language.
- This is usually followed by an activity or game that provides further practice and develops one or more skills – listening, reading, writing or speaking.

Lesson 6

Grammar 2 and Mission Stage 2

This lesson begins with a listening task requiring learners to select a picture by understanding the new language.

- There is a second Gracie's Grammar box which again highlights the target language and gives learners a chance to hear the language and say it correctly.
- The task that follows is usually a dialogue and role play which brings all the new language together and allows learners to try the new language in a natural context.
- In the final part of the lesson, learners use the new language to complete Mission Stage 2. This builds on Mission Stage 1 and again activities usually involve listening and speaking collaboratively to complete a topic-focused task.
- SA Once Mission Stage 2 is completed, learners are directed to complete a reflection and self-assessment from the Mission statement page in the Activity Book.

Lessons 7 and 8

Cross-curricular and video / Cross-curricular consolidation and Mission Stage 3

These two lessons introduce a topic which relates to the main focus of the unit, but which is linked to other subjects in the school curriculum. This encourages learners to think about other learning areas using English and develops their vocabulary further. It also develops critical-thinking skills and encourages broader knowledge of the world around them.

- In the first lesson, learners watch a video which introduces the topic and provides a context to use it.
- A task is provided to help learners focus on the video and understand the topic.
- A variety of practice activities follow: these can involve listening, reading, writing and speaking, and a range of different tasks including choosing pictures, matching, ordering or following instructions. These tasks give learners the chance to practise language, develop their skills and improve their critical thinking.
- The next lesson offers more skills-based activities, developing the knowledge of the learners further and providing more practice of the target language.
- Learners now complete Mission Stage 3 which is the final scaffolded stage of the Mission. This builds on the first two stages and again uses the language and skills that have been practised so far. The activity involves further collaboration to complete a task.
- **SA** Once Mission Stage 3 is completed, learners are directed to complete a reflection and self-assessment from the Mission statement page in the Activity Book.

Lessons 9 and 10

Literature – story focus / response to story and social and emotional skills

In this section learners read and listen to a story and then respond to it. The story uses language from the unit in a context which learners can relate to. The pictures and illustrations support understanding and help learners follow the story as they listen. It also helps them prepare for the activities that follow.

- Each story generally begins with an introductory speaking task which helps the learners to focus on the topic and encourages them to look at the titles and pictures of the story before they read. Learners then listen to the story as they read, which helps bring it to life and understand the narrative.
- Teacher's notes provide comprehension tasks to help support comprehension and to check understanding stage by stage as learners listen and read.
- In the second lesson learners complete follow-up activities using reading, speaking, writing and listening skills. Tasks include answering questions, talking about personal experience related to the topic, discussing ideas and identifying how characters feel. The activities help develop learners' emotional competencies and encourage them to develop social and life skills such as kindness, sharing and politeness.

Lesson 11

Pre A1 Starters skills builder

In Lesson 11 there is a focus on familiarising learners with the Cambridge Pre A1 Starters test. Each lesson focuses either on listening and speaking or reading and writing. It allows learners to develop test strategies and provides tips. It enables them to become familiar with the test rubrics and task types. It also allows both the learners and teacher to see how well they might perform in the Pre A1 Starters test.

- Learners complete tasks typical of Pre A1 Starters. These include writing words, numbers and names, selecting correct and incorrect pictures, colouring in according to instructions, and labelling and matching words and pictures.
- Notes in the Teacher's Book give advice on how to develop learners' test strategies including confidence-building tips.

Lesson 12

Unit review and Mission in action

The final lesson reviews the language covered in the unit through the final Mission stage. This brings together all the previous stages in a collaborative and practical task. As such, it recycles all the language and skills developed in the unit.

- Learners are encouraged to follow all the stages of the Mission, which has a final outcome. This might be acting out a scenario, doing a presentation or showing a final plan or piece of work.
- **SA** Once the Mission in action is completed, learners are directed to complete a final reflection and self-assessment from the Mission statement page in the Activity Book.

Review units

A Review unit is included every three units and appears after Units 3, 6 and 9. Each review is two pages and recycles and consolidates the language from the preceding units. The topics are similar to those in the core units but encourage the learners to apply their new language and knowledge to new contexts.

- Each review begins with an interactive video quiz which learners can do to see how much they can remember. This quiz can be repeated after the review is completed to measure progress.
- This is followed by listening tasks, tasks based on pictures to encourage speaking practice, and personalised writing tasks.

Unit opener page in the Activity Book

The unit opener page in each unit of the Activity Book is actually a page for you and your learners to refer to *throughout* each unit. It has four key parts: My unit goals, a 'can do' statement sunflower, My mission diary and a page reference for the word stack. The following section provides you with the teaching notes for this page of the Activity Book which you can return to as you progress through each unit.

My unit goals

Go through the unit goals with the learners. You can read these or if you prefer you can put them onto the board or a poster). Remember to go back to these at the end of each Mission stage during the unit and review them.

Sunflower

At the end of each Mission stage ask learners to look at the sunflower leaves and read the 'can do' statement, e.g. start with the bottom left leaf after Mission Stage 1 is completed. Ask the learners to add a tick if they agree they have achieved the statement. They can colour the leaf green if they are very confident and orange if they think they need more practice. Quickly check what each learner is doing to get a sense of their own assessment.

My Mission diary

At the end of each Mission stage, use the sunflower to remind learners of the outcome for the Mission stage. Tell them to look at the emoticons in 1, 2 or 3, depending on the stage they have completed, or look at the final set if they have completed the Mission. Tell the learners to think very carefully about how they did on each Mission stage. Ask them to think about the questions they answered, how much they understood and how confident they feel. Learners then choose an emoticon that shows how they feel about their work.

Word stack

The word stack is a personal record for each learner. At the end of each unit ask learners to spend a few minutes looking back at the unit and find a minimum of five new words they have learnt. **Fast finishers and stronger learners** can choose more. Learners write the new words into their word stack with an example sentence. **Extra support** – learners can draw pictures of words they have learnt and check back in their text books to copy the words they have chosen.

Practical techniques for using the word stack

1. Test yourself

- Learners go through their word stack and write a selection of words onto small cards. They can draw a picture on the other side of the card. Put the learners into pairs. Their partner holds up the card to show the picture and the learner says the word.
- Pairs then swap roles.

2. Test each other

- Learners choose a selection of words from their own word stack.
- Put the learners into pairs.
- Learners take it in turns to say a word to their partner. Their partner should draw, mime or give an example sentence of all the words they know. If they are asked a word they don't know their partner should explain or show it to them.

3. K/M/F charts

- This is a play on the K/W/L chart. Learners go through their word stack and choose five words they feel confident about, three they think they know, and two they can't remember.
- They create a poster with the letters *K*, *M*, *F* at the top. *K* is for words they **know**; *M* is for words they **might** know, and *F* is for words they have **forgotten**. They can write the words into the columns or add sticky notes to each column.

Learners then work in small groups of 3 or 4 and present their K/M/F charts to the rest of the group. Other learners in the group should remind them of the three words in the *F* list. If none can remember the words, they should check in their books.

4. Learner quiz

- Learners work in groups of 4 or 5. They look at their word stacks and create three questions to ask the rest of the class about some of the words. The questions can be based on drawings (*What is this? / What are these?*) or on an action (*What do I feel?* – miming angry or happy) or a question (*Is Harry big or small?*).
- Once the learners have prepared their questions, they sit in their groups. Each group takes it in turns to ask one of their questions to the rest of the class.
- The first group to answer gains one point. If any group can ask a question the other learners don't know they get a bonus point.

Sounds and spelling in the Activity Book

When learning another language, pronunciation and spelling are two of the most challenging aspects. English spelling can seem very complicated, but there are many patterns and rules which will help learners achieve success.

There are sounds and spelling practice activities in Lesson two of every unit in the Activity Book. The activities focus on particular sounds that learners often find challenging, or particular spelling patterns that sometimes pose difficulties, such as certain spelling patterns pronounced in different ways, as well as words pronounced the same but spelt differently.

The focus vocabulary used in these activities is drawn from the first vocabulary set of each unit, as well as any relevant revision vocabulary from prior units and levels where appropriate. The activities are designed to practise key sounds or spellings that occur in the words taught in the unit, so that the words and their meanings are already familiar to the learners, therefore making the focus more about sounds and spelling than reading and comprehension.

Be Curious and its methodology: formative assessment and assessment through competencies

Be Curious features a systematic approach to language learning in which **the learner and teacher are in a partnership**. It aims to develop the language and skills of the learner, but also helps them achieve **better life-long progress in learning**.

What does it involve? The *Be Curious* methodology helps teachers and learners to plan learning effectively, measure progress and identify areas for improvement in learning. In practice this means that all activity, inside and outside the classroom, can be integrated with assessment through competencies. More traditional summative assessment still continues. External 'tests' can be used alongside the classroom-focused formative assessment activities. For teachers this should not feel strange: using external assessments to check progress and performance is familiar; monitoring learners' progress and adapting teaching to support them is also routine. *Be Curious* simply combines these elements in a systematic way. In *Be Curious* you will see that classroom activity is designed to allow the teacher to monitor for evidence to measure progress and also includes tasks that are similar to those in formal summative tests such as Cambridge English Pre A1 Starters.

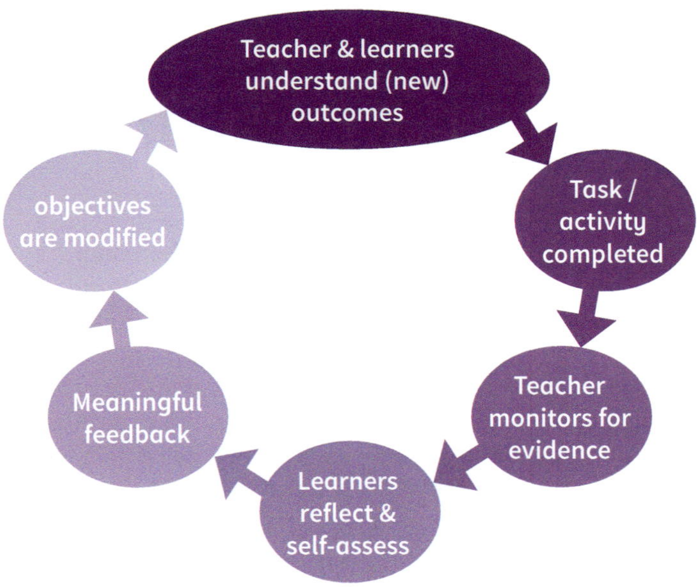

How does it work in the classroom? In *Be Curious* learners are given more independence to understand their own strengths and weaknesses, both immediate (e.g. in a lesson) and longer term (e.g. over a school term). In the classroom this begins with making sure learning objectives are clear to both learner and teacher. In *Be Curious* these are identified by the outcomes at the beginning of each lesson. Once outcomes are established, both the learner and the teacher think about how each activity can support a learning outcome. After the activity is finished they reflect on performance in relation to that outcome and use this evidence to adjust what happens in later lessons – this might be reviewing and practising some language again or moving on more quickly depending on the performance. Normal classroom activities therefore combine learning with assessment to provide meaningful feedback to learners. Being involved in the process helps learners improve outcomes and gain confidence. In addition, if the activities and content are linked to the language and skills of more formal language tests, classroom activities can also be benchmarked against formal tests.

No matter how young a learner might be, this process can help learners develop their skills and learn about the world around them. *Be Curious* aims to develop skills such as collaboration and encourages learners to understand their own progress and think about how they can improve. Learners can begin to do this even when they are young. *Be Curious* therefore includes multistage projects which encourage learners to collaborate and work together helping them develop better life skills, and regular self-assessment stages.

What kind of activities are used in class? *Be Curious* methodology can be integrated into everyday learning to support progress in different ways and these have been integrated into the course:

Be Curious prioritises real-life language and activity. It therefore includes learning activities which reflect **real-world tasks** and offer topics designed to engage the learners.

Be Curious asks teachers and learners to **understand objectives**. Expected outcomes for each lesson are shown at the beginning of each lesson in *Be Curious* and Mission statements are also provided in learner-accessible style; these can be shared in creative ways with the learners. This helps learners understand what they are trying to achieve in each activity they complete.

Using *Be Curious*, learners begin to **reflect on their own performance and measure progress** in achieving those outcomes. Learners complete multistage projects in *Be Curious* and consider how well they have done at each stage of the project using suggested self-assessment techniques. This encourages **autonomy**. Learners are also given opportunities to make choices during their activities and Missions, which encourages self-confidence and independence.

Teachers using *Be Curious* can collect information about the learners through their classroom activities, completion of tasks and self-assessment, and this allows both teacher and learners to **plan learning** more effectively as they work through the material.

Links can be made between classroom activities and some of the performance measures of formal tests so that **formative and summative assessment** is linked together.

Self-assessment guide

It is important for learners to understand the purpose of lessons and to think about how well they achieve learning outcomes. They can begin to do this at a young age: their learning in all areas, not just language, will benefit. In this book, each unit of learning therefore includes stages:

- asking learners to think about what they will learn – making the outcomes for each lesson clear to them
- helping them to think about their progress – asking them to self-assess through simple activities.

When

These stages are labelled **Self-assessment**. You can use any of the techniques explained below at these stages. Choose one of the techniques each time. You can do this at the beginning and end of each lesson and/or at the beginning and end of each unit.

When you do this at the beginning of learning, **encourage the pupils to be honest** – the language will be new, so they should recognise this. They need to be reassured that if you can't do something, knowing this and showing you need more support is a positive way to help yourself. There is an added benefit: when you repeat this assessment at the end of activities, they will be able to recognise that they have learnt. They can also indicate if they are still not confident, which will help you, and them, to see which areas of learning will need more attention.

Techniques for the classroom

1. Thumbs up

Tell the class to use their thumbs to demonstrate how they feel about what they are learning. They can use:

- thumbs up (+ smiling) – 'I feel very confident'
- thumbs mid position (+ neutral face) – 'I think I know this' (optional)
- thumbs down (+ shaking head) – 'I'm not confident'.

2. Red and green cards

These cards can be prepared in advance. Although this takes preparation, these can be reused in class for a long time. Use thick green card and red card and cut these into squares approximately 12 cm x 12 cm. You will need one card of each colour per learner. If possible, laminate the cards. Punch a hole in the top left corner and tie together one red and one green card with string or a treasury tag.

Tell the class to use their cards to demonstrate how they feel about what they are learning. Hold up:

- green for 'confident'
- red for 'not sure'.

Learners can also leave these on their desks as they work, leaving red up if they want help from the teacher. ***Variation:*** If you don't have red/green cards ask learners to draw an empty square on a card and put it on their desk at the beginning of the lesson. During the lesson, stop at an appropriate point and ask them to colour in the square: red for 'I don't understand'; green for 'I understand'.

3. High fives

Tell the class to show how they feel about the learning using 'high fives' (the learner holding out their hand and slapping hands with another learner or the teacher):

- high five (holding the hand up high to slap) – 'I feel very confident'
- low five (holding the hand lower near the waist) – 'I'm not confident'.

Even with a big class you can go around quite quickly to 'high five' or 'low five' each learner.

Alternatively you can ask them to go to one side of the room to 'high five' and to the other side of the room to 'low five' each other, giving you a quick visual of how learners are feeling.

4. K/W/L charts

Before beginning work on new language, create a poster with the letters *K*, *W*, *L* at the top. *K* is for words they **know**; *W* is for words they **would** like to know. Give the learners different words from the activities they are about to do. Ask them which words go into the *K* column and which go into the *W* column. If learners choose to put the words into the K column, they should explain or give an example using the word. After the lesson or activity sequence, go back to the poster and review the words in the *W* column. Learners can move them to the *L* column if they are confident (*L* is for words they have **learnt**) or leave them in the *W* column if not. You can ask them for examples of all the words in the *K* and *L* columns. If any words are left in the *W* column, you may need to teach them again.

Variations:

Have one large poster and the words on cards. Use sticky tack and select learners to come up and pin them into the columns.

- Have several large posters. Divide learners into groups – one poster per group. Choose a group leader to stick the words up for the group or, for a more dynamic activity, allow all the learners to stick up some words. Words can be written on cards with sticky tape on the backs or onto sticky notes – ask the learners to copy the new words out themselves.
- Have several large posters. Divide learners into groups – one poster per group. Give each group a marker pen to write the words into the columns. (They can cross out the words at the end when they change position.)

5. Self-assessment cards

Create a simple self-assessment card and make a 'post box' by using a cardboard box with a 'letter box' cut in the lid. Learners complete their self-assessment and put it into the post box.

An example (which can be adapted for different tasks and activities) is below:

Ask learners which outcomes they are trying to achieve and help them complete the sentences, e.g. *I understand words about clothes.* Then tell them to think about how close they feel to achieving the outcome and to choose a face that shows this.

What we are doing.	**How I feel**
I understand words about	☺ 😐 ☹
I can say	☺ 😐 ☹
I know	☺ 😐 ☹
I don't know	☺ 😐 ☹

6. Sticky notes

Put a large poster on one side of the room with *Hooray! It's OK.* ☺ at the top. Put another on the other side with a confused smiley face (scratching its head) saying *Let's try again*. Learners write or draw something, e.g. a word or phrase they feel confident about and something they aren't sure about, on two different sticky notes. They add the first to the *Hooray* poster and the other to the *Let's try again* poster.

If many learners choose the same word to try again, you may need to revisit it with the whole class. You can ask learners to write their names on the sticky notes to help you identify individual learner's reactions.

7. Mini whiteboards

Give each learner a mini whiteboard if you have these.

Variation:

- You can make them by using laminated card which can be reused a few times.

At appropriate points, stop and ask learners to draw on the card to show how they feel. You can ask them to draw a smiley or frowning face.

Variation:

- Learners write *OK / Not OK* OR write a word/phrase they are confident about at the top and a word or phrase they don't fully understand at the bottom.

They can either hold up their mini whiteboard or leave it on the desk as they work so you can see them as you monitor.

8. Jump up / Sit down

Call out some of the words or language learners have been learning, and ask learners to jump up if they are confident but sit down if they aren't sure. You can do this with more than one item.

9. Paper planes

When looking at the outcomes of a lesson, ask learners to copy some of them, e.g. words, word categories or phrases, onto a piece of paper. Collect these in. After you have finished the activities, give the papers out again. Ask learners to read the lesson outcomes they have worked on. Then show them how to fold the paper into a paper aeroplane shape. (Simple instructions can be found on the internet.) Put a bin or large box at the front of the class. If they are confident about what they have learnt, they should throw their planes into the box. If they are not confident they should throw their planes onto your desk.

Variations:

- Learners screw their papers up into a ball.
- Use ping pong balls and write on them with indelible marker pens.

10. Baskets

Put three plastic baskets or boxes on your desk (a red, a yellow and a green one).

Learners write their names onto pieces of paper and drop their name into the basket that shows how they feel: red – not confident, yellow – OK but need more practice, green – very confident.

Variations:

- If learners have completed a piece of writing or homework task, they can hand this in by placing it into the baskets to show how they feel they have done on that particular task.
- Just have red and green, without yellow, to keep reflection simple.
- Paint or colour three paper plates in the three different colours.
- Have three boxes or baskets, one with a smiley face card on the front, one with a frowning face and one with a neutral face on it. Learners drop their names/work into these.

11. Traffic flags

Get learners to make flags. Give each learner paper. They cut out three large rectangles or triangles of paper and colour or paint them red, green and yellow. Give each learner three drinking straws and sticky tape. Ask them to stick the rectangles/triangles to the straws to make flags. When you complete an activity, the learners wave a flag according to how they feel.

12. Washing lines

Give each child two pegs – preferably one red and one green. Ask them to write their name on both using indelible marker pens. Set up two string lines at the front of the classroom (e.g. across a display board). After an activity, ask the learners to put either their red peg ('I don't understand') or their green peg ('I understand') on the line. If you can't find coloured pegs use simple wooden ones for learners to write on; have two lines (one with the sign *I understand* and one with the sign *Let's try again* next to them).

13. Balloons

Get three balloons: one red, one yellow and one green. If you have a large group, you may need two or three of each colour.

After completing an activity, ask learners to write their names using a soft felt tip pen on the balloon that shows how they feel about the activity. Put the balloons to one side. After you have done follow up, e.g. re-teaching any difficult areas, bring the balloons out again and throw them back and forth asking questions about the words or language covered. At the end the learners can chant *We learnt the words!* and burst the balloons.

Variation:

- Have just two balloons, one red and one green, with no yellow.

14. Sticky spots

Create a poster divided into three columns. In the column headings, write *Hooray, it's OK / I'm not sure / It's not OK – let's try again*. At the end of any activity, give learners a sticky dot or sticky label. Ask them to write their name on it. As they leave the class, they stick their name into one of the columns.

15. Scales

Create a long arrow from cardboard and stick it on the side of the board or on the wall. Inside the very top, draw a smiley face and write *100%*. At the bottom draw a frowning face and write *0%*. (This is re-usable so you only need to prepare it once.) Give out slips of paper and paper clips to the learners. They write their name on the paper. At the end of an activity, ask them to bring up their name and to paper clip it to the edge of the arrow showing where they think they are on the scale.

Teachers' classroom assessment:

As we have seen, *Be Curious* involves assessing learners during everyday activity along with more traditional types of assessment or test-type activities. This information will help the teacher adjust learning aims and lesson plans so that areas of difficulty can be reviewed and areas that are easy can be dealt with quickly. This responsive style of teaching allows better progress. The teacher will also take into account how the learners are feeling: even if a learner answers questions correctly, if they don't feel confident about a particular area they may still need some extra practice.

The teacher's role

To use this approach successfully, during teaching you need to:

a. identify language outcomes clearly at the start of lessons/tasks
b. use 'closing language' regularly to highlight the achievements made
c. monitor effectively during specific activities
d. keep formative assessment notes on the group and individual learners
e. alternatively use check lists to record assessment of skills and life skills (e.g. planning / collaborating / working autonomously / sharing, etc.)
f. encourage students to engage in self-assessment.

After teaching you need to:

a. keep or update anecdotal records
b. use scoring rubrics to measure achievement against external scales
c. use 'portfolio' building / record keeping for individual students.

This will give you a full record of assessment for each learner alongside any results from tests. This can help you when writing reports for learners, making them evidence based and more detailed. It will give you an idea of how well learners are doing against external measures.

Practical techniques for the teacher's role: in class

a) Identifying outcomes

Each unit contains an opening stage which shows you how to set up the Mission clearly for learners. There is a Mission poster to help you track progress in the Activity Book. In this way setting outcomes and reviewing them are built into the materials.

You can:

- tell learners what you will do at the beginning of the lesson
- write the outcomes on the board
- write the outcomes on a poster and stick it on the wall; at the end of the teaching cycle you can then return to this and tick, or encourage a learner to come up and tick the items
- put two posters on the wall: 'What we are learning' 'What we learnt': write each outcome for your lesson on a large card and stick it under the 'What we are learning' poster; at the end of the teaching cycle move or encourage a learner to move the card under the 'What we learnt' poster. All the outcomes from the term can gradually be added here giving a visual record for learners of what they have achieved.

b) Use 'closing language' regularly to highlight the achievement

- After the activity go back to the outcomes and use this to 'close' the task, e.g. *Well done. You have talked about school. You have listened and answered.*
- You can use the language from the outcomes to help close the task.
- If the learners have found something difficult make sure you praise their work even if you need to do more on this area, e.g. *Well done – you have worked hard. You talked about school. Let's try again later and do even better.*

c) Monitor effectively during specific activities

- Once you have set up an activity do a quick check around the room to make sure the learners are 'on task' and provide more guidance if any have not understood what to do. To keep the activity moving it might be necessary to use a little L1 to help them. Try to avoid doing this too much or you will find learners 'switch off' during English instructions as they know you will repeat in L1.
- Once all the learners are on task monitor the group, listening carefully to what they say and looking at their work especially if they are writing words. You may need to feed in words in English or answer questions if they ask you for help.
- If everything is going well you might want to praise their progress briefly in English but don't step in too much. If you always step in, learners will stop doing tasks and expect you to be involved. This is fine sometimes but you want to see how they work and collaborate together and if you are involved all the time you can't do this. Learners will soon get used to you monitoring without intervening.
- Use this time to note how they are doing. If you have a large group make a list of all the learners and plan to monitor different members of the group closely during each activity, e.g. monitor learners 1–5 closely in Activity 1, monitor learners 6–10 closely in Activity 2 and so on. In this way over a few lessons you will have monitored each individual closely.

d) Keep formative assessment notes on the group and individual learners

- You can use monitoring, the activities learners complete and any classroom-based tasks and homework to gather evidence about learner progress.
- Keep a notebook and pen with you during lessons to make notes; alternatively use a mobile device, e.g. tablet.
- You can prepare your notebook in advance with a page or half page for each learner. This can be updated during and after activities. See below for examples of notes on language and the skills of speaking and writing (you could include listening and reading).

Example of notes:

Learner	Overall	Vocab	Grammar	Pron	Speaking	Writing
Maria	Good progress – motivated.	Fine. Good range. Tries new words quickly.	Good word order. Forgets 'am/is/are'.	✗ Word stress	✓ Fluency **?** Turn taking	✓ Spelling
Simone	Not doing homework. Progress limited.	**?** uses a lot of L1	✗ Tends to use single words not sentences.	✓ Accurate when using English. Uses L1 a lot.	**?** Lacks confidence.	✓ Strongest skill. Enjoys copying. Accurate.
Alex	Progress OK but not motivated.	Limited range but remembers.	Pres simp. questions inaccurate.	**?** OK but problem with adding /ə/ before vowels	✓ Fluent **?** Turn taking	**?** OK – has to check text book a lot for words.

e) Use check lists for skills and life skills (planning / collaborating / working autonomously / sharing, etc.)

- Alternatively – or in addition to notes – check lists can help you to keep evidence of progress. The lists need to be prepared in advance and can be based on outcomes and/ or descriptors of level such as those in CEFR. See below for examples of a check list for listening, reading and life skills. (You could include vocabulary, grammar, pronunciation, speaking and writing.) See the next section for information on CEFR.

Example of check list:

	Maria	Simone	Alex
Listening – understanding gist	✓	✗ tries to understand everything	✓
Listening – understanding details	✓ some errors	**?** often incorrect	✓
Listening for specific information	✓ good at predicting strategies	**?** some errors	✓
Reading for gist	✓	✓ slow but can manage	✓
Reading for specific information		✓	✓
Collaborating for group work	✓	✓	✗ not motivated – doesn't do much
Sharing	✓	✓	✓
Working autonomously	✓	✗ tries but lacks confidence	✗ needs encouragement

f) Encourage students to engage in self-assessment

See notes on self-assessment.

Practical techniques for the teacher's role: after class

After teaching you can use the information and evidence you have collected to ensure you have full records for learners. This information can be reviewed, along with the learners' self-assessment, to decide on what kind of teaching and learning will follow as well as to produce reports.

a) Keep or update anecdotal records

You can use your notes to add to any records you keep for learners. If you used a digital device you can cut and paste the notes you made. Along with formal test results, this will give you evidence and detailed information if you need to write reports for your learners.

b) Use scoring rubrics

You can combine in-class assessments with results of class tests, e.g. percentage scores, and all this information can be matched against external standards to give you an idea of how well learners are doing overall. For example, you can look at the 'can do' statements for each skill in CEFR scales.

We really hope you enjoy teaching with *Be Curious* and look forward to supporting you throughout this journey with your learners.

Hello

1 0.02 **Listen. How old are the children?**

2 0.03 **Say the chant.**

3 0.04 **Listen and say the colour.**

Hello Unit learning outcomes

Learners learn to:

- say hello
- understand and use numbers
- ask and answer the question *How old are you?*
- understand and say colours

Materials ten balloons of different colours, blown up, with numbers *1–10* written on them in marker pen (optional), picture from Digital photo bank of a tractor

Key Competences

Understand and say colours; Learn to ask and respond to basic personal questions.

Understand and use numbers 1 to 10.

Chant together as a class.

Self-assessment

- **SA** Say *Open your Pupil's Books at page 4.* Point to the numbers. Say *One, two, three …* Learners continue. Point to the balloons. Ask *What colour is it?* Use self-assessment (see Introduction). Say *OK. Let's learn.*

Warm-up

- Wave. Say *Hello!* Learners wave and repeat. Say *I'm* (*name*). Learners repeat.
- Learners mingle, waving and saying *Hello! I'm* (*name*).

Presentation

- Show learners your balloons. Hold one up and say the colour, e.g. *Red*. Point to other red objects. Learners repeat.
- Repeat with other balloons, e.g. pink, green, orange, yellow. Learners repeat. Throw the balloon to different learners. If they catch it, they repeat the colour.
- Take all the balloons back and point to the numbers. Say *One*. Learners repeat. Continue with numbers *2–10*. Throw balloons to learners. If they catch it, they say the number.
- Say *Look at Pupil's Book page 4*. Point to the farm building and the sign. Say *Look, it's a …* (*farm*). Say *It's the Friendly Farm. Here is Jim Friendly. Here is Jenny Friendly.*
- Say *Show me the numbers*. Learners point. Say the numbers one by one, pointing to each. Learners repeat. Go up from *1* to *10*. Go down from *10* to *1*. Learners repeat.

Pupil's Book, page 4

1 0.02 Listen. How old are the children?

- Say *Open your Pupil's Books at page 4. Look at the picture.*
- Ask a learner *How old are you?* The learner replies. Repeat.
- Point to Jim. Say *It's Jim. How old is he?* Learners guess. Write the words *Jim? Jenny?* on the board.
- Say *Let's find out. Listen.* Play the audio.

Track 0.02

Jim:	Hello, I'm Jim. I'm six.
Jenny:	Hello, I'm Jenny. I'm six.
Jim and Jenny:	We're twins.
Jim:	How old are you?

- Say *Look at Jim and Jenny. They are six. They are twins.*
- Show a picture of a tractor. Ask *What is it?* Say *It's a tractor.* Learners repeat. Clap the stress (on *trac*). Learners repeat. Ask *Where's the tractor? Can you find it?* Learners find the hidden picture of the tractor in the picture on the Pupil's Book page and point to it (on the roof of the barn).

2 0.03 Say the chant.

- Say *Listen and say the chant.* Play the audio, holding up your fingers to show the numbers. Learners chant and show numbers using their fingers.
- Repeat and this time point to the correct coloured balloon on page 4. Learners chant and point.

Track 0.03

1, 2, 3, 4, 5
6, 7, 8, 9, 10 (x2)
Red, blue, red and blue
Yellow, green and orange (x2)
Purple, pink, purple, pink
Purple, pink and grey (x2)
Black, white, black and white
Black and white and brown.

- 10.01 To practise numbers up to 20, use the chant on Pupil's Book page 120.

3 0.04 Listen and say the colour.

- Show the balloons you have. Hold up two of them, e.g. numbers 3 and 4. Ask *What colour is balloon 3?* Learners answer. Repeat with 4.
- Focus on the picture in the Pupil's Book. Ask questions, e.g. *What colour is balloon 2?* (*Blue*) Repeat with two more balloons.
- Play the audio. Learners listen and say the colour.

Track 0.04

1 What colour is balloon 6?
2 What colour is balloon 3?
3 What colour is balloon 5?
4 What colour is balloon 8?
5 What colour is balloon 7?

Key: 6 purple 3 yellow 5 orange 8 grey 7 pink

Activity Book, page 4

See pages TB120–132

Ending the lesson

- Say *This is our lesson. We learnt numbers and colours.*
- Throw all the balloons out to the learners. A learner throws back one and says the number and colour.
- Continue with other learners.
- Say *You can say numbers and colours. Good work.*

Learning outcomes By the end of the lesson, learners will understand when they hear a conversation about how old people are.

New language *How old are you? I'm ... This is ... What's your name? I'm ...*

Recycled language colours, family, names

Materials cards with numbers *1–20* on them (one per learner, repeating numbers if necessary), flashcards of the Friendly Farm characters, audio, video

Key Competences

Read and listen to a story.

Role play a story.

Write the words for the numbers 1 to 10.

Warm-up

- Give out a number card to each learner. Say the numbers. Each time you say a number, the learner with that number jumps up. Continue through the number sequence and then repeat, giving numbers randomly. (Keep a list and tick them off so that all the numbers are covered.)
- If there is time, a stronger learner can come and say the numbers to the rest of the class.

Presentation

- Show the learners the flashcard of Jenny. Point and say *This is Jenny*. Learners repeat. Show the flashcard of Jim. Say *This is Jim*. Learners repeat.
- Point to one learner, turn to a second and introduce them through gesture, saying *This is (Angela). This is (Luis).* Encourage them to say *Hello* and shake hands. Repeat the sequence with new learners.
- Three learners come to the front. Ask the strongest learner to repeat and introduce the other two learners.
- Put learners into groups of three. They take it in turns to introduce each other.

Pupil's Book, page 5

0.05 The Friendly Farm song

- Play the introductory song at the beginning of the cartoon story. Learners listen. Repeat. Learners listen and sing. As they do, tap out the rhythm on the table. Learners copy and tap. Repeat the song. Learners sing and tap.

Track 0.05

The Friendly Farm, The Friendly Farm,
Fun and games on the Friendly Farm,
With the animals in the barn,
Fun and games on the Friendly Farm.

0.05 The Friendly Farm

- Put the flashcards of the Friendly Farm animals on the board. Say *This is* ... (point to the hen) *Henrietta*. Learners repeat. Repeat with the other animals.
- Say *Open your Pupil's Books at page 5*. Ask *Who can you see in the pictures?* Learners name the characters.
- Ask *How old is Rocky? How old is Cameron? Harry? Shelly?* Don't worry if the learners can't answer at this stage. Write the questions on the board. Say *Listen*. Play the audio or video. Learners listen and read.

Track 0.05
The Friendly Farm song + see cartoon on Pupil's Book page 5

- Learners answer the questions in pairs before the class check.
- Play the audio or video again. Pause after frames and check comprehension by asking learners to give the end of sentences:

Frame 2: *This is* ... (point to the cat) (*Cameron*). *And this is* ... (point to the hen and the rooster) (*Henrietta and Rocky*) Frame 3: *Cameron is* ... (*three*) Frame 4: *This is* ... (point to the horse) (*Harry*) *He's* ... (*eight*)

Frame 5: *This is* ... (point to the goat) (*Gracie*) ... *and* ... (point to the sheep) (*Shelly*). Frame 6: *Rocky is* ... (*two*) *How old is Shelly?* (*We don't know.*)

- Play the audio or video again. Put the learners into pairs. Give each pair a role: Cameron, Henrietta, Rocky, Harry, Gracie or Shelly. Learners repeat the speech bubbles for their character.

4 0.06 Listen and correct.

- Say *Listen* and *correct*. Play the audio and pause for learners to correct each sentence.

Track 0.06
1 Cameron's blue and green.
2 Shelly's red.
3 Gracie's yellow.
4 Harry's black.
5 Rocky's pink and purple.
6 Henrietta's grey.

Key: 1 orange and white 2 white 3 grey 4 brown 5 yellow and red (and black/grey) 6 brown

Activity Book, page 5

See pages TB120–132

Ending the lesson

- Display the Friendly Farm animal flashcards on the board. Point and ask *Who is it? How old is he/she?* Learners answer.
- Take down the flashcards and mix them up face down. Hold one up. Show the flashcard with the back facing outwards so learners see the flashcard but not the picture on it. Learners guess who it is. Repeat.

The Friendly Farm

0.05

4 0.06 **Listen and correct.**

1 Our new school

1 **Watch the video. Write or draw a school word.**

mission **Make our classroom English**

In this unit I will:

1. Make labels for the classroom.
2. Choose a new word to learn.
3. Make a class poster.

★ Be the teacher.

Unit 1 learning outcomes

In Unit 1, learners learn to:

- talk about school
- describe where objects are using prepositions
- ask questions using *Where is / Where are … ?*
- ask and answer using *This is / These are*
- read for correct information
- be kind

Materials video, digital poster, coloured pens or pencils, drawing paper

Key Competences

Become familiar with language related to school.

Reflect on their own learning by going through the unit goals.

Write or draw a school word.

Self-assessment

- **SA** Say *Open your Pupil's Books at page 6*. Say *Look at the picture*. Ask *Where is it?* (*A school*) Say *Where are we? We're in school*. Encourage learners to repeat. Say *Point to red/blue/yellow/green*. Learners point. Point to different objects in the picture, e.g. desks, chairs, clocks and board, and ask *What colour is this?* Use self-assessment (see Introduction). Say *OK. Let's learn.*

Warm-up

- Say *Close your books*. Mime closing your book. Learners copy. Ask *Can you remember?* Mime thinking. Say *Hmm … a green chair*.
- Learners call out what they can remember from the picture.

Pupil's Book, page 6

1 Watch the video. Write or draw a school word.

- Say *In this unit we're talking about school*. Say *Let's watch the video*. To introduce the topic of the unit, play the video.
- Say *Look at page 6. Point to the chairs. Point to the desks. Now point to the board*. Show the empty board with space to write. Say *Let's draw on the board*.
- Mime looking around the classroom, seeing something and deciding to draw it. Start to draw. Tell learners *Find something in the school. Draw it and write the word.* Monitor as learners draw. If it is a word they don't know, you can tell them.

  Fast finishers These learners can draw a second item and write the word.

mission Make our classroom English

- Show the digital Mission poster. Say *Let's make our classroom English*. Say *Hello! We speak English!* Wave and encourage the learners to call out *Hello!* and wave back.
- Say *Point to number 1*. Say *We label the classroom*. Act out putting labels on things. Learners copy the mime.
- Say *Point to number 2*. Say *We learn new words*. Act out turning pages in a dictionary. Learners copy.
- Say *Point to number 3*. Say *We make a poster*. Mime drawing a poster and sticking it on the wall. Learners copy.
- Say *Point to number 4*. Say *You'll be the teacher!* Point to yourself and encourage the learners to point to you.
- Say *This is our Mission. Show me the Mission.* Encourage the learners to mime the sequence by saying the words again and acting it out while they copy.
- For ideas on monitoring and assessment, see Introduction.

Activity Book, page 6

My unit goals

- Go through the unit goals with the learners. You can read these or if you prefer you can put them onto the board or a poster.
- You can go back to these unit goals at the end of each Mission stage during the unit and review them.
- Say *This is our Mission page*.

Ending the lesson

- Demonstrate the actions *stand up*, *sit down* and *shake hands*.
- Go around the class pointing and giving each learner a colour: *red*, *green*, *yellow* or *blue*. If you point and alternate between colours, you should end up with roughly equal groups of each colour.
- Say *Hello … blues*. Learners who are blue wave to you. Repeat with red/green/yellow.
- Say *Reds stand up!* Red learners do this. Say *Reds sit down*. Repeat with the other colours.
- Say *Greens say hello*. Greens call out hello. Repeat with other colours.
- Say *Yellows shake hands*. Yellows shake hands with each other. Repeat with other colours. Say *Everyone shake hands*. All learners shake hands.
- If you have any very confident learners, invite them to the front to do the instructions. You can whisper these to help them if they need it.

1 Vocabulary 1

Learning outcomes By the end of the lesson, learners will be able to recognise and use school words.

New language *bag, book, chair, classroom, crayon, desk, pen, pencil, pencil case, rubber, teacher*

Recycled language colours, names, numbers

Materials flashcard of living room, classroom objects (pencil, rubber, school bag, crayon, desk, chair, book, pen, pencil case), audio, video

Key Competences

- Identify and use school vocabulary.
- Chant together as a class.
- Recognise and practise the sounds /p/ and /b/.

Warm-up

- Ask *Where are we?* Chant *We're at school, we're at school.* Learners repeat.

Presentation

- Say *Let's talk about school*. Use classroom objects. Point to yourself. Say *Teacher*. Learners repeat. Repeat with the other classroom objects.
- Choose several learners to come to the front. Give them one classroom object each. One learner holds up their object. The class calls out the word. Continue.
- Learners sit down. Point around the classroom. Learners say the words.

Pupil's Book, page 7

1 (1.01 1.02) Listen and point. Then listen and number.

- Say *Open your Pupil's Books at page 7. Look at the picture.*
- Indicate the caption. Read it.
- Ask *Where's the pencil case?* The class points. Repeat.
- Play Track 1.01. Learners point to the classroom objects.

Tracks 1.01 and 1.02

This morning Jim and Jenny are at their new school.

(1) Teacher:	Hello, Jim. Hello, Jenny. This is your classroom.
(2) Teacher:	I'm Miss Kelly. I'm your teacher.
Jenny:	Hi, Miss Kelly.
(3) Jenny:	Look! I've got my bag. It's green!
Jim:	Hello.
(4) Teacher:	This is your desk, Jenny. It's yellow.
(5) Teacher:	And this is your book.
Jenny:	Ooh. Thank you.
(6) Jenny:	My chair's red. And my book's purple.
Teacher:	Tom and Eva, this is Jenny and this is Jim.
Tom:	Hello, Jenny.
Eva:	Hello, Jim.
(7) Tom:	Look at my pencil, Jim. It's brown.
(8) Tom:	And this is my rubber. It's white.
(9) Jim:	And this is my pen. Look! It's black.
(10) Eva:	Cool! And look at my crayon. It's pink.
(11) Teacher:	Yes, yes, and my pencil case is grey! OK, children. Now, be quiet and sit down, please. Open your books at page 2.

- Say *Look at page 7*. Show the spaces next to the words. Ask *What's number 1?* (*Classroom*) Point out the example.
- Say *Listen and number*. Play Track 1.02. Learners number the school objects. Monitor.
- Ask, e.g. *What's number 2?* Learners point to the objects around the classroom.
- Ask *Where's the tractor? Can you find it?* Learners find the hidden picture of the tractor in the picture on the Pupil's Book page and point to it (on the cupboard).

Key: 2 teacher 3 bag 4 desk 5 book 6 chair 7 pencil 8 rubber 9 pen 10 crayon 11 pencil case

2 (1.03) Say the chant.

- Say *Listen and say the chant*. Play the audio or video. Learners point and chant.

Tracks 1.03

Classroom, bag, teacher (x2)
Desk, chair, book (x2)
Pencil, rubber, pen (x2)
Crayon and pencil case (x2)

3 (1.04) Listen, point and say the colour.

- Focus on the picture. Ask questions, e.g. *What's this?* (*A desk*) *What colour is it?* (*Yellow*) Repeat for all items.
- Play the audio and pause after number 1. Learners call out *Yellow*. Play the rest of the audio. Learners respond.

Track 1.04

1 Where's Jenny's desk? What colour is it?
2 Where's Tom's pencil? What colour is it?
3 Where's Jenny's bag? What colour is it?
4 Where's Eva's crayon? What colour is it?
5 Where's Tom's rubber? What colour is it?
6 Where's Jim's pen? What colour is it?
7 Where's Jenny's chair? What colour is it?
8 Where's the teacher's pencil case? What colour is it?
9 Where's Jenny's book? What colour is it?

- Learners play the same game in pairs.

Key: 1 yellow 2 brown 3 green 4 pink 5 white 6 black 7 red 8 grey 9 purple

Activity Book page 7

See pages TB120–132

Ending the lesson

- Say *This is our lesson. We learnt about school words.*
- **SA** Point to classroom items. Ask *Do you know the words?* Use self-assessment (see Introduct ion). Learners show how they feel.

1 1.01 1.02 **Listen and point. Then listen and number.**

2 1.03 **Say the chant.**

3 1.04 **Listen, point and say the colour.**

1

The Friendly Farm
1.05
1
Look at the bag! Yes, I'm the teacher!
2
Now, this is my classroom. Rocky, where's the pencil?
It's under the desk, teacher.
3
Now you, Shelly. Where's the crayon?
It's on the desk.
4
Now you, Harry. Where's the bag?
It isn't on the desk.
No, it isn't, Harry. It's next to the desk!
5
Where's my bag, Jim?
It's in the barn.
Be quiet! It's Jim and Jenny!
6
Where's the book? It isn't in the bag.
Oops!
Yes, Gracie! Where's the book?

Learning outcomes By the end of the lesson, learners will be able to ask and say where things are and use prepositions of place.

New language *in, next to, on, under*

Recycled language colours, names, school, *It's / They're, It isn't / They aren't*

Materials classroom objects (pen, pencil, crayon, rubber, pencil case, book, bag), flashcard of Gracie, audio, video, digital poster, a soft toy

Key Competences

Read and listen to a story; Identify expressions used to say where things are.

Role play a story.

Warm-up

- Put a pen, pencil, crayon, rubber, pencil case and book into a bag. Show the bag. Ask *What is it?* (*It's a bag.*) Ask *What's in the bag?* Learners guess. As learners suggest items in the bag, say *Yes! The (book) is in the bag!*
- **SA** Use self-assessment to check how well learners think they understand the vocabulary. See Introduction.

Presentation

- Show a flashcard of Gracie. Ask *Who is it?* (*Gracie*) Put it under your desk. Ask *Where's Gracie?* Mime looking. Say *She's under the desk*. Say *under* and indicate 'under' with your hand. Learners repeat.
- Put the flashcard on the desk. Ask *Where's Gracie?* Learners point. Say *She's on the …* Learners say *desk*. Repeat *on*, demonstrating with your hand on the desk. Say *She's on the desk*. Learners repeat.
- Repeat the sequence with *next to* (put the flashcard next to the desk) and *in* (put the flashcard in a desk drawer).
- Repeat, putting the flashcard in different places (on a chair, in a bag, next to a book, etc.) Ask *Where's Gracie?* Give the flashcard to a learner to put somewhere. If they are a stronger learner, they can ask *Where's Gracie?* If not, ask the question and choose the next learner to answer correctly to put the flashcard in a new place. Repeat a few times.

Pupil's Book, page 8

1.05 The Friendly Farm song

- Play the introductory song at the beginning of the cartoon story. Mime a happy face on the first line, do a thumbs up on the second line, and mime waving at the animals on the third line. Learners listen and copy.

Track 1.05
See The Friendly Farm song on page TB5

1.05 The Friendly Farm

- Say *Open your Pupil's Books at page 8*. Ask *Who can you see in the pictures?* Learners name the characters. Ask *What's this?* Point to the crayon. Repeat with other objects (pencil, desk, bag).
- Ask *Who is the teacher? Is the book in the bag?* Write the questions on the board. Say *Listen*. Play the audio or video. Learners listen and read.

Track 1.05
The Friendly Farm song + see cartoon on Pupil's Book page 8

- Learners answer the questions in pairs before the class check (*Gracie is the teacher. No, the book isn't in the bag.*)
- Play the audio or video again. Pause after each frame and check comprehension by asking questions:

  Frame 1: *Who has the bag?* (*Gracie*)
  Frame 2: *Where's the pencil?* (*It's under the desk.*)
  Frame 3: *Where's the crayon?* (*It's on the desk.*)
  Frame 4: *Where's the bag?* (*It's next to the desk.*)
  Frame 5: *Who is coming?* (*Jim and Jenny*)
  Frame 6: *Where is the book?* Say *It's in Gracie's mouth!* Point to your mouth.
- Play the audio or video again. Mime as you play it. Learners copy. Dip down and gesture 'under' with your hands for frame 2, stand up and gesture 'on' with flat palms for frame 3, gesture 'next to' by showing the space next to you for frame 4.
- Put the learners into groups of seven and give each group a role from the sketch (Gracie, Rocky, Shelly, Harry, Cameron, Jenny, Jim). They read the speech bubbles. All learners repeat the mimes as they read.

  Extension Tell learners to cover the cartoon and to try to remember. Ask questions: *Where's the pencil?* (*It's under the desk.*) *Where's the crayon?* (*It's on the desk.*) *Where's the bag?* (*It's next to the desk.*)

Activity Book, page 8

See pages TB120–132

Ending the lesson

- **SA** Repeat the self-assessment technique used at the start of the lesson to see how well learners think they understand the vocabulary. Is there any change?
- Show the class a soft toy. Ask *What's his/her name?* Learners can think of a name.
- Put the soft toy somewhere in the classroom, e.g. on a book. Ask *Where's (name of soft toy)?* Learners answer. Choose a learner to put the soft toy somewhere else. Ask *Where's (name of soft toy)?* Learners answer. Continue, nominating learners to put the soft toy in different places.

  Extra support Learners who find answering difficult can move the soft toy.

1 Language practice 1

Learning outcomes By the end of the lesson, learners will be able to ask and write sentences about where things are, using prepositions.

New language *Where is/are … ? It's / They are in / on / next to / under …*

Recycled language school

Materials In the classroom 1 flashcards, classroom objects, audio, sticky labels (two for each learner), digital Mission poster, Teacher's Resource Book page 14 worksheet

Key Competences

- Learn to use prepositions to talk about where things are.
- Make labels for the classroom.
- Reflect on their own learning.
- Interact with the digital poster.

Warm-up

- Go around the room asking *What is it? (It's a desk.) What are they? (They're crayons.)*

Presentation

- Point to the flashcards in various locations, highlighting single objects. Ask *What is it? How many? Where is it?* (e.g. *It's next to the book.*)
- Point to the objects, highlighting plurals. Ask *What are they? How many? Where are they?* (e.g. *They're on the desk.*)

Pupil's Book, page 9

1.06 Gracie's Grammar

- Say *Open your Pupil's Books at page 9*. Point to Gracie's Grammar box. Write the same sentences on the board.
- Learners copy the sentences.
- Play the audio. Pause for learners to repeat each sentence.

Track 1.06
See Pupil's Book page 9

- Draw a small square desk next to the sentence *It's on the desk*. In a different colour, draw a crayon on the desk.
- Learners draw a picture to illustrate each sentence in their notebooks. Monitor and check.

1 1.07 Listen and stick. Then look, read and write.

- Play the audio. Learners point to the sticker.

Track 1.07

1 Gracie: Where's the rubber, Harry?
Harry: The rubber's on the desk.
Gracie: Very good, Harry.
Shelly: The rubber's on the desk.

2 Gracie: Where are the crayons?
Shelly: The crayons are in the pencil case.
Gracie: Good.

3 Gracie: Where's the pen?
Shelly: The pen's under the book.

4 Gracie: Where are the pencils?
Shelly: The pencils are next to the book.

- Play the audio again. Learners stick in the stickers.
- Say *Look at Activity 1.* Underline *The rubber's* and *The pen's*. Ask *How many? (One)* Underline *The crayons are* and *The pencils are*. Ask *How many crayons? (Three)*
- Say *Read and write the word*. Learners write.

Key: 2 in 3 under 4 next to

mission Stage 1

- Show learners the first stage of the digital Mission poster: 'Labels'. Say *We label the classroom. Let's make labels.* Give out two sticky labels to each learner.
- Learners complete the worksheet task in the Teacher's Resource Book page 14 (see teaching notes on TRB page 7).
- Alternatively, if you do not have the Teacher's Resource Book, give out two sticky labels to each learner.
- Display flashcards of classroom objects. Choose one and ask *What is it?* (e.g. *A pencil case*) Write the word next to it.
- Choose a plural item. Ask *What are they?* (e.g. *Pens*) Write it up.
- Say *Look at the pictures. Choose two. Write two words.*
- Choose five or six stronger learners to come to the front to demonstrate. Ask them *Where is/are (an object)?* If they have this word on their label, they find an example of each object in the room, stick on the sticker and say *Here it is! / Here they are!* The rest of the learners find the object and stick on their label, saying *Here it is!*
- For ideas on monitoring and assessment, see Introduction.

Activity Book, page 9

See pages TB120–132

Activity Book, page 6

- Say *Look at page 6 of your Activity Book*. Review *My unit goals*. Ask *How is your Mission?*
- Learners reflect and choose a smiley face for *My mission diary 1*. Monitor.

Ending the lesson

- **SA** Go back to Stage 1 on the digital Mission poster. Say *We labelled the classroom. Good work*. Add a tick to the 'Labels' stage or invite a learner to do it. Use self-assessment (see Introduction).
- Give out a completion sticker.

Gracie's Grammar

1.06

Where's the crayon?

It's **on** the desk.

It's **under** the book.

It's **in** the pencil case.

It's **next to** the rubber.

1 Listen and stick. Then look, read and write.

1.07

1 The rubber's *on* the desk.

2 The crayons are ________ the pencil case.

3 The pen's ________ the book.

4 The pencils are ________ the book.

mission STAGE 1

Make labels for your classroom.

- Write the words.
- Find, say and stick.

Where are the pencils?

Here they are.

My mission diary
Activity Book page 6

Vocabulary 2 and song

1 Listen and colour. Then sing the song.

1.08

Jim, Jim is in the classroom.
The yellow book is on the bookcase.
The white paper's in the cupboard
and the ruler's under the desk.

Jenny, Jenny's in the playground.
The teacher's next to the window.
The red bag is on the grey wall
and the board's next to the door.
Yes, it is. Yes, it is. Yes, it is.

2 Ask and answer.

Where's the ruler?

It's under the desk.

Learning outcomes By the end of the lesson, learners will have practised the language through song.

New language *board, bookcase, cupboard, door, paper, playground, ruler, wall, window*

Recycled language classroom, colours, *Where is/are ...?*, prepositions

Materials In the classroom 2 flashcards, coloured pens or pencils (including yellow, white, red, grey), audio, video

Key Competences

Learn new classroom vocabulary through a song.

Work in pairs to ask and answer about where things are.

Complete a crossword puzzle.

Warm-up

- Ask *Where are we?* (*We're in the classroom.*) Repeat.
- Ask *Where's (name of learner)?* Learners call out *He/She is in the classroom*.
- The first learner asks *Where's (name of second learner)?* Learners call out *He/She is in the classroom*.
- The second learner asks the question about a third learner.

  Extra support Give learners the sentence to repeat.

  Stronger learners Learners can add extra information after the class say *In the classroom*, e.g. *And she's next to the desk*.
- **SA** Use self-assessment to check how well learners think they understand the vocabulary. See Introduction.

Pupil's Book, page 10

1 1.08 Listen and colour. Then sing the song.

- Say *Open your Pupil's Books at page 10*. Ask the names of the items in the picture. Alternatively, use the flashcards of the classroom. Point to the items and ask *What is it?* (*board, bookcase, paper, cupboard, playground, window, wall, ruler, door*) Learners repeat each word several times.
- Go through the items again and for each one ask *What colour is it?*
- Draw a picture of a ruler and a small bookcase on the board. Ask two stronger learners to come to the front. Give one a blue board marker and one a red board marker. Say *The ruler is red. Colour it in*. The learner with the red pen colours in the ruler quickly. Say *The bookcase is blue. Colour it in*. The learner with the blue pen colours in the bookcase.
- Say *Let's listen and colour*. Show the learners coloured pens or pencils. Say *Find yellow, find red, find white*. Check they have the right pens or pencils. When the learners are ready, play the audio or video. Learners listen and colour.

Track 1.08

Rocky: I'm Rocky-Doodle-Doo and ... here's our song for today: *In the classroom*.

See song on Pupil's Book page 10

- Play the audio or video again if necessary.
- Check answers.
- Play the audio or video again. Learners repeat the song. They hold in the air the pen or pencil of the colours as they hear them.
- Divide the class in half. Give each group a different part of the song. They sing again and wave their pens, but only for their part.

Key: book – yellow, paper – white, bag – red

1.09 **Extension** Once learners are confidently singing along to the song, try singing the karaoke version as a class.

2 Ask and answer.

- Point to the first picture. Learners ask *Where's the ruler?* and answer *It's under the desk*.
- Learners work in pairs to ask and answer about the four pictures. Monitor and check.
- Check answers.
- Show the picture of Rocky in the bottom right-hand corner. Read out the question. Stand next to the board. Learners call out *(Your name) is next to the board*. Stand in a different place. Repeat. Continue around the room.

Key: Where's the paper? It's in the cupboard.
Where's the yellow book? It's on the bookcase.
Where's the board? It's on the wall / next to the door.

Activity Book, page 10

See pages TB120–132

Ending the lesson

- **SA** Repeat the self-assessment technique used at the start of the lesson to see how well learners think they understand the vocabulary. Is there any change?
- Ask a learner to stand up, e.g. next to the window. Ask *Where's (name)?* Learners answer, e.g. (*next to the window*). Choose another learner. Encourage them to stand somewhere different in the room. Ask *Where's (name)?* Learners answer. Continue with different learners. Show them they can go under things, e.g. a desk, or in things, e.g. the cupboard, to make it fun.

  Extra support You can choose weaker learners to stand in different places for this activity.

  Stronger learners You can choose these learners to answer the questions.

1 Language practice 2

Learning outcomes By the end of the lesson, learners will be able to ask and answer what singular and plural nouns are.

New language *What's this? It's a … / What are these? They're …*

Recycled language classroom

Materials small pictures of classroom objects, In the classroom 1 and 2 flashcards or real objects, sticky notes, pieces of paper, audio, video, digital Mission poster

Key Competences

- Learn and practise singular and plural nouns with *this*, *these*, *it's* and *they're*.
- Work together in groups to find new words to learn.
- Reflect on their own learning.
- Interact with the digital poster.

Warm-up

- Give each learner a picture of a classroom object and demonstrate. Go to a learner and point to your own picture. Ask *What is it?* The learner answers. Ask *What colour is it?* The learner answers. The learner asks the same questions, pointing to their own picture. You answer.
- Learners mingle, asking and answering questions.

Pupil's Book, page 11

1 (1.10) What are they talking about? Listen and tick ✓.

- Point to the pictures. Learners say the names of the items (*a bookcase, table and chairs, pencils*).
- Play the audio. Learners listen and tick the picture they are talking about. Check answers.

Track 1.10

Boy: Ooh! Look, Mum! What's this?
Woman: It's a table … and what are these?
Boy: They're chairs.

Key: Picture 2

Presentation

- Draw on the board the outline of a large house with a door. Stick up one sticky note to represent a window.
- Point to the window and ask *What's this?* (*A window*) Say *This is a window*. Learners repeat. Ask *How many?* (*One*)
- Stick up seven more sticky notes. Ask *What are these?* (*Windows*) Say *These are windows*. Learners repeat. Ask *How many?* (*Eight*)

(1.11) Gracie's Grammar

- Write the four sentences from Gracie's Grammar on the board. Read each one and learners repeat.
- Learners copy the sentences in their notebooks.
- Play the audio, pausing so learners can repeat.

Track 1.11
See Pupil's Book page 11

2 Look at the pictures in Activity 1. Ask and answer.

- Point to the pictures and ask *What's this? What are these*? Learners answer.
- In pairs, learners ask and answer about the pictures.

Extension Learners walk around the classroom and ask and answer questions about objects in the room.

Extra support Learners read the questions.

mission Stage 2

- Show learners the second stage of the digital Mission poster: 'Words'. Say *We learn new words*.
- Show learners In the classroom flashcards or real items. Ask the names.
- Say *Look at the classroom*. Find an object they don't know in English. Ask *What's this?* When the learners don't answer, put a coloured sticky note on it as a marker.
- Put learners into small groups. Give out a sticky note to each group. They find something in the room they don't know in English and put a sticky note on it.
- Learners then look around the room and choose one sticky note each. Say *Ask me*. Learners point to the object and ask *What's this? / What are these?* Give each word. Learners repeat several times. Write the words on the board.
- Learners draw what they have chosen on pieces of paper and write the word.

Fast finishers Learners can do a second object.

- Keep the drawings and words for the final Mission stage.

Activity Book, page 11

See pages TB120–132

Activity Book, page 6

- Say *Look at page 6 of your Activity Book*. Review *My unit goals*. Ask *How is your Mission?*
- Learners reflect and choose a smiley face for *My mission diary 2*. Monitor.

Ending the lesson

- **SA** Go back to Stage 2 on the digital Mission poster. Add a tick to the 'Words' stage. Use self-assessment (see Introduction).
- Give out a completion sticker.

1 1.10 What are they talking about? Listen and tick ✓.

1

☐

2

☐

3

☐

1.11 Gracie's Grammar

What**'s this**?	**It's** a window.
What **are these**?	**They're** windows.

2 Look at the pictures in Activity 1. Ask and answer.

What's this? It's a chair. What are these? They're pencils.

mission STAGE 2

Choose a new word to learn.

- Look around your classroom. What words don't you know?
- Ask your teacher. Then draw and say.

What's this? It's a television.

STAGE 2

My mission diary
Activity Book
page 6

Cross-curricular

Be kind at school

1 Watch the video.

2 Who is kind? Look and tick ✓.

1

2

3

4

3 1.12 Listen and number. Then act it out.

a

b

Learning outcomes By the end of the lesson, learners will be able to talk and understand about being kind.

New language *being kind*, *Thank you*, *Are you OK?*

Recycled language classroom objects, *who*, numbers

Materials video, messy board and bookshelf (or desk), flashcard of cake, pictures from Digital photo bank of flowers, a child pushing another child, and a child helping another child with their homework, audio

Key Competences

- Learn and practise vocabulary related to good behaviour at school.
- Learn the value of being kind at school.
- Act out a dialogue.

Warm-up

- Put some words or marks on the board. Ask a learner to come up and clean it for you. Say *Thank you!*
- Show an untidy part of a bookshelf (or pile things in a mess on your desk). Ask learners to help tidy it. Say *Thank you!*

Pupil's Book, page 12

1 Watch the video.

- Say *Let's watch the video*. Learners watch the video about being kind at school and answer the questions at the end of the video.

Presentation

- Say *Let's be kind*. Show the flashcard of a cake. Act out cutting a cake and offering it to the learners. They can mime eating it. Say *I'm kind*.
- Now mime taking cake away and keeping it all yourself. Say *I'm not kind*.
- Show a picture of flowers. Act out giving flowers to learners. Say *I'm kind*. Act out keeping the flowers yourself. Say *I'm not kind*. Check understanding.
- Ask a learner to come up to the front and get him/her to demonstrate coughing a lot. Ask the learner *Are you OK?* The learner stops coughing, recovers, smiles and answers *Yes, thank you*.

2 Who is kind? Look and tick ✓.

- Put up two pictures on the board: one showing a child pushing another child, and another showing a child helping another child with their homework.
- Ask *Who is kind?* Learners point to the picture of the child helping. Tick the picture.
- Say *Open your Pupil's Books at page 12. Look at the pictures. Who is kind?*
- Put the learners into pairs. Learners look and tick pictures. Check answers.

Key: Pictures 1 and 4

3 1.12 Listen and number. Then act it out.

- Say *Look at page 12*. Show the small boxes next to the pictures.
- Say *Listen and number*. Play the audio. Learners listen and number. Monitor.
- Check answers.

Track 1.12

1
Girl 1: Here you are.
Girl 2: Thank you.
2
Boy 1: Are you OK?
Boy 2: Yes, thank you.

Key: Picture a – 2 Picture b – 1

- Put the learners into pairs. Encourage them to act out the dialogues. Monitor and support.

Stronger learners Encourage them to act out their dialogues in front of the class.

Activity Book, page 12

See pages TB120–132

Ending the lesson

- Tell the learners to think of other ways to help each other, e.g. picking up pens, helping with school work, sharing food. Ask them to work in pairs – one learner should act out helping the other, and the person being helped should say *Thank you*.

Extension Learners show their mime to the rest of the class. The class guess how the person is helping. You may need to say the correct words for them, e.g. *Yes, he's helping with school work.*

Learning outcomes By the end of the lesson, learners will be able to talk about sharing and helping and write the words.

New language *help, listen, share, work together*

Recycled language classroom words, *being kind*

Materials building bricks or blocks, pens, pictures from Digital photo bank of people being kind (giving flowers, holding open door, offering drink) and people being unkind (leaving bag on seat where people are standing, children playing in a group and leaving another child on their own), large sheets of paper and coloured pens or pencils

Key Competences

- Learn expressions related to being kind in class.
- Learn about sharing and helping in class; Work together to make a class poster.
- Reflect on their own learning.
- Interact with the digital poster.

Warm-up

- Put learners into groups of four. Say *Let's build a classroom*. Demonstrate that you want the learners to make a model of a classroom using the building bricks, by starting your own model. Create walls and say *Here's the classroom*. Add in more bricks and say *Here's a desk*.
- Say *Work together*. Gesture for the learners to work in a group. Learners build their models.
- When they have finished, ask each group to show the class what they have done, e.g. *It's a desk. It's the board*.

Presentation

- Say *Listen*. Gesture to your ear. Take out some pens. Say *Let's share the pens*. Give out pens to different learners. Encourage them to say *Thank you*. Say *Share*. Learners repeat.
- Say *I need my pens*. Take back one or two pens from a few learners. Choose a confident learner and indicate that you want them to help collect the pens back in. Say *Please help*. The learner helps collect the pens. Check understanding. Say *Help*. Learners repeat.
- Give pencils to a confident learner. Say *Share the pencils with the class*. Encourage the learner to share out the pencils. Other learners say *Thank you*.
- Choose another learner and say *Help me get the pencils*. The learner helps.
- Say *Thank you for helping. We work together.* Say *Work together*. Learners repeat.

Pupil's Book, page 13

4 Look at the poster. Write the words.

- Say *Look at page 13 of your Pupil's Book*. Show the photos. Say *Point to the pen. Point to the books*, etc.
- Show the words and the spaces to write them in. Show the example: *work together.* Say *Write the words.*
- Learners write the words in the spaces. Check answers.

Key: 2 help 3 listen 4 share

mission Stage 3

- Say to the learners *Here's our class. What do we do?* Mime pushing. Ask *Is it OK?* (*No*) Ask *Share?* (*Yes*) Write *share* on the board and draw a simple picture to show this, e.g. stick figures of two learners sharing a book. Ask learners to think of other ideas, e.g. *work together*, *help*, but don't do pictures for these.

  Alternative Use pictures from Digital photo bank of people being kind and unkind.
- Show the class the third stage of the Mission poster: 'Make a class poster'.
- Put the learners into groups of three. Give out large sheets of paper and coloured pens or pencils. Tell the learners to draw some pictures to show class rules and copy words onto the poster.
- Learners work together. Monitor and support. When learners finish, display the posters on the wall.
- For ideas on monitoring and assessment, see Introduction.

Activity Book, page 13

See pages TB120–132

Activity Book, page 6

- Say *Look at page 6 of your Activity Book*. Review *My unit goals*. Ask *How is your Mission?*
- Learners reflect and choose a smiley face for *My mission diary 3*. Monitor.

Ending the lesson

- **SA** Go back to Stage 3 on the digital Mission poster. Add a tick to the 'Make a class poster' stage or invite a learner to do it. Use self-assessment (see Introduction).
- Give out a completion sticker.

4 Look at the poster. Write the words.

help listen share ~~work together~~

Be kind in our classroom

1 work together

2 ______________

3 ______________

4 ______________

mission STAGE 3

Make a class poster.

- How can we be kind at school? Say.
- Write and draw a class poster.

STAGE 3

My mission diary

Activity Book page 6

1 **Look at the pictures. What can you see? Find and tick ✓.**

book	☐	paper	☐	pencil	☐	rubber	☐
crayon	☐	pen	☐	pencil case	☐	ruler	☐

The first day

1.13

Knock! Knock!
It's Lucy at the door.

Hello, Lucy.

Hello, Max.

Lucy and Max are friends. Today is the first day of school.

It's time to pack your bag.

My bag …

It's in the cupboard.

Learning outcomes By the end of the lesson, learners will have read about school and learnt about being organised.

New language *rule, take*

Recycled language prepositions, school, *Where is / Where are … ?*

Materials classroom objects or In the classroom flashcards (pen, pencil, ruler, rubber, book, bag), audio, paper

Key Competences

Read and listen to a story; Revise school vocabulary.

Draw a picture based on verbal information.

Warm-up

- Ask learners to put classroom objects on their desk: a pen, a pencil, a ruler, a rubber, a book and their bag.
- Have similar objects on your desk and a bag of your own. Say *I'm going to school*. Point to your bag. Say *I'm packing my bag*. Say *Here are the things I take to school*. Hold up a pen. Say *I take my pen*. Learners repeat. Continue with the other objects, saying *I take my …* Learners say the sentence with you, filling in the name of the object.
- Put things into your bag one by one. As you do this, chant *I put my pen in the bag. I put my pencil in the bag. I put my ruler in the bag*, etc. Learners listen and join in as you hold up the objects. When everything is ready, say *I'm ready for school!*
- Now learners pack their bags. They put the objects in as you say the sentences. Say *We're ready for school!* Learners repeat.

Presentation

- Say *We are going to read about school*. Say *School rules*. Ask a learner to come to the front. Mime pushing them. Encourage the learners to say *No!* Say *'Don't push' is a school rule*. Mime coming into a room and holding the door for someone and letting them pass. Say *'Be good' is a school rule*. Check understanding of *rule*.
- Learners stand up and mime pushing. Say *No! It's a school rule*. Learners repeat. Learners mime holding a door open for someone. Say *Be good. It's a school rule*. Learners repeat.

Pupil's Book, page 14

1 Look at the pictures. What can you see? Find and tick ✓.

- Say *Open your Pupil's Books at page 14*. Point to the list of words. Read the words with learners.
- In pairs, learners look at the picture and tick the objects they can see.
- Check answers.

Key: book, paper, pencil, crayon, pen, ruler

1.13 The first day

- Focus on the pictures. Look at each picture and ask questions, e.g. *Who is this?* (*Max, Lucy*) *Where is Lucy?* (*At the door*) *Where is the pen?* (*On the table*)
- Say *Read and listen to the first part*. Play the audio. Learners listen and read. Pause the audio at the end of the dialogue on page 14. Ask *Where's Max's bag?* (*In the cupboard*) Ask *What does Max take to school?* Learners suggest ideas. If you have objects or flashcards for what they suggest, put these out on the desk or board. Say *Let's read and listen.*

Track 1.13
See story on Pupil's Book pages 14–15

- Play the rest of the audio. Check if their guesses were correct by holding up or showing the objects/flashcards they suggested and say *Max takes a (name of object)*. Learners say *Yes* or *No*. Put aside any objects that are incorrect. If they missed any, show them the object and say *And Max takes (name of object)*. Ask *Why does Max take a pencil, a pen, a ruler, books and crayons?* Say *It's the school rule!* Learners repeat.
- Ask *But where is Max's bag?* (*In the cupboard*) Point to the rest of the objects and say *Where are these? Listen again.* Play the audio again. Check answers by showing each object and asking *Where is … ?* Learners give answers (pencil – under the chair, pen – on the table, ruler – next to the pen, books – on the bookcase, crayons – on the floor under the window).
- Ask *What's the number 1 rule?* Tap your watch or show a clock. Learners say *Don't be late!* Check understanding.

Activity Book, page 14

See pages TB120–132

Ending the lesson

- Ask learners to pack their bags. Demonstrate *I put my book in the bag*.
- Put learners into pairs. Ask them to pack their bags. They take it in turns to put away items saying what they are doing.
- Monitor and check as learners pack.

1 Literature

Learning outcomes By the end of the lesson, learners will be able to tell simple events in a story.

New language *Oh, yes*

Recycled language classroom objects, prepositions of place, *Where is/are …?*

Materials coloured pencils or pens, classroom objects, e.g. book, pens, pencils, a bag of objects for learners to guess

Social and Emotional Skill: Helping others

- After reading the story, ask learners the questions *Are Max's things in his bag?* (No) *Who helps Max to find his things?* (Lucy) Then say *Lucy wants to help Max. Lucy is Max's friend and friends help each other.*
- Say *Does anyone help you find things? Do you help people to find things they lose? It's important to help people at home and at school.* Talk about ways that learners help each other and help their families at home. Learners can act out helping someone and the rest of the class guess how they're helping. Demonstrate washing up or making the bed. Learners don't need to learn the vocabulary at this point; they just need to recognise ways of helping.
- Have a *Let's be helpful* day. Pre-teach *Can I help you?* Then pick up a pile of books and one learner says *Can I help you?* Say *Yes, please. Thank you.*

Key Competences

- Learn to tell simple events in a story.
- Learn about being organised.
- Act out a story.

Warm-up

- Draw a table on the board. Ask learners to copy it. Give simple instructions, e.g. *Draw a book on the table. Draw a bag under the table.*
- Learners draw what you say. Check and monitor. Allow learners to compare their final drawings.
- Put the learners into pairs.
- Ask the learners to draw their own picture, but not to show their partner.
- Ask each learner to describe their picture to their partner. Their partner tries to draw the same picture. When they have finished, they compare their answers.
- **SA** Use self-assessment to check how well learners think they understand the vocabulary. See Introduction.

Presentation

- Put a few objects in places learners can see, e.g. a book on the table, a bag on a chair, and a pen on the book.
- Ask *Where is my book?* Mime looking until learners answer.
- Say *Oh, yes.* Ask learners to repeat, ensuring that you use correct intonation.
- Repeat with all the objects, getting learners to say *Oh, yes*.

Pupil's Book, page 15

2 Act out the story.

- Say *Act out the story*. Summarise the story, sentence by sentence, using the objects and mime. Mime knocking at the door for the first line. Wave on lines 3 and 4. Mime looking for each *Where's my …?* question. For each answer, point to the object or flashcard. Then mime finding the object and putting it in the bag, e.g. for *It's under the chair*, mime bending down and getting it.
- At the end, mime tapping a watch or pointing to a clock for the last two lines. Learners copy.
- Repeat and encourage the learners to act the story.
- Put learners in pairs. One learner is Max and one is Lucy. Read the dialogue. Learners repeat their line only and act out the actions, e.g. Max mimes looking for the object, Lucy points, and Max mimes getting it, saying *Oh, yes* each time.

3 Ask and answer.

- Put learners into small groups. One learner asks *What's in your school bag?* Learners open their bags and show what they brought with them. They say *Two books and a pencil*, etc.
- When they have shown their objects, they should put them back into their bags. The rest of the group try to remember what they had.

Activity Book, page 15

See pages TB120–132

Ending the lesson

- **SA** Repeat the self-assessment technique used at the start of the lesson to see how well learners think they understand the vocabulary. Is there any change?
- Get out your bag (or prepare a bag and put in different items in advance). Ask *What's in my bag?*
- Put learners into groups of five. Give learners three minutes to think of a list of items in your bag.

  Fast finishers Make sure there is a fast finisher in each group. The fast finisher can make a list of the items the group thinks are in your bag.
- Take the items out of your bag one by one. Learners tick those in their list. They get a point for each correct guess.
- Check which group has the most points at the end.

1

Where's my pencil?

It's under the chair.

Oh, yes.
Take a pencil to school – that's the rule.

Where's my pen?

It's on the table.

Oh, yes.
Take a pen to school – that's the rule.

And where's my ruler?

It's next to your pen.

Oh, yes.
Take a ruler to school –
that's the rule.

Where are my books?

They're on the bookcase.

Oh, yes.
Take your books to
school – that's the rule.

And my crayons?

What are these? The crayons are on the floor, under the window.

Hurry up. It's time to go!
Don't be late for school – that's the number 1 rule!

2 Act out the story.

Where's my pencil?

It's under the chair.

3 Ask and answer.

What's in your school bag?

Two books and a pencil.

1 Look at the pictures. Say the words.

a

b
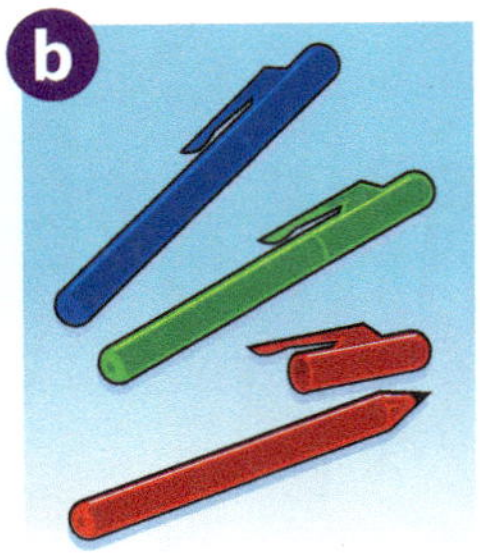
c
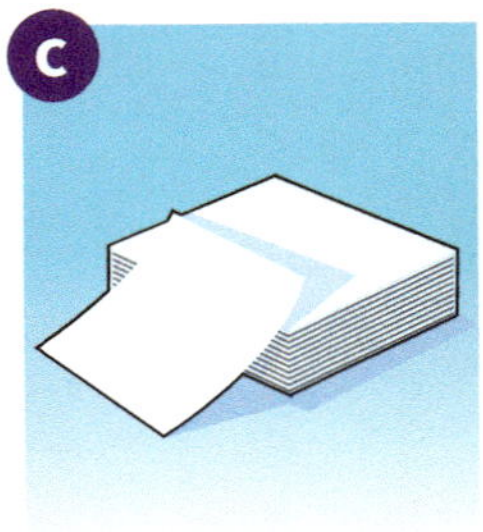
d

e

It's a door.

2 Read and do.

Put a tick (✓) in the box. ☐ Put a cross (✗) in the box. ☐

3 Play the game. Point and say.

This is a rubber.

No. Cross!

This is a door.

Yes. Tick!

4 Look and read. Put a tick (✓) or a cross (✗) in the box. There are two examples.

Examples

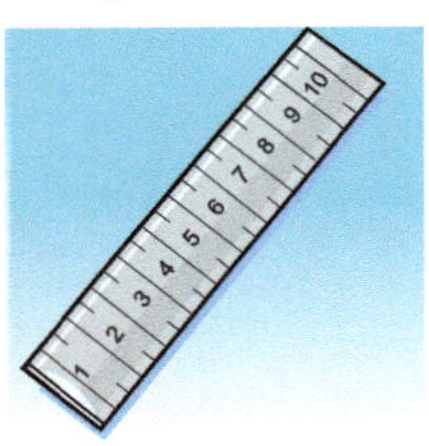

ruler ✓

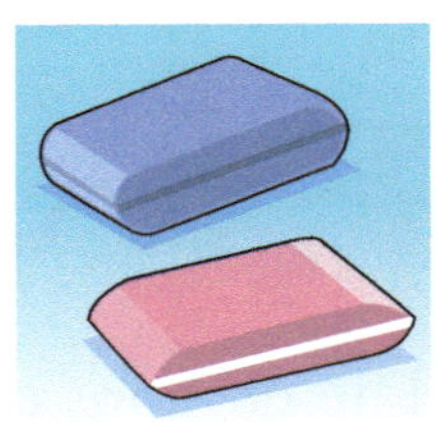

pens ✗

Questions

1
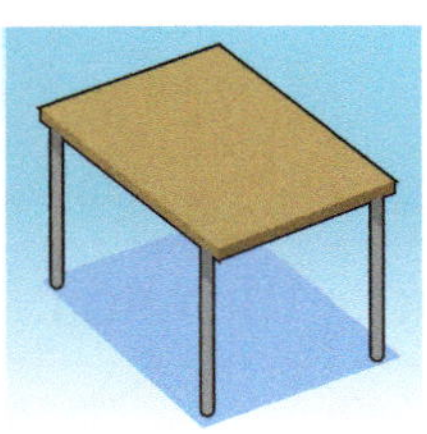

chair ☐

2

bags ☐

Practise writing clear ticks and crosses.

Learning outcomes By the end of the lesson, learners will have read for correct information, learnt how to write clear crosses and ticks, and learnt to read and think before answering.

Recycled language school, *This is / These are …*

Materials some large cards – one with a cross and one with a tick on it, plus a pair of cards for each group of three learners (or blank cards and pens)

Key Competences

- Revise classroom vocabulary.
- Learn to write clear crosses and ticks and to think before answering; Practise activity types found in *Pre A1 Starters* exams.
- Play a vocabulary game in pairs.

Warm-up

- Put learners into groups of three and give them the two cards with a cross and a tick you have prepared.
  Alternative Give learners blank cards and ask them to draw a large cross and a tick on them.
- Show them a tick. Say *It's a tick*. Learners repeat. Repeat with the cross, saying *It's a cross*.
- Say *I am (name of a different teacher)*. The learners quickly hold up the card with the cross. Say *Very good. Cross.* Say *I am (your name)*. Learners hold up the 'tick' card. Say *Very good. Tick.*
  Note: Stop them if they hold up the card before they have heard the sentence properly. Say *No. Think first.* Mime thinking. Then ask the question again.
- Continue to say sentences – some true and some false. These could include saying the colour of something or where it is, e.g. *My book is blue. The pen is on the bag.* Learners respond.
- If you want, you can award points to groups.
- **SA** Use self-assessment to check how well learners think they understand the vocabulary. See Introduction.

Presentation

- Say *Let's do a reading exam*. Write *Reading Exam* on the board.
- Sit down and act out quickly looking at a paper and then writing answers very fast. Say *Is this good?* (*No*)
- Act reading carefully, thinking and then writing answers. Say *Is this good?* (*Yes*) *Very good. Read. Then think.*

Pupil's Book, page 16

1 Look at the pictures. Say the words.

- Point to the pictures one by one. Ask *What's this? / What are these?* as appropriate. Learners answer.

Key: a It's a door. b They are three pens. c It's paper. d They are two chairs. e It's a bookcase.

2 Read and do.

- Draw a cross and a tick on the board. Learners read the sentences and draw in the boxes. Monitor and support.

3 Play the game. Point and say.

- Point to a picture from Activity 1 and say, e.g. *This is a rubber.* (*No*) Gesture to the tick and cross on the board. Encourage learners to say *Cross*. Repeat with a correct example, e.g. *This is a door*, and encourage learners to say *Yes. Tick.*
- Put the learners into pairs. They take it in turns. One points to a picture and says a sentence; the other responds.

4 Look and read. Put a tick (✓) or a cross (✗) in the box. There are two examples.

- Say *Let's read and put ticks and crosses.*
- Read the first example. Point to the tick and learners say *Tick*. Repeat with the second example and *Cross*.
- Say *Very good. Now read and write ticks or crosses.* Learners read the words and put in a tick or cross. Check answers.

Key: 1 ✗ 2 ✗

Activity Book, page 16

See pages TB120–132

Ending the lesson

- **SA** Repeat the self-assessment technique used at the start of the lesson to see how well learners think they understand the vocabulary. Is there any change?
- Point to the monkey at the bottom of Pupil's Book page 16 and read the sentence.
- Give each learner a piece of blank paper. Choose a leader for each group of five. Tell the leaders they will help you.
- Demonstrate on the board. If you have a board timer, set it to count down from ten seconds. If not, tap your watch and say *I have ten seconds*. Count down from ten and as you do so try to write as many neat ticks on the board as you can. Include a very badly written tick. When you reach zero, say *How many ticks?* Count with the learners. Write the total on the board. Then point to the bad tick and say *No. It's very bad.* Take it off the total.
- Tell the leaders to watch as the learners draw and to check everyone stops at the right time. Say *Now you draw ticks.* Say *Go!* Count down as the learners draw.
- Ask them to check how many they drew. Tell the leaders to check the ticks are good and how many each person has.
- Repeat with crosses.
- Ask each group leader who had the most ticks or crosses.

Learning outcomes By the end of the lesson, learners will have revised the language in the unit and role played being a teacher.

Recycled language unit language

Materials a soft ball, flashcards and real classroom objects, learners' drawings from Mission Stage 2

Key Competences

- Revise vocabulary and language learnt in the unit.
- Complete self-assessment tasks and reflect on their own learning.
- Work together in groups to role play being the teacher.

Warm-up

- Ask learners to stand in a circle. Put classroom objects or flashcards into the middle of the circle on the floor.
- Throw a ball to one of the learners. They pick up an object and ask *What's this? / What are these?* They throw the ball. The learner who catches it answers. They put the object somewhere, e.g. under a desk and ask *Where is it?* They throw the ball and the learner who catches it answers. This learner then throws the ball and chooses a new object.
- Check and monitor, making sure all learners are included.

Presentation

- Give learners their drawings and words from Mission Stage 2. If you don't have these, get them to look around the classroom and choose an object.

  Extra support Learners only use words learnt in Unit 1.

  Fast finishers Learners use more than one word and choose their favourite.
- When they all have a new word, go to the front. Say *Hello. I'm (your name). Today I'm the teacher.* Write this up.
- Show a picture. Say *Look! It's a (name of object).* Learners repeat a few times.
- Put the picture somewhere in the classroom. Ask *Where's the (name of object)?* Learners answer.
- Choose a stronger learner and ask them to come to the front and bring their picture.

Pupil's Book, page 17

mission in action!

Be the teacher.

- Point to the sentences on the board. The learner at the front says *Hello. I'm (name). Today I'm the teacher.* Encourage him/her to teach his/her word, showing the picture, pointing to the object and getting the learners to repeat. They put the picture somewhere in the classroom and ask the learners *Where's the (name of object)?* Learners answer. When they have finished, say *Well done! What a good teacher!*
- Put learners into groups of six and give each a number from *1* to *6*. They role play being a teacher. Learner 1 goes first, learner 2 goes second, etc.

  Extra support Tell learners who find this challenging that they will help the teacher by holding up the picture and putting it somewhere in the classroom.

  Fast finishers For learners who will do this easily, encourage them to add extra questions about their word to ask the learners, e.g. *What colour is it?*
- Monitor and support as learners talk.
- For ideas on monitoring and assessment, see Introduction.
- Put the learners into pairs. They go through the unit pages and point to pictures or elements of the unit and say to their partner *Tell me about the (name of an item in the unit).* The partner answers.

Self-assessment

- **SA** Say *Did you like our 'Be the teacher' Mission? A lot?* (cheer) *It's OK?* (smile) *Or Not much?* (shake your head and shrug). Encourage learners to show how they feel.
- Say *Do you know more English?* (Move your hand high to indicate an increase.) Learners respond. If they say *yes*, say *Good! Well done!* If they don't, say *We can try again!*
- Say *Our next Mission is 'All about me'.* Say *How can we do better? Shall we learn more words?* Say *Put your hand up if you want to learn … more words.* (Learners can raise hands.) *More speaking? Writing? Reading? Listening?* (Learners raise hands or not depending on how they feel.)

Activity Book, page 17

See pages TB120–132

Activity Book, page 6

- Say *Look at page 6 of your Activity Book.* Review *My unit goals*. Ask *How is your Mission?*
- Learners reflect and choose a smiley face for *My mission diary* the final stage. Monitor.
- Point to the sunflower. Learners read the 'can do' statements and tick them if they agree they have achieved them. They colour each leaf green if they are very confident or orange if they think they need more practice.
- Point to the word stack sign. Ask learners to look back at the unit and find at least five new words they have learnt. They write them in their word stack.

Ending the lesson

- Go back to the completion stage on the digital Mission poster. Add a tick or invite a learner to do it. Use self-assessment (see Introduction).
- Give out a completion sticker.
- Tell the learners *We made our classroom English. You have finished your Mission! Well done!*

mission in action!

Be the teacher.

My mission diary
Activity Book page 6

★ Say hello to your class.

Hello. I'm Marcus. Today I'm the teacher.

★ Teach the class your word.

Look! It's a television.

★ Put your picture in the classroom.

★ Ask the class a question.

Where's the television?

It's on the desk.

2 All about us

1 **Watch the video. Draw something about you.**

mission Make an *All about me* book

In this unit I will:

1. Share pictures of my family.
2. Talk and write about me.
3. Show my favourite things.
★ Learn about my classmates.

Unit 2 learning outcomes

In Unit 2, learners learn to:

- talk about families and relationships between people
- understand, ask and answer sentences with *he/she*
- use *have/has got, Have/Has … got?, haven't/hasn't got*
- listen to and talk about what people look like
- read about senses and understand disability
- learn about being safe
- listen for detail

Materials video, balloons or ping pong balls, marker pens, coloured pens or pencils, digital Mission poster, a few photos of you with your family

Key Competences

Revise asking for and giving basic personal information.

Reflect on their own learning by going through the unit goals.

Draw a picture about themselves.

Self-assessment

- **SA** Say *Open your Pupil's Books at page 18*. Say *Look at the picture*. Indicate items on the page and ask questions using the language from the unit, e.g. *What is it? What is he/she doing? What colour is this?* Use self-assessment (see Introduction). Say *OK. Let's learn.*

Warm-up

- If possible, bring in balloons – one per learner, plus one extra for you. Inflate them before class. Alternatively, use ping pong balls. Using a marker, draw a smiley face. Write a name and a number (age) on each one.
- Ask the learners to stand up. Say *Hello. I'm (name) and I'm (age)*. Learners repeat, using their own name and age. Repeat. Ask *What's your name?* Learners repeat. Ask *How old are you?* Learners repeat. Point to a stronger learner. Say *Hello. What's your name?* The learner responds. Ask *How old are you?* The learner responds. Continue going around, with the learners asking and answering.
- Say *OK. Ready to catch?* Show them the balloon (or ball) and mime throwing and catching it.
- Say *You all need one balloon/ball*. Throw them quickly. Learners try to catch one. Keep one for yourself. Say *This is you*. Show your balloon and the name and age. Say *Hello. I'm (name on balloon) and I'm (age on balloon)*. Turn to a learner and ask *What's your name? How old are you?* The learner replies, using the information on their balloon.
- Learners turn to their partner and ask and answer.

  Alternative Learners can work in groups of six to eight.

Pupil's Book, page 18

1 Watch the video. Draw something about you.

- Say *In this unit we're talking about families*. Say *Let's watch the video*. To introduce the topic of the unit, play the video.
- Say *Look at page 18*. Point to the empty space. On the board, draw a sketch of your face and a simple object or pet, e.g. your car or your cat. Point and say *This is me. This is my car/cat*. Do a mime and make an associated noise, e.g. mime driving and the sound of a car engine, or stroking a cat and a miaow. Learners copy. Say *My favourite thing* and draw a smiley face and a heart next to it. Say *Me and my car/cat*, do the mime and make the noise. Learners repeat.
- Learners draw small pictures about themselves.
- Put learners into pairs. They show their drawing to their partner and say *Me and my (object)* and make an appropriate noise or mime.

mission Make an *All about me* book

- Show the digital Mission poster. Say *This is our Mission*.
- Say *All about me! Point to number 1. My family*. Repeat *fa-mi-ly* and clap on each syllable. Show a few photos of you with your family. Learners repeat *fa-mi-ly* and clap.
- Say *Point to number 2*. Show them the picture. Say *Me!* Point to yourself. Learners copy. Say *Number 2* and learners mime. Say *One, family* and clap on the syllables; say *Two, me!* and point to yourself. Repeat.
- Say *Point to number 3*. Show them the toys. Say *Favourite things!* Make a heart symbol with your fingers and thumbs and smile. Learners copy. Say *Three* and repeat.
- Go through sequence 1–3 again, calling out the numbers for learners to join in.
- Say *All about me!* Repeat the whole sequence. Say *This is our Mission*.

Activity Book, page 18

My unit goals

- Go through the unit goals with the learners. You can read these or put them onto the board or a poster.
- You can go back to these unit goals at the end of each Mission stage during the unit and review them.
- Say *This is our Mission page*.

Ending the lesson

- Write up the words *family*, *me* and *friends* on the board. Give learners one minute to look at the spelling.
- Rub the words off the board. Say the words. Learners write them.
- They check in pairs. Write the words on the board again.

2 Vocabulary 1

Learning outcomes By the end of the lesson, learners will be able to understand and talk about families.

New language *brother, dad, family, father, grandfather, grandma, grandmother, grandpa, mother, mum, sister, twins*

Recycled language colours, names, numbers

Materials Family flashcards, T-shirt flashcard, a scarf to cover learners' eyes, a picture from Digital photo bank of twins, audio, video

Key Competences

- Identify and name family members.
- Chant together as a class.
- Recognise and say words with letters *th* and *t*.

Warm-up

- Split the class into groups of four. Each group stands in a line facing you. Ask *Can you find something red?* The first person in each line needs to find a red object as fast as possible. The fastest gets a point. They sit down. Continue.

Presentation

- Put up the flashcard of Jenny. Ask *Who's this?* (*Jenny*)
- Add the flashcard of Mrs Friendly above Jenny. Ask *Who's this?* (*Mrs Friendly*) Say *Yes. It's Jenny's mother.*
- Add the flashcard of Mr Friendly next to Mrs Friendly and teach *father*. Add the flashcard of Jim next to Jenny and teach *brother* and *sister*.Repeat for *grandmother* and *grandfather*. Say *They are a family. Family.*

Pupil's Book, page 19

1 2.01 2.02 Listen and point. Then listen and number.

- Say *Open your Pupil's Books at page 19. Look at the picture.*
- Indicate the caption and read it. Say *It's a family.*
- Ask *Where's Mr Friendly?* The class points. Repeat.
- Play Track 2.01. Learners point to the people.

Tracks 2.01 and 2.02

Meet the Friendly family. This is Mrs Friendly. She's Jim and Jenny's mother.

Mrs Friendly: Hello.

This is Mr Friendly. He's Jim and Jenny's father.

Mr Friendly: Hello.

This is Grandma Friendly. She's Jim and Jenny's grandmother.

Grandma Friendly: Hello.

And this is Grandpa Friendly. He's Jim and Jenny's grandfather.

Grandpa Friendly: Hello.

Today the Friendly family are playing a game at home.

(1) Jenny: Are you … Grandma?
Grandma: No, it isn't Grandma. I'm here.
(2) Jenny: Are you Grandpa?
Grandpa: No, I'm Grandpa. I'm here.
(3) Jenny: Are you Mum?
Mrs Friendly: No, it isn't Mum. I'm here.
(4) Jenny: Are you Dad?
Mr Friendly: No, I'm Dad. I'm here.
(5) Jenny: So, you're my brother.
Jim: Yes, I'm your brother …
(6) Jim: … and you're my sister.
Jenny: Yes! You're a boy. I'm a girl …
Jim and Jenny: … and we're twins.
(7) All the adults: We're the Friendly family.

- Say *Look at Jenny. She's playing a game*. Ask *Who does Jenny find? Let's listen.* Play Track 2.01 again. (*Jim*) Say *Yes. They are twins*. Show a picture of twins.
- Say *Listen and number.* Play Track 2.02. Learners number.

Key: 1 Grandma 2 Grandpa 3 Mum 4 Dad 5 brother 6 sister 7 family

2 2.03 Say the chant.

- Say *Listen and say the chant*. Play the audio or video. Learners chant.

Track 2.03

(1) Boy, girl, twins,
sister and brother. (x2)
(2) Dad, father, mum, mother. (x2)
(3) Grandpa, grandfather,
Grandma, grandmother. (x2)
(1) Boy, girl, twins,
sister and brother. (x2)

3 2.04 Listen, point and say the colour.

- Show the T-shirt flashcard. Say *It's a T-shirt*.
- Ask questions about the picture on page 19, e.g. *Who's this?* (*Jenny*) *What colour is her T-shirt?* (*Purple*)
- Play the audio. Learners listen and say the colour.

Track 2.04

Where's the grandfather? What colour is his T-shirt?
Where's the mother? What colour is her T-shirt?
Where's the sister? What colour is her T-shirt?
Where's the grandmother? What colour is her T-shirt?
Where's the brother? What colour is his T-shirt?
Where's the father? What colour is his T-shirt?

Key: blue yellow purple orange green red

Activity Book, page 19

See pages TB120–132

Ending the lesson

- **SA** Show the Family flashcards. Ask *Do you know the words?* Use the self-assessment technique (see Introduction). Learners show how they feel.

Vocabulary 1

2

1 2.01 2.02 **Listen and point. Then listen and number.**

2 2.03 **Say the chant.**

3 2.04 **Listen, point and say the colour.**

The Friendly Farm

2.05

Learning outcomes By the end of the lesson, learners will understand when they hear a conversation about family members.

New language *eggs, He's/She's, she/he*

Recycled language colours, family, names

Materials Family flashcards, photos of your mother, father, sister or brother, grandmother and grandfather – either real or found on the Internet, Friendly Farm animals flashcards, audio, video

Key Competences

Read and listen to a story; Identify the present simple of the verb *to be*.

Role play a story in pairs.

Warm-up

- Place the Family flashcards on the floor. As you put them down, learners chant each family word, e.g. *Mother* for Mrs Friendly. Ask three learners to come to the front. Say a word, e.g. *Father*. Learners stand by the flashcard of Mr Friendly. Repeat with different family words and different learners.
- **SA** Use self-assessment to check how well learners think they understand the vocabulary. See Introduction.

Presentation

- Show the learners a photo of your mother. Ask *He or she?* (*She*) Say *Yes. She's my mother.* Learners repeat. Show a photo of your father. Ask *He or she?* (*He*) Say *Yes. He's my father.* Repeat with different photos and family members.

Pupil's Book, page 20

2.05 The Friendly Farm song

- Play the introductory song at the beginning of the cartoon story. Learners listen. Repeat. Learners listen and sing. As they do, clap hands quickly twice each time the word *Friendly* appears. Repeat the song. Learners sing and clap.

Track 2.05

See The Friendly Farm song on page TB5

2.05 The Friendly Farm

- Put the flashcards of the Friendly Farm animals on the board. Ask *Where's Gracie?* Learners point. Ask *Is she a horse?* (neigh like a horse) (*No – she's a goat.*) *What colour is she?* (*White*)
- Repeat with the other Friendly Farm animal flashcards. Learners point to the flashcard. Then ask questions about the character.
- Say *Open your Pupil's Books at page 20*. Ask *Who can you see in the pictures?* Learners name the characters. Ask *What are these?* Point to the eggs. Say *Eggs*. Learners repeat.
- Ask *Who is Rocky's brother? Who is Rocky's sister?* Write the questions on the board. Say *Listen*. Play the audio or video. Learners listen and read.

Track 2.05

The Friendly Farm song + see cartoon on Pupil's Book page 20

- Learners answer the questions in pairs before the class check.

Stronger learners Learners can say *Eggs*.

Extra support Learners can point to the eggs.

- Play the audio or video again. Pause after frames and check comprehension by asking learners to give the end of sentences.

Frame 2: *Shelly isn't Rocky's …* (*sister*) *She is Rocky's …* (*friend*)

Frame 3: *Harry isn't Rocky's …* (*brother*) *Harry is Rocky's …* (*friend*)

Frame 5: *Show me Rocky's brother and sister.* (Learners point to the eggs.)

Frame 6: *It's a boy. He's Rocky's …* (*brother*) *It's a girl. She's Rocky's …* (*sister*)

- Play the audio or video again. Put the learners into pairs. Give each pair a role: Rocky or Henrietta. Learners repeat the speech bubbles for their character.

Extension Put the flashcards of the Friendly Farm animals on the board. Say *I'm Rocky*. Point to Gracie. Ask *Is she my mother?* (*No, she isn't.*) Ask *Is she my friend?* (*Yes, she is.*)

- Put learners into pairs to role play the dialogue. Monitor and check.

Fast finishers These learners can find and copy the family words.

Activity Book, page 20

See pages TB120–132

Ending the lesson

- **SA** Repeat the self-assessment technique used at the start of the lesson to see how well learners think they understand the vocabulary. Is there any change?
- Display the Family flashcards on the board. Point to the different characters and say *He or she?* Learners answer.
- Say *I'm Jim*. Point to different family members, e.g. Mr Friendly. Ask *Is he my mother?* (*No, he isn't.*) Repeat, pointing to a few characters and finishing on the correct flashcard.

Stronger learners These learners can come to the front, point to the characters and ask *Is she my … ? / Is he my … ?* and other learners answer.

Learning outcomes By the end of the lesson, learners will be able to ask and answer questions using *he* and *she* pronouns.

New language *Who is he/she? He's my … / She's my …*

Recycled language family, names

Materials pictures of people the learners know (girls and boys), photos of your family, Family flashcards, digital Mission poster, large sheets of paper, coloured pens or crayons, learners' family photos (optional), glue (optional)

Key Competences

- Learn to ask and answer questions with the verb *to be* and *he* and *she* pronouns.
- Work in pairs to ask and answer questions about their families.
- Make a page about their families for the *All about me* booklet.
- Interact with the digital poster.

Warm-up

- Show a picture of a girl. Encourage learners to say *She's a girl*. Show a picture of a boy. Learners say *He's a boy*. Show the rest of the pictures of the people learners know quickly. Learners call out the correct sentence.

Presentation

- Show the Family flashcards. Show Mrs Friendly. Ask *Who is she?* (*She's Mrs Friendly*.) Say *Yes. Listen. Who is* ***she****?* Say ***She****'s Jenny's mother.* Say *Who is she?* Learners repeat. Say *She's Jenny's mother*. Learners repeat.
- Show the photo of your mother. Learners ask *Who is she?* Say *She's my mother.* As you say *my*, point to yourself. Repeat with father, sister, brother and grandparents.

Pupil's Book, page 21

2.06 Gracie's Grammar

- Say *Open your Pupil's Books at page 21*. Point to Gracie's Grammar box. Write the same sentences on the board. Point to *she*. Ask *Boy or girl?* (*Girl*) Repeat with *he*.
- Learners copy the sentences.
- Play the audio. Pause for learners to repeat each sentence.

Track 2.06
See Pupil's Book page 21

- Rub out the words *she* and *he*. Choose a confident learner to write the correct words back in the spaces.
- Choose two learners. Point to one and ask *Who is he/she?* The other learner answers *He's/She's (name)*. *He's/She's my friend*. Repeat with other learners.

1 2.07 Listen and stick. Then look, read and write.

- Learners look at the stickers and say the people.
- Play the audio for learners to point to the correct sticker.

Track 2.07
1 Who's he?
Jenny: This is Dad. He's my father.
2 Who's she?
Jenny: This is Mum. She's my mother.
3 Who's he?
Jenny: This is Jim. He's my brother.
4 Who's he?
Jenny: This is Grandpa. He's my grandfather.

- Play the audio again. Learners stick in the stickers.
- Say *Look at the sentences*. Point to sentences 1–4. Say *Look, read and write*. Learners write. Check answers.

Key: 2 mother 3 brother 4 He's

mission Stage 1

- Show learners the first stage of the digital Mission poster: 'My family'. Say *My family*. Repeat *fa-mi-ly* and clap on the syllables. Encourage the learners to repeat and clap.
- Give out two large sheets of paper to each learner and ask them to fold the paper to make their booklet. Give out coloured pens or pencils. Encourage each learner to create a front page. They draw and colour a design with the title *All about me* to create their own booklet
- Say *Let's show our families*. Show the class pictures of your family. Put them up on the board. Point and say *She's my* … and encourage learners to complete, e.g. *mother*.
- Learners draw pictures of their family or stick on photos inside the first page. They write the name of the person next to each picture. Monitor and support.
- In pairs, learners point and ask about each other's photos, e.g. *Who is she? She's my mother.*

  Extension Learners stand up. They move around, asking and answering questions, e.g. *Who is he/she?*
- For ideas on monitoring and assessment, see Introduction.

Activity Book, page 21

See pages TB120–132

Activity Book, page 18

- Say *Look at page 18 of your Activity Book*. Review *My unit goals*. Ask *How is your Mission?*
- Learners reflect and choose a smiley face for *My mission diary 1*. Monitor.

Ending the lesson

- **SA** Go back to Stage 1 on the digital Mission poster. Say *We talked about our family. Good work*. Add a tick to the 'My family' stage. Use self-assessment (see Introduction).
- Give out a completion sticker.

Gracie's Grammar

2.06

Who **is she**? **She's** Jenny. **She's** a girl.
Who **is he**? **He's** Jim. **He's** a boy.

1 2.07 **Listen and stick. Then look, read and write.**

1 This is Dad. He's my father.
2 This is Mum. She's my ______.
3 This is Jim. He's my ______.
4 This is Grandpa. ______ my grandfather.

mission STAGE 1

Make a *Family* page for your *All about me* book.

- Stick photos or draw pictures of your family.
- Write their names.

My mission diary
Activity Book page 18

Vocabulary 2 and song

1 2.08 Listen and do the actions. Then sing the song.

Move your body, Jenny.
Move your tail, Cameron.
Move your body, Jenny.
Move your tail, Cameron.
Move, move your body.
Move your legs and your feet.
Move, move your body
and now put your arms up.
Chorus
Stop! Now move your head.
Touch your hair and your face.
Move, move your body.
Touch your ears and your nose.
Chorus
Stop! Now close your eyes.
Open your mouth
and clap your hands.
Move, move your body.
Touch your ears and your nose.
Chorus

2 2.10 Listen and follow.

Learning outcomes By the end of the lesson, learners will have practised the language through song.

New language *arm, body, ear, eye, face, feet, foot, hair, hand, head, leg, mouth, nose, tail, move*

Recycled language colours, names

Materials Parts of the body flashcards, audio, video, pictures of people with different hair colours (brown, black, red, blond)

Key Competences

- Learn the parts of the body.
- Listen to a song and do the actions.
- Complete a crossword puzzle.

Warm-up

- Ask the learners to stand up. Say *Let's move our bodies*. Demonstrate moves as you do them so learners can copy. Say *Up* and stretch to the ceiling. Say *Down* and crouch to the floor. Say *Round* and turn 360 degrees. Repeat the sequence. Repeat again in a different order.
- **SA** Use self-assessment to check how well learners think they understand the vocabulary. See Introduction.

Presentation

- Introduce new words by pointing to parts of your body, e.g. point to your leg and say *Leg*. Learners repeat. Wave your leg. Learners copy and repeat. Continue with *feet* (hold up one and then another in the air), *hands* (wave), *hair* (rub it), *face* (point), *eyes* (point and blink), *mouth* (point and open and close), *ears* (push forward with fingers), *nose* (put finger on the end and waggle), *head* (waggle back and forward). Gesture to your whole body and say *Body*. Repeat several times for each item, waving each body part. Learners repeat and copy.
- Now point to different parts of the body and learners call out the word. Alternatively, use the Parts of the body flashcards. Demonstrate *move*. Give instructions, e.g. *Move your arms*. Learners follow your instructions. Repeat, asking learners to move different parts of the body.
- In groups, learners take it in turns to point to different body parts. The other learners say the words.

  Extra support Learners just point to the parts of the body and listen to the answers.

Pupil's Book, page 22

1 2.08 Listen and do the actions. Then sing the song.

- Say *Open your Pupil's Books at page 22*. Point to the picture in Activity 1.

Point to different characters in the picture and ask *Who is he/she?* Learners answer.

- Say *Show me Grandpa. Show me his head … arms … feet.* Learners point to the parts in the picture as you say them.
- Play the audio or video. Learners listen and do the actions.

  Track 2.08

  Rocky: I'm Rocky-Doodle-Doo and … here's our song for today: *Move your body!*

  See song on Pupil's Book page 22
- Play the audio or video again. Learners listen and do the actions. Monitor. Repeat the audio if necessary.
- Point to Cameron in the picture. Point to his tail. Ask *Is it a leg?* (No) Say *It's a tail*. Learners repeat.
- Play the audio or video again. Learners repeat the song, doing actions, first in small sections and then the whole song.
- Divide the class into three. Give each group one of the verses of the song to perform. They all join in with the chorus. Once they have practised the song, ask them to stand up and perform it.

  2.09 **Extension** Once learners are confidently singing to the song, try singing the karaoke version as a class.

2 2.10 Listen and follow.

- Say *Look at Activity 2. Listen and follow.* Learners listen and point to the body parts, tracing their way through the maze.

  Track 2.10

  1 an ear, a foot, an arm, two hands, two ears, a body, a leg
  2 black hair, a face, a mouth, a nose, two feet, brown hair, a tail, two legs, a head, two green eyes
- Repeat the audio.
- Check the answers.
- Show the picture of Rocky in the bottom right-hand corner.
- Encourage learners to answer the question, saying their hair colour (*brown/black/red/blond*).
- Show some pictures of people with different coloured hair and say the hair colours. Learners repeat.
- Read Rocky's question again. Learners answer. Support as necessary.

Activity Book, page 22

See pages TB120–132

Ending the lesson

- **SA** Repeat the self-assessment technique used at the start of the lesson to see how well learners think they understand the vocabulary. Is there any change?
- Take the Family flashcards and use thin paper to trace an outline without filling in any details. Put the traced outlines up onto the board.
- Learners guess who each character is.
- If they get the characters quickly, point to two of the outlines and learners say the relationship, e.g. *It's Jim and Jenny. They are brother and sister. They are twins.*

2 Language practice 2

Learning outcomes By the end of the lesson, learners will be able to use *have got* to describe their hair and eyes and their families.

New language *have/has got, haven't/hasn't got, Have/ Has … got?*

Recycled language colours, family, parts of the body

Materials audio, video, coloured pens or pencils, digital Mission poster

Key Competences

- Learn to use *have got / haven't got* to describe people.
- Make a class survey about family members.
- Draw and write about themselves.
- Reflect on their own learning.
- Interact with the digital poster.

Warm-up

- Draw two faces on the board and say They are twins. Draw black hair and blue eyes. Nod and say They've got … (*black hair*). They've got … (*blue eyes*). Learners repeat. Shake your head and say They haven't got brown hair. Learners repeat.
- Rub out one face. Repeat the whole sequence, using *She's got … Has she got … ? She hasn't got …*
- Point to yourself and describe your hair and eyes. Ask *What about you?* Say *Have you got black hair?* Learners repeat. Say *Have you got brown eyes?* Learners repeat. Say the questions several times.

Pupil's Book, page 23

1 (2.11) Who is talking? Listen and tick ✓.

- Point to each picture. Ask, e.g. *Has he got black hair?* Learners answer, e.g. *Yes, he has.*
- Say *Listen. Who's talking?* Play the audio or video. Learners listen and tick the correct person.

Track 2.11

Girl: Look at my pictures, Sam. They're pictures of me and my brother and sister.
Sam: Oh, they've got black hair. You haven't got black hair.
Girl: No, I haven't. I've got brown hair, and I've got green eyes.
Sam: Have your brother and sister got green eyes?
Girl: No, they haven't. My sister has got blue eyes and my brother has got brown eyes.

Key: Picture 2

(2.12) Gracie's Grammar

- Look at Gracie's Grammar box. Play the audio, pausing after each sentence. Learners repeat.

Track 2.12
See Pupil's Book page 23

- Write the sentences on the board. Rub out *I've*, *They've* and *Have*. Ask the learners to read the sentences and fill in the spaces as they speak.
- Point to the question *Have you got red hair?* Ask and answer. In pairs, learners ask the question and describe themselves, e.g. *Have you got red hair? No, I haven't got red hair.*

Fast finishers Learners can write a sentence about themselves.

2 Ask and answer. Tick ✓ or cross ✗.

- Say *Let's talk about families*. Choose a strong learner. Ask *Have you got a brother?* Encourage the learner to answer *Yes* or *No*. Learners repeat the question. Say *Have you got a sister?* Learners repeat.
- Demonstrate the task. Copy the first question from Activity 2 onto the board and draw the three small boxes. Demonstrate, asking three learners and putting a tick or cross in each box according to their answers.
- Learners mingle. They ask and answer questions and tick.

mission Stage 2

- Show learners the second stage of the digital Mission poster: 'This is me'.
- Give learners their *All about me* booklet. Demonstrate by drawing a picture of yourself on the board. Use gestures to show it is you. Say and then write sentences about yourself.
- Learners draw and write about themselves.
- When they finish, put out the *All about me* booklets opened at the *This is me* pages. Show each one and ask *Who is it?* Learners guess which of their classmates it belongs to, e.g. *He's (name)* or *She's (name)*. Once they have guessed, ask questions, e.g. *Good. Has (name) got brown hair?* Learners answer. Repeat with a variety of *This is me* pages.
- For ideas on monitoring and assessment, see Introduction.

Activity Book, page 23

See pages TB120–132

Activity Book, page 18

- Say *Look at page 18 of your Activity Book*. Review *My unit goals*. Ask *How is your Mission?*
- Learners reflect and choose a smiley face for *My mission diary 2*. Monitor.

Ending the lesson

- Go back to Stage 2 on the digital Mission poster. Add a tick to the 'This is me' stage or invite a learner to do it. Use self-assessment (see Introduction).
- Give out a completion sticker.

1 Who is talking? Listen and tick ✓.

2.11

1 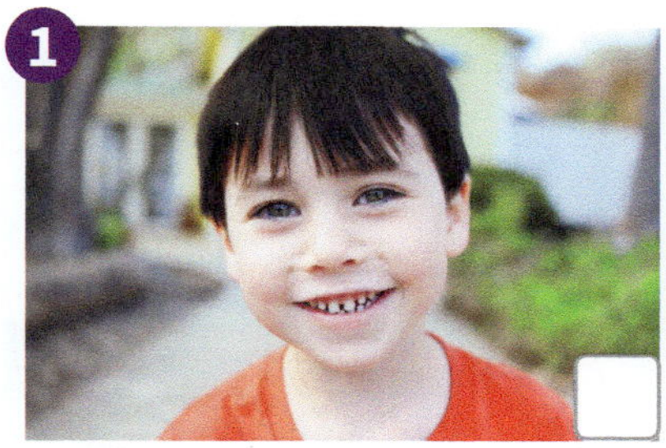

2 

3 

Gracie's Grammar

2.12

I**'ve got** brown hair.	I **haven't got** black hair.
They**'ve got** blue eyes.	They **haven't got** green eyes.
Have you **got** red hair?	Yes, I **have**. / No, I **haven't**.

2 Ask and answer. Tick ✓ or cross ✗.

		______	______	______
1	Have you got a brother?	☐	☐	☐
2	Have you got a sister?	☐	☐	☐
3	Have you got twins in your family?	☐	☐	☐

mission STAGE 2

Make a *This is me* page for your *All about me* book.

- What do you look like? Draw, say and write.

I've got brown hair and green eyes.

My mission diary
Activity Book page 18

Cross-curricular

Using our senses

1 Watch the video.

2 2.13 Listen and say. Look and match.

1
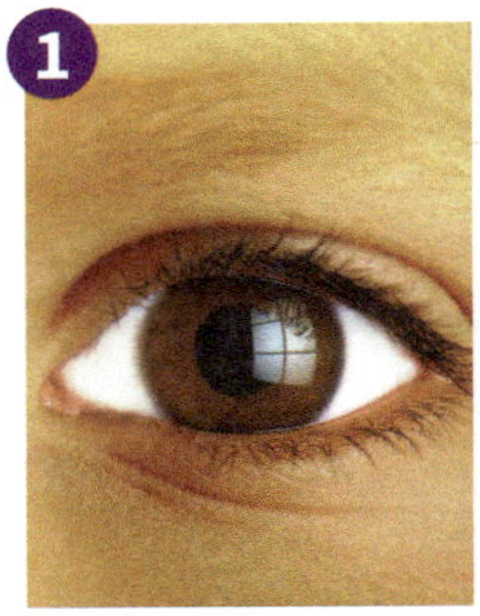
see

2
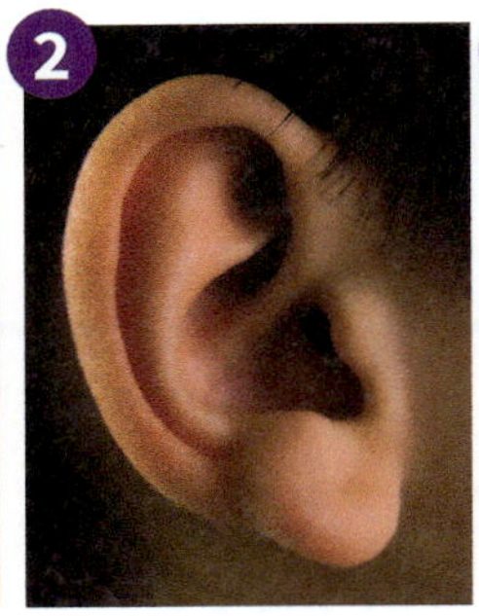
hear

3
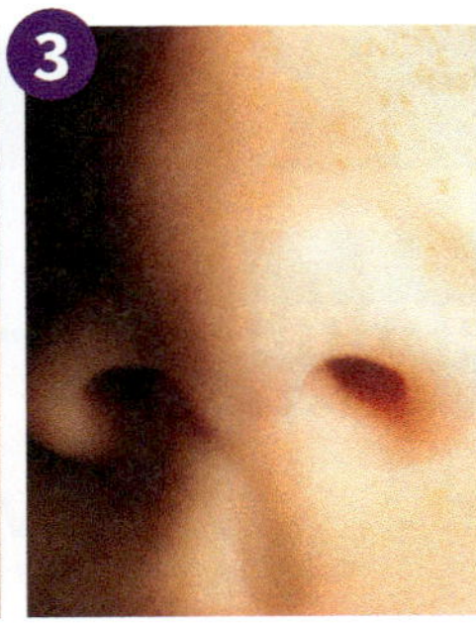
smell

4

taste

5

touch

a

b
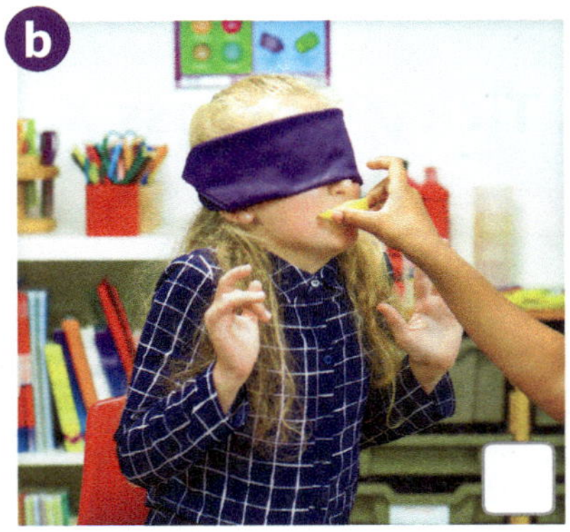

c
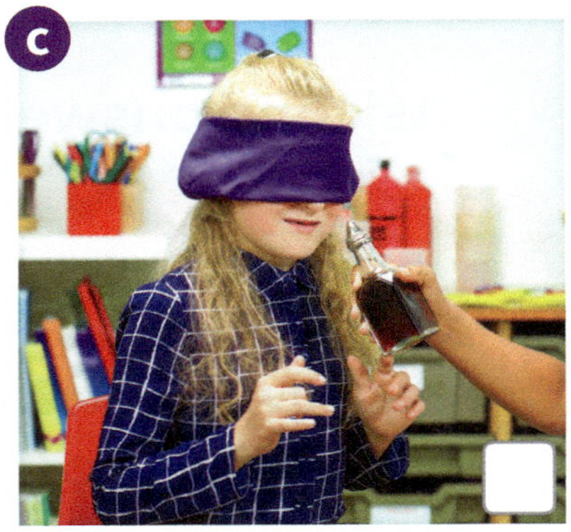

d

e

3 Play the senses game.

Learning outcomes By the end of the lesson, learners will be able to describe senses and understand disabilities.

New language *hear, see, smell, taste, touch*

Recycled language *have/has got*, parts of the body

Materials video, a dropper with orange juice and water, pictures from Digital photo bank of things you can taste (lemons, pizza), smell (perfume, smoke) and hear (a tablet, a road drill)

Key Competences

Learn specific language to talk about Science in English.

Learn about their senses.

Work together to play a game.

Warm-up

- Point to your head and say *head*. Learners repeat. Gesture to your face. Learners say *face*. Gesture to your nose. Learners say *nose*. Repeat with eyes. Point to your tongue. Say *tongue*. Learners repeat. Correct pronunciation in each case.
- Put learners into pairs. They take it in turns to show a part of their head or face and their partner says the word.

Pupil's Book, page 24

1 Watch the video.

- Say *Let's watch the video*. Learners watch the video about using our senses and answer the questions at the end of the video.

Presentation

- Say *Open your Pupil's Books at page 24*. Focus on pictures 1–5 at the top. Ask *What is it?* (*1 eye, 2 ear, 3 nose, 4 mouth/ tongue, 5 hands*). Learners repeat.
- Say *Point to your eyes*. Learners point. Say *We see with our eyes*. Say *see*. Learners repeat. Go through the sequence again, pointing to the different parts of the face. Ask learners to point to their ears. Say *ears*. Learners repeat. Say *We hear with our ears*. Ask learners to point to their nose. Say *nose*. Learners repeat. Say *We smell with our nose*. Learners repeat. Ask learners to point to their mouth. Say *mouth*. Learners repeat. Say *We taste with our mouth*. Learners repeat. Show the hands. Say *hands*. Say *We touch with our hands*. Learners repeat.
- Repeat the sequence, pointing to your eyes, ears, nose, mouth and hands. Learners say the names. Now repeat and learners say what we can do with each part of the body.

2 (2.13) Listen and say. Look and match.

- Show learners the words under the pictures. Play the audio. Learners repeat the words. Correct pronunciation.

Track 2.13
See Pupil's Book page 24

- Put learners into pairs. They match the pictures 1–5 with photos above. Check answers.

Key: b 4 c 3 d 2 e 1

3 Play the senses game.

- Tell learners to close their eyes and name things they can hear in the classroom. (Clap hands, open and close a door, walk loudly, etc.)
- Fill a dropper with orange juice and water. Drop two drops on the learners' tongues. Ask them what they can taste.
- Show the learners different objects, e.g. a pen, a rubber, a crayon. Learners close their eyes and an object is placed in their hands for them to name.

Activity Book, page 24

See pages TB120–132

Ending the lesson

- Put learners into groups of three or four. Give each group three cards. Ask them to write a word on each card: *taste, smell, hear*.
- Show pictures from the Digital photo bank on the board. These are a mixture of things they can taste (lemons, pizza), smell (perfume, smoke) and hear (a tablet, a road drill). Show the photos in random order and learners hold up the appropriate word card as quickly as possible. Some photos may have more than one answer. Alternatively, use flashcards of chocolate, flowers and guitar.
- Now ask learners to work in pairs. Tell them to think of one more thing for each category. If they don't know the word, they can draw a picture, e.g. a piano for *hear*.
- Monitor and give words to learners if they have drawn pictures.
- When they have finished, ask a few learners to give the word they added to each category.

2 Cross-curricular

Learning outcomes By the end of the lesson, learners will be able to understand how to help a blind person.

New language *blind, dog, favourite (thing)*

Recycled language *hear, help, see, smell, taste, touch*

Materials examples of things you like to smell (e.g. a flower or fruit), taste (food), hear (music) and touch (picture of a pet), digital Mission poster, a scarf

Key Competences

- Read a text.
- Learn about blind people and how to help them.
- Draw their favourite things to do using each of the senses.
- Reflect on their own learning.
- Interact with the digital poster.

Warm-up

- Say to learners *Stand up. Show me your eyes.* Learners point. *Show me your ears.* Learners point. Continue with *nose, mouth* and *hands*.
- Ask a learner to come up and lead the same sequence.

Pupil's Book, page 25

4 Look, read and match.

- Say *Open your Pupil's Books at page 25*. Show the photo of the blind person. Ask *Can she see?* Gesture to your eyes. (*No*) Say *No. She's blind*. Learners repeat. Ask *Can she hear?* Gesture to your ears. (*Yes*) Repeat with *smell, taste* and *touch*. Point to the guide dog. Say *dog*. Learners repeat. Point to the traffic light. Say *traffic light*. Learners repeat.
- Point to the picture of the guide dog again. Say *Look! Can the dog see?* (*Yes*) Say *The dog can see and help.*
- Show learners sentences 1–3 and pictures a–c. Learners match the sentences with the pictures.
- Check answers.

Key: a 3 b 2 c 1

mission Stage 3

- Show the class the third stage of the Mission poster: 'Favourite things'. Make a heart shape with your fingers and thumbs.
- Show the class something you like to smell, e.g. a flower or fruit. Say *My favourite thing to smell!* Mime pleasure. Show them something you like to eat – lick your lips and show pleasure. Say *My favourite thing to taste!* Repeat with something you like to hear, e.g. your favourite music and say *My favourite music*, and touch, e.g. a picture of a pet and say *touch* as you mime stroking the pet. Say *My favourite things to smell, taste, hear and touch.* Write the sentence on the board.
- Learners complete the worksheet task in the Teacher's Resource Book page 24 (see teaching notes on TRB page 17).
- Alternatively, if you do not have the Teacher's Resource Book, say *Draw your favourite things*. Give out the *All about me* booklets. Learners draw a page showing their favourite things. Monitor as they draw and give words they want to know.

  Stronger learners They can write the words with their pictures.

  Extra support Learners can draw a picture and you write in the word for them as they work. Monitor and guide.

  Alternative Learners could plan this at home and bring in some real examples.
- Put the class in groups of three. Each learner shows their pictures and says *My favourite thing to see/hear/smell/touch/taste*. The other learners guess what the pictures are.
- For ideas on monitoring and assessment, see Introduction.

Activity Book, page 25

See pages TB120–132

Activity Book, page 18

- Say *Look at page 18 of your Activity Book*. Review *My unit goals*. Ask *How is your Mission?*
- Learners reflect and choose a smiley face for *My mission diary 3*. Monitor.

Ending the lesson

- **SA** Go back to Stage 3 on the digital Mission poster. Add a tick to the 'Favourite things' stage or invite a learner to do it. Use self-assessment (see Introduction).
- Give out a completion sticker.

4 Look, read and match.

Some people can't see. They are blind. They use their other senses to help them. Today there are many things to help blind people.

1 They can read books with their hands.
2 They can hear traffic lights.
3 A guide dog can see for them.

a

b

c
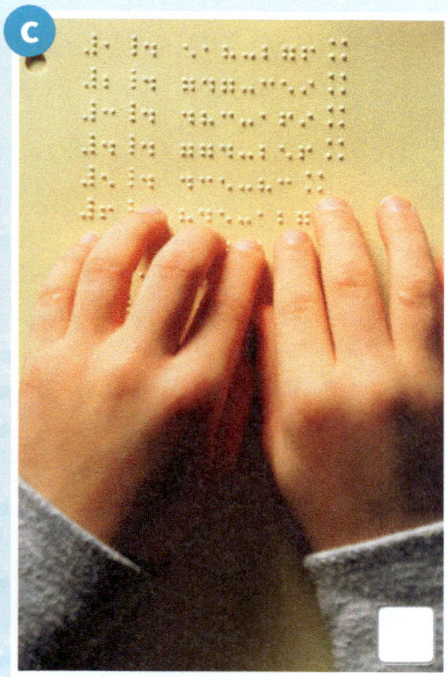

mission STAGE 3

Make a *Favourite things* page for your *All about me* book.

- Think about your favourite things to see, hear, smell, taste and touch.
- Draw them.
- Learn the words in English.

STAGE 3

My mission diary

Activity Book page 18

Literature

1 **Look at the pictures. What is the game? What's your favourite game?**

2.14

Sara's favourite game

I'm Pablo. I live with my mum, dad, grandma and grandpa. Today my cousin Sara is here too. Sara's got black hair and brown eyes.

Sara's favourite game is *Hide and Seek*. I close my eyes and I count to ten, and Sara hides.

Today she's hiding in the cupboard in the kitchen. She's in the cupboard in the kitchen ... again! She always hides ... Oh, she isn't there. 'Sara?' I say. 'Where are you?'

Learning outcomes By the end of the lesson, learners will have read about playing a game.

New language *game, hide*

Recycled language *cupboard, favourite (thing),* describing someone, family, names

Materials small ball and three cups (either different colours or with a number written on each), flashcard of board game and picture from Digital photo bank of skipping game, coloured pens or pencils

Key Competences

- Read and listen to a text about a game.
- Learn about the game *Hide and Seek*.
- Order events in a story using visual clues.

Warm-up

- Ask learners to watch. Put a ball into a cup. Turn it upside down and add two more cups upside down. Move the cups around really fast. Ask *Where is the ball?* Learners point and say the colour or number of the cup. If they find it first time, say *Well done!* and repeat. As you put the ball in, say *I'm going to hide the ball*. As you move the cups, say *Find the ball*.
- If you have time, ask a learner to come up and do the same thing. Say *Hide the ball*. Say to the other learners *Find the ball*. The other learners guess where it is.

Presentation

- Say *We are going to read about Sara's favourite game.* Demonstrate hiding, e.g. go behind a cupboard or curtain. Say *I am hiding*. Come out and choose a learner. Say *(Name), hide!* The learner hides. Ask the other learners *Where is (name)?* They point and say *He's/She's there*. The learner comes out.
- Repeat with two more learners if there is time.

  Extension Learners say where the person is hiding, e.g. *Suzi is under the table.*

Pupil's Book, page 26

1 Look at the pictures. What is the game? What's your favourite game?

- Ask learners *What is your favourite game?* Show the flashcard of a board game and the picture from Digital photo bank of a skipping game. Learners point. Say *Game*. Learners repeat.
- Point to the picture of Pablo. Say *This is Pablo*. Ask questions about how he looks, e.g. *Has he got blue eyes?* (*No*) Point to Sara. Say *This is Pablo's cousin.* Ask questions about her, e.g. *Is she a boy or a girl?* (*Girl*) *Has she got black hair?* (*Yes*)
- Ask *What is the game?* Learners try to answer. Don't worry if they can't at the moment. Say *Sara is hiding*.
- Ask learners *What is your favourite game?* Learners answer.

2.14 Sara's favourite game

- Focus on the pictures. Look at each picture and ask questions, e.g. Picture 1: *Who is it?* (*Pablo/Sara*) *Where are they?* (*At home*) Picture 2: *Where is Sara?* (*Hiding*) Picture 3: *Is she in the cupboard?* (*Yes, Yes, No*) Picture 4: *Is she next to the bookcase?* (*No*) If learners can't answer the questions, don't give the answers yet.
- Ask learners to guess where Sara is hiding. Say *Let's find out!*
- Say *Read and listen to the first part*. Play the audio. Learners listen and read. Pause the audio after paragraph 2. Ask *What is Sara's favourite game?* (*Hide and Seek*) Pause the audio at the end of page 26. Ask *Is she in the cupboard?* (*No*)

  Track 2.14
  See story on Pupil's Book pages 26–27
- Say *Read the next part*. Show them the paragraphs on page 27. Ask *Where is Sara?* Play the audio. Check if their guesses were correct.

Activity Book, page 26

See pages TB120–132

Ending the lesson

- Say *Let's play a game*. Play 'I spy'. Write on the board *I spy with my little eye something beginning with …* Explain that learners must find something beginning with the letter you say.
- Say *I spy with my little eye something beginning with 'd'.* If necessary, write *d* on the board. Learners guess what it could be. (*desk*) Repeat with another object of your choice.
- Now encourage a learner to give the clue. If possible, they say the whole sentence, but if they can't, they can just give the letter. If necessary, give them suggested words and help them say the letter, writing it on the board for the other learners to see.

Learning outcomes By the end of the lesson, learners will have talked about games.

New language *find, Here he/she is!*

Recycled language *game*, numbers, prepositions of place

Materials flashcards from the units so far, pictures of famous cartoon characters or people that the learners know

Social and Emotional Skill: Showing concern for others

- After reading the story, ask learners the questions *What game do Pablo and Sara play?* (*Hide and Seek*) *Is it Sara's favourite game?* (*Yes*) *Is it Pablo's favourite game?* (*No*) *Why does he play?* (*To make Sara happy*) Ask *In the game, is Sara in the cupboard?* (*No*) Say *No. Pablo wants to find Sara. He's sad she's not in the cupboard and worried.* Explain in L1 that he shows concern for her.
- Draw a big heart on the board and say *Think of your brother, sister or cousin. How do you feel?* And point to the heart. Say *Yes, you love them.*
- Ask the learners if they play with their little brother or sister or cousin. Ask *What games do you like? What games does your little brother, sister or cousin like? Do you play games you don't want to play with them?* Point out that it's important to play with them even if sometimes you don't want to. It's good to think of other people. Tell learners it makes them happy to play with a big brother, sister or cousin and that it's important to think about how they feel.
- Learners tell you what games they play. Learners draw themselves playing with their sister, brother, cousin or friend at a game they want to play. Each learner tells you who they're playing with and what they're playing as you go around.

Key Competences

- Revise the prepositions of place through a text.
- Act out a story.
- Ask and answer questions about the games they play.

Warm-up

- Say *Let's play Hide and Seek.*
- Send three learners out of the class. Choose another learner to hide. When they are hidden, bring in the three learners. Encourage the class to say *Where's (name of learner hiding)?*
- The three learners look. As they do, the class can ask questions, e.g. *Is he/she under the desk?* Encourage the learners to say *No, he/she isn't*. Continue until they find the hidden learner. Finally they say *Yes, he/she is!* When they find the learner, encourage them to say *Here he/she is!*
- **SA** Use self-assessment to check how well learners think they understand the vocabulary. See Introduction.

Presentation

- Hide the Family flashcards around the room. Tell the learners *The Friendly family are hiding. Where are they?* Mime looking around the classroom. Mime finding one of the cards and say, e.g. *Ah! Here's Grandma Friendly. She's under the window.*
- Encourage the learners to look for the other characters. When they find a card, they say, e.g. *Here's Mr Friendly! He's in the cupboard.*

Pupil's Book, page 27

2 Act out the story.

- Say *Act out the story*. Summarise the story with questions and mime. Mime Sara hiding and Pablo counting. Learners copy. Say *Sara! Where are you?* Learners repeat. Mime Pablo looking in the cupboard (open a door). Say *Is she in the cupboard? No, she isn't.* Learners repeat. Ask *Is she next to the bookcase? No, she isn't.* Mime looking next to the bookcase. Say *Is she in the garden? No, she isn't.* Mime looking in the garden. Say *Is she under the table? Yes, she is!* Mime looking under the table (bend down and then point as if you have found her).
- Repeat and encourage the learners to act out the story.

3 Ask and answer.

- Ask *Who do you play with?* Suggest answers, e.g. *Your brother? Your sister? Your friends? Your cousins?* Learners answer (*I play with my …*).
- Put up some pictures of famous cartoon characters or people that the learners know. Ask *Who do you want to play with?* Learners choose their favourite character.

Activity Book, page 27

See pages TB120–132

Ending the lesson

- **SA** Repeat the self-assessment technique used at the start of the lesson to see how well learners think they understand the vocabulary. Is there any change?
- Choose some flashcards from the units so far. Put sticky notes over them until they are covered. Write a number on each sticky note. Ask the learners to choose numbers. Encourage the learners to give you a number. Move the sticky note with that number to reveal a small part of the picture. Learners try to guess what the picture is.
- Repeat with different flashcards.

2

Is she next to the bookcase?
No, she isn't. 'Sara?' I say.
'Where are you?'

Is she in the garden?
No, she isn't. 'Sara!' I say.
'Where *are* you?'

Mum, Dad, Grandma and Grandpa come to help, but we can't find Sara anywhere! Then Grandma sees Sara's crayons on the table. 'Is she under the table?' she says.

'Yes!' says Mum. 'She is! Hello, Sara!'

'Sara!' I say.

2 Act out the story.

Sara! Where are you?

Is she in the cupboard?

No, she isn't.

Is she next to the bookcase?

3 Ask and answer.

Who do you play with?

I play with my cousins.

1 Read and number.

a

b

c

1 The blue crayon is next to the book.

2 The red crayon is on the book.

3 The blue crayon is on the book.

2 Look and read. Write *yes* or *no*.

Examples

The children have got crayons. ___yes___

The baby is on the chair. ___no___

Questions

1 The bag is on the table. ______

2 The mother has got a book. ______

3 Six people have got black hair. ______

Learning outcomes By the end of the lesson, learners will have read to find specific information and responded.

Recycled language colours, family, *Have you got … ?*

Materials large paper and pen for each group, a watch or timer, a bell or whistle (optional), a picture of a baby, from Digital photo bank, audio, paper, coloured pens or pencils, an example mask

Key Competences

Listen for specific information; Practise activity types found in *Pre A1 Starters* exams.

Solve word puzzles with visual clues.

Warm-up

- Put learners into groups of five. Give each group a large piece of paper. Choose a strong learner in each group and give them a pen.
- Say *Let's remember!* Tell them they have one minute for each part of the game. Show your watch or, if you have a timer, set the timer. Ask *How many words can you remember?* Check they understand they have to write as many words as they can. The learner with the pen in each group writes. The learners in the group say words. Say *Write down colours*. Give one minute. After one minute, ring a bell or blow a whistle. If you don't have this, call *Stop!* Check with each group how many words they wrote. Repeat with *Write down family words*. Check how many words they have.
- Pick out two or three words from each list. Ask learners to cover their lists. Say the words slowly. Learners try to write the words with the correct spelling.
- To check, ask learners to spell out the words and write them onto the board, correcting any errors.
- **SA** Use self-assessment techniques to check how well learners think they understand the vocabulary. See Introduction.

Presentation

- Say *Let's do a reading exam!* Write *Reading Exam* on the board.
- Say *First use your sight.* Say *Read first. Think. Then write your answer.* Repeat this. Write the words *Read*, *Think* and *Write* on the board in that order. Ask *Which is number 1?* (*Read*) Ask *Which is number 2?* (*Think*) Say *So number 3 is …* (*Write*)
- Make a chant and clap rhythmically, saying *Read, think, write.* Learners repeat and clap.

Pupil's Book, page 28

1 Read and number.

- Say *Open your Pupil's Books at page 28.* Point to the pictures. Ask *What colour are the crayons?* (*Blue and red*)
- Point to each picture and ask *Where is the crayon?* (*On the book / Next to the book*) Show the sentences under the pictures. Ask the learners to read them.
- Put learners into pairs. Ask them to match the pictures.
- Check answers.

Key: a 3 b 1 c 2

2 Look and read. Write *yes* or *no*.

- Say *Don't forget: Read, think, write.* Learners repeat the chant and clap.
- Say *We read. We think. We write 'yes' or 'no'.*
- Put a picture of a baby on the board. Write *It's a chair.* Learners say *No*. Write *no* next to the sentence. Say *No, it's a baby.*
- Tell the learners to look at the picture. Ask questions: *Is it a family?* (*yes*) *Is there a table?* (*yes*) *Are there some chairs?* (*yes*) *Are the crayons on the table?* (*no*) *Is there a bag?* (*yes*) *What colour is the bag?* (*purple*) *Is the book on the table?* (*no*)
- Show learners the sentences. Say *Read the sentences. Think. Write yes or no.* Learners read the sentences and write their answers.
- Put them into pairs to check answers. Check answers with the group.

Key: 1 no 2 yes 3 no

- Say *Well done. You read, thought and wrote. Good job!*

Activity Book, page 28

See pages TB120–132

Ending the lesson

- **SA** Repeat the self-assessment technique used at the start of the lesson to see how well learners think they understand the vocabulary. Is there any change?
- Say *Let's make a mask.* Find an outline of a mask shape or draw one on the board for learners to copy. Learners draw on hair, eyes and other features. When they finish colouring, show an example mask you have made. Ensure it is different from your normal features, e.g. if you are dark-haired, make it red-haired.
- Encourage learners to ask questions, e.g. *Have you got brown eyes?* Holding the mask to your face, give answers true for the mask, e.g. *No, I haven't. I've got blue eyes.*
- Learners mingle, holding up their masks, asking and answering questions.

  Fast finishers Learners can write the sentences at the end or swap masks with a friend and ask more questions.

Learning outcomes By the end of the lesson, learners will have revised the language in the unit and talked about their *All about me* books.

Recycled language unit language

Materials a photo of your family, *All about me* books

Key Competences

- Revise vocabulary and language learnt in the unit.
- Complete self-assessment tasks and reflect on their own learning.
- Work together in groups to talk about their *All about me* booklets.

Warm-up

- Say *Let's make some questions!* Write the number *1* and *Family* on the board and put up a photo of your family. Write *2 My face* on the board and stick up the mask from the previous lesson. Write *3 My favourite things* on the board and next to it add *see/smell/hear/touch/taste*.
- Say *Think of a question for each one*. Give an example. Point to *1* and the picture and say *Is she my mother?* Point to number *2* and say *Have I got brown hair?* Learners work in groups and think of questions. Monitor while they work.
- Check answers by pointing to *1–3*. Learners call out different questions. Write them on the board. Add some if they can't think of any.

Presentation

- Say *Classmates*. Point to all the learners. Say *Classmates* again. Learners repeat. Say *Let's ask questions!* Draw a question mark on the board. Learners repeat *Let's ask questions!*
- Say some sentences, e.g. *My eyes are brown. He is my classmate. Have you got blue eyes? Apples are my favourite fruit. Is this your favourite book?* Learners call out *Question* if the sentence you say is a question.
- Say *Let's find out about our classmates!*

Pupil's Book, page 29

mission in action!

Learn about your classmates.

- Learners sit in groups of five. Give out their *All about me* books.
- Demonstrate showing a book page by page. For each page, point to the questions on the board and say *Ask questions*. Learners ask suitable questions. Answer each one.
- Learners work in groups. They take it in turns to show their *All about me* books and the other learners ask questions. They answer.

Extra support Give these learners two questions written down that they can ask.

Fast finishers Ask them to work with another fast finisher and to tell them about a classmate from their group, e.g. *(Name) has got a sister. His favourite thing to smell is chocolate.*

- Point to the picture of the Friendly family on Pupil's Book page 19. Say *Tell me about him*. Point to Jim. Learners say, e.g. *He's Jim. He's a boy. He's Jenny's brother.* Learners repeat the activity in pairs, choosing anything they want from the unit.
- For ideas on monitoring and assessment, see Introduction.

Self-assessment

- **SA** Say *Did you like our 'All about me' Mission? Show me.* Say *Good?* (Demonstrate stretching your hand up high.) *OK?* (Hold your hand mid level.) *Or not so good?* (Hold your hand lower.) Learners show you.
- Say *Did you do better than the last Mission – Being a teacher? Better?* (Move your hand up.) *Or not?* (Move your hand down.) Praise or say *OK. We can try again.*
- Say *Our next Mission is 'Let's make a farm'.* Ask learners to stand up. *What can you do better next time?* Point to the left. Say *Writing*. Point to the right. Say *Reading*. Learners move to the side they think they need. Repeat with *Speaking* and *Listening*. Say *Well done*.

Activity Book, page 29

See pages TB120–132

Activity Book, page 18

- Say *Look at page 18 of your Activity Book.* Review *My unit goals.* Ask *How is your Mission?*
- Learners reflect and choose a smiley face for *My mission diary* the final stage. Monitor.
- Point to the sunflower. Learners read the 'can do' statements and tick them if they agree they have achieved them. They colour each leaf green if they are very confident or orange if they think they need more practice.
- Point to the word stack sign. Ask learners to spend a few minutes looking back at the unit and find a minimum of five new words they have learnt. They write the new words into their word stack.

Ending the lesson

- Go back to the completion stage on the digital Mission poster. Add a tick or invite a learner to do it. Use self-assessment (see Introduction).
- Give out a completion sticker.
- Tell the learners *You have finished your Mission! Well done!*

mission in action!

Learn about your classmates.

My mission diary
Activity Book page 18

Look at your classmates' *All about me* books. Ask questions.

Who's this?
She's my mum.

Show your *All about me* book. Answer your classmates' questions.

These are my favourite things.
What's this?
It's a flower.

3 Fun on the farm

1 **Watch the video. Choose and write a name for the farm.**

mission Make a farm

In this unit I will:

1. Draw and describe a farm animal.
2. Play a game with the animals.
3. Make a farm and write about it.

★ Show our farm.

Unit 3 learning outcomes

In Unit 3, learners learn to:

- talk about animals
- use adjectives describing appearance and feelings
- use *Has it got … ? Yes, it has / No, it hasn't* to ask and describe
- read and write words about animals accurately
- read and listen to information about how animals help us

Materials video, picture from Digital photo bank of a farm, flashcards of classroom and living room (to illustrate 'home'), digital Mission poster, flashcards of tree, sheep, board, teacher, pen, book and pictures of tractor and field

Key Competences

Become familiar with language related to the farm.

Reflect on their own learning by going through the unit goals.

Work together to choose a name for a farm.

Self-assessment

- **SA** Say *Open your Pupil's Books at page 30*. Say *Look at the picture*. Indicate items on the page and ask questions using the language from the unit, e.g. *What is it? What are the animals? How many cows are there? What colour are the cows?* Use self-assessment (see Introduction). Say *OK. Let's learn*.

Warm-up

- Put up three pictures of places: a farm, home (flashcard of living room) and classroom (flashcard). Point to each picture in turn. Ask *Where is it?* Learners say *Farm/Home/School*. Repeat. Learners say each word several times.
- Do a mime for an activity that would fit one of the places, e.g. writing at a desk. Ask *Where am I?* Learners say *At school*. Do another mime, e.g. relaxing and watching TV. Ask *Where am I?* Learners say *At home*. Repeat for *On the farm*, e.g. mime digging.
- Learners work in groups of four. They take it in turns to mime activities. The other learners guess where they are.

Pupil's Book, page 30

1 Watch the video. Choose and write a name for the farm.

- Say *In this unit we're talking about animals*. Say *Let's watch the video*. To introduce the topic of the unit, play the video.
- Keep the three pictures of places on the board. Next to the school, write three possible names, e.g. *Friendly School* (draw a smiley face), *Sunny School* (draw a sun symbol), *Cool School* (draw a smiley face with sunglasses).
- Say the names of the schools. Ask *Which name shall we choose?* Show the learners they can put up their hand for the name they like best. Say the names one by one and the learners vote. Count the votes and say *OK. Let's name the school (learners' choice)!*
- Say *Look at page 30*. Point to the farm. Say *Let's choose a name for the farm!* Put the learners into groups of six. They think of a name for the farm.

  Fast finishers Learners can think of a few different ideas in their groups and then vote on their favourite.

  Extra support Learners can be given some different names to choose from.
- Point to the empty sign in the picture on page 30. Learners write the name and can add an emoticon or picture if they want.

mission Make a farm

- Show the digital Mission poster.
- Point to the farm. Ask *What is it?* Learners say *A farm*. Say *Yes! It's a farm.*
- Point to the empty space in the middle. Say *Oh! There are no … (animals)*. Point to Stage 1 at the bottom and say *I know!* (as if you had a great idea) *We'll draw an animal.*
- Say *Point to number 2*. Learners point. Say *And we'll play a game!*
- Say *Point to number 3*. Learners point. Say *And we will choose animals and write about our farm*. Say with excitement *Let's make a farm!* Encourage them to jump and smile. Say *This is our Mission*.

Activity Book, page 30

My unit goals

- Go through the unit goals with the learners. You can read these or if you prefer you can put them onto the board or a poster.
- You can go back to these unit goals at the end of each Mission stage during the unit and review them.
- Say *This is our Mission page*.

Ending the lesson

- Get two large sheets of paper. Write *Farm* on one and *Classroom* on the other. Stick them at each end of the classroom.
- Show learners flashcards/pictures of different things – encourage them to run to the correct side of the room according to where you find the things in the pictures. Say the words as you show each picture (e.g. for farm: tree, sheep, tractor, field, and for classroom: board, teacher, pen, book).

  Stronger learners Choose these learners to call out the words. Other learners answer.

3 Vocabulary 1

Learning outcomes By the end of the lesson, learners will be able to recognise and use animal words.

New language *cat, chicken, cow, dog, donkey, duck, goat, horse, pet, sheep, spider*

Recycled language colours, names, numbers

Materials flashcards from previous units, Farm animals flashcards, pictures from Digital photo bank of families with pets, e.g. cats or dogs (and/or your own photos if you have a pet), audio, video

Key Competences

- Identify and name animals.
- Chant together as a class.
- Practise numbers by counting animals.
- Identify the sound /k/.

Warm-up

- Use flashcards from previous units: pen, desk, grandmother, etc. Reveal the picture. Learners repeat the word.

Presentation

- Hold up a Farm animal flashcard, e.g. cow, facing towards you and away from the learners. Make the sound of a cow mooing. Ask *What is it?* (*It's a cow.*) Turn the flashcard around and say *It's a cow*. Learners repeat several times. Say *Make a cow sound*. Learners make a mooing sound.
- Go through the same process with each animal card.
- Show a picture of a cat or dog. Say *This is my pet*. Ask *Have you got a pet?* Learners say *Yes* or *No*. Ask *What pet have you got? A cat? A dog?* Learners answer.

Pupil's Book, page 31

1 3.01 3.02 Listen and point. Then listen and number.

- Say *Open your Pupil's Books at page 31. Look at the picture.*
- Indicate the caption and read it. Say *It's a farm*.
- Ask *Where's Jim? Can you find him?* The class points. Repeat with different people. Ask *Where's the donkey?* Learners point. Ask *How many?* (*One*) Repeat, asking the names and how many.
- Say *Listen and point*. Play Track 3.01. Learners point to the animals in the picture.

Tracks 3.01 and 3.02

This afternoon Tom and Eva are on the farm with Jim and Jenny.

(1) Jim: This is our farm and these are our animals.
Tom: Ooh, a sheep.
Jim: Yes, she's Shelly.
(2) Jim: And that's Gracie, our goat.
(3) Jim: OK, Cameron. Good boy.
Eva: Is he your pet cat?
Jim: Yes.
(4) Jim: And we've got a pet dog. Look – she's black and white.
(5) Jenny: This is Harry. He's our horse. Look at his tail! It's black.
Eva: Hmm.
(6) Jenny: We've got three cows.
(7) Jenny: And a donkey.
Eva: Ooh, it's a grey donkey!
(8) Eva: Are they your ducks?
Jenny: Yes, they are. We've got two ducks.
(9) Jim: Look, Tom. This is Henrietta and this is Rocky. They're chickens.
(10) Tom: And this black spider? What's his name?
Jenny: Ha ha. I don't know. It isn't our spider!
Tom: Aagh!

- Display the Farm animal flashcards on the board. Say *Look at page 31*. Point to the flashcards and ask *What's number 1?* (*Sheep*) Play number 1 of the audio. Write number *1* on the board, next to the sheep flashcard.
- Play Track 3.02. Learners number the animals.

Key: 2 goat 3 cat 4 dog 5 horse 6 cow 7 donkey 8 duck 9 chicken 10 spider

2 3.03 Say the chant.

- Play the audio or video. Learners point and chant.

Track 3.03

Cow, horse, dog (x2)
Chicken and goat (x2)
Duck, sheep, cat (x2)
Donkey and spider (x2)

3 3.04 Listen and say the animal.

- Focus on the picture. Ask questions, e.g. *What's this?* (*A horse*) *What colour is it?* (*Brown*) *How many?* (*One*)
- Make a chicken noise. Ask *What's this?* (*A chicken*) Play the audio. Learners say the animal or animals.

Track 3.04

1 What's this? [a chicken]
2 What are these? [dogs]
3 What's this? [a cow]
4 What are these? [cats]
5 What's this? [a horse]
6 What are these? [sheep]
7 What's this? [a donkey]
8 What are these? [ducks]

Key: 1 chicken 2 dogs 3 cow 4 cats 5 horse 6 sheep 7 donkey 8 ducks

Activity Book, page 31

See pages TB120–132

Ending the lesson

- **SA** Say *We learnt about animals*. Show the flashcards. Ask *Do you know the words?* Use the self-assessment technique (see Introduction). Learners show how they feel.

1 3.01 3.02 **Listen and point. Then listen and number.**

2 3.03 **Say the chant.**

3 3.04 **Listen and say the animal.**

The Friendly Farm

3.05

Learning outcomes By the end of the lesson, learners will be able to understand when they hear adjectives.

New language *big, long, nice, old, short, small, young*

Recycled language animals, colours, names

Materials Farm animal flashcards, Family flashcards, Friendly Farm animal flashcards, audio, video

Key Competences

Read and listen to a story; Identify and learn adjectives in context.

Act out a story.

Warm-up

- Draw a large fence on the board and write *Farm*. Say *Here's my farm.* Say *Which animals are on my farm? Let's listen!* Make the sound of a horse. Learners say *Horse*. Say *Yes, there's a horse on my farm*. Stick the horse flashcard in the farm. Learners repeat *Horse* and make the animal noise. Continue going through the animals.
- **SA** Use self-assessment to check how well learners think they understand the vocabulary. See Introduction.

Presentation

- Put up the flashcard of Grandpa Friendly on the board. Ask *Who is this?* (*Grandpa*) Say *Grandpa is old*. Mime an old person walking, e.g. with a stick. Repeat the sequence with Grandma Friendly. Say *Old*. Put up a flashcard of Jenny. Ask *Is Jenny old?* (*No*) Say *No, she isn't. Jenny is young.* Mime a young person full of energy. Say *Young*. Learners repeat. Repeat with Jim. Point to the four flashcards randomly. Learners say *Young* or *Old*.
- Use flashcards of Mr Friendly and Jim to demonstrate *tall* and *short* following a similar sequence.
- Use flashcards of Harry and a spider to demonstrate *big* and *small* following a similar sequence. Add flashcards of the other animals. Point randomly. Learners say *Big* or *Small*.
- Add a flashcard of Cameron. Ask *Who is it?* (*Cameron*) *What is it?* (*A cat*) Say *Cameron is a nice cat*. Say *Nice* and smile. Learners repeat *Nice*.
- Point to Cameron's tail. Ask *What is it?* (*Tail*) Say *Tail*. Learners repeat. Say *The tail is long*. Indicate *long* with your hands. Learners repeat. Move your hands together. Say *Short*. Learners repeat.

Pupil's Book, page 32

3.05 The Friendly Farm song

- Say *The Friendly Farm is big*. Hold your arms outwards to indicate *big*.
- Play the introductory song at the beginning of the cartoon story. As it plays, gesture *big* each time the word *farm* appears. Learners listen. Repeat. Learners listen, gesture and sing.

Track 3.05
See The Friendly Farm song on page TB5

3.05 The Friendly Farm

- Hide the Friendly Farm animal flashcards around the room. Ask *Can you find a small animal?* Mime looking. Show the spider flashcard. Ask *What is it?* (*A spider*) *Is it small?* (*Yes*)
- Ask four learners to come to the front. Ask *Can you find a big animal?* When the first learner finds a flashcard, they hold it up. Ask *Is it big?* If it is big, keep the flashcard. Repeat the sequence with four new learners searching. Continue until you have collected all the flashcards.
- Say *Open your Pupil's Books at page 32*. Ask *Who can you see in the pictures?* Learners name the characters. Ask their names and colours.
- Ask *Who is young? Who is old? Who is short?* Write the questions on the board. Say *Listen*. Play the audio or video. Learners listen and read.

Track 3.05
The Friendly Farm song + see cartoon on Pupil's Book page 32

- Learners answer the questions.
- Play the audio or video again. Pause after each frame and check comprehension:
  Frame 1: *The spider is …* (*small*).
  Frame 2: *Harry is …* (*big*) *and his tail is …* (*long*).
  Frame 3: *Cameron is …* (*long*).
  Frame 4: *Gracie is …* (*old*).
  Frame 5: *Gracie isn't …* (*young*).
  Frame 6: *Now Cameron isn't …* (*long*). *He's …* (*short*).
- Point to frame 3. Ask *Is Cameron nice?* (*Yes*) *Is he short?* (*No, he's long.*)
- Play the audio or video again. Divide the class into groups of four and give each group a role. Learners repeat the speech bubbles for their character.

Activity Book, page 32

See pages TB120–132

Ending the lesson

- **SA** Repeat the self-assessment technique used at the start of the lesson to see how well learners think they understand the vocabulary. Is there any change?
- Divide the class into two groups. Choose two confident learners to come to the front – one from each group. Draw a line to divide the board in half. Give each learner a board pen and tell them to draw what their team says.
- Stand in front of the board, facing the class, with the two learners behind you. Hold up the first Farm animal flashcard. Learners call out the animal and *Small* or *Big*. The first learner to complete a drawing wins a point for the team. Continue with all of the Farm animal flashcards.

3 Language practice 1

Learning outcomes By the end of the lesson, learners will be able to use adjectives accurately when speaking and writing.

New language article + adjective + singular noun, adjective + plural noun

Recycled language food, names

Materials sets of cut up sentences (one set per three to four learners). Each set contains the four sentences from Gracie's Grammar on different coloured card cut up into single words, Farm animal flashcards, coloured pens or pencils, digital Mission poster

Key Competences

- Learn to use adjectives accurately.
- Work together to play a guessing game.
- Colour a picture based on verbal information.
- Reflect on their own learning.
- Interact with the digital poster.

Warm-up

- Learners stand in a circle. Stand in the centre. Learners walk around anti-clockwise. Clap your hands and say *Chicken*. Learners walk like a chicken and make chicken sounds. Clap again and shout *Horse*. Learners gallop and make a horse sound. Continue with other animals.

Presentation

- Draw a big spider. Write *It's a spider big* on the board. Ask *OK?* Learners say *No*. Rub out *spider big* and write *big spider*. Ask *OK?* Learners say *Yes*.
- Draw a second spider. Write *They is big spiders*. Ask *OK?* Learners say *No*. Look puzzled. Learners say *They're*. Correct the sentence. Underline *It's* from the first sentence and ask *How many spiders?* (*One*) Underline *They're* from the second sentence. Ask *How many spiders?* (*Two*)
- Rub out the spiders and draw one very small spider. Point to the sentence *It's a big spider*. Shake your head. Say *It* … (shake head)… ***isn't*** *a big spider*. Learners repeat. Draw a second small spider. Point to *They're big spiders*. Shake your head. Learners say *They* ***aren't*** *big spiders.*
- Take out the sets of cut up sentences. Learners rebuild the sentences, putting the cards into the correct order.

Pupil's Book, page 33

3.06 Gracie's Grammar

- Say *Open your Pupil's Books at page 33*. Point to Gracie's Grammar box. Write the same sentences on the board.
- Underline the adjectives: *nice*, *big*, *young*, *old*. Ask *Nice cat or cat nice?* Learners say *Nice cat*. Say *Yes – good*. Repeat with the other examples.
- Play the audio. Pause for learners to repeat each sentence.

Track 3.06
See Pupil's Book page 33

1 3.07 Listen and stick. Then look, read and write.

- Learners look at the four stickers. They do not stick them in yet. Point and ask, e.g. *Is it big?* (*Yes*) *Is it old?* (*No*)
- Play the audio for learners to point to the correct sticker.

Track 3.07
1 Is it an old cat? No, it isn't. It isn't an old cat.
2 Are they young cats? Yes, they are. They're young cats.
3 Is it a small cat? Yes, it is. It's a small cat.
4 Are they short cats? No, they aren't. They aren't short cats.

- Play the audio again. Learners stick in the stickers.
- Say *Look, read and write*. Learners write.

Key: 2 young 3 small 4 short

mission Stage 1

- Show learners the first stage of the digital Mission poster: 'Draw an animal'. Say *Let's draw!*
- Learners complete the worksheet task in the Teacher's Resource Book page 34 (see teaching notes on TRB page 27).
- Alternatively, if you do not have the Teacher's Resource Book, quickly show learners all the Farm animal flashcards. They call out the name of each one.
- Learners use coloured pens or pencils to draw an animal.
- Learners stand up. Each learner should make the noise of their animal. The group call out the name. The learner shows their picture and says *Yes!* They sit down. Continue around the class until all learners are sitting.
- Keep the animal pictures safe, to use again for Stage 2.

Activity Book, page 33

See pages TB120–132

Activity Book, page 30

- Say *Look at page 30 of your Activity Book*. Review *My unit goals*. Ask *How is your Mission?*
- Learners reflect and choose a smiley face for *My mission diary 1*. Monitor.

Ending the lesson

- Go back to Stage 1 on the digital Mission poster. Say *We drew an animal. Good work*. Add a tick to the 'Draw an animal' stage or invite a learner to do it. Use self-assessment (see Introduction).
- Give out a completion sticker.

Gracie's Grammar

3.06

He's a **nice** cat.

We're **young** boys and girls.

It isn't a **big** spider.

They aren't **old** chickens.

1 3.07 **Listen and stick. Then look, read and write.**

~~old~~ short small young

1 It isn't an old cat.

2 They're ________ cats.

3 It's a ________ cat.

4 They aren't ________ cats.

mission STAGE 1

Choose an animal for your farm.

- Draw your farm animal.
- What does it look like? Write and say.

It's a big horse.

My mission diary

Activity Book page 30

Vocabulary 2 and song

1 3.08 **Listen and act out the animals. Then sing the song.**

She's a funny dog
with a brown nose and a long tail.
She's a funny dog.

He's a sad dog
with a black nose and a brown tail.
He's a sad dog.

I've got a happy dog.
My happy dog's in the park.
She's a beautiful dog.
I've got a happy dog.
My happy dog's in the park.
We're in the park!
Different dogs in the park, yeah!
Different dogs in the park.

He's an ugly dog
with a pink nose and a short tail.
He's an ugly dog.

She's an angry cat
with a black nose and a black tail.
She's an angry cat.

Chorus

2 **Look at the picture. Play the game.**

It's a dog with a pink nose and a short tail.

Is it the ugly dog?

Yes, it is!

I love dogs! Have you got a pet?

Learning outcomes By the end of the lesson, learners will have practised the language through song.

New language *angry, beautiful, funny, happy, sad, ugly*

Recycled language animals, colours, numbers, parts of the body

Materials Adjectives flashcards, plastic drinking straws (five per pair of learners), pictures from Digital photo bank of a park in sunshine, a park in the rain, a beautiful garden, an ugly garden and a dog rolling on its back happily in the grass, a soft ball, audio, video, paper, coloured pens or pencils

Key Competences

Learn and practise new adjectives for description through a song.

Act out a song.

Play a guessing game in pairs.

Warm-up

- Say *Let's make some dogs and cats*. Hold up a straw. Say *The dog has got a black nose and a white tail*. Colour the very end of the straw black. Colour the other end of the straw white – make this a slightly longer section. Say *It has got a black nose and a white tail*. Write the sentence on the board. Learners copy.
- Learners make the dogs and a cat from straws according to the description. Write under the first sentence:
  The dog has got a pink nose and a short tail. (use a pink pen and twist the other end of the straw so it is short)
  The cat has got a black nose and a black tail. (use black)
  The dog has got a brown nose and a long tail. (use brown)
  The dog has got a black nose and a brown tail. (use black and brown)
- Say *Show me your pets.* As you call out the descriptions, learners hold up their straw animals.
- **SA** Use self-assessment to check how well learners think they understand the vocabulary. See Introduction.

Pupil's Book, page 34

1 3.08 Listen and act out the animals. Then sing the song.

- Show a picture of a park in the sun. Say *It's a park*. Learners repeat. Say *The park is nice*. Learners repeat.
- Show a picture of a dog rolling over on its back in the grass. Ask *What is it? (A dog) Is it happy? (Yes)* Laugh and point and mime rolling. Say *It's funny!* Learners repeat.
- Show a picture of a park in the rain. Say *I'm not in the park*. Look sad. Say *I'm sad*. Learners repeat. Say *I'm in the house. But … oh no!* Look and sound angry. Say *No jumping. No ball.* Say *I'm angry.* Learners repeat.
- Say *I'm happy*. Learners mime *happy* and repeat. Say *I'm sad*. Learners mime *sad* and repeat. Continue with *angry*.
- Show a picture of a beautiful garden with flowers. Say *I'm in the garden*. Learners repeat. Say *The garden is beautiful*. Learners repeat. Show a picture of the ugly garden. Say *I'm in the garden*. Ask *Is it beautiful?* Learners say *No*. Say *It's ugly* and make a disgusted face. Learners repeat.
  Alternative Use the Adjectives flashcards to teach *angry, beautiful, funny, happy, sad, ugly*.
- Say *Open your Pupil's Books at page 34*.
- Play the audio or video. Learners listen and point.

Track 3.08

Rocky: I'm Rocky-Doodle-Doo and … here's our song for today: *Different dogs in the park*.

See song on Pupil's Book page 34

- Play the audio or video again. Learners hold up their straw dogs and cats for the correct description.
  3.09 **Extension** Once learners are confidently singing to the song, try singing the karaoke version as a class.

2 Look at the picture. Play the game.

- Say *Look at the picture on page 34*. Point to the animals one by one, saying *The happy dog, the ugly dog, the angry cat, the funny dog, the sad dog*. Ask *Which one?* Read the clue: *It's a dog with a pink nose and a short tail.* Learners say *Is it the ugly dog?*
- In pairs, learners describe a dog or cat and their partner asks *Is it the (happy/ugly/angry/funny/sad) dog/cat?*
- Teach the word *pet* by telling the learners about your pet. Say, e.g. *I've got a dog. My dog is my pet.*
- Show the picture of Rocky in the bottom right-hand corner. Read out the question. Learners call out their answers.

Activity Book, page 34

See pages TB120–132

Ending the lesson

- **SA** Repeat the self-assessment technique used at the start of the lesson to see how well learners think they understand the vocabulary. Is there any change?
- Draw a simple outline of a dog four times. Colour each dog differently.
- Learners draw and colour in their choice of colours. They number the pictures 1–4.
- Say *Hmm … I'm thinking of one dog. It's got a brown nose and a long black tail.* Learners guess which dog you have chosen, e.g. *Is it number 3? (Yes)* In pairs, learners describe and guess.

3 Language practice 2

Learning outcomes By the end of the lesson, learners will be able to ask about features of animals using *Has it got … ?*

New language *It's got … It hasn't got … Has it got … ? Yes, it has. No, it hasn't.*

Recycled language animals, colours, parts of the body

Materials a large picture of a cat or a dog and a 'tail' made of string or cotton wool with sticky tack on the end, a scarf or similar blindfold, audio, video, donkey flashcard, coloured pens or pencils, digital Mission poster

Key Competences

- Learn and practise *has got* / *hasn't got* to make descriptions.
- Learn about features of animals.
- Play a guessing game to revise the newly learnt vocabulary.
- Reflect on their own learning.

Warm-up

- Display the large picture of a cat or a dog. Ask *What is it? (Cat/Dog)* Say *Oh no! It hasn't got a …* Show the tail. Learners say *tail*.
- Choose a confident learner and use a scarf or similar to cover their eyes. Put the 'tail' in their hand so they hold it at the top where the sticky tack is. Turn the learner around a couple of times and then put them near the board so they know where to put their hand. Say *Put on the tail!* The learner tries to add the tail in the right place. If they get it close, say *Well done!* If not, say *That's funny!*
- Repeat with one or two more learners.

Pupil's Book, page 35

1 3.10 Which duck is he talking about? Listen and tick ✓.

- Point to the photos. Ask the learners to describe each one.
- Say *Listen. Which animal is the boy talking about?* Play the audio.

Track 3.10

Boy: This is my favourite photo from my trip to the farm. It's a photo of a duck on the farm. It isn't a young duck. It's got a big white body and it's got orange feet. It hasn't got a long tail. It's got a short, white tail.

Key: Picture 2

3.11 Gracie's Grammar

- Show the flashcard of a donkey. Ask *Has it got a tail? (Yes)* Say *Yes, it has*. Learners repeat. Ask *Has it got small ears? (No)* Say *No, it hasn't*. Learners repeat. Ask *Has it got a long face? (Yes, it has.)* Say the three questions and answers again. Learners repeat both questions and answers.
- Point to Gracie's Grammar box. Play the audio. Learners repeat.
- Put the learners into pairs. They take it in turns to say the sentences. Play the audio, pausing so learners can repeat.

Track 3.11

See Pupil's Book page 35

2 Think of an animal. Describe it for your partner to draw.

- Draw a funny animal, e.g. with three legs and three tails, but don't show the learners. Tell them to listen and draw what you say. Describe your animal, e.g. *My animal is big. It's got three legs. It's got three tails.* Ask learners to show what they have drawn. Show your original drawing.
- Tell the learners to think of their own animal and draw it, but not show anyone.
- Put the learners in pairs. Learners describe their animal to their partner who should draw it. They swap roles. Once they have finished, they can compare their pictures.
- While they compare, they can describe the animal their partner asked them to draw, e.g. *Your animal is small. It's got four eyes.*

Extra support Give a list of possible sentence stems for learners to use while they describe their animal.

mission Stage 2

- Show learners the second stage of the digital Mission poster: 'Play a game'.
- Take out learners' animal pictures from Mission Stage 1.
- Learners look again at their own picture. Then they mingle in the class without showing their pictures to each other. They ask and answer questions and try to find out which animal their classmate drew.
- For ideas on monitoring and assessment, see Introduction.

Activity Book, page 35

See pages TB120–132

Activity Book, page 30

- Say *Look at page 30 of your Activity Book.* Review *My unit goals.* Ask *How is your Mission?*
- Learners reflect and choose a smiley face for *My mission diary 2.* Monitor.

Ending the lesson

- **SA** Go back to Stage 2 on the digital Mission poster. Add a tick to the 'Play a game' stage or invite a learner to do it. Use self-assessment (see Introduction).
- Give out a completion sticker.

1 3.10 Which duck is he talking about? Listen and tick ✓.

1

2

3

3.11 Gracie's Grammar

It's **got** long ears.
Has it **got** a long face?

It **hasn't got** small feet.
Yes, it **has**. / **No**, it **hasn't**.

2 Think of an animal. Describe it for your partner to draw.

My animal has got a big body.

My animal has got long ears.

My animal has got a short tail.

mission STAGE 2

Play a guessing game with your animals.

Has it got long ears?

Yes, it has.

Is it beautiful?

No, it isn't.

It's the donkey.

Yes, it is.

My mission diary
Activity Book page 30

Cross-curricular

What do animals give us?

1 **Watch the video.**

2 3.12 **Look and match. Then listen and check.**

1 

cow

2 

chicken

3 

sheep

4 

bee

a 

wool

b 

milk

c 

honey

d 

eggs

3 **Tick ✓ the things that come from animals.**

Learning outcomes By the end of the lesson, learners will be able to understand the link between food and animals.

New language *eggs, honey, milk, wool*

Recycled language animals

Materials some milk, a jar of honey, two bowls, some disposable plastic teaspoons, paper, coloured pens or pencils, audio, video, four large cards

Key Competences

- Learn specific language to be able to talk about Science in English.
- Learn about what animals give us.
- Work in pairs to identify things that come from animals.

Warm-up

Note: Before doing this activity, check if any learners have a dairy or honey/pollen allergy.

- Put some milk in a bowl and some honey in another bowl. Don't tell learners what it is. Ask a few learners to come to the front. Give them a spoon of milk to try. Ask *Is it nice?* Learners respond. Repeat with honey.
- Ask *What is it?* Learners respond. If they guess correctly and say the word in L1, say the word in English. Learners repeat.

Pupil's Book, page 36

1 Watch the video.

- Say *Let's watch the video.* Learners watch the video about things animals give us and answer the questions at the end of the video.

2 3.12 Look and match. Then listen and check.

- Point to the animal pictures one by one. Ask *What is it?* (*Cow, chicken, sheep, bee*)
- Point to the other pictures one by one. Ask *What is it?* (*Wool, milk, honey, eggs*) Say each word. Learners repeat several times.
- Point to the milk. Ask *Which animal has got milk?* (*Cow*) Show the match between the pictures of the cow and the milk.
- Learners continue, matching the foods with the animals.
- Play the audio. Learners listen and check their answers.

Track 3.12

Animals give us a lot of things. Cows give us milk. Chickens give us eggs. Sheep give us wool. And bees … [sound of buzzing bees] give us honey.

Key: 2 d 3 a 4 c

3 Tick ✓ the things that come from animals.

- Point to each picture. Ask *What is it?* (*An egg, crisps, chicken, a hat*) Say *Crisps are …* Learners say *potatoes*. Say *This hat is …* Learners say *wool*.
- Ask *Which things are from animals?*
- Put learners into pairs. They tick the correct pictures.
- Check answers. Say the words so that learners can repeat any new ones, e.g. *Wool*.
- In pairs, learners look at the units they have studied so far and find as many animals as they can. Check which pair has found the most animals.
- Repeat the task. This time, ask them to find things that come from animals. Check which pair has found the most items.

Key: the egg the chicken the hat

Activity Book, page 36

See pages TB120–132

Ending the lesson

- Learners work in pairs. They take it in turns to make an animal noise and their partner says the name of the animal.

  Extension Learners sit in a circle. Stand in the middle and act out an animal, e.g. walk like a chicken, flapping your arms and clucking. Learners call out *Chicken*. Bring a learner into the centre to act out an animal. Learners call out the answer. Keep going, giving all learners a turn.

  Larger class Divide the class into two or three smaller circles once you have demonstrated the activity.

Learning outcomes By the end of the lesson, learners will be able to read about animals and understand if information is correct. They will understand the source of food.

New language *alpaca, cut, Peru*

Recycled language animals, colours, *have/has got*, numbers

Materials two large cards – one with *Animal* and one with *No animal* on it, sticky tack, small cards with pictures of food (eggs, cheese, apples, meat, cereal, sausages, milk, tea, spaghetti, potatoes) – one per learner, an egg, an apple and a ball of wool (or pictures), pictures from Digital photo bank of a sheep with a heavy coat and of a sheared sheep, a world map showing Peru, Farm animals flashcards, learners' pictures of animals from Mission Stage 1, coloured pens and pencils

Key Competences

- Read for specific information.
- Learn facts about alpacas.
- Work in groups to make their farm and write about it.
- Reflect on their own learning.
- Interact with the digital poster.

Warm-up

- Display the card with the word *Animal* on one side of the room, and the card with *No animal* on the other.
- Show an egg or a picture of an egg. Ask *What is it?* (*Egg*) Say *Chickens have got eggs. Chickens give us eggs. Animals give us eggs.* Show an apple or a picture of an apple on a tree. Say *It's an apple. Animals haven't got apples.*
- Point to the cards on the wall. Say *Egg*. Go to the *No animal* card. Ask *OK?* Learners say *No!* Go to the *Animal* card. Say *Yes. Chickens have got eggs. OK?* Learners say *Yes*. Show the apple. Learners call out *No animal*.
- Give out the small cards with food pictures on them – one per learner. Learners go to the side of the room with the correct card on the wall, according to their food. Check quickly. Collect the cards and redistribute. Repeat.

  Extra support Give learners pictures of the egg/apple rather than new words.

  Fast finishers Ask them which animal the food is from.

Presentation

- Show learners a ball of wool or a picture. Ask *What's this?* (*Wool*) Learners repeat. Ask *Have animals got wool?* Learners respond. Say *Yes. Sheep have got wool. Sheep have got hair. We make wool with sheep hair.*
- Show the picture of a sheep with a heavy coat and the picture of a sheared sheep. Say *We cut the hair.* Gesture cutting. Point to the sheared sheep.
- Point to the picture of the sheep. Say *It's a horse*. Learners say *No!* Say *It's black*. Learners say *No!*

Pupil's Book, page 37

4 Read the article. Then read the sentences and write *yes* or *no*.

- Point to the picture. Ask *Where is it?* Say *It's in Peru.* Show Peru on a world map.
- Ask *What can you see? Let's find out! Which animal is it? What has it got? Read.*
- Learners read to find out the animal. Then ask *Which animal is it?* (*Alpaca*) Ask *What has it got?* (*Wool*)
- Say *Read again. Write yes or no.* Learners read and write.

Key: 2 no 3 yes 4 yes

mission Stage 3

- Draw a farm on the board with a space in the middle of the fence. Leave a space on one side for sentences. Say *Look at our farm!*
- Hold up some Farm animals flashcards. Say *Let's put some animals on the farm!* Learners call out the animals they want. Stick them on the board. Ask *What has our farm got? How many? What colour?* Build up sentences on the board, e.g. *Our farm has got two cows and three chickens and a dog. The cows are black and white. The cows give us milk …*
- Divide the class into groups. Give each group a large piece of paper. Learners draw a farm and fence.
- Give out the animal pictures that learners drew in Stage 1. They stick their animal pictures in the farm. They write sentences.
- Keep the farm pictures safe for the Mission completion in a later lesson.
- For ideas on monitoring and assessment, see Introduction.

Activity Book, page 37

See pages TB120–132

Activity Book, page 30

- Say *Look at page 30 of your Activity Book*. Review *My unit goals*. Ask *How is your Mission?*
- Learners reflect and choose a smiley face for *My mission diary 3*. Monitor.

Ending the lesson

- **SA** Go back to Stage 3 on the digital Mission poster. Add a tick to the 'Choose animals' stage. Use self-assessment (see Introduction).
- Give out a completion sticker.

4 Read the article. Then read the sentences and write *yes* or *no*.

Alpaca wool

Do you know this animal? This is an alpaca. It's got four legs and long hair. Alpacas live in the Andes Mountains in Peru.

The hair of an alpaca is like the hair of a sheep. It's called wool. People cut the wool.

Then people clean the wool. They use the wool to make clothes. They use lots of colours. How many colours can you see?

1 Alpacas have got two legs. no
2 Alpacas have got short hair. ______
3 Alpacas live in Peru. ______
4 People make things from alpaca wool. ______

mission STAGE 3

Make your farm and write about it.

- In groups, put your farm animals together.
- Write about your farm and its animals.

Our farm has got two chickens, two cows and a donkey. The chickens give us eggs.

My mission diary
Activity Book page 30

Literature

1 **Look at the cows. What colour are they in the pictures?**

How cows got their spots

3.13

Cathy is a young white cow. She lives with her mum on a big farm. There are horses, sheep and chickens. There are also lots of flies. 'Ouch! Ouch! Ouch! Go away!'

'Use your tail,' says her mum. But Cathy's tail is very short and the flies are not scared of her.

One day she tells a friend about her problem. 'Follow me!' says Little Horse and he jumps into some black mud.

'Come on! Jump in!' he shouts.

Text type: A fantasy story

Learning outcomes By the end of the lesson, learners will have read about animals on a farm and learnt about helping each other.

New language *bite, dirty, flies, mud*

Recycled language adjectives describing appearance and feelings, animals

Materials photos of a house (e.g. your house) and pictures from Digital photo bank of animal homes (a chicken coop, a field, a pond, a stable)

Key Competences

- Read and listen to a story.
- Order events in a story using visual clues.
- Write and draw what scares them.

Warm-up

- Show learners a photo of your house (or a house from the Internet). Say *This is my home*.
- Ask learners to think about where animals live. Show them the pictures of a chicken coop, a field, a pond and a stable.
- Learners work in pairs and say which animal lives in each place.

  Extra support Show learners animal names (*chicken*, *horse*, *duck*, *cow*) and ask them to match them with the places.

  Stronger learners Learners can try to do this activity alone.
- Go through the answers. Learners should find: *chicken coop – chicken, field – cow (and horse), pond – duck, stable – horse*.

Presentation

- Point to the picture of the mud on Pupil's Book page 38. Say *Mud*. Learners repeat.
- Point to the flies in the picture. Ask *What are these?* Say *Flies*. Learners repeat several times. Ask *Are flies nice?* (*No*) Say *Flies can bite*. Mime a fly biting at you and say *Ouch!* Say *Bite* and mime. Learners repeat and copy several times.

Pupil's Book, page 38

1 Look at the cows. What colour are they in the pictures?

- Show the pictures on Pupil's Book pages 38 and 39. Say *Point to the cows*. Ask *What colour are the cows?* (*White/ brown*) *Have they got spots?* Draw spots on the board. Learners say *No*.

3.13 How cows got their spots

- Say *Open your Pupil's Books at pages 38 and 39*. Focus on the pictures. Look at each picture and ask questions, e.g. Picture 1: *Which animals can you see?* (*Horses, sheep, cows, chickens*) Show Cathy, the young cow. Say *This is Cathy. Is she old or young?* (*Young*) *Has she got a long or short tail?* (*Short*) Picture 2: *What is this?* Point to the horse. (*A horse*) *Where is it?* (*In mud*) *Why?* (*To stop the flies*) Picture 3: *Has Cathy got spots?* (*Yes*) *Are the other cows kind?* (*No*) Picture 4: *Are the cows happy?* (*No – sad*) *Why?* (*The flies bite them.*) If learners can't answer the *why* questions, don't give the answers yet.
- Use the artwork to teach *dirty*.
- Ask learners to guess what happens in the story.
- Say *Read and listen to the first part*. Show them page 38. Play the audio. Learners listen and read. Pause the audio at the end of page 38. Ask *Why is Cathy sad?* (*The flies bite her.*) *Can she use her tail?* (*No – it's short.*) *Where is she with the horse?* (*In the mud*)

  Track 3.13

  See story on Pupil's Book pages 38–39
- Say *Read the next part*. Show them the first paragraph on page 39. Ask *Are the other cows kind?* Play the audio for this part. Check if their guesses were correct. (*No – they laugh at her.*)
- Ask them to look at the last paragraph and the fourth picture. Ask *Are the cows happy?* (*No – sad*) *Why?* (*The flies bite them.*) Say *Read and listen*. Play the rest of the audio. Check answers.
- Say *Act out the story*. Say *Cathy can't use her tail*. Mime swishing a pretend tail. Say *The flies bite her. Ouch, ouch, ouch!* Learners copy. Say *The horse shows her the mud*. Mime rolling in mud. Learners copy. Say *Cathy has black spots!* Mime looking at your spots in surprise. Learners copy. Say *The cows laugh at Cathy*. Mime laughing and then Cathy looking sad. Learners copy. Say *Now the flies are here! They bite the cows. Ouch, ouch, ouch!* Mime being bitten by flies again.
- Repeat and encourage the learners to act the story.

Activity Book, page 38

See pages TB120–132

Ending the lesson

- Tell learners to each choose an animal and make it into an anagram, e.g. *cow – owc*. Monitor and check.
- Put learners into pairs. Ask them to give their anagram to their partner. Their partner tells them the word. Repeat, giving each learner a new partner.

Learning outcomes By the end of the lesson, learners will have read about animals on a farm and learnt about helping each other.

New language *bite, flies, mud*

Recycled language adjectives describing appearance and feelings, animals

Materials flashcard of an animal you like (e.g. giraffe), flashcard of zoo, paper for each learner, coloured pens or pencils

Social and Emotional Skill: Identifying the feelings of others

- After reading the story, ask learners *How does Cathy feel when the other cows laugh at her?* (*Sad*) *How does she feel when the flies don't bite her?* (*Happy*) *Who helps Cathy feel happy?* (*Little Horse*) Remind learners that in the story, the other cows laugh at Cathy and it isn't kind to laugh at others. You should think about how others feel. Say *In the class everyone is different. (Javier) has got brown hair. (Maria) has got black hair. (Andrea) has got red hair.* Point out we are all different and we are all unique and that's good. It's not kind to laugh at friends. We are all friends in the same class.
- Play a game to demonstrate the idea of playing together, being part of a group. The learners stand in a circle. Give numbers to each learner but not in order. Stand in the circle with a ball and say *One*. Then throw the ball to the person with that number. That person then throws to number two and so on. Say *We need all the numbers to play the game. We need everyone in the class*. Ask *Do you want to make other people happy or sad?* (*Happy*) Point out that it's good for everyone to play. It's good to be kind and make people feel happy. It's sad when one person doesn't play with the others.
- Role play in pairs:
  A: Hello. What's your name?
  B: (Mia). What's your name?
  A: (Alex). Do you want to play with me?
  B: Yes, please.
  A: Let's play ball.

Key Competences

Read and listen to a story.

Learn the value of helping each other;
Think about how other people feel.

Warm-up

- Tell learners to look at the pictures on pages 38 and 39 and think of the most important words for each part of the story, e.g. *Cathy, short tail, mud*. They note down the key words.
- Ask each pair to compare their list with another pair.
- In pairs, learners tell the story again. Make sure they use the key words.
- **SA** Use self-assessment techniques to check how well learners think they understand the vocabulary. See Introduction.

Pupil's Book, page 39

2 How do they feel? Read and circle.

- Mime *happy*. Ask *How do I feel?* (*Happy*) Mime *sad*. Ask *How do I feel?* (*Sad*) Repeat with *angry* and *surprised*.
- Learners copy.
- In pairs, learners take turns acting the four emotions. Their partner tells them which feeling they are miming.
- Say *Look at Activity 2. Look at the faces. How do they feel?* Learners guess the answers. Say *Listen and read*. Play Track 3.13 all the way through.
- Check answers.

Key: 2 happy 3 sad 4 surprised

3 Ask and answer.

- Show flashcards of different animals. Choose one you like, e.g. a giraffe. Learners say the name. Ask questions, e.g. *What colour is it? Has it got a long or short neck? Has it got big eyes?*
- Learners draw an animal they like. Monitor, telling them the name of the animal if they don't know it.
  Extra support Write the name for them and give them a few sentences about the animal, e.g. *It's big and brown. It's got four legs.*
  Fast finishers Learners write sentences describing their animal.
- When they finish, ask learners to sit in groups of six. They show their animal and describe it to their group.

Activity Book, page 39

See pages TB120–132

Ending the lesson

- **SA** Repeat the self-assessment technique used at the start of the lesson to see how well learners think they understand the vocabulary. Is there any change?
- Show learners the flashcard of the zoo and check meaning. Learners show the animals they have drawn. Together, choose animals for the zoo.

3

When Cathy stands up, her beautiful white coat is very dirty. 'Look!' the young cows laugh. 'Cathy's got big black spots!' Suddenly lots of flies come from behind the house.

'Run!' says Cathy's mum.

'Hide!' shout the young cows.

When the flies go, lots of the young cows have bites. 'Ouch!' they cry. 'Ouch!'

'I haven't got any bites!' laughs Cathy. 'Thank you, Little Horse.' Now lots of white cows have black spots so flies don't bite them.

2 How do they feel? Read and circle.

1 When the flies bite Cathy, she feels:

2 When Little Horse helps Cathy, she feels:

3 When the young cows laugh at Cathy, she feels:

4 When Cathy sees that she hasn't got any bites, she feels:

3 Ask and answer.

What's your favourite animal?

It's a donkey.

Pre A1 Starters

1 Look and say the animals. Which letter do they start with?

It's a cow.

Letter C.

2 How many letters? Count and circle.

1	c o w	2 / (3) / 4 letters	3	d u c k	3 / 4 / 5 letters
2	d o n k e y	4 / 5 / 6 letters	4	s h e e p	5 / 6 / 7 letters

3 Look at the picture. Look at the letters. Write the words.

Example

h o r s e

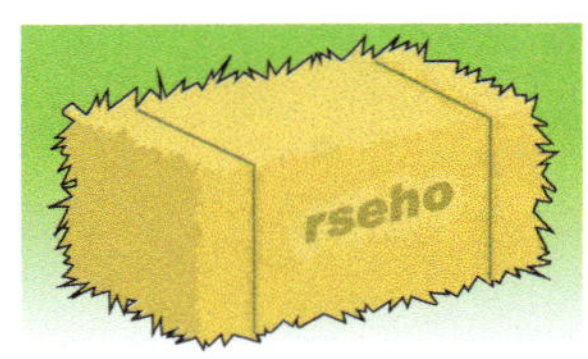

Questions

1

c h _ _ _ _ _

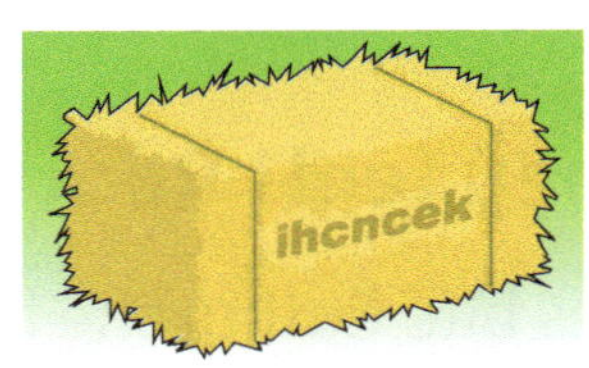

2

d _ _

3

g _ _ _

Look at your answer. Has it got all the letters?

Learning outcomes By the end of the lesson, learners will have written animal words with the correct spelling.

New language *frog*

Recycled language animals

Materials flashcard of spider, coloured pens or pencils

Key Competences

- Learn and practise the correct spelling of animal words.
- Solve a puzzle to practise spelling.
- Practise activity types found in *Pre A1 Starters* exams.

Warm-up

- Show a picture of a spider. Ask *What is it?* (*Spider*) Say *Yes. Spider. Let's make the word.*
- Write the word *spider* up on the board, mixed up. Invite a learner to the front. The learners tell him/her how to write the word.
- Ask *How many letters?* Point to each letter and count them.
- Ask the learners to write the word out in their books. Check clarity of handwriting. Say *You wrote nice letters. Well done.*
- **SA** Use self-assessment to check how well learners think they understand the vocabulary. See Introduction.

Presentation

- Say *Let's do a writing exam!* Write *Writing Exam* on the board.
- Write *spidr* on the board. Ask *Is this good?* (*No*) Rub out the *r* and write *er*. Ask *Is this good?* (*Yes*) Say *Think. Then write.*
- Write up some animal words with incorrect spelling, e.g. *hors – horse*, *chiken – chicken*, *got – goat*, *seep – sheep*.
- Put the learners into pairs. Ask them to find the spelling mistakes and write out the words correctly.
- Check spelling with the whole class. Choose learners to say the correct spellings and to write them up on the board.
- Say *Think. Then write. Check your writing.*

Pupil's Book, page 40

1 Look and say the animals. Which letter do they start with?

- Say *Open your Pupil's Books at page 40*. Point to the animals in the picture one by one. Ask *What's this?* (*Cow, sheep, duck, chicken, donkey, spider, bee*) Give the new word for learners to repeat: *Frog*.
- Point to the cow. Ask *What letter does it start with?* (*Letter c*) Write *cow* on the board and underline the *c*.
- Point to the rest of the animals again, asking *What is it? What letter does it start with?* Learners answer.
- If learners need more practice naming the letters of the alphabet, use the alphabet chant on page 120.

Key: sheep. Letter S. donkey. Letter D. (frog. Letter F.) duck. Letter D. (bee. Letter B.) chicken. Letter C. spider. Letter S.

2 How many letters? Count and circle.

- Say *How many letters? Count and circle.* Show number 1 and say *Cow. How many letters?* Say the letters one by one and count as you do: *C – one*, *O – two*, *W – three*. Ask *How many letters?* (*Three*) Show them the example circle round *3*.
- Learners complete the rest.
- Check answers.

Key: 2 6 letters 3 4 letters 4 5 letters

3 Look at the picture. Look at the letters. Write the words.

- Point out the exam tip at the bottom of Pupil's Book page 40. Say *Look at your answer. Has it got all the letters?*
- Show the first picture. Ask *What is it?* (*Horse*) Say *Let's spell it!* Spell out the letters. Point to the other pictures, for learners to say the names. Say *Write the words. Be careful!*
- Learners write. Monitor and check.

  Extra support Learners look at the Pupil's Book, find the animal and copy.

  Fast finishers Learners try to remember the spellings.
- Write the correct spellings up on the board.

Key: 1 chicken 2 dog 3 goat

Activity Book, page 40

See pages TB120–132

Ending the lesson

- **SA** Repeat the self-assessment technique used at the start of the lesson to see how well learners think they understand the vocabulary. Is there any change?
- Choose some animals. Put learners into groups of three. Ask one to write. Say the name of the animals slowly: *Dog, cow, horse, sheep*. Learners work together to write them.
- Show the correct spellings. Learners check and get one point for each correct answer.
- Draw a picture of a cow on the board. Make a head using a *C* shape; make the body using an *O* shape; add a wiggly tail in a *W* shape. Say *Look at my letters in the cow.*
- Put learners into pairs. Tell them to think of an animal and draw it, hiding the letters in the drawing.
- When learners have finished, each pair shows their picture to the class. The other learners guess which animal it is.

Learning outcomes By the end of the lesson, learners will have revised the language in the unit and made a farm.

Recycled language unit language

Materials large paper, coloured pens or pencils, dice, counters

Key Competences

Revise vocabulary and language learnt in the unit.

Complete self-assessment tasks and reflect on their own learning.

Work in groups to present their farm to the rest of the class.

Warm-up

- Say *Let's ask questions!*
- Tell learners to find their animal from Mission 1. Tell them they will ask and answer questions. On the board, write:
  1 *Have you got ... ?*
  2 *What colour ... ?*
  3 *Has it got . . ?*
  4 *Is it ... ?*
  5 *Can you spell it?*
- Give examples, e.g. *1 Have you got a dog/cat/goat/chicken? 2 What colour is it? 3 Has it got four legs? 4 Is it nice/ beautiful/ugly? 5 Can you spell it?*
- Learners work with a partner and ask and answer questions about their animal.

Presentation

- Write on the board: *Show your farm.*
- Show an example farm – draw a farm building and fence on the board. Say *Here is my farm*. Stick up some flashcards of animals in the middle. Say *Here are the horses. And here are the cows* and so on.
- If you prefer, show flashcards and allow the learners to select animals to go on the farm. Ask the names and write these next to the animals.
- Say *Here is my farm.*

Pupil's Book, page 41

mission in action!

Show your farm.

- Say *You will show the class your farm*. Give an example, e.g. *My farm has got three cows, three pigs, a goat, three chickens and a cat. The cows are big. They are black and white. The chickens give us eggs.* Point as you show the farm.
- Put the learners into their groups from Stage 3 and give them each their group farm picture. Tell the learners to talk in their group and describe their farm.
- Ask a few confident learners to come to the front and show their farms.
- Ask the learners to say what they like about the farms they see, e.g. *I like the horses and the farm house.*
- Point to the picture of an animal from the unit, e.g. a sheep. Say *Tell me about this*. Learners say, e.g. *It's a sheep. It's nice. It's got four legs. It's got wool.* Learners repeat the activity in pairs, choosing anything from the unit.
- For ideas on monitoring and assessment, see Introduction.

Self-assessment

- **SA** Say *Did you like our 'Let's make a farm' Mission?* Put a picture of a smiley face on the wall at one end of the class and a picture of a frowning face on the opposite wall. Demonstrate that if learners loved the Mission, they stand near the smiley face and if they didn't, they stand near the frowning face.
- Say *Did you do better than the last Mission – All about me? Better? Or not?* Ask them to stand near the smiley or frowning face. Praise or say *OK. We can try again.*
- Say *Our next Mission is 'Have a picnic'.* Ask learners to stand up. *What can you do better next time?* Ask them to choose one thing and tell their partner, e.g. *I can write more words. I can read more.* Say *Well done*. Monitor and make notes of their ideas.

Activity Book, page 41

See pages TB120–132

Activity Book, page 30

- Say *Look at page 30 of your Activity Book*. Review *My unit goals*. Ask *How is your Mission?*
- Learners reflect and choose a smiley face for *My mission diary* the final stage. Monitor.
- Point to the sunflower. Learners read the 'can do' statements and tick them if they agree they have achieved them. They colour each leaf green if they are very confident or orange if they think they need more practice.
- Point to the word stack sign. Ask learners to spend a few minutes looking back at the unit and find a minimum of five new words they have learnt. They write the new words into their word stack. See Introduction for techniques and activities.

Ending the lesson

- Go back to the completion stage on the digital Mission poster. Add a tick or invite a learner to do it. Use self-assessment (see Introduction).
- Give out a completion sticker.
- Tell the learners *You have finished your Mission! Well done!*

mission in action!

Show your farm.

My mission diary
Activity Book page 30

★ **Talk about your farm.**

Our farm has got three cows.

And it's got a donkey.

★ **Talk about the animals.**

The donkey has got long ears.

The sheep are happy.

★ **Talk about what the animals give us.**

The cows give us milk.

3

Review • • • Units 1–3

1 Watch the video and do the quiz.

2 3.14 Listen and tick ✓.

1 This is my sister.

2 This is my brother.

3 This is my cat.

4 This is my horse.

3 Look at the picture and remember. Ask and answer.

Where's the red book?

It's on the purple chair.

Learning outcomes By the end of the lesson, learners will have consolidated language from Units 1–3.

Recycled language *have/has got, Have/Has … got?, haven't/hasn't got, he/she,* prepositions, school, *This is / These are, Where is / Where are … ?*

Materials two sheets of A3 paper, flashcards from Units 1–3, video, coloured pens or pencils, audio

Warm-up

- Divide the board into two halves or put up two sheets of A3 paper and stick them on the wall at a level the learners can write on. Take out the flashcards for Units 1–3, mix them up and divide them randomly into two equal piles. Put the flashcards face down at the back of the room.
- Divide the learners into two groups and ask them to stand in two lines facing the board. Give the learner at the front of each line a marker pen.
- The learner at the front of each line should run to the back, turn over the first flashcard and then run to the board and write the name of the object, animal or person. If they don't know the word, they can put the flashcard to the bottom of the pile and try the next one.
- If they can write the word, you take the flashcard from them and they pass the marker pen to the next learner in their line. The next learner runs and writes the next word.
- Learners keep going until all the flashcards are finished.

Extra support Learners can be selected to assist you by collecting the completed flashcards and reading the words aloud to you as the other learners add them.

Pupil's Book, page 42

1 Watch the video and do the quiz.

- Show the video to learners.
- Ask learners to do the quiz. Check their answers to see how much the learners can remember.
- Repeat this at the end of the Review unit and compare the results to measure progress.

2 3.14 Listen and tick ✓.

- Ask three learners to come to the front. Point to each learner. Ask, e.g. *What colour is her hair? What colour are her eyes? Has she got a pencil? Has she got a long tail? Is she happy or sad?* Learners answer.
- Ask *Which learner am I talking about*? Describe one of them, e.g. *This learner has got brown hair and brown eyes. She is happy.* Learners choose.
- Say *Open your Pupil's Books at page 42.* Point to the pictures in Activity 2. Ask learners what they can see in each picture. (e.g. *She has got brown hair, but she has got black hair.*) Say *Let's listen and tick the picture we hear about.*
- Play the audio. If necessary, pause after number 1 and check. Then play the rest of the audio. Learners complete the task.

Track 3.14

1 Girl: This is my sister. She's got black hair and blue eyes.
2 Boy: This is my brother. He's sad today. He hasn't got a crayon.
3 Girl: This is my cat, Fluffy. She's grey and she's got a short tail.
4 Boy: This is my horse. My horse is beautiful. He's got a long, black tail and he's happy.

- Check answers.

Key: 1 c 2 b 3 b 4 a

3 Look at the picture and remember. Ask and answer.

- Put some objects on the desk, e.g. a bag, a book, a pencil case, pens and a rubber. Ask *Where is the book?* (e.g. *On the desk*) Encourage the learners to give more detail (e.g. *It's on the desk next to the pencil case.*)
- Ask about the different objects.
- Put the learners into pairs. Ask them to write three sentences about the objects. Give an example, e.g. *The red bag is under the white desk.*
- Say *Look at Activity 3.* Point to the picture. Encourage learners to ask questions about the picture, e.g. *Where is the pink bag? Where is the red book?* Other learners answer.
- Put the learners into pairs – A and B. Tell all the learners to look and try to remember the picture. Tell the learners who are 'A' to close their Pupil's Books. Tell the learners who are 'B' to look at the picture and ask their partner questions. Monitor and support.
- After a few minutes, ask them to swap roles and repeat.

Activity Book, page 42

See pages TB120–132

Ending the lesson

- Draw a rough sketch of objects, but don't show learners. Tell the learners to listen and draw what you describe, e.g. *There's a desk. There's a red bag under the desk. There's a blue pen on the desk. There's a white rubber next to the pen.* When learners finish, compare their drawings with yours.

Extension Put learners into pairs. Write a list of objects on the board (e.g. *desk, chair, bookcase, pens, pencils, ruler, rubber, bag, teacher, board*). Tell learners to draw a picture, including at least five objects. They describe their picture to their partner and the partner draws. They compare drawings.

Learning outcomes By the end of the lesson, learners will have consolidated language from Units 1–3.

Recycled language animals, appearance, colours, families, *There is / There are*, *Who … ?*

Materials flashcards from Units 1–3, photos of your family and pets (or pictures from the Internet), coloured pens or pencils, audio, video

Warm-up

- Show Friendly Farm and Farm animals flashcards. Each time you show one, ask questions, e.g. *What/Who is it? Has he got black hair? Has it got four legs?* Learners answer.
- Hide one of the flashcards behind your back without showing learners which one, e.g. a horse.
- Demonstrate the task. Ask *Which picture have I got? Ask me questions.* Choose a learner. Say *Have you got an animal or a person?* The learner repeats. Say *It's an animal.* Choose another animal. Say *Has it got two legs or four legs?* The learner repeats. Say *It's got four legs*. Ask *Can you ask about the colour? What colour …* (*is it?*) Say *It's brown*. Say *Another question?* Mime or gesture a tail by waving your arm behind you like a tail. Ask *Has it got …* (*a tail?*) Say *Yes, it has*. Ask *Is it a cat? No*. Encourage learners to ask about other animals until they guess *horse*. If they don't get it, do a horse impression to help.
- Continue with other flashcards. Encourage the learners to ask questions until they guess what the animal is.

  Extension Put the learners into groups of six. Give them a selection of flashcards face down. Learners take it in turns to pick up a flashcard without showing the group. The other learners ask them questions about their flashcard following the same sequence.

Pupil's Book, page 43

4 3.15 Listen and follow. Draw lines.

- Say *Open your Pupil's Books at page 43*. Point to the words in Activity 4. Ask *Which red words can you see?* (*legs, arm, red, brown, green, I'm, four*) Repeat with *blue, pink, purple* and *green*.
- Say to the learners *Listen and point*. Give a sentence, e.g. *He's got brown hair*. Learners point. Check they have linked the words.
- Say *Now listen and draw lines*. Play the audio.

  Track 3.15

  This is my young brother, Sam. He's four. He's got short brown hair and big green eyes. (x3)
- Check answers.

5 Draw you and your family or pets. Then write.

- Show photos of your family and pets to the learners (or use pictures from the Internet). Say, e.g. *This is my sister. She has got blonde hair and green eyes. She is tall. My cat is called Sunny. He is black and white. He has got a long tail.*
- Put learners into pairs. Ask them to describe their family and pets to their partner.
- Say *Open your Pupil's Books at page 43*. Show the empty box and ask the learners to draw pictures of their family and pets. Learners draw.
- Show the sentences with spaces under the picture. Learners complete the sentences.

  Fast finishers Learners can write additional descriptions under the picture. Then ask them to work in pairs to show and describe their pictures to each other while you monitor and support other learners.

Activity Book, page 43

See pages TB120–132

Ending the lesson

- Say *Look at Pupil's Book page 43 Activity 4*.
- Divide learners into six groups. Assign a colour to each group from the colours in Activity 4 (*red, pink, purple, green, light blue, dark blue*). Point to the colour to show each group.
- Tell each learner to write down the words in Activity 4 which are in their colour. Give them two minutes to remember.
- Now ask learners to cover their words and write them again from memory.
- Put the learners into new groups with one learner of each colour. Ask them to try to make new sentences, e.g. *She's five. / She's got beautiful hair.*
- Repeat the video and quiz.

4 3.15 **Listen and follow. Draw lines.**

legs · beautiful · old · red · big · green

ugly · my · arm · hair · and

This · is · brown · feet · eyes.

I'm · young · short · got · ears

She's · brother, · small · He's

He's · got · Sam. · He's · four. · hasn't

5 **Draw you and your family or pets. Then write.**

This is me. I've got ______________________ .

This is my ____________ . ____________ *got* ____________

______________________________________ .

This is my ____________ . ______________________

______________________________________ .

4 Food with friends

1 Watch the video. Draw your picnic food.

mission Organise a picnic

In this unit I will:

1. Find out what food my friends like.
2. Buy food for our picnic.
3. Write and share a recipe.
4. Have a picnic.

Unit 4 learning outcomes

In Unit 4, learners learn to:

- talk about food
- understand, ask and talk about likes/dislikes
- make and respond to offers
- make predictions and eliminate incorrect answers
- read about a balanced diet
- share

Materials video, real picnic food (apples, bread, juice and chocolate) and blanket (optional), Food 1 and 2 flashcards, paper plates, coloured pens or pencils, digital Mission poster

Key Competences

Become familiar with language related to food.

Reflect on their own learning by going through the unit goals.

Draw their favourite food.

Self-assessment

- **SA** Say *Open your Pupil's Books at page 44*. Say *Look at the picture*. Indicate items on the page and ask questions using the language from the unit, e.g. *What is it? What is he/she doing? What colour is this?* Use self-assessment (see Introduction). Say *OK. Let's learn.*

Warm-up

- If possible, bring into class a blanket and some food (or use flashcards). Make a picnic on the floor. As you put down items, model each word: *Picnic*, *apples*, *bread*, *juice*, *chocolate*. The learners repeat each word after you. Point to items and the learners say the words. Do this several times, adding claps for word stress, e.g. *picnic* – clap on *pic*, *apple* – clap on *ap*.
- Put out an empty paper plate. Say *I like chocolate. Mmm.* Show learners some chocolate. Mime enjoyment. Draw a picture of chocolate on the plate.

Pupil's Book, page 44

1 Watch the video. Draw your picnic food.

- Say *In this unit we're talking about food.* Say *Let's watch the video*. To introduce the topic of the unit, play the video.
- Say *Look at page 44*. Point to the empty plate (or give out real paper plates). Learners draw pictures of their favourite food on the plate. Monitor. Tell each learner the name of the food they have drawn.

  Fast finishers Learners can draw a second item and write the words.

mission Organise a picnic

- Show the digital Mission poster. Say *Point to the picnic.*
- Say *Let's have a picnic.* Say *Point to number 1*. Say *First we need food*. Rub your stomach as if hungry and learners copy. Say *Number 1* and gesture for them to rub their stomachs.
- Say *Point to number 2*. Show them the shop picture. Say *We need to buy food*. Mime choosing things in a shop and putting them in your basket. Learners copy. Say *Number 2* and gesture for them to mime. Say *One* and rub your stomach; say *Two* and mime shopping. Repeat.
- Say *Point to number 3*. Show them the picture of the recipe. Say *We make the food*. Mime reading the recipe and cooking (e.g. mixing). Learners copy. Say *Three* and repeat. Go through mimes 1–3, calling out the numbers for learners to mime.
- Say *Point to number 4*. Show them the arrow leading back to the picnic picture. Say with excitement *Let's have a picnic!* Encourage them to jump and smile. Say *Four* and learners jump again. Repeat the whole sequence, getting the learners to mime as you call out the numbers. Say *This is our Mission*.

Activity Book, page 44

My unit goals

- Go through the unit goals with the learners. You can read these or if you prefer you can put them onto the board or a poster.
- You can go back to these unit goals at the end of each Mission stage during the unit and review them.
- Say *This is our Mission page*.

Ending the lesson

- Put the numbers *1* to *5* on the board. Put a picture of a picnic under one, and the following flashcards under the others: juice, apple, bread and chocolate. Call out the words and encourage learners to give you the correct number, e.g. *Apples*. (*Three*) Repeat a few times.

  Stronger learners Choose these learners to call out the words. Other learners answer.

  Extra support Choose less confident learners to call out the numbers and the rest of the class answers.

4 Vocabulary 1

Learning outcomes By the end of the lesson, learners will be able to recognise and use food words.

New language *banana, bread, burger, cake, chicken, chocolate, lemonade, mango, salad, water*

Recycled language colours, names, numbers

Materials Food 1 flashcards, audio

Key Competences

- Identify and say food vocabulary.
- Chant together as a class.
- Revise the numbers 1 to 10 by labelling the food pictures.
- Play a game in pairs to revise the language they've learnt.

Warm-up

- Hold up each Food 1 flashcard and say the words. Learners repeat. Say *Remember the words!*

Presentation

- Hold up a flashcard of a countable noun, e.g. banana. Ask *What is it? (It's a banana.)* Ask *How many?* Learners say the number. Say, e.g. *Two bananas*. Learners repeat. Repeat with all countable nouns (*burger, mango*).
- Hold up a flashcard of an uncountable noun, e.g. water. Ask *What's this? (It's water.)* Repeat with other uncountable nouns (*bread, cake, chicken, chocolate, lemonade*).

Pupil's Book, page 45

1 4.01 4.02 Listen and point. Then listen and number.

- Say *Open your Pupil's Books at page 45. Look at the picture.*
- Indicate the caption and read it. Say *It's a picnic.*
- Ask *Where's the (banana)?* Repeat.
- Play Track 4.01. Learners point to the food items in the picture.

Tracks 4.01 and 4.02

This afternoon the Friendly family are having lunch in the garden.

(1) Mrs Friendly:	I've got three burgers. Jim! Have you got your burger?
(2) Jim:	Yes, thanks, Mum. And I've got the mango.
(3) Mrs Friendly:	I've got some chicken here too.
(4) Mrs Friendly:	OK. Where's the bread?
(5) Jenny:	It's on the table. It's next to the lemonade.
(6) Jenny:	We've got some water too.
(7) Mr Friendly:	I've got the cake.
(8) Mr Friendly:	Who's got the bananas?
Jenny:	I've got them.
(9) Mrs Friendly:	OK, put them on the floor next to the salad, please, Jenny.
Jenny:	Yes, of course.
(10) Jim:	Who's got the chocolate?
Mrs Friendly:	It's on the … Oh, no! Gracie's got it! She's got the chocolate in her mouth.
All:	Oh, Gracie!

- Display the flashcards on the board and number them *1–10*. Say *Look at page 45*. Ask *What's number 1? (Burger)* Quickly take down the flashcards.
- Play Track 4.02. Learners number the food items *1–10*.
- Ask *Number 1? (Burger)* Put the flashcard back up above number 1. Ask *Number 2? (Mango)* Continue.

Key: 2 mango 3 chicken 4 bread 5 lemonade 6 water 7 cake 8 banana 9 salad 10 chocolate

2 4.03 Say the chant.

- Say *Listen and say the chant*. Play the audio or video.
- Divide the class into four groups. Say *Chant when I point*. Play the audio or video and point to the first group for the first two lines, the second group for the next two lines, etc. They all chant the final verse together. Repeat.
- Say *Chant*. Groups chant from memory.

Track 4.03

Banana, bread, burger (x2)
Chocolate, chicken, cake (x2)
Water, mango, salad (x2)
And le-mo-nade (x4)

3 4.04 Listen and say *yes* or *no*.

- Focus on the picture. Ask *Who's got the cake? (Mr Friendly's got the cake.)* Play the audio and pause after each sentence. Learners respond *Yes* or *No*.

Track 4.04

1 Jenny's got the cake.
2 The bread's on the table.
3 Jim's got some chicken.
4 Gracie's got the chocolate.
5 The mango is on the table.
6 Jenny's got the bananas.
7 The lemonade's next to the water.
8 Mrs Friendly's got four burgers.

- Learners work in pairs to play the same game.

Key: 1 no 2 yes 3 no 4 yes 5 no 6 yes 7 yes 8 no

Activity Book, page 45

See pages TB120–132

Ending the lesson

- **SA** Say *We learnt about picnic food*. Show the flashcards. Ask *Do you know the words?* Use the self-assessment technique (see Introduction). Learners show how they feel.
- Say *We did listening and speaking*. Gesture 'listening' and 'speaking' and indicate they should use their thumbs.
- Say *You listened to the words well. Good job!*

Vocabulary 1

1 4.01 4.02 **Listen and point. Then listen and number.**

2 4.03 **Say the chant.**

3 4.04 **Listen and say *yes* or *no*.**

The Friendly Farm
4.05
1
Gracie!
I'm sorry, but I like chocolate.
2
Do you like chocolate, Cameron?
Yes, I do.
3
I like chocolate and
I like cake, bananas,
bread, books and socks!
4
I don't like
books.
I like
books.
But, Rocky, you
read books. You
don't eat books!
5
What do you
like, Harry?
I don't like books or
chocolate. I like mangoes.
6
What do you
like, Shelly?
I like water. I can see
my face in water.

Learning outcomes By the end of the lesson, learners will be able to understand when they hear a conversation about likes and dislikes.

New language *I/You/We like / don't like … Do I/you/we like … ?*

Recycled language colours, food, names

Materials real picnic food (apples, bread, juice and chocolate) and blanket (optional), audio, video, Food 1 flashcards, Friendly Farm animal flashcards

Key Competences

- Read and listen to a story; Identify expressions used to talk about likes and dislikes.
- Mime the animals they hear in a song.
- Role play a story in groups.

Warm-up

- Place the real food (or flashcards) on the blanket. Point to each item. Learners chant each word. Repeat. Cover the food and remove one item. Ask which is missing. Repeat until you have removed all of the items.
- **SA** Use self-assessment to check how well learners think they understand the vocabulary. See Introduction.

Presentation

- Show the learners Food 1 flashcards of the food and encourage them to call out the words.
- Draw a large heart symbol on one side of the board and a heart crossed out on the other side. Show a Food 1 flashcard, e.g. salad. Say *I like salad*. Repeat while miming pleasure. Put the flashcard on the board next to the big heart. Learners repeat *I like salad*. Do the same with two or three more items.
- Now show a new flashcard. Say *I don't like burgers*. Mime dislike. Learners repeat. Stick the flashcard next to the crossed out heart. Do the same with two or three more items. Take the flashcards down.

Pupil's Book, page 46

4.05 The Friendly Farm song

- Play the introductory song at the beginning of the cartoon story. Learners listen and sing. Learners choose an animal to mime. Repeat the song with the mimes.

Track 4.05
See The Friendly Farm song on page TB5

4.05 The Friendly Farm

- Hide the Friendly Farm animal flashcards around the room. Ask *Where's Gracie?* Mime looking. Show the flashcard. Ask *Is she a cat?* (*No, she's a goat.*) *What colour is she?* (*White*)
- Repeat with the other Friendly Farm animal flashcards. Ask *Where's … ?* Learners find the flashcard. Then ask questions about the character.
- Say *Open your Pupil's Books at page 46*. Ask *Who can you see in the pictures?* Learners name the characters. Ask *What's this?* Point to the chocolate. Repeat with other objects and food.
- Ask *Who likes chocolate? Who likes books? Who likes water?* Write the questions on the board and put flashcards of each item on the board. Say *Listen*. Play the audio or video. Learners listen and read.

Track 4.05
The Friendly Farm song + see cartoon on Pupil's Book page 46

- Learners answer the questions in pairs before the class check.
- Play the audio or video again. Pause after each frame and check comprehension by asking learners to give the end of sentences, e.g. *Gracie likes … Cameron likes …*
- Ask questions to show third person short answers. Model an example: *Does Gracie like chocolate?* Say *Yes, she does*. Work through each frame asking questions and giving short answers. The class repeat several times. Note the model of the negative form in frame 4. Ask *Does Harry like books?* (*No, he doesn't.*)

Extension Call out a mixture of correct and incorrect sentences, e.g. *Gracie likes cake. Harry likes chocolate*. Learners jump up and shout *No, he/she doesn't!* for incorrect sentences.

- Put learners into groups of six to role play the dialogue. Monitor and check.

Extra support Ask some of the learners to listen and choose the best group to perform their dialogue.

Activity Book, page 46

See pages TB120–132

Ending the lesson

- **SA** Repeat the self-assessment technique used at the start of the lesson to see how well learners think they understand the vocabulary. Is there any change?
- Display the character and Food 1 flashcards on the board. Point to them when you speak about them. Say *Gracie likes …* Encourage the learners to finish the sentence by pointing to the Food 1 flashcards. When they call out a correct answer, e.g. *Chocolate*, mime pleasure and say *Yum*. Gesture for the learners to repeat.
- Say *Harry likes books*. Then shake your head and indicate this is wrong. Say *Harry …* Learners finish the sentence: *Harry doesn't like books*. Mime dislike and say *Yuck*. Gesture for the learners to repeat.
- Give the beginning of sentences using the characters. Learners complete the sentences and mime/say *Yum/Yuck*.

4 Language practice 1

Learning outcomes By the end of the lesson, learners will be able to ask and answer questions about likes and dislikes.

New language *like / don't like*: *I like chocolate. Harry likes mangoes. I don't like books. Harry doesn't like chocolate. Do you like chocolate? Does Harry like shoes?*

Recycled language food, names

Materials Food 1 flashcards, coloured pens or pencils, digital Mission poster

Key Competences

- Learn to talk about likes and dislikes.
- Work together asking and answering questions with *like*.
- Reflect on their own learning.
- Interact with the digital poster.

Warm-up

- Put a heart symbol on the right side of the room and a crossed out heart symbol on the left side.
- Ask the learners to stand up. Call out *Apples*. By miming and using sounds, show that the learners should jump to the right if they like apples and left if they don't. Point to those on the right and say *You like apples*. Point to the left and say *You don't like apples*.
- Repeat with different types of food.

Presentation

- Show a selection of flashcards from earlier lessons. Encourage the learners to say *I like …* or *I don't like …*
- Choose a few confident learners and ask them about different foods and drinks, e.g. *(Name), do you like burgers?*

Pupil's Book, page 47

4.06 Gracie's Grammar

- Say *Open your Pupil's Books at page 47*. Point to Gracie's Grammar box. Write the same sentences on the board. Draw a heart next to *I like chocolate.* Draw a crossed out heart next to *I don't like books*.
- Learners copy. Encourage learners to copy the other four sentences and draw a heart or crossed out heart for each.
- Play the audio. Pause for learners to repeat each sentence.

Track 4.06

See Pupil's Book page 47

- Now rub out the words *chocolate* and *books*. Show the learners a flashcard, e.g. burgers. Point to the sentence stems and the spaces. Tell them *Write a sentence for you – 'I like …' or 'I don't like …'* Monitor to check the sentences are correct. Repeat with two or three more flashcards.

1 4.07 Listen and stick. Then look, read and write.

- Ask the learners to look at the four stickers. They do not stick them in yet. Ask them to predict what each person might like or not like, e.g. *What does Grandpa like?*
- Play the audio for learners to point to the correct sticker.

Track 4.07

1	Jim:	Mum, do you want chicken or burgers?
	Mrs Friendly:	Oh, a burger, please, Jim. I like burgers.
2	Jenny:	What's your favourite food, Dad? Do you like chips?
	Mr Friendly:	No, I don't. I don't like chips, but I like bananas. They're my favourite food.
3	Jim:	Grandma, do you want some lemonade?
	Grandma:	No, thank you, Jim. I want some water, please. I don't like lemonade.
4	Jenny:	Grandpa, do you like burgers?
	Grandpa:	Hmm. No, I don't like burgers, but I like chicken.

- Play the audio again. Learners stick in the stickers.
- Say *Look at the sentences*. Point to sentences 1–4. Show the spaces. Say *Look, read and write*. Learners write.

Key: 2 chips 3 doesn't like 4 likes

mission Stage 1

- Show learners the first stage of the digital Mission poster: 'Food?' Say *Let's choose food*.
- Show the class Food 1 flashcards. Ask the names of the food. Ask a confident learner, e.g. *Do you like chips?* The learner answers. Repeat with other items and different learners.
- Ask learners to choose five of the flashcards and copy them. Learners write the word next to each picture.
- Learners stand up. They move around, asking and answering questions using the pictures they have drawn, e.g. *Do you like burgers? Yes, I do.* They put ticks or crosses next to the pictures.

Activity Book, page 47

See pages TB120–132

Activity Book, page 44

- Say *Look at page 44 of your Activity Book*. Review *My unit goals*. Ask *How is your Mission?*
- Learners reflect and choose a smiley face for *My mission diary 1*. Monitor.

Ending the lesson

- **SA** Go back to Stage 1 on the digital Mission poster. Say *We chose food. Good work.* Add a tick to the 'Food?' stage. Use self-assessment (see Introduction).
- Give out a completion sticker.

4.06 Gracie's Grammar

I **like** chocolate.
I **don't like** books.
Do you **like** chocolate?

Harry **likes** mangoes.
Harry **doesn't like** chocolate.
Yes, I **do**. / No, I **don't**.

1 4.07 Listen and stick. Then look, read and write.

1 Mum likes burgers.
2 Dad doesn't like ______.
3 Grandma ______ lemonade.
4 Grandpa ______ chicken.

mission STAGE 1

Find out what food your friends like. Choose food for your picnic.

Do you like burgers?

Yes, I do.

STAGE 1

My mission diary
Activity Book page 44

Vocabulary 2 and song

1 4.08 Listen and draw. Then sing the song.

Do you like fruit?
Yes, I do.
Do you like juice?
No, I don't ...

I like apples.
I like oranges.
I like grapes
but I don't like juice ...

Do you like salad?
Yes, I do.
Do you like meat?
No, I don't ...

I don't like burgers.
I don't like sausages.
I don't like meatballs
but I like beans ...

2 Read, think and say. Compare with your classmates.

Think of ...

- one thing you eat or drink for breakfast.
- two things you eat or drink for lunch.
- three things you eat or drink for dinner.

Learning outcomes By the end of the lesson, learners will have practised the language through song.

New language *apple, beans, fruit, grapes, juice, meat, meatballs, orange, sausage*

Recycled language *I/You/We like / don't like ... Do I/you/we like ... ?*

Materials Food 1 and 2 flashcards, audio, a simple drawing you have done of an apple, paper, coloured pens or pencils, video

Key Competences

Practise newly learnt language through a song.

Talk about their eating habits in pairs.

Warm-up

- Introduce new items using Food 2 flashcards or mime. Show a flashcard of *juice* and mime drinking. Learners repeat and mime. Do this for the other words: *fruit* (mime picking from trees), *grapes* (popping them into your mouth), *apples* (taking a bite), *oranges* (peeling), *salad* (mixing the leaves), *meatballs* (putting on a fork and biting). Repeat the words several times.
- Mime without speaking. The class calls out the words. Put learners into groups of four or five. Learners take it in turns to mime to each other and guess words.
- **SA** Use self-assessment techniques to check how well learners think they understand the vocabulary. See Introduction.

Pupil's Book, page 48

1 4.08 Listen and draw. Then sing the song.

- Say *Open your Pupil's Books at page 48*. Alternatively, use the Food 1 and 2 flashcards. Ask the names of the food items. Learners repeat any words not covered in the warm-up.
- Play the audio or video. Learners listen and mime actions.

Track 4.08

Rocky: I'm Rocky-Doodle-Doo and ... here's our song for today: *What do you like?*

See song on Pupil's Book page 48

- Indicate the face icons. Demonstrate the task: learners will add a smile or sad mouth to each icon as they listen to the song.
- Play the audio or video again. Learners listen and draw. Monitor. Repeat the audio if necessary.
- Check answers.
- Play the audio or video again. Learners repeat the song, doing actions, first in small sections and then the whole song. Once they have practised the song, ask them to stand up and perform it.
- Divide the class into groups. Give each group a different part of the song. They sing again, but only their part.

Key: juice ☹ apple ☺ orange ☺ grapes ☺ salad ☺ meat ☹ burger ☹ sausage ☹ meatballs ☹ beans ☺

4.09 **Extension** Once learners are confidently singing to the song, try singing the karaoke version as a class.

2 Read, think and say. Compare with your classmates.

- Draw three symbols on the board: a semi-circle sun coming up, a full sun and a moon. Point to the rising sun. Say *I eat bread and apples for breakfast*. Point to the full sun. Say *I eat meatballs for lunch*. Point to the moon. Say *I eat chicken and salad for dinner*.
- Say *Look at page 48*. Show learners Activity 2. Say, e.g. *I eat an apple for breakfast*. Repeat with two things for lunch and three things for dinner.
- Put the class in pairs. Learners tell their partner their ideas. Monitor and check.
- Show the picture of Rocky in the bottom right-hand corner. Read out the question. Encourage learners to call out their answers.

Activity Book, page 48

See pages TB120–132

Ending the lesson

- **SA** Repeat the self-assessment technique used at the start of the lesson to see how well learners think they understand the vocabulary. Is there any change?
- Check learners have paper and coloured pens or pencils. Show them a simple drawing you have done of an apple.
- Say *Draw a picture of food*. Monitor as learners draw.
- Use your picture. Demonstrate moving around the class and asking *Do you like apples?* Encourage learners to answer. If a learner says *Yes*, give them your picture. Tell them to ask and answer questions and swap pictures if both partners say *Yes*. Monitor as they mingle.
- When the task is over, choose a confident learner. Ask *What food do you have now?* The learner answers, e.g. *Grapes*. Ask *And do you like grapes?* The learner answers. Repeat with different learners.

Learning outcomes By the end of the lesson, learners will be able to make requests and offers, and say *yes/no*.

New language *Can I have some chocolate, please? Here you are. Would you like some cake? Yes, please. / No, thank you. ice cream*

Recycled language food

Materials Food 1 and 2 flashcards, classroom objects and paper money (optional), audio, coloured pens or pencils, Presentation Plus (video and digital Mission poster)

Key Competences

Learn and practise questions with *Would you like…?* and *Can I have…?*

Learn to make and respond to polite requests and offers.

Work together to role play shopping for food.

Interact with the digital poster.

Warm-up

- Give each group a classroom object. Circulate, asking, e.g. *Can I have a pen, please?* Learners answer *Here you are* and give you the object.
- Circulate again. Ask *Would you like (name of object)?* Learners say *Yes, please* or *No, thank you*.

Pupil's Book, page 49

1 4.10 Which food does she buy? Listen and tick ✓.

- Use the artwork to teach the word *ice cream*.
- Play the audio. Learners listen and tick the food the girl buys. Check answers.

Track 4.10

Girl:	Good morning.
Shopkeeper:	Good morning.
Girl:	Can I have some chocolate, please?
Shopkeeper:	I'm sorry. I haven't got any chocolate. Would you like an apple?
Girl:	No, thank you.
Shopkeeper:	Would you like some ice cream?
Girl:	Oh, yes, please.
Shopkeeper:	Here you are.
Girl:	Thank you.

Key: Picture 2

4.11 Gracie's Grammar

- Act out the sentences, demonstrating the request and response. Learners repeat.
- Divide the class into two. Half are the customer and half are the shopkeeper. Play the audio, pausing so learners can repeat the lines of their character.

Track 4.11
See Pupil's Book page 49

- Swap roles and repeat.

2 Read and say the dialogue. Act it out.

- In pairs, learners read the dialogue.
- Ask pairs to cover the dialogue and act it out.

Extension Put out on a table some classroom objects that learners know, e.g. a pen, a pencil and a book. Encourage the learners to ask for the items by saying *Can I have …?* Give out the objects to a learner who asks correctly. Point to one of the learners with an object and then demonstrate they should ask you *Would you like …?* Take back the object. Repeat with different learners.

mission Stage 2

- Show learners the first stage of the digital Mission poster: 'Buy food?'
- Learners complete the worksheet task in the Teacher's Resource Book page 44 (see teaching notes on TRB page 37).
- Alternatively, if you do not have the Teacher's Resource Book, show learners the Food 1 and 2 flashcards and ask them the names.
- Put learners into groups of four. Ask them to draw six food items from the list and write the prices underneath. Get each group to set up a shop display.
- Give out paper money if possible.
- Divide each group of four into pairs. One pair goes shopping; the other pair acts as shopkeepers. Tell the shoppers to use their shopping list, circulate and buy what they need for the picnic. They tick the items off their list.
- When the activity slows down, the pairs swap over.

Activity Book, page 49

See pages TB120–132

Activity Book, page 44

- Say *Look at page 44 of your Activity Book*. Review *My unit goals*. Ask *How is your Mission?*
- Learners reflect and choose a smiley face for *My mission diary 2*. Monitor.

Ending the lesson

- Go back to Stage 2 on the digital Mission poster. Add a tick to the 'Buy food?' stage or invite a learner to do it. Use self-assessment (see Introduction).
- Give out a completion sticker.

1 4.10 Which food does she buy? Listen and tick ✓.

1 

2 

3 

4.11 Gracie's Grammar

Can I have some chocolate, **please**? Here you are.

Would you like some ice cream? Yes, **please**. / No, **thank you**.

2 Read and say the dialogue. Act it out.

A Can I have some apples, please?

B I'm sorry, I haven't got any apples. Would you like some oranges?

A Yes, please.

B Here you are.

A Thank you.

mission STAGE 2

Buy the food for your picnic.

Can I have some chicken, please?

Here you are.

STAGE 2

My mission diary

Activity Book page 44

Cross-curricular

Making a recipe

1 Watch the video.

2 4.12 Tick ✓ the ingredients. Then listen and check.

pasta ☐

meat ☐

onions ☐

potatoes ☐

rice ☐

cheese ☐

carrots ☐

tomatoes ☐

3 4.13 Listen and number.

a  ☐

b  ☐

c  ☐

d  1

Learning outcomes By the end of the lesson, learners will be able to understand a recipe and words for cooking.

New language *ingredients, meat, onions, pasta, tomatoes*

Recycled language food, numbers, talking about likes and dislikes

Materials paper, coloured pens or pencils, audio, video, four large cards

Key Competences

- Learn about ingredients and methods of cooking.
- Listen for specific information.
- Order stages of a recipe using visual clues.

Warm-up

- Give out paper and coloured pens or pencils. Show learners how to draw a grid with six squares (two columns and three rows) and number them *1–6*.
- Demonstrate that you will say a word and they should draw a picture of it in any square. Read out the words: *Apple, water, bread, grapes, cake, juice*. Give a minute for them to draw each picture quickly.
- Put learners into pairs. Demonstrate questions: choose a learner and ask *Is number 1 an apple?* Encourage the learner to answer: *Yes, it is. / No, it isn't.* When you get the correct answer, say *Good – one point!* Show that they get a point when they find the correct answer.
- Tell learners to find out which pictures their partners have in each square by asking questions. Learners complete the activity.
- Ask each pair who had the most points at the end.

Pupil's Book, page 50

1 Watch the video.

- Say *Let's watch the video*. Learners watch the video about making a recipe and answer the questions at the end of the video.

2 4.12 Tick ✓ the ingredients. Then listen and check.

- Say *Open your Pupil's Books at page 50*. Focus on the large photo of the dish of food. Ask *What is it?* (*Spaghetti Bolognese*) Ask *Do you like Spaghetti Bolognese?*
- Point to the food items around the dish. Use the photos to teach the new food words. Learners repeat the words. Check understanding of *ingredients*.
- Learners work in pairs and guess which ingredients are in the Spaghetti Bolognese. Check their ideas.
- Say *Listen and check*. Play the audio.

Track 4.12

Hello! Today I'm making my favourite dish – Spaghetti Bolognese. I've got onions, tomatoes, meat, pasta and cheese.

Key: onions, tomatoes, meat, pasta, cheese

3 4.13 Listen and number.

- Focus on the pictures and ask learners the names of the food, e.g. say *Pasta* and the class repeats. Ask learners which picture comes first in the recipe. Encourage them to guess the sequence, e.g. point to a picture and ask *Is this number 1?*
- Play the audio. Learners listen and write numbers to show the order. Check.

Track 4.13

OK. Let's make Spaghetti Bolognese!
I cut the onions. I cook the onions in a pan.
I add the meat. I cook the meat with the onions.
Now, the meat is brown. I put the tomatoes in the pan too.
I cook the pasta in water.
It's ready! I eat my Spaghetti Bolognese with cheese on top. Yum!

Key: a 2 b 4 c 3 d (1)

Activity Book, page 50

See pages TB120–132

Ending the lesson

- Write *Meat, Fruit, Vegetables, Drink* onto four large cards. Stick them on the board. Ask the learners to stand near the board. Choose four learners and tell them a word each: *Chicken, salad, water, mangoes*. They stand under the correct sign. Repeat with different learners and words.

Learning outcomes By the end of the lesson, learners will be able to read a recipe.

New language *cook, cut, mix, omelette*

Recycled language cooking, describing likes and dislikes

Materials pictures of food from Digital photo bank, flashcards of water and juice, large copies of the reading text or cut up copies of the text (optional), digital Mission poster

Key Competences

- Read a recipe.
- Draw and write the ingredients for their own recipe.
- Reflect on their own learning.
- Interact with the digital poster.

Warm-up

- Put some pictures of popular foods around the room. Include eggs, onions, meat, ice cream, and flashcards of water and juice. Point and ask the names. Learners repeat.
- Ask learners to go and stand by their favourite food.
- Choose one group to say the sentence *I like (name of food)*.
- Ask the different groups to say the sentence for their food.
- Now demonstrate they should stand near a food they don't like. Encourage them to say the sentence *I don't like (name of food)*.
- A few different groups say their sentence.

Presentation

- Mime some cooking words and teach them: *mix, cut, cook*. Learners repeat and mime the words.
- Say *Mix*. Show the class they should go and stand next to suitable pictures, e.g. for *mix* they can choose eggs. Say *Cut*. Learners stand next to a picture of food you can cut. Repeat with *cook*.

Pupil's Book, page 51

4 Read and circle the food words. Then number the pictures.

- Say *Open your Pupil's Books at page 51*. Focus on the picture. Ask the name of the food (*omelette*). Ask learners if they like omelettes. Ask which ingredients they think might be in the omelette. Write their ideas on the board.
- Learners read the text and circle the food words. Put learners into pairs to check their answers. Check with the whole class and see if the guesses were correct.

Alternative Put up on the walls two or three enlarged versions of the text. Put learners into groups and assign one of the texts to each. Check they know which is their group by asking them to point to their text. Get each group to stand in a line in front of the text. Say *Go!* Each learner takes it in turn to run to the text and circle one of the food words, then pass the pen to the next person in line. The first group to finish wins.

- Demonstrate the ordering task. Put learners in pairs to number the pictures.

Key: cheese onion tomatoes omelette
a 5 b 3 (c 1) d 4 e 2

Alternative Copy and cut up the text into strips. Give one set of strips to each group of three learners. Get them to put the papers in order using the pictures to guide them.

- Learners read the text again.

mission Stage 3

- Set this Mission stage so that the class can complete or prepare it at home if possible.
- Show the class the third stage of the Mission poster: 'Recipe'.
- Tell the class to choose their favourite food for a sandwich. Show them your own favourite sandwich and tell them the ingredients, e.g. *In my sandwich I put chicken and salad*. Write the sentence on the board.
- The class create their sandwich recipes using the model. They draw pictures and label with ingredients.

  Stronger learners These can write sentences as in the model.

  Extra support Learners can draw a picture and label it. Monitor and guide.
- Put the class in groups of three. Each learner mimes making their sandwich. The other learners guess what ingredients are being used.
- For ideas on monitoring and assessment, see Introduction.

Activity Book, page 51

See pages TB120–132

Activity Book, page 44

- Say *Look at page 44 of your Activity Book*. Review *My unit goals*. Ask *How is your Mission?*
- Learners reflect and choose a smiley face for *My mission diary 3*. Monitor.

Ending the lesson

- Go back to Stage 3 on the digital Mission poster. Add a tick to the 'Recipe' stage or invite a learner to do it. Use self-assessment (see Introduction).
- Give out a completion sticker.

4

4 **Read and circle the food words. Then number the pictures.**

HOW TO MAKE ... *an omelette!*

1. You need two eggs, some cheese, an onion and some tomatoes.
2. Mix the eggs. Cut the onion and the tomatoes.
3. Cook the eggs for four minutes.
4. Put the cheese, onion and tomato on the eggs.
5. Fold the omelette and cook it for one more minute.

a

b

c

1

d

e

mission STAGE 3

Make and share your recipe.

My favourite sandwich
This is a monster sandwich. It's got chicken, cheese and salad. Yum!

STAGE 3

My mission diary
Activity Book page 44

Literature

1 **Talk to a friend. What food do you like to eat on picnics?**

4.14

A picnic with friends

Mia and Matt want to go on a picnic.

'Can we cook burgers in the woods, Mum?'

'No, but you can take sandwiches and fruit.'

Mia likes egg sandwiches. Matt wants chicken sandwiches. He wants lemonade too.

'Would you like a banana or a watermelon?'

'A banana, please,' says Mia.

'A banana and a watermelon, please,' says Matt.

Now they're in the woods. They've got sandwiches, fruit, lemonade and ... chocolate!

'Would you like some chocolate, Matt?'

'Yes, please!' Matt likes chocolate.

'Here you are.'

Text type: A real-life story

Learning outcomes By the end of the lesson, learners will have read about a picnic, learnt about a balanced diet and learnt about sharing.

New language *birds, clothes, scarecrow*

Recycled language describing likes and dislikes, food, making offers and suggestions

Materials pictures from Digital photo bank of a desert, woods, a scarecrow, birds, clothes and a watermelon, flashcards of beach, apple, mango and banana, paper for each learner, coloured pens or pencils

Key Competences

- Revise the language they've learnt through a story.
- Learn about balanced diets.
- Learn the value of sharing.
- Complete a wordsearch.

Warm-up

- Ask learners to think about a picnic. Show them some pictures and flashcards of places, e.g. a desert, a beach, the woods. Check understanding of *woods*. Learners repeat the word.
- Ask *What is a good place for a picnic?* Say *I like the beach*. Encourage them to offer ideas.

Presentation

- Say *We are going to read about Mia and Matt's picnic*. Show a picture of a scarecrow. Say *This is a scarecrow*. Check understanding. Learners repeat the word. Show a picture of birds. Ask *What are these?* Say *Birds*. Learners repeat the word. Show a picture of clothes. Ask *What are they?* Say *Clothes*. Learners repeat.

Pupil's Book, page 52

1 Talk to a friend. What food do you like to eat on picnics?

- Put the class into groups of four. Ask *What food do you like to eat on picnics? Is it the same?* Learners talk about what they like. Monitor. When they finish, ask some of the groups *What do you like to eat?*
- Check their ideas.

4.14 A picnic with friends

- Say *Open your Pupil's Books at page 52*. Focus on the pictures. Look at each picture and ask questions, e.g. Picture 1: For each character, *Who is it?* (*Mia, Matt, Mum*) *Where are they?* (*At home*) Picture 2: *Which picnic food do they like?* (*Melon, bananas*) Picture 3: *What is the food?* (*Chocolate, sandwich, melon, bananas*) Picture 4: *Where are the clothes?* (*On the watermelon*) *Why?* (*To scare the birds*) Picture 5: *Where are the clothes now?* (*On Mia and Matt*) *Why?* (*The picnic is finished.*) If learners can't answer the 'why' questions, don't give the answers yet.
- Ask learners to guess what happens in the story.
- Say *Read and listen to the first part*. Show them paragraph 1. Play the audio. Learners listen and read. Pause the audio after picture 1. Ask learners to predict: *What sandwiches does Matt like? Which fruit does Mia like?*

Track 4.14
See story on Pupil's Book pages 52–53

- Say *Read the next part*. Show them paragraph 2. Play the audio for picture 2. Check if their guesses were correct.
- Ask them to look at picture 3. Ask *Where are they?* (*In the woods*) *What food has Mia got?* (*Chocolate*) Say *Read and listen*. Show them paragraph 3 and play the audio for picture 3. Check answers.
- Say *Look at pictures 4 and 5. What is the problem?* Learners predict. Say *Read and listen to the rest of the story*. Show them paragraphs 4 and 5. Play the rest of the audio. Check answers. (*The birds are eating the food.*)
- Say *Act out the story*. Summarise the story, sentence by sentence, and mime. Encourage the learners to copy. Say *Get the picnic food ready*. Mime packing. Say *Sandwiches, watermelon, bananas and chocolate.* Mime putting each food item into the basket. Say *Let's go to the woods*. Mime walking and putting out the picnic. Say *Eat some chocolate*. Mime eating. Say *Oh no! The birds like the picnic.* Mime waving birds away. Say *Let's make a scarecrow*. Mime building one. Say *Come and eat the crumbs, birds!* Mime throwing crumbs down for birds.
- Repeat and encourage the learners to act the story.

Activity Book, page 52

See pages TB120–132

Ending the lesson

- Give out paper to each learner. Divide the class into three. Tell them *Draw picnic food and write the word*. Say to one group *Draw a drink*. Say to the second group *Draw something sweet – cake or chocolate*. Say to the third group *Draw meat or fish or sandwiches*. Monitor and support.
- Tell them *We need to make a picnic*. Write *chocolate* and *cake* on the board. Say *Is it a good picnic?* Encourage the learners to say *No*. Rub out *chocolate* and write *sandwich*, *water*. Say *Is it a good picnic?* Encourage the learners to say *Yes*. Tell the learners *Find friends for a good picnic*. Show your own picture and word, e.g. *chicken*, and demonstrate finding friends, e.g. a learner with cake or fruit or similar, and then another with a drink. Learners mingle and find other learners with foods to make a good picnic together.

Learning outcomes By the end of the lesson, learners will have talked about feelings and learnt about sharing.

New language *happy, sad*

Recycled language *birds*, clothes, food, describing likes and dislikes, making offers and suggestions, *scarecrow*

Materials two pictures – happy and sad face emoticons (optional), flashcards of fruit (e.g. apple, mango, banana) and picture of watermelon from Digital photo bank, audio

Social and Emotional Skill: Sharing

- After reading the story, ask the learners simple questions: *Can the children cook burgers in the woods?* (*No*) *How do the children in the story feel?* (*Sad*) Say *Yes, they feel sad, but they accept it's a rule. It's important to follow rules.* Say *Matt and Mia share the food in the picnic. Mia shares her chocolate with her brother.* Ask *What does Mia say?* (*Would you like some chocolate, Matt?*) *What does Matt say?* (*Yes, please!*) Say *Matt is very polite. It's important to share things and be polite.* Ask *What do we share in the classroom?* (e.g. *Crayons, toys*)
- Hand out a worksheet to colour. Place two boxes of crayons on each table. Say *We have two boxes for everyone. Let's share the crayons. We take turns. What colour would you like, (Juan)? (Juan), can I have the red crayon, please?* Continue with all the crayons. The learners ask politely when they want a different crayon.
- After completing Pupil's Book Activity 2, hand out two pieces of card to each learner. They draw a happy face on one and a sad face on the other. Ask *How do you feel today?* The learners hold up one of their cards. If the pupils know more emotions, you can make a range of face cards.

Key Competences

Learn to talk about their feelings.

Reflect on how other people feel; Talk in pairs about their eating habits.

Warm-up

- Draw a happy face emoticon on the board (or put up a picture). Draw a sad face emoticon. Ask *How do the children feel at the end of the story?* Learners point to the emoticon. Ask *How do the birds feel?* Learners point to the emoticon.
- Act out the story again using summary sentences as in the previous lesson. Encourage the learners to act too.
- **SA** Use self-assessment techniques to check how well learners think they understand the vocabulary. See Introduction.

Presentation

- Point to the happy face emoticon on the board and say *happy*. Learners repeat. Point to the sad face emoticon and say *sad*. Learners repeat.
- Make a happy face. Say *I'm …* Learners say *happy*. Make a sad face. Say *I'm …* learners say *sad*.
- Ask learners to look at the units they have done so far. Ask *Who is happy?* Learners find pictures of characters looking happy. Ask *Who is sad?* Learners find pictures of characters looking sad.

Pupil's Book, page 53

2 How do they feel? Read and circle.

- Say *Look at Activity 2. Look at the faces. How do they feel?* Learners guess the answers. Say *Read and circle*. Learners read the story all the way through.
- Check answers.

Key: 2 happy 3 sad 4 happy

- Tell learners to close their books. Ask them to write *happy* and then *sad*. Check the spelling.

3 Ask and answer.

- Show flashcards and/or pictures of different fruit (e.g. apple, mango, banana, watermelon). Point. Learners say the names.
- Say *I like fruit. I like apples and mangoes. I like watermelon. Do you like fruit?* Learners answer.
- Ask and answer with a confident learner: *Where do you have lunch? (I have lunch at home.) Who do you have lunch with? (I have lunch with my friend, (name).)* Learners have similar conversations in pairs.

Activity Book, page 53

See pages TB120–132

Ending the lesson

- **SA** Repeat the self-assessment technique used at the start of the lesson to see how well learners think they understand the vocabulary. Is there any change?
- Learners draw a picture of a food item and write the word.
- Learners stand in a circle. Take a picture from a stronger learner. Demonstrate the activity. Hold up the picture and say *I like (food in picture)*. Encourage the learner who drew it to say *No! I like (food)* and collect their picture.
- Take all the pictures, mix them up and hand them out again randomly.
- Choose a learner to start. He/She holds up their picture and says *I like …* The owner of the picture says *No! I like (food)* and takes it. Continue around the circle until all learners have their pictures back.

4

But what's this? Birds!

'Hey! Go away!'

'We need a scarecrow,' says Mia. They put the watermelon and some clothes on a stick. The birds don't like the scarecrow. They fly away! Mia and Matt finish eating.

But what about the crumbs? 'We don't need the scarecrow now,' says Matt. So Mia takes the scarecrow down.

'Come on, birds,' calls Matt. 'Come and eat the crumbs!'

It's good to share your picnic with friends!

2 How do they feel? Read and circle.

1 When the children can't cook burgers in the woods, Matt feels: 

2 When Matt sees the chocolate, he feels: 

3 When the birds arrive, Matt feels: 

4 At the end of the story, the children feel: 

3 Ask and answer.

Where do you have lunch?

At home.

Who do you have lunch with?

With my family.

1 **Look at the pictures in Activity 3. What can you see?**

I can see …

2 4.15 **Look at Activity 3 and listen. Which picture is <u>not</u> correct?**

It isn't picture … because …

3 4.16 **Listen and tick (✓) the box. There is one example.**

What food would Dan like?

A ☐

B ✓

C ☐

1 Where's Lucy's book?

A ☐

B ☐

C ☐

Think about what's different in pictures A, B and C.

Learning outcomes By the end of the lesson, learners will have listened for information, made predictions and eliminated incorrect answers, learnt how to listen well in an exam and learnt how to improve word stress.

New language *kiwi*

Recycled language colours, food, prepositions of place

Materials a few sentences on paper (*I like lemonade, but I don't like chicken. Matt and Mia like egg and chicken sandwiches. Cut the onion and tomatoes. Does Cameron like chocolate?*), Food 1 and 2 and Friendly Farm animal flashcards, picture of kiwi from Digital photo bank, audio, paper, coloured pens or pencils

Key Competences

Learn to listen for specific information, to make predictions and to eliminate incorrect answers; Practise activity types found in *Pre A1 Starters* exams.

Warm-up

- Pick ten learners to stand in a line at the front of the class. Choose a sentence from the ones you have prepared on paper, e.g. *I like lemonade, but I don't like chicken.*
- Whisper it to the first learner in the line. The learner whispers it to the next learner. They continue whispering down the line. The last learner says the sentence out loud.
- See if it is the same as the original sentence. Show the learners the sentence and say it aloud so they can hear if it is correct. Say *Well done!* or *Let's try again.*
- Repeat with new learners and sentences.
- **SA** Use self-assessment to check how well learners think they understand the vocabulary. See Introduction.

Presentation

- Say *Let's do a listening exam*. Write *Listening Exam* on the board.
- Sit down and act out speaking. Say *Is this good?* (*No*) Act out looking out of the window and fidgeting. Ask *Is this good?* (*No*) Act out looking very nervous and panicked. Ask *Is this good?* (*No*)

Pupil's Book, page 54

1 Look at the pictures in Activity 3. What can you see?

- Use a picture to teach the word *kiwi*.
- Say *Open your Pupil's Books at page 54*. Point to the pictures. Ask *What's this?* Learners say the words.

Key: kiwi, grapes, banana, book, chair, desk, school bag, table

2 4.15 Look at Activity 3 and listen. Which picture is <u>not</u> correct?

- Point to the three food pictures. Say *Let's find a picture that is **not** correct. Listen and point*. Play the audio. Do the example together. Then learners do number 1 in pairs.

Track4.15

Example

Mum: Would you like a banana, Dan?

Dan: Yes, please.

1

Lucy: Dad, where's my book?

Dad: I don't know, Lucy. Is it on your desk?

Lucy: It isn't, Dad.

Key: Example It isn't picture A because there isn't a banana. 1 It isn't picture B because it's on the desk.

3 4.16 Listen and tick (✓) the box. There is one example.

- Point out the exam tip at the bottom of the page. Say *Look at the pictures*. Show the first set. Ask *What is different in pictures A, B and C?* Learners give ideas. Repeat with the second set of pictures.
- Say *Now listen and tick*. Play the audio. Learners listen and tick the pictures. Check answers.

Track4.16

What food would Dan like?

Mum: Would you like a banana, Dan?

Dan: Yes, please, and can I have some grapes?

Mum: OK. And would you like a kiwi too? It's your favourite.

Dan: No, thanks, Mum. I don't want one today.

Can you see the tick? Now you listen and tick the box.

One Where's Lucy's book?

Lucy: Dad, where's my book?

Dad: I don't know, Lucy. Is it on your desk?

Lucy: It isn't, Dad. And it isn't on the chair in my bedroom. Oh no!

Dad: Look, Lucy – there it is, in your school bag!

- Say *Well done. When you listened, you didn't talk* (mime chatting), *you listened hard* (mime fidgeting) *and you didn't feel worried* (mime being nervous). *Good job!*

Key: 1 C

Activity Book, page 54

See pages TB120–132

Ending the lesson

- **SA** Repeat the self-assessment technique used at the start of the lesson to see how well learners think they understand the vocabulary. Is there any change?
- In pairs, learners spell out food words on one another's backs and guess the words.

Learning outcomes By the end of the lesson, learners will have revised the language in the unit and had a picnic, offering and sharing food and saying what they like and dislike.

Recycled language unit language

Materials Food 1 and 2 flashcards, paper, coloured pens or pencils, a template picture of a sandwich with ingredients labelled for learners needing extra support (optional), paper plates, dice, counters, real food and drink (optional), digital Mission poster

Key Competences

- Revise vocabulary and language learnt in the unit.
- Complete self-assessment tasks and reflect on their own learning.
- Role play the value of sharing.

Warm-up

- Put learners into groups. Say *Let's do a quiz.*
- Put the Food 1 and 2 flashcards on the board. Ask for examples of the following and give a point for each correct answer:

  A drink
  Something we eat for breakfast
  Something we eat for dinner
  A food we can cook

Presentation

- Write on the board:

  My favourite sandwich *My favourite drink*
- Give out paper and coloured pens or pencils. Say *Draw your favourite sandwich. Draw your favourite drink. Write the ingredients.* Learners draw and label.

  Extra support Give out a template picture of a sandwich with the ingredients labelled.

  Fast finishers Learners can add extra food, e.g. cake or fruit, and write sentences about the sandwich.
- Put the learners into pairs. Say *Tell your partner about your food. What is in your sandwich? How did you make it?*

Pupil's Book, page 55

mission in action!

Have a picnic.

- Learners sit in their Mission groups, as if having a picnic. Make one of each group the Mission leader. Say *Your job is to help me.* Give paper plates to the Mission leader and ask them to hand out the plates to their group. Learners put their food pictures onto their plates.
- Demonstrate showing your picnic food, telling them what is in your sandwich and what your drink is. Learners say if they like or dislike your food. The Mission leader points around the group so each learner will explain their food and the other learners say if they like it or not.
- Learners role play sharing and eating food. Mime offering your food and ask *Would you like a chicken sandwich? Would you like some juice? Can I have some chocolate?* Remind them to say if they like something.

  Extra support Instead of asking questions, learners answer *Yes, please* or *No, thank you.*

  Fast finishers Ask learners to choose the best food from the picnic and offer it to a fast finisher in a different group.
- Point to the banana in the picture. Say *Tell me about this.* Learners say, e.g. *It's a banana. It's yellow.* Repeat with other pictures on the page and in the unit, e.g. *Tell me about this.* (*It's a picnic. There are apples.*) Learners repeat the activity in pairs.
- For ideas on monitoring and assessment, see Introduction.

Self-assessment

- **SA** Say *Did you like our 'Have a picnic' Mission?* Learners show a thumbs up, thumbs down or thumbs in the middle.
- Say *Did you do better than the last Mission? Better? Or not?* (Learners show thumbs up or down.) Praise or say *OK. We can try again.*
- Say *Our next Mission is 'Let's have a party'. What do you want to learn?'* (*I want to speak more. I want to spell words about parties.*)

Activity Book, page 55

See pages TB120–132

Activity Book, page 44

- Say *Look at page 44 of your Activity Book.* Review *My unit goals.* Ask *How is your Mission?*
- Learners reflect and choose a smiley face for *My mission diary* the final stage. Monitor.
- Point to the sunflower. Learners read the 'can do' statements and tick them if they agree they have achieved them. They colour each leaf green if they are very confident or orange if they think they need more practice.
- Point to the word stack sign. Ask learners to spend a few minutes looking back at the unit and find a minimum of five new words they have learnt. They write the new words into their word stack. See Introduction for techniques and activities.

Ending the lesson

- **SA** Go back to the completion stage on the digital Mission poster. Add a tick. Use self-assessment (see Introduction).
- Give out a completion sticker.
- Tell the learners *You have finished your Mission! Well done!*

mission in action!

Have a picnic.

My mission diary
Activity Book page 44

★ Make some food for the picnic.

★ Present your food to the class.

Look! This is my sandwich.

★ Have a picnic.

Would you like a banana?

Can I have some water, please?

★ Talk about the food at the picnic.

Yum! I like grapes.

Me too.

5 Happy birthday!

1 Watch the video. Draw a toy.

mission Have a present-giving party

In this unit I will:

1. Ask my friends about their toys.
2. Choose a present for my friend.
3. Make and write a card.

★ Give the present.

Unit 5 learning outcomes

In Unit 5, learners learn to:

- talk about toys
- ask and describe who things belong to, using possessive pronouns and *'s*
- explain what someone wants and doesn't want, using *Does … want? Yes, he/she does. No, he/she doesn't.*
- describe shapes
- read about and learn how to say sorry
- listen for specific numbers and names

Materials video, a small gift (e.g. bag of dried fruit or sweets) wrapped in many layers of paper, music for the game, Toys 1 and 2 flashcards, coloured pens or pencils, four squares of blank card or paper per learner, digital Mission poster, Friendly Farm animal flashcards, Food 1 and 2 flashcards

Key Competences

Work together to play a game.

Reflect on their own learning by going through the unit goals.

Draw their favourite toy.

Self-assessment

- **SA** Say *Open your Pupil's Books at page 56.* Say *Look at the picture. Point to red/green/pink/white.* Point to different objects in the picture and ask *What colour is this?* Point to the present. Ask *What's this?* Say *It's a present.* Say *Present.* Repeat and clap your hands on the stressed syllable: *pre-sent.* Learners repeat several times and clap the stress. Use self-assessment (see Introduction). Say *OK. Let's learn.*

Warm-up

- Play 'Pass the parcel'. Use the small gift wrapped in many layers of paper. The learners sit in a circle. Play some music. Say *Pass the present.* Learners pass the present around the circle. Pause the music. Say *Stop!* The learner holding the parcel unwraps the first layer of paper. Start the music again. Say *Pass the present.* Learners pass the parcel. Continue until the final layer is unwrapped. Say *Here's the present!* Let the learners share the fruit or sweets.

Pupil's Book, page 56

1 Watch the video. Draw a toy.

- Say *In this unit we're talking about toys.* Say *Let's watch the video.* To introduce the topic of the unit, play the video.
- Say *Look at page 56.* Say *It's a party!* Say *Party* and clap the stress (*par-ty*). Learners repeat. Ask *Do you like parties?* (*Yes, I do. / No, I don't.*)
- Hold up the Toys 1 and 2 flashcards. Ask *What are these?* Say *Toys.* Learners repeat. Point to different toys. Ask *Do you like it?* (*Yes, I do. / No, I don't.*)
- Point to the empty space. Ask *Which toy do you like? Draw your toy.* Learners draw a picture of their favourite toy in the space. Tell each child the name of the toy they have drawn.

  Fast finishers Learners can write the word.

mission Have a present-giving party

- Give each learner four squares of paper.
- Show the digital Mission poster. Say *Point to the party.*
- Say *Let's have a party! Point to number 1.* Learners point. Say *We'll ask about toys.* Write *Toys* on the board. Learners copy the word onto one square of paper. Say *Toys.* Learners repeat and hold up their word.
- Say *Point to number 2.* Say *We'll choose a present.* Write *Present* on the board. Learners copy the word onto a second square of paper. Say *Present.* Learners repeat and hold up their word.
- Say *Point to number 3.* Say *We'll make a card.* Write *Card* on the board. Learners copy the word onto a third square of paper. Say *Card.* Learners repeat and hold up their word.
- Say *Point to number 4.* Say *We'll give a present.* Say *Present.* Learners repeat and hold up their second word again.
- Point back to the words at the top of the poster. Say with excitement *Let's have a party!* Encourage learners to jump and smile. Write *Party* on the board. Learners copy the word onto a fourth square of paper. Say *Party.* Learners repeat and hold up their word. Say *Four – Let's have a party!* Repeat the whole sequence.
- Say *This is our Mission.*

Activity Book, page 56

My unit goals

- Go through the unit goals with the learners. You can read these or if you prefer you can put them onto the board or a poster.
- You can go back to these unit goals at the end of each Mission stage during the unit and review them.
- Say *This is our Mission page.*

Ending the lesson

- Show Friendly Farm animal and Food 1 and 2 flashcards. Learners say the words. Say *Let's see who is at my party! Let's see the food at my party!*
- Put the learners into groups of five and give each learner a number 1 to 5. Each group sits in a circle with a sheet of paper in the middle. Call out *One!* Learner 1 from each group comes up and looks at a flashcard. They go back to their group and sketch the character or food. The group guess the word. Continue until all flashcards have been drawn and named.

5 Vocabulary 1

Learning outcomes By the end of the lesson, learners will be able to recognise and use toy words.

New language *ball, bike, car, doll, house, kite, plane, robot, favourite*

Recycled language colours, numbers

Materials Toys 1 flashcards, coloured pens or pencils, audio, video

Key Competences

- Identify and name toys.
- Chant together as a class; Say a rhyme.
- Identify and say words starting with the letter 'h'.

Warm-up

- Write on the board:
  a) 9 5 10 b) 6 1 7 9 10 c) 6 7 2 8 2 4 9
- Write a 'secret code' on the board:
  1=A 2=E 3=G 4=N 5=O 6=P 7=R 8=S 9=T 10=Y
- In pairs, learners use the code to find words (a) toy, b) party, c) present).

Presentation

- Mime throwing a ball. Ask *What is it? (It's a ball.)* Show the flashcard of a ball. Say *Ball*. Learners repeat.
- Continue with different flashcards: kite – hold the strings and look up; robot – robot movement; car – driving; bike – get on and ride; doll – hug and dress up the doll; house – open the windows; plane – flying motion with arms.
- Ask *Which toy is your favourite?* Learners answer.

Pupil's Book, page 57

1 5.01 Listen and point. Then listen again and colour the toys.

- Say *Open your Pupil's Books at page 57. Look at the picture.*
- Indicate the caption and read it.
- Ask *Where's the doll?* The class points. Repeat with different toys. Add questions, e.g. *Is it big? Is it small?*
- Ask *Where's the tractor? Can you find it?* Learners find the picture and point (on the farm house).
- Say *Listen and point*. Play Track 5.01. Learners point to the toys in the picture.

Track 5.01

Today is Jim and Jenny's birthday.

Tom: Look, Jim! I'm on your bike.
Jim: No, that isn't my bike. I've got an orange bike. It's next to your grey robot. You're on Jenny's bike.
Tom: Oh!
Jim: Look at my cool, new kite, Grandma. It's big and blue. It's my birthday present. It's my new favourite toy.
Grandma: Ooh, yes. That's fantastic! And look at my red and grey plane. This is my favourite toy. Where's Jenny?
Jim: Here she is. She's got a new red car. That's her birthday present.
Jenny: Hi, Jim. Where's Eva?
Jim: She's playing with the toy house. It's yellow. And she's got a doll.
Eva: Look at the ball, Dolly. Look at the plane, Dolly. The plane! Cameron!
Cameron: Miaow!

- Say *Where is Cameron? And where is the plane? Let's listen.* Play Track 5.01 again. Ask *Where is Cameron? (In the tree) And where is the plane? (Next to Cameron in the tree)*
- Say *Listen and colour.* Play Track 5.01 again. Learners colour.

Key: kite – blue house – yellow

2 5.02 Say the chant.

- Say *Listen and say the chant.* Play the audio or video. Learners point and chant.

Track 5.02

Car, ball, doll, bike (x2)
House, plane, robot, kite (x2)
(Repeat)

- Play the chant again and mime. Learners chant and copy.

3 5.03 Listen and say *yes* or *no*.

- Describe the picture, using correct and incorrect information. Learners say *yes* or *no*.
- Play the audio. Pause for learners to call out *Yes* or *No*.

Track 5.03

1 Jenny's in the car.
2 The robot's under the orange bike.
3 Eva's got a doll.
4 The ball's next to Cameron.
5 The house is Grandma's favourite toy.
6 Jim likes his new blue kite.
7 Cameron's in the plane.
8 Jim's got a red bike.

Key: 1 no 2 no 3 yes 4 no 5 no 6 yes 7 no 8 no

Activity Book, page 57

See pages TB120–132

Ending the lesson

- **SA** Say *We learnt about toys*. Show the flashcards. Ask *Do you know the words?* Use the self-assessment technique (see Introduction). Learners show how they feel.
- Say *You can say the words well. Good work.*
- Ask learners to bring in photos of their families next lesson.

Vocabulary 1

5

1 5.01 **Listen and point. Then listen again and colour the toys.**

2 5.02 **Say the chant.**

3 5.03 **Listen and say *yes* or *no*.**

5

The Friendly Farm

5.04

Learning outcomes By the end of the lesson, learners will be able to understand when they hear possessive pronouns and the possessive *'s*.

New language *whose, his, her, their, 's*

Recycled language *favourite, have got, present,* toys

Materials audio, video

Key Competences

Read and listen to a story; Identify *Whose…?* possessive adjectives and possessive *'s* to talk about possessions.

Role play a story in groups.

Warm-up

- Say *Stand up*. Learners stand. Say *Show me your hands*. Learners wave their hands in the air. Say *Turn around*. Learners turn around. Say *Sit down*. Learners sit. Point to a girl. Ask *Boy or girl?* (*Girl*) Point to a boy. Ask *Boy or girl?* (*Boy*)
- Give instructions for learners to carry out: *Girls, stand up. Girls, show me your hands. Girls, sit down.* Repeat for boys. *Girls, stand up. Turn around. Sit down.* Repeat for boys.
- **SA** Use self-assessment techniques to check how well learners think they understand the vocabulary. See Introduction.

Presentation

- Choose a girl and ask *Have you got a bag?* (*Yes*) She puts the bag on her desk. Say *Look. It's (María)'s bag*. Learners repeat. Point to a boy. Ask *Is it (José)'s bag?* (*No*) Say *No. It's (María's) bag*. Learners repeat. Say *It's her bag*, pointing to her. Learners repeat.
- Choose a different learner, preferably a boy. Ask *Have you got a book?* If the learner says *Yes*, show the book and put it on his desk. Say *Look. It's (David)'s book*. Learners repeat. Point to a different learner, preferably a girl. Ask *Is it (Lupita)'s book?* Learners say *No*. Say *No. It's (David)'s book*. Learners repeat. Say *It's his book*. Learners repeat several times.
- Choose another learner, preferably a girl, and repeat the sequence with a pen. Choose a fourth, preferably a boy, and repeat with a rubber.
- Take the four items to the front of the room and ask the four learners to stand at the front. Hold up the first item. Ask *Whose bag is this?* Point to the four learners at the front. The learners say *It's (María)'s bag*. Repeat with the three other items. Show the bag. Point to one of the four learners. Ask *Is it his bag?* Learners say *No*. Encourage them to point to the correct learner and say *It's her bag*.
- Hold up the bag. Say *Whose bag is it?* Learners repeat. Say *Whose*. Learners repeat. Repeat with different items.
- Hold up each item once more. Learners ask, e.g. *Whose bag is it?* and answer, e.g. *It's (María's) bag*.

Pupil's Book, page 58

5.04 The Friendly Farm song

- Play the introductory song at the beginning of the cartoon story. Learners listen and sing. Ask *Can you remember?* Learners sing the song from memory. Repeat.

Track 5.04
See The Friendly Farm song on page TB5

5.04 The Friendly Farm

- Say *Open your Pupil's Books at page 58*. Ask *Who can you see in the pictures?* Learners name the characters. Ask *What's this?* Point to the car. Repeat with other objects.
- Ask *Whose birthday is it?* (*Jim and Jenny's birthday*) *Who likes cars?* (*Jenny*) *Who likes kites?* (*Jim*) *Does Cameron like the birthday present?* (*No, he doesn't.*) Say *Listen*. Play the audio or video. Learners listen and read.

Track 5.04
The Friendly Farm song + see cartoon on Pupil's Book page 58

- Learners answer the questions in pairs before the class check.
- Play the audio or video again. Pause after each frame and check comprehension. Frame 1: *What's Jim's favourite toy?* (*Kite*) Frame 2: *Whose car is it?* (*Jenny's*) Frame 3: *Do Jenny and Jim like dolls?* (*No*) Frame 4: *What is Jenny's favourite toy?* (*Car*) Frame 5: *What is their birthday present?* (*Plane*) Frame 6: *Is Cameron happy?* (*No – he doesn't like the plane*) Say *Cameron doesn't like the kite and he doesn't like the plane.*
- Play the audio or video again. Choose six confident learners and give each a role. Ask them to read aloud the speech bubbles.
- Put the learners into groups of six to role play the dialogue. Monitor and check.

  Extension Point to the toys in the pictures. Ask *Whose is it?* Learners answer.

Activity Book, page 58

See pages TB120–132

Ending the lesson

- **SA** Repeat the self-assessment technique used at the start of the lesson to see how well learners think they understand the vocabulary. Is there any change?

5 Language practice 1

Learning outcomes By the end of the lesson, learners will be able to use possessive pronouns and *'s* for possession accurately.

New language *Whose ... is this? It's his/her ... It's ...'s ...*

Recycled language toys

Materials pictures of toys cut in half, Toys 1 flashcards, Friendly Farm flashcards, Food flashcards, audio, digital Mission poster

Key Competences

- Learn to use possessive pronouns and 's for possession.
- Do a class survey about toys.
- Reflect on their own learning.
- Interact with the digital poster.

Warm-up

- Give out the pictures of toys cut in half. Learners mingle and find their other half. Pairs tell the class their toys.

Presentation

- Show a flashcard of Cameron, but cover it so only his tail shows. Ask *Whose tail is it? (Cameron's)*.
- Stick up four flashcards: Mr Friendly, Mrs Friendly, Jim and Jenny. Next to each one, stick a flashcard of an object, e.g. a hamburger, a cake, a kite and a car. Point to an object. Say *Whose*. Learners ask *Whose hamburger is this?* Point to Mr Friendly. Learners say *This is Mr Friendly's hamburger*. Repeat with the other objects.
- Point to the car. Point to Mr Friendly. Ask *Is it his car? (No)* They point to Jenny and say *It's her car*. Repeat with other objects and people.

Pupil's Book, page 59

5.05 Gracie's Grammar

- Say *Open your Pupil's Books at page 59*. Point to Gracie's Grammar box. Write the sentences on the board. Underline *Whose*. Underline *his*, *her*, *their* and *'s* in any examples.
- Play the audio. Pause for learners to repeat each sentence.

Track 5.05
See Pupil's Book page 59

1 5.06 Listen and stick. Then look, read and write.

- Play the audio for learners to point to the correct sticker.

Track 5.06

1 Mr Friendly: What's your favourite toy, Jim?
Jim: My favourite toy is my kite.
2 Mr Friendly: What's Grandma's favourite toy?
Jim: It's her plane.
3 Jim: What's Eva's favourite toy?
Jenny: It's her doll.
4 Jenny: What's Tom's favourite toy?
Jim: It's his robot.

- Play the audio again. Learners stick in the stickers.
- Write the sentences with spaces on the board. Choose learners to come to the board and fill in the spaces.

Key: 2 plane 3 's, her 4 's, his

mission Stage 1

- Show learners the first stage of the digital Mission poster: 'Toys'. Say *Let's ask about toys!* Learners find out which toys their friends like, to help them choose a toy as a present for their friend in Stage 2.
- Learners do the worksheet in the Teacher's Resource Book page 54 (see notes on TRB page 47 Activity 1).
- Alternatively, if you do not have the Teacher's Resource Book, show the flashcards of toys and ask the names.
- Draw a table on the board:

Do you like ...	*A:*	*name*	*name*	*name*
balls?				
kites?				
planes?				

- Point to Learner A and write their name in the first column. Demonstrate asking questions and adding ticks or crosses to the table, e.g. *Do you like balls? (Yes)* Add the tick. *Do you like kites? (No)* Add the cross.
- Learners copy the blank table. They choose three toys to ask about.
- Learners stand up. They move around, asking and answering questions, e.g. *Do you like balls? Yes, I do.* They put ticks or crosses in their table.
- Keep the completed tables safe to refer to again in a later lesson, for Stage 2.

Activity Book, page 59

See pages TB120–132

Activity Book, page 56

- Say *Look at page 56 of your Activity Book*. Review *My unit goals*. Ask *How is your Mission?*
- Learners reflect and choose a smiley face for *My mission diary 1*. Monitor.

Ending the lesson

- **SA** Go back to Stage 1 on the digital Mission poster. Say *We asked about toys. Good work.* Add a tick to the 'Toys' stage. Use self-assessment (see Introduction).
- Give out a completion sticker.

5.05 Gracie's Grammar

Whose bike is this? It's **Jim's** bike. **His** bike's orange.

Whose car is this? It's **Jenny's** car. **Her** car's red.

Whose house is this? It's **Jim and Jenny's** house. **Their** house is yellow.

1 5.06 Listen and stick. Then look, read and write.

1 Jim's favourite toy is his kite.

2 Grandma's favourite toy is her ________.

3 Eva ________ favourite toy is ________ doll.

4 Tom ________ favourite toy is ________ robot.

mission STAGE 1

Ask your friends about their toys.

Do you like kites? Yes, I do.

Have you got a kite? No, I haven't.

STAGE 1

My mission diary
Activity Book page 56

Vocabulary 2 and song

1 5.07 Listen and circle. Then sing the song.

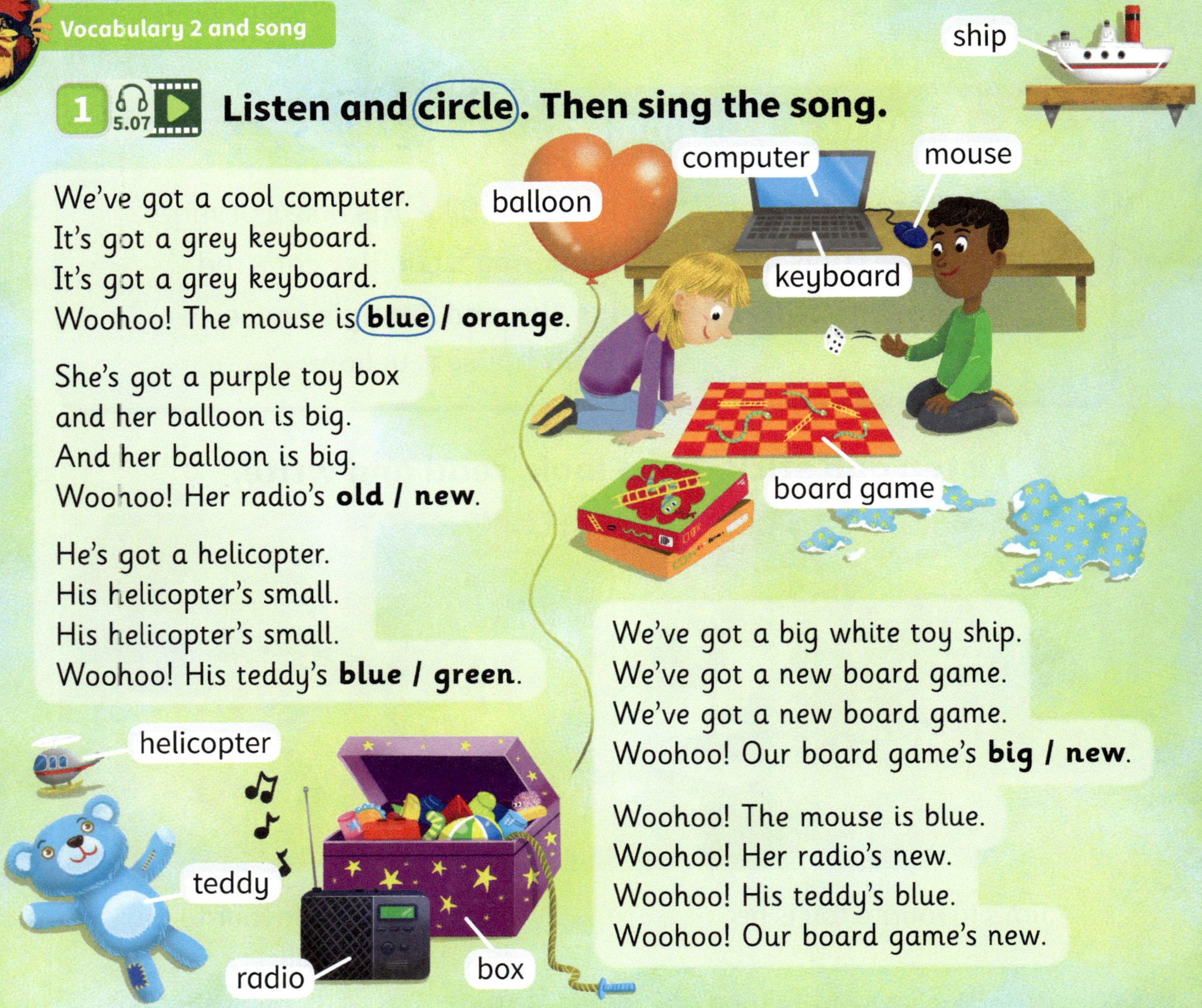

We've got a cool computer.
It's got a grey keyboard.
It's got a grey keyboard.
Woohoo! The mouse is **blue** / **orange**.

She's got a purple toy box
and her balloon is big.
And her balloon is big.
Woohoo! Her radio's **old** / **new**.

He's got a helicopter.
His helicopter's small.
His helicopter's small.
Woohoo! His teddy's **blue** / **green**.

We've got a big white toy ship.
We've got a new board game.
We've got a new board game.
Woohoo! Our board game's **big** / **new**.

Woohoo! The mouse is blue.
Woohoo! Her radio's new.
Woohoo! His teddy's blue.
Woohoo! Our board game's new.

2 Write the toys.

Learning outcomes By the end of the lesson, learners will have practised the language through a song.

New language *balloon, board game, box, computer, helicopter, keyboard, mouse, radio, ship, teddy, new, old*

Recycled language colours, *big, small, have/has got*

Materials an old book in bad condition and a new book, an old pencil and a new pencil, card or paper (two pieces per three learners), pictures from Digital photo bank of old and new bags, Toys 2 flashcards, eight large cards with one word on each (*computer, keyboard, mouse, teddy, helicopter, balloon, board game, ship*), a simple drawing of two toys (e.g. a robot and a ball), a cardboard box with *Toy box* written on it, some cardboard boxes (one per five learners), paper and coloured pens or pencils, audio, video

Key Competences

Learn new toys vocabulary through a song.

Listen to a song and do the actions.

Complete and interpret a Venn diagram.

Warm-up

- Show the learners an old and a new book. Ask *What are these?* (*Books*) Show the old one. Say *It's an old book*. Show the new one. Say *And this is a new book*. Say *Old*. Learners repeat. Say *New*. Learners repeat. Repeat the procedure with *What's this?* (*A pencil*), etc.
- Give out two pieces of card or paper per group of three learners. Write *old* on the board. Learners copy it onto one of the cards. Write *new* on the board. Learners copy it onto the second card.
- Show them the old pencil. Learners hold up the card that says *old*. Show them the new pencil. Learners hold up the card that says *new*.
- Show some pictures of old and new bags from Digital photo bank. Learners quickly hold up their cards.
- **SA** Use self-assessment to check how well learners think they understand the vocabulary. See Introduction.

Pupil's Book, page 60

1 5.07 Listen and circle. Then sing the song.

- Display Toys 2 flashcards of a computer with keyboard and mouse, a teddy, a helicopter, a balloon, a ship and a board game. Point and say the names. Learners repeat.
- Give out the eight large cards to eight learners: *computer, keyboard, mouse, teddy, helicopter, balloon, board game, ship*.
- Learners with cards come to the front one by one and show their cards. The other learners point to the object. The learner sticks the card to the board on the correct object.
- Write *big/small* under the balloon flashcard. Write *old/new* under the computer flashcard.
- Ask a learner to come to the board. Say *It's a new keyboard*. The learner circles the word *new*. Say *It's a big balloon*. The learner circles *big*.
- Say *Open your Pupil's Books at page 60*. Ask the names of the items. Learners repeat the words. Ask the colours. Show the toy box. Say *Look – the toys are in the toy box*. Say *Toy box*. Learners repeat.
- Play the audio or video. Learners listen and point.

Track 5.07

Rocky: I'm Rocky-Doodle-Doo and … here's our song for today: *Our cool toys!*

See song on Pupil's Book page 60

- Learners listen and circle the correct word.

Fast finishers These learners can write sentences, e.g. *It's a big balloon. It's a new computer.*

5.08 **Extension** Once learners are confidently singing to the song, try singing the karaoke version as a class.

2 Write the toys.

- Learners look at the Venn diagram. Say *Which toys has she got? Write them here.* Point to the circle for the girl. Say *Which toys has he got? Write them here.* Point to the circle for the boy. Say *Which toys have the girl and the boy got? Write them here.* Point to the overlapping section of the circles.
- Put the class in pairs. Learners read and write.
- Show the picture of Rocky in the bottom right-hand corner. Read out the question. Encourage learners to answer .

Activity Book, page 60

See pages TB120–132

Ending the lesson

- **SA** Repeat the self-assessment technique used at the start of the lesson to see how well learners think they understand the vocabulary. Is there any change?
- Say *Draw two pictures of toys*.
- Take out a cardboard box with *Toy box* written on it. Put your pictures into the box. Demonstrate, asking *Is the computer in the toy b* They ask each other about the toys in the toy box.
- Ask some confident learners to tell the class about the group's toy box, e.g. *In our toy box we've got a teddy, two balls, a computer, a plane and a balloon.*

Learning outcomes By the end of the lesson, learners will be able to say what someone wants or doesn't want.

New language *Does he/she want … ? Yes, he/she does. No, he/she doesn't. He/She wants …*

Recycled language toys

Materials pictures from Digital photo bank of a big red ball and a small blue ball, wrapping paper and sticky tape (optional), audio, Toys 1 and 2 flashcards, coloured pens or pencils, digital Mission poster

Key Competences

- Talk about what someone wants or doesn't want.
- Act out a dialogue.
- Choose and draw a present for their friend.
- Reflect on their own learning.
- Interact with the digital poster.

Warm-up

- Put up a picture of a big red ball and a small blue ball. Say *Look at the balls*. Point and ask questions: *What colour is it? Is it big or small?*

Pupil's Book, page 61

- Choose a learner and show them the balls. Ask *This one or this one?* The learner chooses one. Say to the class *(Name) wants the (big red) ball*. Learners repeat. Write the sentence on the board and underline the *s* in *wants*.
- Point to the first learner. Point to the ball she didn't choose. Say *Does (she) want this ball?* Learners repeat. Write *Does she want this ball?* on the board. Put a cross next to the ball she didn't choose. Say *No, she doesn't*. Learners repeat. Write *No, she doesn't* on the board. Point to the correct one. Say *Does she want this ball?* Say *Yes, she does*. Tick the correct one. Write *Yes, she does*. Learners repeat.

1 5.09 Which toy do they buy? Listen and tick ✓.

- Play the audio or video. Learners listen and tick the toys they buy.

Track 5.09

Alice:	Mum, it's Mark's birthday today.
Mum:	Oh, yes. What does he want for his birthday, Alice?
Alice:	Hmm. I don't know.
Mum:	Does he want a big grey robot?
Alice:	No, he's got a robot. Oh! He wants a teddy.
Mum:	Does he want a big one or a small one?
Alice:	He wants a small one.
Mum:	OK. Can we have the small brown teddy, please?
Shopkeeper:	Yes. Here you are.

Key: Picture 3

5.10 Gracie's Grammar

- Play the audio of Gracie's Grammar. Learners repeat.

Track 5.10
See Pupil's Book page 61

2 Read and say the dialogue. Act it out.

- Put the learners into pairs and give them a role: A or B.
- Each pair reads the dialogue. Correct pronunciation.
- Pairs cover the dialogue and act it out.

Extra support Learners can keep the dialogue to read.

mission Stage 2

- Show learners the second stage of the digital Mission poster: 'Choose toys'.
- Show learners the Toys 1 and 2 flashcards and ask the names.
- Say *Let's choose a present for our friends!*
- Learners pick a name out of a hat to see who they will be giving a present to.
- Say *Think about your friend. Does he or she want a teddy? Or a computer? Or a ball?* Ask them to choose a toy for their friend and draw it, but not show them. Learners can refer back to the tables they completed in Stage 1 for toys that learners like.
- Pair the learners with someone they aren't giving a present to. Learners say *My present is for …* Partners try to guess the present, e.g. *Does she want a doll? (No, she doesn't.) Does she want a car? (Yes, she does.) Does she want a red one? (No. She wants a green one.)*
- Learners complete the worksheet task in the Teacher's Resource Book page 54 (see notes on TRB page 47).
- Alternatively, if you do not have the TRB, give out wrapping paper and sticky tape. Each learner wraps their present and writes the person's name on it.
- Collect the presents and keep them for later.

Activity Book, page 61

See pages TB120–132

Activity Book, page 56

- Say *Look at page 56 of your Activity Book.* Review *My unit goals*. Ask *How is your Mission?*
- Learners reflect and choose a smiley face for *My mission diary 2*. Monitor.

Ending the lesson

- **SA** Go back to Stage 2 on the digital Mission poster. Add a tick to the 'Choose toys' stage. Use self-assessment (see Introduction).
- Give out a completion sticker.

1 5.09 Which toy do they buy? Listen and tick ✓.

1  ☐

2  ☐

3  ☐

5.10 Gracie's Grammar

Does he **want** a teddy? **Yes**, he **does**. / **No**, he **doesn't**.

What **does** he **want**? He **wants** a helicopter.

2 Read and say the dialogue. Act it out.

A What does your friend want?

B I think he wants a kite.

A Does he want the big orange one?

B No, he doesn't want that one.

A Does he want the small yellow one?

B Yes, he does.

mission STAGE 2

Choose a present for your friend.
Draw, wrap and say.

I think my friend wants a teddy.

Does he want a big teddy or a small teddy?

STAGE 2

My mission diary

Activity Book page 56

Cross-curricular

Shapes around us

1 Watch the video.

2 5.11 Listen and say.

1 circle

2 square

3 triangle

4 rectangle

3 Look at the toys. What shapes can you see?

I can see four triangles.

It's the kite!

Learning outcomes By the end of the lesson, learners will be able to understand shapes and how they can be described.

New language *shape, circle, rectangle, square, triangle*

Recycled language toys

Materials video, audio, a computer or flashcard of computer, paper cut into shapes (circles, squares, triangles), glue, sheets of paper

Key Competences

- Learn language related to shapes.
- Learn about shapes.
- Identify shapes in objects and things around us.

Warm-up

- Draw a red circle on the board. Draw a blue square. Draw a yellow triangle. Point to each. Ask *What colour is this?* Learners answer.
- Put learners into groups of four or five. Say *Choose a colour*. Ask each group which colour they have chosen. Say *Look around. How many things can you see with your colour?* Give an example: *Green. I can see five things: a pen, a bag, a chair, a book and the trees outside the window.* Point to each item as you say it. Learners see how many objects they can find around them. Give them one minute. Check answers, getting learners to point for objects they don't know in English.

Presentation

- Go back to the shapes on the board. Make the shapes with your hands: circle, square and triangle. Say *These are different shapes*. Say *Shapes*. Learners repeat.
- Say *Look at the red shape. It's a circle.* Learners repeat several times. Say *Draw a circle.* Monitor.
- Say *Look at the blue shape. It's a square.* Learners repeat several times. Say *Draw a square.* Monitor.
- Say *Look at the yellow shape. It's a triangle.* Learners repeat several times. Say *Draw a triangle.* Monitor.
- Now draw a rectangle around all the other shapes up on the board. Say *It's a rectangle. Look. Two sides are big.* Show with your hands the longer sides of the rectangle. Say *Rectangle*. Learners repeat several times. Say *Draw a rectangle.* Monitor.
- Say *Choose your favourite shape: the circle, square, triangle or rectangle.* Ask each group the shape they have chosen. Ask *How many things have got your shape?* Point out an example of each one, e.g. *The board is a rectangle. The clock is a circle. The book is square. The chair makes a triangle.* Give learners one minute to find examples for their shape. Check answers, getting learners to point for objects they don't know in English.

Pupil's Book, page 62

1 Watch the video.

- Say *Let's watch the video*. Learners watch the video about shapes and answer the questions at the end of the video.

2 5.11 Listen and say.

- Ask learners to point to the different shapes. Say *Circle*. Learners point. Repeat with the other shapes.
- Play the audio. Pause so learners can repeat.

Track 5.11
See Pupil's Book page 62

3 Look at the toys. What shapes can you see?

- Show learners a computer or the flashcard of the computer. Ask *What's this?* (*Computer*) *What shape is the computer?* (*Rectangle*) Show a round button. Ask *What shape is this?* (*Circle*)
- Learners look at the picture. Point to each item and ask *What is it?* Learners answer.
- Ask *What shapes can you see?* Learners answer.
- Read out the example with a confident learner: *I can see four triangles.* (*It's the kite!*)
- Learners work in pairs, describing the shapes and guessing the toys in the same way.

Activity Book, page 62

See pages TB120–132

Ending the lesson

- Put learners into groups of three. Give each group cut out shapes (triangles, circles and squares), glue and a sheet of paper.
- Tell learners to create a toy or object by sticking the shapes onto the paper.
- When they have finished, ask each group to show what they have made. The class guess what their artwork shows, e.g. *It's a doll's house.*

Learning outcomes By the end of the lesson, learners will be able to describe a toy and the shapes of things around them.

Recycled language colours, parts of the body

Materials large sheets of paper (one per four learners), paper for each learner, coloured pens or pencils, pictures of paintings containing shapes from Digital photo bank, some shapes drawn on pages (e.g. a small triangle, a big square and a small rectangle; two large circles and a small square; a large rectangle and a small circle inside it)

Key Competences

- Read and complete a description of a toy.
- Make and write a card for their friend.
- Reflect on their own learning.
- Interact with the digital poster.

Warm-up

- Draw on the board some clear shapes that represent objects, e.g. a circle (a ball), a square with legs (a table), a triangle and a rectangle (a house with a roof).
- Point to the outlines and ask *What is it?* Learners answer.
- Point to the different shapes in each outline and ask *What shape is it?* Learners answer.

Pupil's Book, page 63

4 Look, read and write.

- Say *Open your Pupil's Books at page 63*. Learners look at the picture. Ask *What colour is it?* (*Green and grey*) *What colour are its eyes?* (*Red and yellow*)
- Ask *Can you see any circles?* Learners point to, e.g. its eyes. Ask *Are there any squares?* Learners point to, e.g. its body.
- Learners read the sentences and write the words in the spaces. Check answers.

Key: red, square, circles, rectangle, rectangles

5 Look around your classroom. What shapes can you see?

- Point to the board. Ask *What shape is it?* (*Rectangle*) Point to the clock. Ask *What shape is it?* (*Circle*)
- Put learners into groups of four. Give out a large sheet of paper to each group. Using pens, learners divide the paper into four. Write *circle*, *rectangle*, *triangle*, *square* on the board. Learners copy each word onto the top of each section.
- Give learners five minutes to write as many things as they can see in each section, according to shape. If they don't know a word, they can do a drawing.
- After five minutes, stop the activity and check answers. The winning group is the one with the most items. If learners have drawn pictures of items that might be useful for them to know, teach the word to the class.

mission Stage 3

- Show the class the third stage of the Mission poster: 'Card'.
- Say *Pictures have lots of shapes*. Show learners some pictures of paintings and see if learners can see the shapes in the pictures. Ask *Which is your favourite picture?*

  Extension Put up some copies of famous paintings. Place them around the room like an art gallery. Learners walk around and decide which picture they like best.
- Now learners stand in small groups – a few learners near each picture. They find examples of shapes in the pictures. Say *Circle*. Learners point to any circles they can see. Repeat with the other shapes.
- Now say *Let's make a card!* Put learners into pairs or ask them to find a partner.
- Give paper to each learner. Show them how to fold it in half to make a card shape. Say *My card is for (name)*. Write *To (name) From (your name)* on the inside of the card. Learners write their own message for their partner.
- Say *Now let's make a picture for the card with shapes!* Show them an example, drawing and overlapping shapes and colouring in.
- Learners draw their cards. Monitor. As you check, point to the shapes learners are drawing and ask what shape and colour they are.
- When all the learners have finished, get them to work in small groups (but not with the person their card is for) and show their cards. They describe the shapes, e.g. *It has got a circle and a square.*
- For ideas on monitoring and assessment, see Introduction.
- Collect the cards and keep them for later.

Activity Book, page 63

See pages TB120–132

Activity Book, page 56

- Say *Look at page 56 of your Activity Book*. Review *My unit goals*. Ask *How is your Mission?*
- Learners reflect and choose a smiley face for *My mission diary 3*. Monitor.

Ending the lesson

- Go back to Stage 3 on the digital Mission poster. Add a tick to the 'Card' stage or invite a learner to do it. Use self-assessment (see Introduction).
- Give out a completion sticker.

4 Look, read and write.

square circles ~~green~~ rectangle red rectangles

This is my toy robot. It's got two green arms, two green legs and two __________ feet. Its head is a green __________. Its eyes are red and yellow __________. Its mouth is a white __________. Its body is a green square with two big grey __________. It's cool!

5 Look around your classroom. What shapes can you see?

Look! The board is a rectangle.

mission STAGE 3

Make and write a card for your friend.

- Draw a shapes picture on the card.
- Write a message in the card.

My mission diary
Activity Book page 56

Literature

1 **Look at the pictures. What toys can you see? What's your favourite toy?**

5.12 The twins and their robots

Dora and Cora are twins. They like toys. They've got a teddy, a car, a plane, a monster and an alien. But Dora's favourite toy is a robot. Its name is Bill. Cora's favourite toy is a robot too. Its name is Jill.

One day, Dora says, 'Can I play with Jill, please?'

'Yes,' says Cora. 'Here you are. And can I play with Bill, please?'

'Yes,' says Dora. 'Here you are.'

Dora and Cora like their new robots. The twins are very happy.

Learning outcomes By the end of the lesson, learners will have read about toys and learnt about saying sorry.

New language *alien, angry, Can I have …, please?, I'm sorry, monster, my*

Recycled language asking for something, *Here you are*, toys

Materials Toys 1 and 2 flashcards, either real soft toy alien and monster or pictures from Digital photo bank of toy alien and monster, audio

Key Competences

Read a text about sharing toys.

Think about the importance of sharing and saying sorry; Work in groups to talk about their favourite toys.

Warm-up

- Ask learners to think about their toys. Ask *What's your favourite toy?* Learners answer.
- Show five flashcards of toys. Ask learners the names. Hold up one of the flashcards, e.g. a car. Say *This is my favourite toy*. Point to yourself. Mix the flashcards up and then put them up on the board face down. Say *Can you find my favourite toy?* Learners point. Show the flashcard they point to. If they are wrong, say *Try again!* When they find the car, say *Well done! My favourite.* Mix the cards up again and repeat.

Presentation

- Say *We are going to read about Dora and Cora. They are twins. They have favourite toys.*
- Say *They like aliens and monsters.* Show your soft toys or pictures of an alien and a monster. Say *This is an alien*. Learners repeat. Say *This is a monster*. Learners repeat.
- Say *Is this my favourite toy?* Say *My favourite*, pointing to yourself. Learners repeat. Hold up the alien or monster and ask *Is this my favourite?* (*No*) Ask *What's my favourite toy?* (*Car*)
- Now offer the car flashcard, the alien and the monster to three learners, saying *Here you are*. Say *I'm sharing*.
- Act out changing your mind. Look at the car flashcard. Say *I want my car. I'm angry.* Act out *angry*. Say *Angry* and act it out. Learners copy and repeat. Go and take back the car flashcard without speaking to the learner. Ask *Is it OK?* Learners say *No*. Indicate the learner and say *Is he/she angry?* Learners say *Yes*. Go back to the learner and say *I'm sorry*. Learners repeat several times.
- Go to the second learner with the alien. Say *Can I have the alien, please?* Take the card. Say *Is it OK?* Learners say *Yes*. Say *Can I have the alien, please?* Learners repeat.
- Go to the third learner. Encourage learners to help you ask *Can I have the monster, please?* Learners repeat several times.

Pupil's Book, page 64

1 Look at the pictures. What toys can you see? What's your favourite toy?

- Put the class into groups of three. Say *Open your Pupil's Books at page 64. What toys can you see?* Learners call out. Say *What's your favourite toy? My favourite toy is a car.* Learners talk about what they like, using *My favourite toy is …* Monitor.
- Check their ideas.

5.12 The twins and their robots

- Guide learners to look at each picture and ask questions, e.g. Picture 1: *Who are they?* (*Cora and Dora*) *What colour is Cora's name?* (*Red*) *What colour is Dora's name?* (*Yellow*) *How many robots are there?* (*Two*) Picture 2: *Which one is Cora's?* (*The red robot*) *Which one is Dora's?* (*The yellow robot*) Picture 3: *Are the twins happy or sad?* (*Happy*) *Why?* (*They are sharing toys.*) Picture 4: *Are they happy now?* (*No – they are sad.*) *Why?* (*Because they want their robots back*) Picture 5: *Are they happy now?* (*Yes*) *Why?* (*Because they said sorry*) If learners can't answer the 'why' questions, don't give the answers yet.
- Ask learners to guess what happens in the story.
- Say *Read and listen to the first part*. Play the audio. Learners listen and read. Pause the audio at the end of page 64. Ask *Who has Cora's robot?* (*Dora*) *And who has Dora's robot?* (*Cora*) *Are they happy?* (*Yes*) Ask *Why are they sad later?* Learners suggest ideas.

  Track 5.12
  See story on Pupil's Book pages 64–65
- Say *Look at page 65. Read the next part.* Show them the rest of the story. Play the rest of the audio. Check if their guesses were correct. (*They want their robots back.*)
- Say *Look at picture 5. Are they happy now?* (*Yes – they said sorry.*) Check answers.

Activity Book, page 64

See pages TB120–132

Ending the lesson

- Put learners into pairs. Ask Learner A of each pair to take out a pen. Encourage Learner B to take the pen from them. Ask Learner As *Are you happy or angry?* (*Angry*) Encourage Learner Bs to say *I'm sorry*.
- Tell each pair to repeat. Then swap roles and repeat.
- Now tell Learner Bs to say *Can I have the pen, please?* Encourage Learner As to give the pen and say *Here you are*. Repeat the sequence. Then ask learners to swap roles and repeat.

Learning outcomes By the end of the lesson, learners will have read about toys and learnt about saying sorry.

New language *alien, angry, Can I have …, please? I'm sorry, monster, my*

Recycled language toys, asking for something, *Here you are*

Materials three sets of letter cards per group of four learners (five blue with the letters *HAPPY*; five red with the letters *ANGRY*; five yellow with the letters *SORRY*), audio

Social and Emotional Skill: Saying sorry

- After reading the story, say *Dora and Cora have toy robots. They are playing with their robots. They share their robots. They are happy. When Dora says 'Jill is MY robot' and Cora says 'Bill is MY robot', are Dora and Cora happy?* (*No, they are angry.*)
- Ask *Is it nice to be angry? How can you stop being angry?* (*Say sorry*) *Do the twins say sorry?* (*Yes*) *How do they feel?* (*Happy*)
- Demonstrate a situation where it's important to say sorry. Walk past a child's desk and knock something over. Don't say sorry. Do the same again, but this time say sorry. Encourage learners to say how they felt each time. The learner feels better when you say sorry.
- When there are problems in class between learners, encourage them to think about what happened and how the other person feels to get the apology to come from them. Ask *What happened? How do you think (Maria) feels?* When they say sorry, ask *How are you feeling now?*
- When learners say sorry, encourage them to say the following sentences (in their own language) so learners recognise what they have done and think about how they can improve: *I'm sorry because … This is wrong because … In the future I will … Will you forgive me?*

Key Competences

- Read a text.
- Act out a story.
- Work in pairs to talk about the toys they play with.

Warm-up

- Tell learners to get out a pen, rubber or pencil. Put them into pairs. They ask for their partner's object, e.g. *Can I have the pen, please?* and answer politely: *Yes. Here you are.*
- **SA** Use self-assessment techniques to check how well learners think they understand the vocabulary. See Introduction.

Presentation

- Give out letter cards to the learners: five blue for *HAPPY* (a different letter on each), five red for *ANGRY* and five yellow for *SORRY*. In groups, learners sort the cards into words.
- Say each word for learners to mime.
- In pairs, learners write each word from memory.

Pupil's Book, page 65

2 Act out the story.

- Say *Act out the story*. Summarise the story sentence by sentence, and mime. Put learners into pairs. Learners copy with their partner as you act the story. Say *Cora and Dora are happy with their robots*. Act playing happily. Say *They share robots*. Act swapping robots. Learners swap with their partner. Say *Cora wants her robot back. And Dora wants her robot back*. Act angry. Learners copy. Say *Now Dora and Cora are sorry*. Look sorry and act offering a robot. Say *Now they are happy again*. Act happy.
- Repeat. The learners act the story.
- Now ask the learners to read the story and act it out again, reading out some of the sentences.

Fast finishers Learners can try to remember the sentences as they act and speak from memory.

Extra support Learners read some of the dialogue, using the text to help.

3 Ask and answer.

- Choose a confident learner. Ask *Have you got a brother or sister?* (e.g. *I've got a brother.*) Ask *What toys do you play with?* (e.g. *My ball and my doll.*)
- Learners ask and answer in pairs.

Activity Book, page 65

See pages TB120–132

Ending the lesson

- **SA** Repeat the self-assessment technique used at the start of the lesson to see how well learners think they understand the vocabulary. Is there any change?
- Write the words *happy*, *sad*, *angry*, *sorry* on the board. Mime the word *happy*. Ask *Am I happy, sad, angry or sorry?* Learners answer.
- Put learners into pairs. They take it in turns to act out an adjective and their partner guesses.
- Draw a basic emoticon on the board. Ask learners to copy it three times. Tell learners to draw onto the emoticon and make a happy one, an angry one and a sorry one.
- Once they have finished, they show their emoticons to their partner. Their partner writes *happy*, *angry* or *sorry* under each one.

5

'Jill is *my* robot,' says Dora.
'No, she isn't!' says Cora. 'Jill's *my* robot!'
'Bill is *my* robot,' says Cora.
'No, he isn't!' says Dora. 'Bill's *my* robot!'
Oh, no! The twins are very angry now.

'Can I have Bill, please, Cora?' says Dora.
'OK,' says Cora. 'Here you are. I'm sorry, Dora.'
'Can I have Jill, please, Dora?' says Cora.
'OK,' says Dora. 'Here you are. I'm sorry, Cora.'
The twins are happy again.

2 Act out the story.

Can I play with Bill, please?

Yes. Here you are.

3 Ask and answer.

Have you got a brother or sister?

I've got a brother.

What toys do you play with?

My ball and my doll.

1 Practise with a friend. Say and write.

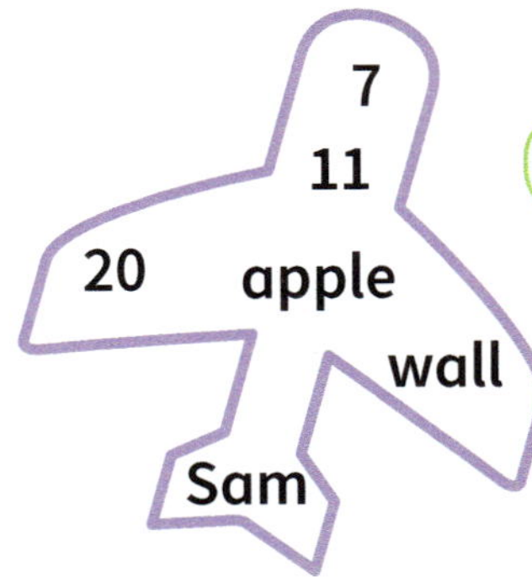

Kite. That's K-I-T-E.

2 Ask and answer.

Where do you live?

I live in Lime Street.

How do you spell that?

It's L-I-M-E.

3 Read the questions. Is the answer a name or a number?

4 5.13 Listen and write a name or a number. There are two examples.

Examples

What's Mark's family name?

Small

How old is Mark?

7

Questions

1 How many kites has Mark got?

____

2 Where does Mark live?
In ______________ Street

3 What number is Mark's house?

____

Go to page 120. Practise the alphabet and numbers 1–20.

Learning outcomes By the end of the lesson, learners will have listened for numbers and names.

Recycled language letters, names, numbers, toys

Materials Toys 1 and 2 flashcards, audio

Key Competences

- Listen for names and numbers.
- Practise activity types found in *Pre A1 Starters* exams.
- Work in pairs to ask and answer about the road where they live.

Warm-up

- Tell the learners to stand in a circle.
- Say *Let's say the first letter of our names!* Start with a confident learner, e.g. *I'm Eli and my name has got an E.*
- Go around the circle in this way.
- SA Use self-assessment to check how well learners think they understand the vocabulary. See Introduction.
- If your learners need more practice of the alphabet, go to page 120 and listen to the alphabet chant and do the activity.

Pupil's Book, page 66

1 Practise with a friend. Say and write.

- Say *Open your Pupil's Books at page 66.*
- Learners work in pairs. One learner has the teddy and the other has the plane.
- Learners now spell out their words. Learners who have the plane close their books. The learner with the teddy says, e.g. *Kite. That's K-I-T-E.* The other learner listens (without looking at the Pupil's Book) and writes the word. The first learner continues with all of the words in the teddy.
- The learners then swap roles and repeat, with the second learner spelling out the words in the plane.
- Check spellings with the words in the shapes.

2 Ask and answer.

- Read out the example questions and answers.
- In pairs, learners ask and answer.

3 Read the questions. Is the answer a name or a number?

- Say *Name*. Learners repeat. Say *Number*. Learners repeat.
- Ask *Which is the answer – a name or a number? 'What's her name?'* Learners say *Name*. Say *'How old is she?'* Learners say *Number*.
- Say *We can listen for numbers and names.*
- Show the examples in Activity 4. Ask *What's Mark's family name? (Name) How old is Mark? (Number)*
- In pairs, learners say *Name* or *Number* for 1–3.

4 (5.13) Listen and write a name or a number. There are two examples.

- Say *Look at Activity 4. Let's listen to the example.*
- Play the first part of the audio and look at the answers.

Track 5.13

Woman: Is this your friend?
Boy: Yes. His name's Mark Small.
Woman: Mark Small? S-M-A-L-L?
Boy: Yes, that's right. It's his birthday today.
Woman: How old is Mark?
Boy: He's seven.
Woman: Seven?
Boy: Yes.

Can you see the answers? Now you listen and write a name or a number.

1 Woman: Does Mark want a beautiful kite?
Boy: No, he doesn't. He's got three kites in his toy cupboard.
Woman: Three! That's a lot!
Boy: Yes, they're new … from his mum and dad.

2 Woman: And where does Mark live?
Boy: In Pear Street.
Woman: Is that P-E-A-R?
Boy: That's right. Pear Street is next to his old school.

3 Woman: OK. And where is his party?
Boy: It's at his house.
Woman: Which number is it?
Boy: Number 15.
Woman: 15. Right, come on!

Now listen again.
[Repeat track]

- Play the rest of the audio. Learners write the names or numbers.
- Check answers.
- Say *Well done. When you listened, you found the numbers and names. Good job!*

Key: 1 3 2 Pear 3 15

Activity Book, page 66

See pages TB120–132

Ending the lesson

- SA Repeat the self-assessment technique used at the start of the lesson to see how well learners think they understand the vocabulary. Is there any change?
- Place flashcards of toys face down on a desk at the front of the room.
- Ask a learner to come up and look at the toy on the card without showing the rest of the class. The learner acts out the toy on the card, e.g. for *ball* they could act throwing and catching; for *robot* they could do robot movements. The rest of the class calls out the name of the toy.

Learning outcomes By the end of the lesson, learners will have revised the language in the unit and had a present-giving party, giving cards and presents and guessing what the present is.

Recycled language unit language

Materials sets of cards with the unit words on them: one set per four learners (e.g. *angry, sorry, robot, ball, circle, square, triangle, monster*), party music and balloons (optional), cards and presents made earlier in the unit

Key Competences

- Revise vocabulary and language learnt in the unit.
- Complete self-assessment tasks and reflect on their own learning.
- Role play having a present-giving party.

Warm-up

- Say *Let's play a game!* Put learners into groups of four. Give each group a set of unit word cards face down on the desk between them. Show them how to play. Learners take it in turns to take a card.
- They give clues to their group by acting the words as in the Ending the lesson activity from the previous lesson, but this time they work in smaller groups. If the group guesses, the next learner can take a card and repeat. The groups continue until all the words are complete.
- At the end, go through the words and act out each word together, checking learners remember them all.

Presentation

- Write on the board:
  Giving a present
  Giving a card
- Act out giving a present. Say *Here is your present.* Learners repeat. Act out receiving a present. Say *Thank you!* Learners repeat. Say *Cool! It's a robot. I love robots!* Learners repeat. Say *Great! I love it.* Learners repeat.
- Go through the sequence again for giving a card. Say *Cool! It's got triangles. I love it.* Learners repeat. Say *Great! I love it.* Learners repeat.

Pupil's Book, page 67

mission in action!

Have a present-giving party.

- If possible, play some party music and put out some balloons.
- Say *Let's have a party!*
- Bring out the presents and cards the learners made earlier in the unit.
- Encourage the learners to give their card to their friend. Make sure they talk about the cards as they give them, using the phrases just learnt.
- Now learners collect the present they made. Tell them to work in pairs. They each try to guess what the toy is, e.g. *Is it a kite? (No, it isn't.) Is it a robot?*
- Learners open their presents and respond, e.g. *Yes, it's a robot! Great. I love robots.*
- Point to pictures of toys in the unit. Say *Tell me about this toy*. Learners say, e.g. *It's a teddy. It's small and brown.* Learners repeat the activity in pairs, asking each other about the unit content.
- For ideas on monitoring and assessment, see Introduction.

Self-assessment

- **SA** Say *Did you like our 'Have a party' Mission? A lot?* (cheer and jump) *It's OK?* (smile) *Or not much?* (shake your head and shrug). Encourage learners to show how they feel.
- Say *Did you do better than the last Mission – Have a picnic? Better?* (move your hand up) *Or not?* (move your hand down).
- If they say *yes*, say *Good! Well done! Tell me one thing you did better.* Each learner gives one idea. If you have a big class, they can tell partners.
- Say *Our next Mission is 'Act out a wildlife tour'.* Say *How can we do better? Tell me one thing you will do better.*

Activity Book, page 67

See pages TB120–132

Activity Book, page 56

- Say *Look at page 56 of your Activity Book.* Review *My unit goals.* Ask *How is your Mission?*
- Learners reflect and choose a smiley face for *My mission diary* the final stage. Monitor.
- Point to the sunflower. Learners read the 'can do' statements and tick them if they agree they have achieved them. They colour each leaf green if they are very confident or orange if they think they need more practice.
- Point to the word stack sign. Ask learners to spend a few minutes looking back at the unit and find a minimum of five new words they have learnt. They write the new words into their word stack. See Introduction for techniques and activities.

Ending the lesson

- Go back to the completion stage on the digital Mission poster. Add a tick or invite a learner to do it. Use self-assessment (see Introduction).
- Give out a completion sticker.
- Tell the learners *You have finished your Mission! Well done!*

mission in action!

Have a present-giving party.

My mission diary
Activity Book page 56

★ **Give the card to your friend.**

Here you are, Carla.

Thank you, Hugo. I can see a circle and two triangles.

★ **Give the present to your friend.**

Here you are.

Thank you!

★ **Your friend plays a guessing game.**

I think it's a doll.

No, it isn't.

Is it a robot?

★ **Your friend opens the present.**

Cool! It's a robot. I like robots!

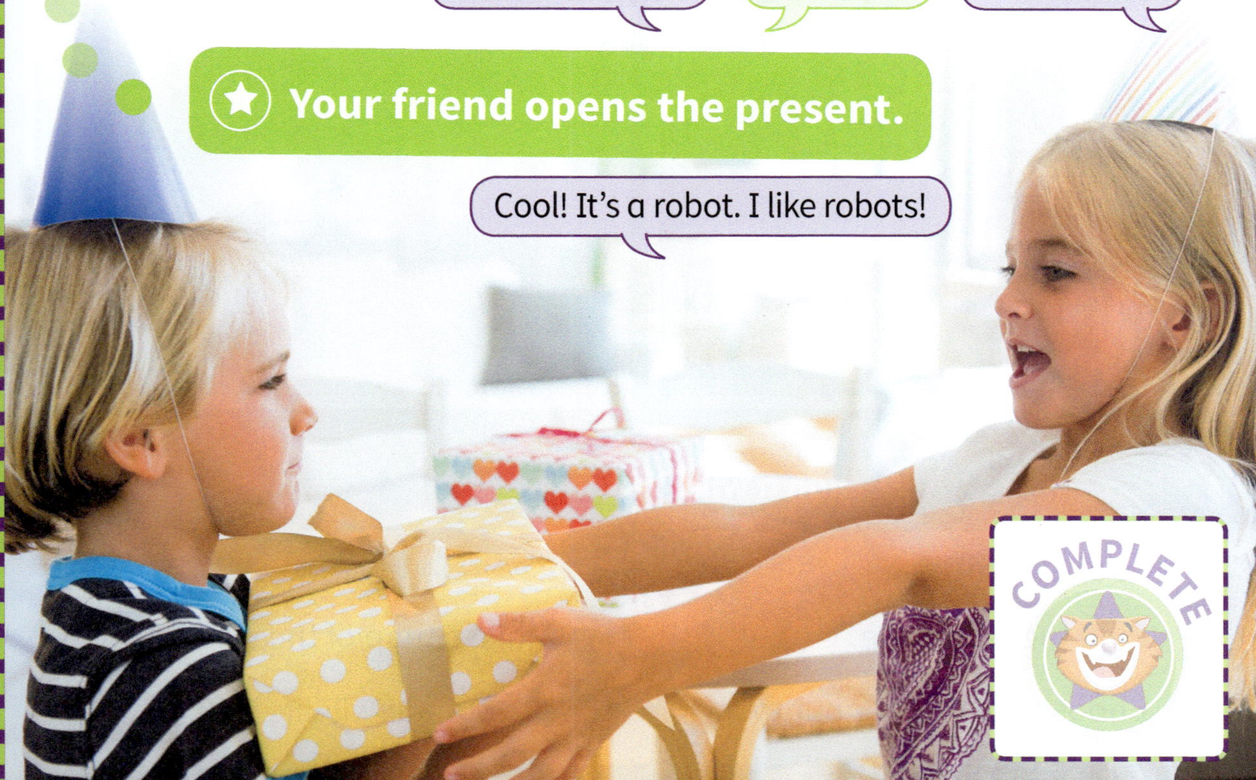

6 A day out

1 Watch the video. Draw an animal.

mission Plan a wildlife tour

In this unit I will:

1. Play the bus game.
2. Choose animals for our tour.
3. Make a map of the wildlife park.

★ Act out our wildlife tour.

Unit 6 learning outcomes

In Unit 6, learners learn to:

- talk about animals
- say if they don't know something
- make and respond to suggestions using *Let's*
- describe where animals live
- read about animals in a zoo and guess how the writer feels
- complete sentences using picture and word clues

Materials video, pictures from Digital photo bank of an African plain and trees in a jungle, real picnic food (apples, bread, juice and chocolate) and blanket (optional), pieces of paper the same size as the blank space on the Pupil's Book page (one per learner), flashcards of food, paper plates, coloured pens or pencils, digital Mission poster

Key Competences

Become familiar with language related to animals.

Reflect on their own learning by going through the unit goals.

Draw a picture of an animal.

Self-assessment

- **SA** Say *Open your Pupil's Books at page 68*. Say *Look at the pictures*. Indicate items on the page and ask questions using the language from the unit, e.g. *What are they?* Say the names of the animals (*parrots*, *zebras*, *giraffes*). Learners repeat. Point again and ask *What colour are they?* (parrots – *yellow*, *blue*, *green*, *black and white*; zebras – *black and white*; giraffes – *brown and orange*).
- Use self-assessment (see Introduction). Say *OK. Let's learn.*

Warm-up

- Show a picture of a tree and an African plain. Ask learners *Where can you see … ?* Point to the parrots. Learners point to the tree. Repeat with zebras and giraffes (*African plain*).

Pupil's Book, page 68

1 Watch the video. Draw an animal.

- Say *In this unit we're talking about animals*. Say *Let's watch the video*. To introduce the topic of the unit, play the video.
- Say *Look at page 68*. Point to the space on the page. Learners draw a picture of an animal on a piece of paper the same size as the blank space on the Pupil's Book page. Monitor. Tell each child the name of the animal they have drawn.

  Fast finishers Learners can draw a second item and write the words.

- Say *I'll do a tour*. Learners hold up their pictures and make the noise of their animal. Tour around the room pretending to take photos and pointing to their pictures saying *Look! A (name of animal)*. Finish and say *A wildlife tour*. Say *Wildlife tour*. Learners repeat. Invite four or five learners to do a 'tour' around the classroom, pretending to take photos. The other learners make animal noises.

mission Plan a wildlife tour

- Show the digital Mission poster.
- Say *Let's see some animals*. Say *Point to number 1*. Say *We'll play a game*. Learners chant *Play a game!* Repeat.
- Say *Point to number 2*. Say *We'll choose animals*. Learners chant *Animals*. Repeat. Point back to number 1 and learners chant *Play a game!* Point to number 2 and learners chant *Animals*. Repeat.
- Say *Point to number 3*. Say *We'll make a map*. Learners chant *Map*. Say *Three* and repeat. Go through numbers 1–3, encouraging learners to chant.
- Say *Point to number 4*. Say *We'll do a wildlife tour*. Learners chant *Wildlife tour!* Repeat the whole sequence, getting the learners to chant as you call out the numbers. Say *This is our Mission*.

Activity Book, page 68

My unit goals

- Go through the unit goals with the learners. You can read these or you can put them onto the board or a poster.
- You can go back to these unit goals at the end of each Mission stage during the unit and review them.
- Say *This is our Mission page*.

Ending the lesson

- Act out taking photos. Learners copy.
- Split the class into two and ask half the learners to stand around the edge of the room holding their animal pictures. The other half do a tour and go to their friends and take a photo. The learner holding the picture says the name of the animal and the 'touring' learner repeats it.
- After a few minutes, learners swap roles: the touring learners stand with pictures and the rest go around taking photos.

  Alternative Put learners into groups of six and tell them to get out the animal pictures they have drawn. Try to group the learners so that each member of the group has a different animal picture. Learners put up their pictures on the wall. Learners in each group present their tour to the other learners – each says the name of the animals they have on the tour and the rest of the class repeat. The learners on the tour take photos. Once each group has finished, a new group presents their tour.

- If appropriate, learners can stick their animal pictures on the blank space on the Pupil's Book page.

Learning outcomes By the end of the lesson, learners will be able to recognise and use words about things we see around us.

New language *bus, bus stop, car, flower, garden, lorry, motorbike, park, shop, train, tree*

Recycled language *like/likes, don't like / doesn't like,* numbers

Materials Vehicles and places flashcards and flashcard of bike, two large pictures of a park and a street scene, coloured pens or pencils, audio, video

Key Competences

- Identify and name vehicles and places.
- Chant together as a class.
- Identify and practise the /eɪ/ sound.

Warm-up

- Cover up the flashcard of the bike and then reveal the edge. Ask learners *What is it?* Learners guess. Gradually reveal more of the flashcard until they say *It's a bike.* Repeat the process with the flashcard of a garden. Ask *What is it?* (*It's a garden.*)

Presentation

- Show two large pictures of a park and a street scene. Point to the park. Ask *What is it?* (*A park*) Learners repeat. Point to the street scene. Ask *What is it?* (*A street*) Learners repeat.
- Hold up the flashcard of the lorry. Ask *What is it?* Say *Lorry*. Learners repeat. Invite a learner to the front. Ask *Where can we find a lorry?* The learner sticks the flashcard up on the street or the park picture. Repeat with the other flashcards.
- Take down the flashcards. Learners say each word.
- Give out the flashcards. Give instructions, e.g. *Put the tree in the park. Put the bus stop next to the shop.*

Pupil's Book, page 69

1 6.01 Listen and point. Then listen again and draw. What does Mrs Friendly like?

- Say *Open your Pupil's Books at page 69.*
- Indicate the caption and read it.
- Ask *Where's the house?* The class points. Ask *Is it old or new?* (*Old*) Repeat with different objects, e.g. *Where's the lorry? Is it old or new?* (*Old*) *What's this?* (*Bus stop*) *Where is it?* (*Next to the garden*) *What colour is the bus stop?* (*Blue*)
- Ask *Where's the tractor? Can you find it?* Learners find the picture and point (on the bridge).
- Play the audio. Learners point to the items in the picture.

Track 6.01

Today Jim and Jenny are at Bellevue Park.

Jim:	This is a beautiful park, Dad. Look at the old house with the garden in front of it.
Mrs Friendly:	Do you want to look at the flowers and trees?
Jenny:	No, Mum. It's got old cars, lorries and motorbikes.
Mrs Friendly:	Hmm.
Mr Friendly:	Oh, yes. That's nice.
Jim:	Look, Dad! It's got a small train too. Can we go on the train?
Mr Friendly:	I don't know. Hmm, it is a big park.
Mrs Friendly:	It's got a bus. Look – it's next to the blue bus stop.
Jim:	Yes, and the bus is next to the toyshop.
Mr Friendly:	Look, the park's got some animals too.
Mrs Friendly:	Oh, oh, yes. I don't like lorries, motorbikes or shops, but I like trees, flowers and animals.
All:	Aah!

- Ask *What does Mrs Friendly like?* Play the audio again. Learners complete the faces – a smile if she likes it and a frown if she doesn't. (*Trees, flowers and animals*)

2 6.02 Say the chant.

- Divide the learners into 11 pairs. Give each one a word from the chant to draw.
- Play the audio or video. Learners point and chant.
- Groups chant and hold up their pictures.

Track 6.02

Park, garden, flower, tree (x2)
Car, lorry, motorbike (x2)
Train and bus (x2)
Bus stop and toyshop (x2)

3 6.03 Listen and say *yes* or *no*.

- Focus on the picture. Ask questions, e.g. *What's this?* (*A train*) *Is it big or small?* (*Small*) *What colour is the lorry?* (*Blue*) Repeat for all items.
- Say *The motorbike is new.* Ask *OK?* (*No*) *Is the motorbike old or new?* (*Old*) Play the audio. Learners call out *Yes* or *No*.

Track 6.03

1 Is the park small?
2 Is the house new?
3 Has the park got flowers?
4 Has the house got a garden?
5 Has the park got a plane?
6 Is the bus stop next to the sho
7 Can they look at motorbikes?
8 Can they go to a bookshop?

Key: 1 no 2 no 3 yes 4 yes 5 no 6 no 7 yes 8 no

Activity Book, page 69

See pages TB120–132

Ending the lesson

- Say *We learnt about the park and the street.* Show the flashcards. Ask *Do you know the words?* Use self-assessment (see Introduction). Learners show how they feel.
- Say *We did listening and speaking. You can say the words well. Good work.*

1 6.01 **Listen and point. Then listen again and draw. What does Mrs Friendly like?**

2 6.02 **Say the chant.**

3 6.03 **Listen and say *yes* or *no*.**

The Friendly Farm
6.04
1
Jenny and Jim are at Bellevue Park with their mum and dad.
There are old cars and motorbikes there.
And animals.
2
There's a big lorry.
Is there? What's in it?
I don't know, but we can look.
3
Are there new animals?
I don't know, but I don't like it.
4
Cameron doesn't like it! There's a lorry and animals!
Animals! Are there new animals in the lorry?
We don't know.
5
It's OK everyone. There are young trees and flowers in the lorry. There aren't any new animals.
They're for Grandpa's new garden.
6
It's OK, Henrietta. There aren't any animals. There are flowers for Grandpa's new garden. I like flowers.

Learning outcomes By the end of the lesson, learners will be able to understand when they hear a conversation about things around us using *There is/are* and *There isn't/ aren't.*

New language *There is/are, There isn't/aren't, I don't know*

Recycled language adjectives, likes and dislikes, objects we see around us

Materials empty bowl, words on slips of paper (*train, motorbike, lorry, car, bus stop, garden, tree, shop, park, flower*), large sheets of paper and marker pens (one per group of four learners), thick string or sticky tape, boxes (one large box labelled *Shop*, two smaller boxes labelled *Car*, a tall box labelled *Bus stop*, two or three small boxes labelled *Tree*, a narrow box labelled *Motorbike*, three very small boxes labelled *Flowers*), flashcards of Jenny and Jim, Vehicles and places flashcards, audio, video

Key Competences

- Read and listen to a story.
- Role play a story.
- Order the events of a story using visual clues.

Warm-up

- Play 'Spelling bowl'. Put the words (*train, motorbike, lorry, car, bus stop, garden, tree, shop, park, flower*) in a bowl. Choose a learner to take out a paper and spell out the word, e.g. *G-A-R-D-E-N*.
- Put learners in groups and give each group a large piece of paper and a marker pen. They choose a group 'writer'. Read out the words one by one. The group spell the word for the writer.
- **SA** Use self-assessment techniques to check how well learners think they understand the vocabulary. See Introduction.

Presentation

- Create a street in the classroom. Say *Let's make a street*. Put down lines of sticky tape or long pieces of string to form a street on the floor. Say *Here's the street*. Show learners the cardboard box labelled *Shop*. A learner puts the shop box on the street. Say *There's a shop in the street*. Learners repeat. Continue with the other boxes.
- Point to the street. Ask, e.g. *Is there a shop? (Yes, there is.) Are there trees?* (*Yes, there are.*)
- Point to the cars. Ask *Are they new?* Shrug and say *I don't know*. Learners repeat. Ask *What colour is the bus stop?* Learners say *I don't know*.
- A few learners 'walk along the street' and describe, e.g. *There is a bus stop. There are trees.*

Pupil's Book, page 70

6.04 The Friendly Farm song

- Play the introductory song at the beginning of the farm cartoon story. Mime a happy face on the first two lines, do a thumbs up on the third line and mime waving at the animals on the fourth line. Learners listen and watch. Repeat. Learners listen, sing and copy the actions. Repeat.

Track 6.04

See The Friendly Farm song on page TB5

6.04 The Friendly Farm

- Say *Open your Pupil's Books at page 70*. Ask *Who can you see in the pictures?* Learners name the characters. Ask *What's this?* Point to the lorry. Ask *Is it big or small?* (*Big*) Point to the trees and flowers. Ask *What are these?*
- Ask *Where are Jenny and Jim? Are there new animals in the lorry? Are there trees and flowers in the lorry?* Write the questions on the board and put flashcards of Jenny, Jim, the lorry, the tree and the flower on the board. Say *Listen*. Play the audio or video. Learners listen and read.

Track 6.04

The Friendly Farm song + see cartoon on Pupil's Book page 70

- Learners answer the questions in pairs before the class check (*At Bellevue Park. No, there aren't. Yes, there are.*)
- Play the audio or video again. Pause after each frame and check comprehension by asking questions, e.g. Frame 1: *Are there animals at Bellevue Park?* (*Yes*) Frame 2: *Where's the lorry?* (*On the farm/street*) Frame 3: *Does Cameron like the lorry?* (*No*) Frame 4: *Are there animals in the lorry?* (*We don't know.*) Frame 5: *What's in the lorry?* (*Young trees and flowers*) Frame 6: *Are there any animals?* (*No*) *Is Gracie happy?* (*Yes*)
- Say *I don't know* and shrug to show this idea. Say *We don't know* and repeat the gesture. Play the audio or video again. Learners listen and shrug when *I/We don't know* is heard.
- Put learners into groups of six to role play the dialogue. Monitor and check.

Activity Book, page 70

See pages TB120–132

Ending the lesson

- **SA** Repeat the self-assessment technique used at the start of the lesson to see how well learners think they understand the vocabulary. Is there any change?
- Put flashcards onto the board in a 3 x 3 grid shape, spaced apart: *train, motorbike, lorry, car, bus stop, garden, tree, shop, flower*.
- Draw a grid shape around the flashcards. Point to each square. Learners say the word.
- Gradually remove the flashcards. Continue to drill and point to each space for learners to say the word.

Learning outcomes By the end of the lesson, learners will be able to use *There is/isn't/are/aren't* accurately to describe where objects are.

New language *Are there … ? / Is there … ?, There is/are/isn't/aren't …*

Recycled language classroom words

Materials small beanbag, Vehicles and places flashcards, In the classroom flashcards, building blocks, square pieces of paper, picture of a street scene, audio, digital Mission poster

Key Competences

- Learn to use *there is / isn't / are / aren't* accurately.
- Work together to play a game.
- Colour a picture based on the information given in a written text.
- Reflect on their own learning.
- Interact with the digital poster.

Warm-up

- Put flashcards on the floor. Learners take it in turns to throw a beanbag and say the flashcard it lands on.

Presentation

- Put a large square piece of paper on your desk. Say *This is a classroom*. Take some building blocks and put them onto the square on one side. Say *There is a board in the classroom*. Ask *How many boards?* (*One*) Say *There **is** a board*. Learners repeat.
- Add eight blocks in islands or lines. Say *There are desks in the classroom*. Ask *How many desks?* (*Eight*) Say *There **are** desks*. Learners repeat.
- Repeat with a cupboard, chairs, the door, windows.
- Ask *Are there any trees?* Say *There aren't any trees*. Learners repeat. Ask *Is there a car?* Say *No, there isn't a car*. Learners repeat. Repeat with *train* and *shops*.

Pupil's Book, page 71

6.05 Gracie's Grammar

- Say *Open your Pupil's Books at page 71*. Point to Gracie's Grammar box. Write the sentences on the board. Put four flashcards down the side of the board: car, lorries, train, shops. Say *There's a car*. Learners point to the car. Draw a tick next to the car. Say *There isn't a train*. Learners point to the train. Say *There **isn't** a train*. Take down the train flashcard. Repeat with the lorries and shops flashcards. Ask *Are there any animals?* (*No, there aren't.*)
- Read *There's a car. There isn't a train*. Ask *How many?* (*One*) Read *There are two lorries. There aren't any shops*. Ask *How many lorries?* (*Two*) Read *Are there any animals?* Underline the verbs.
- Play the audio. Pause for learners to repeat.

Track 6.05

See Pupil's Book page 71

1 6.06 Listen and stick. Then look, read and write.

- Play the audio for learners to point to the correct sticker.

Track 6.06

1 Jenny: Look at this photo of Bellevue Street!
Grandpa: Are there any cars?
Jenny: Yes, there are. They're in front of the toyshop.
2 Grandma: Is there a lorry?
Jim: Yes, there is. It's next to the cars.
3 Jim: There's a bus next to the bus stop.
Grandpa: Is it a new one?
Jim: No, it isn't. It's an old, blue one.
4 Jenny: There are two motorbikes too!
Grandma: Are they next to the bus stop?
Jim: No, they aren't. They're in front of the trees.

- Play the audio again. Learners stick in the stickers.
- Say *Look, read and write*. Learners complete the sentences.

Key: 2 There is 3 There is 4 There are

mission Stage 1

- Show learners the first stage of the digital Mission poster: 'Play a game'. Say *Let's play a game*.
- Set up chairs in the shape of a bus. Point to the first flashcard and say *Look! There's a motorbike*. Learners repeat. Choose learners at the front of the bus. Point for them to say *Look! There's a motorbike …* Say *and* as you point to the second flashcard. The learner says *and a lorry*. Learners repeat *Look! There's a motorbike and a lorry*. Continue with more and more flashcards. If learners can't remember the word, put them at the front of the bus and start again.

Activity Book, page 71

See pages TB120–132

Activity Book, page 68

- Say *Look at page 68 of your Activity Book*. Review *My unit goals*. Ask *How is your Mission?*
- Learners reflect and choose a smiley face for *My mission diary 1*. Monitor.

Ending the lesson

- **SA** Go back to Stage 1 on the digital Mission poster. Say *We played a game. Good work*. Add a tick to the 'Play a game' stage. Use self-assessment (see Introduction).
- Give out a completion sticker.

Language practice 1

6

6.05 Gracie's Grammar

There's a car. **There isn't** a train.

There are two lorries. **There aren't** any shops.

Are there any animals? Yes, **there are**. / No, **there aren't**.

1 6.06 Listen and stick. Then look, read and write.

1 There are some cars.

2 ______________ a lorry.

3 ______________ a bus.

4 ______________ two motorbikes.

mission STAGE 1

Play the bus game.

Look! There's a motorbike.

There's a motorbike and a lorry.

There's a motorbike, a lorry and a park!

STAGE 1

My mission diary
Activity Book page 68

Vocabulary 2 and song

1 Listen and act out the animals. Then sing the song.

6.07

We're all at the zoo.
Look at the animals ...
Bear, there's a bear.
Snake, there's a long snake.
There's a green crocodile.

Monkey, there's a monkey.
Tiger, there's a tiger.
There's a grey elephant.

Chorus

Lizard, there's a lizard.
Giraffe, there's a giraffe.
There are two polar bears.

Hippo, there's a hippo.
Zebra, there's a zebra.
There's a green crocodile.

Chorus

2 Play the game. Correct your friend.

There's a small bear.

No, there isn't. There's a big bear.

There's a red and yellow zebra.

No, there isn't. There's a black and white zebra.

There isn't a zoo in my town. Is there a zoo in your town?

Learning outcomes By the end of the lesson, learners will have practised the language through song.

New language *bear, crocodile, elephant, giraffe, hippo, lizard, monkey, polar bear, snake, tiger, zebra, zoo*

Recycled language *There is/are …*

Materials Zoo animals flashcards, flashcards of zoo, cat and dog, audio, video

Key Competences

- Learn new animal words through a song.
- Act out a song.
- Play a game in pairs to practise the new language.
- Complete a crossword puzzle.

Warm-up

- Show the flashcard of the zoo. Ask *Where is it?* Say *It's the zoo.* Learners repeat. Ask *What can we see at the zoo?* (*Animals*)
- Show the flashcard of the cat. Ask *Is there a cat at the zoo?* (*No*) Show the flashcard of the tiger. Ask *Is there a tiger at the zoo?* (*Yes*) Repeat with a dog and an elephant.
- **SA** Use self-assessment techniques to check how well learners think they understand the vocabulary. See Introduction.
- Learners sit (or stand) in a circle. Show the first flashcard to the first learner and say *This is a bear*. Repeat.
- The learner passes the flashcard clockwise to the next learner and says *This is a bear*. The learners continue to pass the flashcard until it has gone all the way round the circle.
- Continue with a couple more flashcards. When learners are confident, give a second flashcard to a learner to pass anti-clockwise at the same time as a flashcard going clockwise. The flashcards will cross in the middle.
- Once all the flashcards have gone around the circle, put them on the board. Point to each one. Learners say the word. Point again and show an action for each animal. Learners repeat and do the actions. (Actions: snake – wiggle your hand, bear – wiggle as if rubbing your back on a tree, crocodile – touch wrists and open your hands like a crocodile mouth, giraffe – pull hands apart to indicate a long neck, hippo – make a round shape by holding out arms and joining hands at the front like a wide jaw, lizard – hold your arms out and bent to the sides with hands flat like lizard feet moving, monkey – scratch under your armpits, tiger – snarl and hold up your hands like claws, zebra – toss your head like a mane and hold your hand behind like a swishing tail, polar bear – hold out hands like big paws in a swimming motion.)
- Point to the flashcards one by one. Learners say the words and do the actions.

Pupil's Book, page 72

1 6.07 Listen and act out the animals. Then sing the song.

- Say *Open your Pupil's Books at page 72*. Ask the names of the animals. Ask questions, e.g. *Where is the crocodile?* (*Next to the elephant*) *Is it blue?* (*No, it's green.*)
- Play the audio or video. Learners listen and do the actions.

Track 6.07

Rocky: I'm Rocky-Doodle-Doo and … here's our song for today: *Animals at the zoo*.

See song on Pupil's Book page 72

- Play the audio or video again. Learners listen, sing and do the actions. Monitor. Repeat the audio or video if necessary.
- Play the audio or video again. Learners repeat the song, doing actions first in small sections and then the whole song. Once they have practised the song, ask them to stand up and perform it.

6.08 **Extension** Once learners are confidently singing to the song, try singing the karaoke version as a class.

2 Play the game. Correct your friend.

- Point to the picture in Activity 1. Say *There's a small bear*. Encourage the learners to say *No, there isn't. There's a big bear.* Say *There's a red and yellow zebra.* (*No, there isn't. There's a black and white zebra.*)
- Put the class in pairs. Learners say sentences that are not correct. Their partner corrects them. Monitor and check.

Fast finishers Learners can write sentences about their own zoo, e.g. *In my zoo there is a big yellow snake. There is a tiger. There are two monkeys.*

- Show the picture of Rocky in the bottom right-hand corner. Read out the question. Encourage learners to call out their answers.

Activity Book, page 72

See pages TB120–132

Ending the lesson

- **SA** Repeat the self-assessment technique used at the start of the lesson to see how well learners think they understand the vocabulary. Is there any change?
- Learners stand or sit in a circle. Demonstrate the task: stand in the centre of the circle and do an animal action from the song. Learners call out the name of the animal.
- Choose a learner to stand in the middle and do an animal action. The learners call out the name. Continue until as many learners as possible have had a chance to go in the middle of the circle.

Learning outcomes By the end of the lesson, learners will be able to make suggestions and agree to suggestions.

New language *Let's … That's a good idea. / OK.*

Recycled language animals, *zoo*

Materials Zoo animals flashcards, coloured pens or pencils, eight playing-card-sized papers per learner, sticky tack (to put pictures on the wall), audio, video, digital Mission poster, buttons or counters

Key Competences

Learn to make and respond to suggestions.

Act out a dialogue.

Work together in groups to prepare a wildlife tour.

Reflect on their own learning.

Warm-up

- Draw an empty zoo map with spaces on the board. Stick up Zoo animals flashcards at the edge of the board. Say *Let's make a zoo.*
- Ask *Which animals shall we put in the zoo?* Learners point. Say *Let's have a (tiger) in the zoo*. Learners repeat. Say *A tiger. That's a good idea.* Learners repeat. Put the tiger flashcard in the zoo.
- Pick learners to come up and choose an animal. As they choose, encourage them to say *Let's have a/an (name of animal) in the zoo*. Learners respond *That's a good idea.*

Pupil's Book, page 73

1 6.09 Which game do they play? Listen and tick ✓.

- Say *Open your Pupil's Books at page 73*. Point to the first picture. Ask *What is it? (A frog)* Point to the second picture. Ask *What is it? (A car)* Point to the third picture. Ask *What is it? (Red)*
- Play the audio or video. Learners listen and tick the game they play. Check answers.

Track 6.09

Girl: Let's play a game.
Boy: OK. What would you like to play? Do you want to play 'Colour snap'?
Girl: No, let's play 'Animal snap'.
Boy: Ooh, yes. I like 'Animal snap'.
Girl: OK. Let's make our game.
Boy: That's a good idea.

Key: Picture 1 (Animal snap)

6.10 Gracie's Grammar

- Act out the sentences, demonstrating the request and response. Learners repeat.
- Divide the class into two. Half say the suggestions and the other half answer. Then reverse roles. Play the audio, pausing so learners can repeat the lines.

Track 6.10
See Pupil's Book page 73

2 Read and say the dialogue. Act it out.

- In pairs, learners read the dialogue a few times.
- Give out blank playing cards (four per learner). They draw two identical pictures of each animal.
- In groups of five, learners put their pictures together, mix them up and act out 'Animal snap'.

mission Stage 2

- Show learners the second stage of the digital Mission poster: 'Animals'.
- Show the Zoo animals flashcards and ask the names.
- Put learners into groups of three and give them four extra pieces of paper. Ask them to draw four animals and keep one each of the animal snap cards. They write the names under each animal. Get each group to set up a display.
- Give out a counter or button to each learner.
- Put two groups together. The first group show their display and say the names of the animals. The three learners in the second group each choose their favourite animal from the pictures and put down a counter on that animal. They say *Let's have (a monkey) on the tour*.
- Swap the groups over.
- Learners put away the animals not chosen for their tour and stick their three animals onto the wall with sticky tack. They stand near their pictures.
- Say *I'm going on a wildlife tour*. Walk around the room looking at the animals and pretending to take photos. As you pass, each group should tell you about their animals, e.g. *There is a monkey, a lizard and a snake*.
- Keep the pictures safe for Mission Stage 3 in a later lesson.

Activity Book, page 73

See pages TB120–132

Activity Book, page 68

- Say *Look at page 68 of your Activity Book*. Review *My unit goals*. Ask *How is your Mission?*
- Learners reflect and choose a smiley face for *My mission diary 2*. Monitor.

Ending the lesson

- SA Go back to Stage 2 on the digital Mission poster. Add a tick to the 'Animals' stage. Use self-assessment.
- Give out a completion sticker.

1 6.09 Which game do they play? Listen and tick ✓.

1

☐

2

☐

3

☐

6.10 Gracie's Grammar

Let's play a game.	That's a good idea.
Let's make our game.	OK.

2 Read and say the dialogue. Act it out.

A Let's make our game.
B Oh, yes. That's a good idea.
A Let's colour the elephants grey.
B OK. That's nice.

mission STAGE 2

Choose animals for your wildlife tour.

Let's look at the elephants.

OK. Let's look at the zebras too.

My mission diary
Activity Book page 68

Cross-curricular

Animals in the wild

1 Watch the video.

2 Tick ✓ the animals that live in the jungle.

3 Help the other animals get home.

Learning outcomes By the end of the lesson, learners will be able to talk about where animals live.

New language *whale, live, lives*

Recycled language animals, colours

Materials Zoo animals flashcards, pictures from Digital photo bank of a frog, a whale, jungle and grassland, flashcards of house, zoo, sea and cat

Key Competences

Learn to talk about where animals live.

Learn about animal habitats; Complete a classification activity.

Warm-up

- Split the learners into two groups and ask them to stand in two lines in front of you.
- Show a Zoo animal flashcard. The learners at the front of each line play. The first learner who names the animal correctly gets a flashcard. At the end of the game, the team with the most flashcards wins.
- Show the learners two new pictures: a frog and a whale. Ask *What's this?* Say *Frog*. Learners repeat. Say *Whale*. Learners repeat.

Pupil's Book, page 74

1 Watch the video.

- Say *Let's watch the video.* Learners watch the video about animals in the wild and answer the questions at the end of the video.

2 Tick ✓ the animals that live in the jungle.

- Put up flashcards of the house and the sea, and a picture of a jungle. Point to each one. Say the word. Learners repeat.
- Show the flashcard of the cat. Say *The cat lives here*. Point to the sea. Learners say *No*. Point to the jungle. Learners say *No*. Point to the house. Learners say *Yes*. Say *The cat lives in the house*. Learners repeat several times.
- Repeat using a picture of a whale and the flashcard of the tiger.
- Say *Open your Pupil's Books at page 74*. Focus on the photos of the animals. Ask *What is it?* Learners answer.
- Put learners into pairs. They tick the animals that live in a jungle.
- Check answers.

Key: 1 frog 2 snake 3 monkey

3 Help the other animals get home.

- Point to animals 1–3. For each one, ask *What is it?* (*Whale, polar bear, giraffe*)
- Ask *Where does it live?* Learners point.
- Say *Let's see*. Learners trace the maze and find out which animal lives in which place.
- Check answers by getting learners to point to the places.

Key: 1 whale – b sea 2 polar bear – c Arctic 3 giraffe – a grassland

Activity Book, page 74

See pages TB120–132

Ending the lesson

- Put a picture in each corner of the room: flashcards of sea and house, and pictures of jungle and grassland. Demonstrate the game. Stand in the middle of the room and close your eyes. Say *Go!* Learners run to one of the corners. Say the name of an animal, e.g. *Whale*. All the learners standing by the sea picture stay in the game. The rest sit down.
- Repeat with new animals until only one learner is left as the winner.
- Play a few times and then see how many points each learner has.

  Alternative The learners standing in the correct place get a point each time. Repeat a number of times. If you want, choose learners to come to the middle and call out the animal names (make sure they keep their eyes shut). At the end, check how many points each learner has.

Learning outcomes By the end of the lesson, learners will be able to read about animals, where they live and what they eat.

New language *boa, penguin, rhino, cold, hot, climb, drink, eat, swim*

Recycled language animals

Materials a ball, Zoo animals flashcards, large pieces of card, paper, coloured pens or pencils, Teacher's Resource Book page 64

Key Competences

- Read and write a description of an animal.
- Learn about different animal habitats.
- Work in groups to make a map of their wildlife park and present it to the rest of the class.
- Reflect on their own learning.
- Interact with the digital poster.

Warm-up

- Learners stand in a circle. Tell the learners to think of an animal name. Throw a ball to one of the learners and say *Frog*. The learner says *It's green* or *It lives in the jungle*.
- The learner throws the ball to another learner saying the name of another animal. They can say either the colour or the place where it lives. Ensure all learners have a turn.

Presentation

- Mime some action words and teach them: *climb, eat, drink*. Learners repeat and mime the words. Ask learners to think of some animals that can climb, e.g. *monkey, cat*. Ask them what different animals eat and drink, e.g. *Tigers eat meat*.
- Mime being hot. Say *I'm hot*. Learners repeat. Mime being cold. Say *I'm cold*. Learners repeat. Ask learners which animals live in a hot place.
- Show the flashcard of the monkey. Write sentence stems on the board:

  This is a …
  It lives in the …
  It is … in the jungle.
  It … trees.
  It … fruit.
- Ask learners to complete the sentences by pointing to the picture and miming. Learners write:

  This is a monkey.
  It lives in the jungle.
  It is hot in the jungle.
  It climbs trees.
  It eats fruit.

Pupil's Book, page 75

4 Read and write the animals.

- Say *Open your Pupil's Books at page 75*. Focus on the pictures. Ask the names of the animals (*rhino, frog, boa, penguin*). Point to each one and ask learners where they think each animal lives. Write their ideas up.
- Learners read the texts and write the animal names. Put learners into pairs to check their answers. Check with the whole class and see if the guesses about the places they live were correct.

  Fast finishers Learners can use the text as a model and write some sentences about one of the other animals.

Key: 1 penguin 2 boa

mission Stage 3

- Show the class the third stage of the Mission poster: 'Map'.
- Learners complete the worksheet task in the Teacher's Resource Book page 64 (see notes on TRB page 57).
- Alternatively, if you do not have the Teacher's Resource Book, divide the learners into groups of five and give each group a large piece of card. Write *Wildlife Park* on the board. Ask the learners to copy the title onto their card.
- Learners draw different areas, e.g. a jungle area / an area with grass / a water area / a cold area with ice. They stick each area onto their park.
- Give out pictures that learners drew in Stage 2 of the Mission. Learners choose one of their animal pictures, label the animal and stick it into the correct part of the park.
- Learners bring their wildlife park map to the front and present it to the rest of the class, e.g. *The monkeys are in the jungle. The penguins are here – it is cold.*

  Stronger learners Learners can write sentences on the map about the animal and its home.

  Extra support Learners can copy the name of their animal from the book.
- For ideas on monitoring and assessment, see Introduction.

Activity Book, page 75

See pages TB120–132

Activity Book, page 68

- Say *Look at page 68 of your Activity Book*. Review *My unit goals*. Ask *How is your Mission?*
- Learners reflect and choose a smiley face for *My mission diary 3*. Monitor.

Ending the lesson

- Go back to Stage 3 on the digital Mission poster. Add a tick to the 'Map' stage or invite a learner to do it. Use self-assessment (see Introduction).
- Give out a completion sticker.

4 Read and write the animals.

1 This animal lives in Antarctica. It lives near the sea. It can swim and it can eat fish and drink sea water. It's very cold in Antarctica. The animals stand together so they don't get cold. What is it?
It's a ____________________.

2 This animal lives in the hot jungle. It hasn't got any legs but it can climb trees. It eats birds, frogs and other small animals in the jungle. What is it?
It's a ____________________.

mission STAGE 3

Make a map of your wildlife park.
Put the animals in their habitats.

The monkeys are in the jungle.

My mission diary
Activity Book page 68

Literature

1 **Look at the pictures. Which animals can you see? Which is your favourite animal?**

6.11 When we go to the zoo

When we go to the zoo,
There are lots of things to see.
Tall giraffes with long thin necks,
Eating leaves from a tree.

Big grey elephants, swinging their trunks,
Looking for something to do.
But I really like the monkeys,
When we go to the zoo.

When we go to the zoo,
We watch the animals play.
Penguins jumping in a pool,
Eating fish all day.

Learning outcomes By the end of the lesson, learners will have read about a visit to the zoo and the animals you can see.

New language *bamboo, flamingo, jump, leaves, lion, play, roar, roll, scary, sleep, swing*

Materials Zoo animals flashcards, flashcard of zoo, pictures from Digital photo bank of a lion, flamingos, a panda with bamboo, a penguin

Key Competences

- Read about a visit to the zoo.
- Learn about zoos.
- Make their own zoo poem.

Warm-up

- Ask learners to think about a zoo. Put out four flashcards of animals (monkey, snake, tiger, frog). For each one, ask *What sound does a (monkey) make?* Learners make monkey noises. Repeat for each animal.
- Add some new flashcards to the pile (hippo, elephant, giraffe, crocodile, zebra, polar bear). Tell learners to look at the pictures for one minute and remember.
- Hide the flashcards. Give two minutes. In pairs, learners write down as many of the names as they can remember.
- Check how many each pair could write. Show the flashcards again one by one. Learners check to see if they remembered.

Presentation

- Say *We are going to read about the zoo*. Show the flashcard of the zoo. Then show a picture of a lion. Say *This is a lion*. Learners repeat the word. Ask *What sound does a lion make?* Make a roaring sound. Learners copy. Say *Lions roar*. Learners repeat. Mime sleeping. Say *And lions sleep*. Learners repeat and copy.
- Show a picture of flamingos. Ask *What are these?* Say *Flamingos*. Learners repeat the word. Say *Flamingos stand on one leg*. Stand on one leg. Learners repeat and copy.
- Show the flashcard of the elephant. Ask *What is it?* (*Elephant*) *What colour is it?* (*Grey*) Point to the trunk. Ask *What is it?* Say *Trunk*. Learners repeat. Swing your arm out in front of your face like a trunk and say *Elephants swing their trunks*. Learners copy and repeat.
- Go back to the previous pictures. As you point, learners say *Lions roar and sleep. Flamingos stand on one leg. Elephants swing their trunks.* They do the action or noise.
- Show a picture of a panda with bamboo. Ask *What is it?* Say *A panda*. Learners repeat. Say *Pandas roll*. Mime rolling. Learners repeat and copy. Point to the bamboo. Say *Pandas eat bamboo*. Mime eating a bamboo stick. Learners repeat and copy.
- Show a picture of a penguin. Ask *What is it?* (*Penguin*) *What colour is it?* (*Black and white*) Say *Penguins jump*. Mime jumping into water. Learners copy and repeat.
- Show the flashcard of the giraffe. Ask *What is it?* (*Giraffe*) *What colour is it?* (*Orange and brown*) Say *Giraffes eat leaves*. Mime eating leaves. Learners repeat and copy.
- Go back to the panda, penguin and giraffe pictures/ flashcard in turn, encouraging learners to repeat and do the actions.
- Repeat the words and actions for all the pictures and flashcards.

Pupil's Book, page 76

1 Look at the pictures. Which animals can you see? Which is your favourite animal?

- Say *Open your Pupil's Books at page 76*. Focus on the pictures. Learners say the names of the animals they can see.
- Use mime to teach the word *scary*.
- Put the learners into pairs. They tell their partner their favourite animal.

6.11 When we go to the zoo

- Look at each picture and ask questions: *What are they? What colour are they? Do they have long legs? Do they have a tail?* Learners name and describe each animal they can see.
- Say *Read and listen to the first part*. Show them verse 1. Play the audio. Learners listen and read. Pause the audio after the first picture to ask questions. *What are they?* (*They are giraffes.*) *What are they doing?* (*Eating leaves*)
- Continue telling learners to read and listen to each verse and pause after each verse to ask questions: *What are they?* (*They are elephants.*) *What are they doing?* (*Swinging their trunks*) *What are they?* (*They are penguins.*) *What are they doing?* (*Jumping*) *What are they?* (*They are tigers/crocodiles/lions.*) *What are they doing?* (*Sleeping/ Swimming/Roaring*) *What are they?* (*They are flamingos.*) *What are they doing?* (*Standing on one leg*) *What are they?* (*They are pandas.*) *What are they doing?* (*Rolling and eating bamboo*) *What are they?* (*They are monkeys.*) *What are they doing?* (*Playing and eating bananas*)

Track 6.11
See story on Pupil's Book pages 76–77

Activity Book, page 76

See pages TB120–132

Ending the lesson

- Learners work in pairs. They take it in turns to act as one of the animals in the poem, e.g. an elephant swinging its trunk. Their partner guesses which animal in the zoo they are acting out.

Learning outcomes By the end of the lesson, learners will have summarised a story, answered questions about it and understood how the writer feels by looking for clues.

New language *really love*

Recycled language adjectives, animals, *favourite*

Materials audio, coloured pens or pencils, Zoo animals flashcards, picture from Digital photo bank of panda, flashcards of park and beach, picture from Digital photo bank of cinema

Social and Emotional Skill: Understanding and expressing feelings

- After reading the story, ask *Which is the author's favourite animal?* (*Monkey*) *What does the author say?* (*I really like/love the monkeys when we go to the zoo.*) Choose three animals, e.g. lizard, giraffe, panda, and show the flashcards/picture. Point to the lizard and make a disgusted face. Say *I don't like lizards*. Draw a cross on the board. Learners repeat. Point to the giraffe and smile. Say *I like giraffes*. Draw a heart on the board. Learners repeat. Point to the panda and look very happy. Say *But I really love pandas*. Draw three hearts on the board. Say *Pandas are my favourite*. Learners repeat. If necessary, repeat with three more animals.
- Ask learners to look at the pictures on pages 76–77. Ask *Which is your favourite animal?* Ask volunteers to come to the front of the class and mime their favourite animal. Encourage learners to say *I really like* ... or *I really love* ... The rest of the class guesses the animal.

Key Competences

- Answer questions about a text.
- Think about the importance of respecting the animals.
- Work in pairs to ask and answer questions about the zoo.

Warm-up

- Call out the names of the animals in the story again, using summary sentences to describe what they are doing, e.g. *Giraffes eat leaves from the trees*. Learners act out the animal actions as in the previous lesson.
- Put learners into pairs. Ask them to act out the sentences. Their partner tries to remember the sentence and say it again. Monitor and support if they can't remember.
- Once the learners have tried different sentences, call learners to the front one by one to act out their sentences and encourage the rest of the class to say the sentences.
- **SA** Use self-assessment to check how well learners think they understand the vocabulary. See Introduction.

Presentation

- Draw a happy face emoticon on the board. Draw a sad face emoticon. Ask *How do you feel about the animals?*
- Show flashcards of different animals. Learners point to the emoticon showing their reaction. They say *I like (giraffes)* or *I don't like (giraffes)*.

Pupil's Book, page 77

2 Answer the questions.

- Say *Open your Pupil's Books at page 77*. Read Activity 2. Put the learners in pairs. They find the animals and count them. Check answers.
- Ask *Which is the author's favourite animal?* Check the meaning of *author*. Learners work in pairs. Check answers. Ask learners *Why?* Learners answer.

Key: 1 Nine animals (ten if you count fish)
2 Monkeys 3 Because the author says 'I really love the monkeys'.

3 Ask and answer.

- Choose a confident learner. Ask *Who do you go to the zoo with?* (e.g. *I go with my grandpa*.) Ask *What zoo animals do you love?* (e.g. *I love the zebras*.)
- Learners ask and answer in pairs.

Stronger learners Learners can give their own answers.

Extra support Learners can point to the pictures. Give them a sentence and the learner repeats.

Activity Book, page 77

See pages TB120–132

Ending the lesson

- **SA** Repeat the self-assessment technique used at the start of the lesson to see how well learners think they understand the vocabulary. Is there any change?
- Learners choose an animal and write three sentences about it, e.g. *I have a long neck. I eat leaves. I am orange and brown.*
- Put the learners into groups of five. They read their sentences. The other learners guess which animal they are.

Extra support Learners can be given gapped sentences on strips of paper with the name of the animal and they complete the sentences.

Fast finishers Learners can write their own sentences for two animals.

6

Tigers sleeping, crocodiles swimming,
And scary lions roaring too.
But I really like the monkeys,
When we go to the zoo.

When we go to the zoo,
There are lots of things that are fun.
Pink flamingos with long thin legs,
Standing on only one.

Black and white pandas rolling about,
Eating sticks of bamboo.
But I really love the monkeys,
When we go to the zoo.

2 Answer the questions.

1. How many animals are in the poem?
2. Which is the author's favourite animal?
3. How do you know?

3  Ask and answer.

Who do you go to the zoo with?

I go with my grandpa.

What zoo animals do you love?

I love the zebras.

1 Read and write the names of the animals.

mouse

snake

bird

monkey

frog

1 It's green and it likes water. _____frog_____
2 It's got a long body and it hasn't got legs. ______________
3 It lives in the trees and it's got a long tail. ______________
4 It's small and it's got a long tail. ______________
5 It's small and it can fly. ______________

2 Look at the picture in Activity 3. Say three things about the animals.

3 Read this. Choose a word from the box. Write the correct word next to numbers 1–3. There is one example.

body

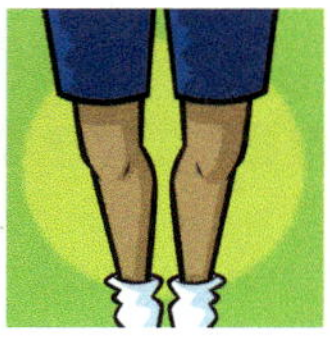

legs

meat

handbag

eyes

tablet

Tigers are very big cats! A tiger's _____body_____ and tail are orange and black. A tiger has got two (1)______________. It walks or runs on four (2)______________ and it eats (3)______________.

There are two extra words.

Learning outcomes By the end of the lesson, learners will have read to find out detailed information and written animal words accurately.

New language *bird, mouse/mice*

Recycled language adjectives, animals, colours

Materials pictures from Digital photo bank of a mouse and a bird, sticky notes with animal names written on them (one per learner), paper, coloured pens or pencils

Key Competences

Read to find out detailed information in a text; Practise activity types found in *Pre A1 Starters* exams.

Work in pairs to describe an animal.

Warm-up

- Play 'Hangman'. Draw a picture of a cliff dropping down to the sea. Draw a shark fin in the sea. Write the numbers *1–6* spaced out along the top of the cliff.
- Choose a word from the unit and write up a line for each letter in the word, e.g. *crocodile* would be _ _ _ _ _ _ _ _ _ .
- Learners call out letters. If they say a letter that is in the word, write it in the relevant space. If the letter is not in the word, tick one of the numbers, starting with *1*, at the top of the cliff.
- Learners try to fill in all the letters and guess the word before they reach *6* and lose.
- Write the letters they have said at the side of the board.
- **SA** Use self-assessment techniques to check how well learners think they understand the vocabulary. See Introduction.

Presentation

- Say *Let's do a reading exam*. Write *Reading Exam* on the board. Say *First look at the pictures. Then read and think.*
- Show a picture of a mouse and a picture of a bird. Point and ask *What is it?* (*Mouse/Bird*) Learners repeat. Teach the plural form *mice*. Ask *What colour is it?* (*White/Grey*) Ask *Can it fly?* Mime flapping wings. Say *Fly*. Learners repeat. Point to the mouse. Ask *Can it fly?* (*No*) Point to the bird and ask *Can it fly?* (*Yes*)
- Write two sentences on the board:
  1 *It's got a long tail and big ears.*
  2 *It hasn't got big ears.*
- Ask *Which animal is number 1?* (*Mouse*) *And 2?* (*Bird*)
- Underline the word *tail*. Say *The picture and the word 'tail' helped us answer.*

Pupil's Book, page 78

1 Read and write the names of the animals.

- Say *Open your Pupil's Books at page 78*. Say *Remember. First look at the pictures and then read.*
- Point to the pictures. Ask *What's this?* Learners say the words.
- Point to the sentences. Say *Look for the words that help.* Read number 1 out and the answer. Write on the board *It's green and it likes water*. Say *Look – 'green' and 'water' helped us answer.*
- Learners work in pairs and answer the questions.
- Check answers. Point to the words that helped: *2 long body, hasn't got legs, 3 trees, tail, 4 small, long tail, 5 small, fly.*

Key: 2 snake 3 monkey 4 mouse 5 bird

2 Look at the picture in Activity 3. Say three things about the animals.

- Learners work in pairs. Point to the large picture in Activity 3. Ask *What are they?* (*Tigers*) *How many legs have they got?* (*Four*) Say *Very good. Let's say more.*
- Learners work in pairs and say three more things about the tigers.

3 Read this. Choose a word from the box. Write the correct word next to numbers 1–3. There is one example.

- Show the learners the text under the tiger picture. Read the first two sentences. Point to the word *body* on the right. Show it again in the sentence. Say *Look at the pictures. Then write the word.*
- Point out the exam tip at the bottom of the page. Ask *How many words have you got?* Point to the potential answers. (*Six*) Point to the sentences. Ask *How many spaces?* Count with the learners, including the space for *body*. (*Four*) Say *Two words are wrong.*
- Say *Now write the correct words*. Learners read and write.
- Check answers.
- Say *Well done. You looked at the picture and found words that help. Good job!*

Key: 1 eyes 2 legs 3 meat

Activity Book, page 78

See pages TB120–132

Ending the lesson

- **SA** Repeat the self-assessment technique used at the start of the lesson to see how well learners think they understand the vocabulary. Is there any change?

Learning outcomes By the end of the lesson, learners will have revised the language in the unit and had a wildlife tour, suggesting where to go on the tour and giving information about the animals.

Recycled language unit language

Materials Zoo animals flashcards, hand-drawn map of a wildlife park (with fences and different areas, e.g. monkeys in an area with trees, crocodiles in a pool, elephants in an open area), paper, coloured pens or pencils, dice, counters

Key Competences

Revise vocabulary and language learnt in the unit.

Complete self-assessment tasks and reflect on their own learning.

Work in groups to act out their wildlife tour.

Warm-up

- Say *Let's play 'True or false'.*
- Show a line down the centre of the room and make one side 'True' and the other 'False'.
- Hold up a flashcard of an animal and say different things each time, e.g. its name, or colour, a description of its appearance or what it eats. If learners think it is true, they jump on the true side; if not, they jump on the false side, e.g. *It eats leaves* (showing a tiger – false).
- Repeat with learners talking about other animals.

Presentation

- Write on the board: *My wildlife tour*
- Show the map of the wildlife park that you have drawn. Say *Let's start at the monkeys. Next let's go to the elephants. Next let's go to the crocodiles.* As you explain, draw an arrow on the map.
- Show learners how to do the tour. Point to your own wildlife map. Go back to the beginning of your route. Say *Let's see the monkeys first. Monkeys have got long tails. They play games. Then let's go to the elephants. They are big and grey. They like water.*

Pupil's Book, page 79

mission in action!

Act out your wildlife tour.

- Put learners into groups of three or four. Use the wildlife park maps from Stage 3 of the Mission.
- Learners plan a route. They can draw arrows onto the map and make a list of the different animals in the order they will see them on the tour.
- Learners work in their groups and plan what to say about each animal. Two learners should take the role of different animals and act the actions and noises of each animal. One or two learners should explain the tour. In groups, learners practise their tour.
- Put each group of learners with a second group. Each group acts out their wildlife tour for the others. Encourage the learners who are watching to pretend to take photos.

  Extra support Learners write down a sentence about one of the animals. When they act out the tour, they can either play the role of the animal or read their sentence.

  Fast finishers Learners can add an extra animal at the end of the tour.
- Point to a picture in the unit. Say *Tell me about this animal.* Learners say, e.g. *It's a whale. It's grey. It lives in the sea.* Learners repeat the activity in pairs.
- For ideas on monitoring and assessment, see Introduction.

Self-assessment

- **SA** Say *Did you like our 'Act out a wildlife tour' Mission? Show me.* Say *Good?* (Demonstrate stretching your hand up high, mid-level or lower.) Learners show you.
- Say *Did you do better than the last Mission – Have a party? Better?* (move your hand up) *or not?* (move your hand down). Praise or say *OK. We can try again.*
- Say *Tell me things you can do now …* Learners suggest ideas (*We can say what we like. We can talk about animals.*)
- Say *Our next Mission is 'Have a sports day'.* Say *How can we do better? Tell me one thing the class will do better.* (e.g. *We can listen more carefully.*)

Activity Book, page 79

See pages TB120–132

Activity Book, page 68

- Say *Look at page 68 of your Activity Book.* Review *My unit goals.* Ask *How is your Mission?*
- Learners reflect and choose a smiley face for *My mission diary* the final stage. Monitor.
- Point to the sunflower. Learners read the 'can do' statements and tick them if they agree they have achieved them. They colour each leaf green if they are very confident or orange if they think they need more practice.
- Point to the word stack sign. Ask learners to spend a few minutes looking back at the unit and find a minimum of five new words they have learnt. They write the new words into their word stack. See Introduction for techniques and activities.

Ending the lesson

- Go back to the completion stage on the digital Mission poster. Add a tick or invite a learner to do it. Use self-assessment (see Introduction).
- Give out a completion sticker.
- Tell the learners *You have finished your Mission! Well done!*

mission in action!

Act out your wildlife tour.

My mission diary
Activity Book page 68

★ Design a tour around your wildlife park.

Let's see the monkeys first.

Then, let's go to the rhinos.

★ Plan what to say about the animals.

What can we say about the monkeys?

Let's talk about their habitat.

Good idea.

Let's talk about their food.

★ Act out a tour of your wildlife park.

This is a rhino. Rhinos are big and grey.

They live in grasslands.

COMPLETE

Review • • • Units 4–6

1 Watch the video and do the quiz.

2 6.12 Listen and follow. Draw lines.

It's – Kim's
a
big
flower
got
brown
cake.
birthday
She's
today.
He's
She's
wants
lizard
board game.
and
seven
a
She's
She
likes
robot
today.
wants
crocodile
white
polar bear
seven.
they
street
small
a

3 Talk to a partner. Find eight differences.

a

b

In picture A, there is an orange kite in the cupboard.

In picture B, the kite is green.

Learning outcomes By the end of the lesson, learners will have consolidated language from Units 4–6.

Recycled language offers, possessive pronouns and *'s*, toys, *want/wants, Does … want? Yes, he/she does. No, he/ she doesn't.*

Materials flashcards from Units 4–6, video, audio

Warm-up

- Show some Toys and Zoo animals flashcards. Ask learners *What is it? What colour is it? Tell me about it.* Learners describe them.
- Tell the learners to choose one of the toys or animals. Put them into groups of four. Each learner describes their chosen flashcard. Other learners try to guess which it is.

  Extra support You can give learners sentences describing one of the flashcards with the name written underneath. They can read the clues to their teammates.

  Fast finishers Learners can remember and describe more than one flashcard.

Pupil's Book, page 80

1 Watch the video and do the quiz.

- Show the video to learners.
- Ask learners to do the quiz. Check their answers to see how much the learners can remember.
- Repeat this at the end of the Review unit and compare the results to measure progress.

2 6.12 Listen and follow. Draw lines.

- Say *Open your Pupil's Books at page 80.* Point to the words in Activity 2. Ask *Which animal words can you see? (lizard, polar bear, crocodile) Which toys can you see? (board game)*
- Ask learners to work in pairs. Tell them to use the words and try to make sentences.
- Check ideas.
- Say *Listen and point. She wants a small white polar bear.* Learners point.
- Say *Good. Now listen and draw lines.* Show them the line between *It's* and *Kim's*.
- Play the audio. Learners complete the task.

  Track 6.12

  It's Kim's birthday today. She wants a small white polar bear and a board game. She's got a big brown cake. She's seven today. (x4)
- Learners compare their answers.
- Check answers with the class by asking the learners for each word and writing it up on the board so they can check the lines they have drawn.

3 Talk to a partner. Find eight differences.

- Ask learners to look at the pictures. Ask *Where is it? (A bedroom) Can you see a bed? (Yes) Can you see a table? (Yes) Are they the same? (Yes)*
- Ask *Where is the kite? (In the cupboard) What colour is it in the first picture? (Orange) What colour is it in the second picture? (Green) Are they the same? (No – they are different colours.)*
- Put learners into pairs. Say *Find the differences in the pictures. There are eight.*
- Learners work together and find the differences.
- Check answers.

Key: In picture A, there is a big teddy on the bed.
In picture B, the teddy is small.
In picture A, there are two long snakes under the table.
In picture B, the snakes are short.
In picture A, there are two giraffes in the car.
In picture B, there are two teddies in the car.
In picture A, there is a board game on the floor.
In picture B, there is a robot on the floor.
In picture A, there is a crocodile in the box.
In picture B, there is a lizard in the box.
In picture A, there is a poster of a banana on the wall.
In picture B, there is a poster of an apple on the wall.
In picture A, there is a train on the bookcase.
In picture B, there is a lorry on the bookcase.

- Put learners into pairs. Say *Look at the picture. What toy do you want?* Learners tell their partner.
- Check by asking learners to report back about their partner, e.g. *What does (Lucia) want? (She wants the crocodile.)*

Activity Book, page 80

See pages TB120–132

Ending the lesson

- Ask learners to think about the toys they have at home. Put them in pairs. Tell them to talk about their toys and find two toys they have that are the same and two toys that are different.
- Choose a confident learner to demonstrate. Say *I've got a teddy. It's white and brown. It's big. Have you got a teddy?* If the learner says *yes*, say *OK. We have both got a teddy. We've got the same toy.* If the learner says *no*, ask them to tell you about a toy they have got. Say *Oh, I haven't got (a train). OK. I have got a teddy and you have got a train. They're different.* Repeat until you have an example of two similar and two different toys.
- Learners talk in pairs.
- When they finish, select a few different pairs to report back.

Learning outcomes By the end of the lesson, learners will have consolidated language from Units 4–6.

Recycled language food, *Do you / Does she like … ?*, likes/dislikes

Materials flashcards from Units 4–6 (or real toys), audio

Warm-up

- Display a selection of real toys if possible or Toys 1 and 2 flashcards if not. Put learners into groups of three or four. Tell each group to choose a toy they want.
- Give the groups four minutes to write a description of the toy they want. The best description will win the toy.
- One learner from each group gives a description to win the toy for the rest of the lesson.
- Collect the toy at the end of the lesson.

Pupil's Book, page 81

4 6.13 Listen and draw. What do the children like?

- Say *Open your Pupil's Books at page 81*. Point to the table in Activity 4. Point to each picture in the heading row of the table. For each one, ask *What is it?* (*Mango, banana, bread, hamburger, chocolate, ice cream, water, chicken*)
- Draw on the board pictures of a smiley face and a frowning face. Say *Listen and point*. Say *I like mangoes, bananas, chocolate and chicken*. Learners point to the smiley face. Say *I don't like hamburgers or ice cream*.
- Say to the learners *Listen and draw a happy or sad face*.
- Play the audio for Alice. Pause and check answers.
- Play the rest of the audio.

Track 6.13

Alice
Boy: Hi, Alice. Do you like bread?
Alice: Yes, I do.
Boy: Do you like ice cream?
Alice: No, I don't.

Tom
Girl: Hi, Tom. Do you like burgers?
Tom: No, I don't, and I don't like chicken. I don't eat meat.
Girl: Do you like bananas?
Tom: Yes, and I like mangoes and water.

May
Boy: Hi, May. Do you like ice cream?
May: Yes, I do. My favourite is mango ice cream. I really like mangoes.
Boy: What other food do you like?
May: I like bread, burgers, chicken and chocolate.

Matt
Girl: Hi, Matt. Do you like water?
Matt: No.
Girl: Do you like bananas?
Matt: No, I don't.
Girl: Do you like mangoes?
Matt: Yuck, no.
Girl: What do you like?
Matt: I like burgers and chocolate! Yum!

- Ask *Which person eats very healthy food?* (*Tom*) *Which person eats food that is not healthy?* (*Matt*)
- Put learners into pairs. They draw an extra line at the in their notebooks. They interview each other and draw smiley or sad faces according to their partner's answers.

Key: Alice: ☺ bread ☹ ice cream; Tom: ☺ bananas, mangoes, water ☹ burgers, chicken; May: ☺ ice cream, mangoes, bread, burgers, chicken, chocolate; Matt: ☺ burgers, chocolate ☹ water, bananas, mangoes

5 Write about you.

- Say *Open your Pupil's Books at page 81*. Choose learners to read out the questions in Activity 5.
- Ask a different learner to answer one of the questions.
- In pairs, learners ask and answer the questions.
- When the learners have finished, they write their answers to the questions.

  Fast finishers Learners can ask more than one learner. (Pair fast finishers together.)

Activity Book, page 81

See pages TB120–132

Ending the lesson

- In groups of two or three, learners choose a famous person or character from a film or book they like.
- They create an 'ID' for the person they have chosen. Write some questions on the board to help them, e.g. *What's your name? How old are you? Have you got a bike/car? Have you got a pet? Do you like orange juice / water? What's your favourite food? What do you want for your birthday?*
- If they don't know some details, they can make them up.

  Extension Learners tell their descriptions to a different group without saying the name. The second group try to guess which person is being described.
- Repeat the video and quiz.

4 6.13 Listen and draw. What do the children like?

Alice								
Tom								
May								
Matt								

5 Write about you.

What's your name?

____

How old are you?

____

What's your teacher's name?

____

Have you got a bike?

____

Have you got a board game?

____

Do you like orange juice?

____

What's your favourite food?

____

What toy do you want for your birthday?

____

7 Let's play!

1 **Watch the video. Draw your hobby.**

mission Plan a sports day

In this unit I will:

1. Practise some activities.
2. Choose an activity.
3. Prepare a warm-up routine.
★ Act out the sports day.

Unit 7 learning outcomes

In Unit 7, learners learn to:

- talk about hobbies and activities
- understand, ask and talk about activities and actions using the present continuous tense
- ask for and understand permission using *can/can't*
- read to learn about a healthy lifestyle
- understand about a healthy lifestyle
- learn about helping friends

Materials video, item that represents your own hobby (e.g. book / walking boots / cooking implement), a ball, a paintbrush, a DVD, a musical instrument (e.g. guitar or recorder), four pictures from Digital photo bank (a child in a sports kit, a person with an easel, a person listening to music, a person at the cinema), sets of cards with letters (one set of three cards – letter *D*, letter *A* and letter *Y*; one set of six cards for each group of six learners: *S*, *P*, *O*, *R*, *T*, *S*), coloured pens or pencils, digital Mission poster

Key Competences

Become familiar with language related to hobbies.

Reflect on their own learning by going through the unit goals.

Draw a picture of their favourite hobby.

Self-assessment

- **SA** Say *Open your Pupil's Books at page 82*. Say *Look at the picture*. Ask *How many people are there?* (*Four*) Say *Point to blue/white/brown/pink*. Point to the skateboard, the football and the guitar. Ask *What is this?* Use self-assessment (see Introduction). Say *OK. Let's learn.*

Warm-up

- Show the item that represents a hobby you enjoy, e.g. a book. Say, e.g. *I like reading books. It's my hobby.* Check understanding of *hobby*. Say *hobby*. Clap on the stressed syllable. Learners repeat.
- Hold up a ball, a musical instrument, a paintbrush and a DVD. As you show each item, ask *What's this?* Say the word (*a ball, a guitar/recorder, a paintbrush, a film*).
- Display four pictures: a child in a sports kit, a person with an easel, a person listening to music, and a person at the cinema.
- Hold up the first item and ask *Whose ball is it?* Learners point to the picture of the child in the sports kit. Say *Yes – he/she likes sports. Football is his/her hobby*. Repeat for each item (instrument – person listening to music; paintbrush – person with easel; DVD – person in cinema).

Pupil's Book, page 82

1 Watch the video. Draw your hobby.

- Say *In this unit we're talking about hobbies and activities.* Say *Let's watch the video*. To introduce the topic of the unit, play the video.
- Say *Look at page 82*. Show the space on the page. Say *Let's draw a picture of your hobby.*
- Learners draw a picture of their hobby. Monitor and check. Tell each learner the name of their hobby.

  Fast finishers Learners can write a short sentence for their hobby, e.g. *Gaming is my hobby.*

  Extra support Learners can just repeat the name of their hobby when you monitor.

mission Plan a sports day

- Show the digital Mission poster. Say *We plan a sports day.*
- Say *Point to number 1*. Say *We practise some activities.* Mime running and throwing. Say *Number 1* and gesture for learners to repeat and copy.
- Say *Point to number 2*. Say *We choose an activity*. Mime thinking and deciding, as if choosing an activity. Learners copy. Say *Number 2* and gesture for them to copy. Say *One* and mime running and throwing; say *Two* and mime thinking and deciding. Repeat.
- Say *Point to number 3*. Say *We warm up*. Jump up and down. Learners copy. Say *Three* and repeat. Go through mimes 1–3, calling out the numbers for learners to mime.
- Say *Point to number 4*. Say with excitement *Let's have a sports day!* Mime winning a race, raising your arms and celebrating. Learners copy. Say *Four* and learners jump again. Repeat the whole sequence, the learners miming as you call out the numbers. Say *This is our Mission*.

Activity Book, page 82

My unit goals

- Go through the unit goals with the learners. You can read these or put them onto the board or a poster.
- You can go back to these unit goals at the end of each Mission stage during the unit and review them.
- Say *This is our Mission page*.

Ending the lesson

- Call three learners to the front. Give each one a letter card randomly (one is *D*, the second is *A*, the third is *Y*). Learners hold up the cards so everyone can see the letters. Ask the other learners which order they should stand in to create a word. The other learners tell them the order so that the cards create the word *DAY*.
- Divide the learners into groups of six. Give out the other letters cards (*S*, *P*, *O*, *R*, *T*, *S*) – one set to each group.
- Learners create a word by lining up and holding up their cards. The first group to order the cards correctly wins.

Learning outcomes By the end of the lesson, learners will be able to recognise and use words or phrases to describe sports and activities.

New language *music, play basketball/football/tennis, play the guitar/piano, ride a bike, sport, swim, watch TV*

Recycled language *I'm sorry, Let's ..., like*

Materials Sports and hobbies 1 flashcards, audio

Key Competences

- Identify and name sports and hobbies.
- Chant together as a class.
- Say a rhyme to practise the 's' sound.

Warm-up

- Write the words *Music* and *Sport* on the board. Mime playing the piano and ask *Music or sport?* (*Music*) Continue with other music and sport activity mimes.

Presentation

- Display the Sports 1 flashcards on the board in a line. Point and say the words, e.g. *Play tennis*. Learners repeat.

Pupil's Book, page 83

1 7.01 7.02 Listen and point. Then listen and number.

- Say *Open your Pupil's Books at page 83. Look at the picture.*
- Indicate the caption. Read it.
- Ask *Where's the person swimming?* The class points. Repeat with different activities.
- Play Track 7.01. Learners point to the activities.

Tracks 7.01 and 7.02

This morning the children are at the Community Centre.

(1) Eva:	Let's play tennis. Tennis is fun.
(2) Jenny:	Oh, no. I want to play football. Football is my favourite.
(3) Eva:	OK, not tennis or football. Let's play basketball. Basketball's nice.
(4) Tom:	Basketball's nice, but ... let's ride our bikes.
(5) Jim:	Hmm. Sport's fine, but what about music? I want to play the piano.
(6) Jim:	... or let's play the guitar.
(7) Jenny:	Ugh! No, thank you. I'd like to swim.
Mr Friendly:	Oh dear! I'm sorry, kids. The Community Centre isn't open today.
Jim:	Oh, no! It's closed.
Tom, Jenny, Eva:	Closed?
(8) Tom:	Don't worry. Let's watch television. Let's watch sport on television.
Mr Friendly:	I know. Let's go to the farm. Would you like to ride Harry?
Tom:	Oh, great. Yes, please. Let's go now.

- Ask *Where do they go? Why?* Play Track 7.01 again. Ask *Where do they go?* (*The farm*) *Why?* (*To ride Harry because the Community Centre is closed*)
- Display the Sports and hobbies 1 flashcards on the board and number them *1–10*. Say *Look at page 83*. Indicate the spaces next to the words and show the example. Quickly take down the flashcards.
- Say *Listen and write*. Play Track 7.02. Learners number the activities *1–8*. Monitor.
- Ask *Number 1?* (*Play tennis*) Put the flashcard back up over number *1*. Continue until the sequence is rebuilt.

Key: 1 play tennis 2 play football 3 play basketball 4 ride a bike 5 play the piano 6 play the guitar 7 swim 8 watch television

2 7.03 Say the chant.

- Play the audio or video and do the actions: 1 watching TV and changing channels, 2 kicking a football / throwing a ball into a basketball net / hitting a tennis ball, 3 playing a guitar, playing the piano, 4 swimming, riding a bike.
- Repeat the audio or video. Learners chant and mime.
- Divide the class into two. Play the audio or video. The first group chants and the second group mimes. Then swap.

Track 7.03

Watch, watch, watch
Watch television (x2)

Play, play, play
Football, basketball, tennis (x2)

Play, play, play
The guitar, the piano (x2)

Swim, swim, swim
Ride a bike, ride a bike (x2)

3 7.04 Listen and say the activity.

- Play the audio and pause for learners to complete the sentences.

Track 7.04

1	Jim:	Let's play ...	5	Jim:	I want to ...
2	Jenny:	I want to play ...	6	Jim:	Let's ...
3	Eva:	Let's play ...	7	Jenny:	I'd like to ...
4	Tom:	Let's ...	8	Tom:	Let's ...

Key: 1 tennis 2 football 3 basketball 4 ride our bikes 5 play the piano 6 play the guitar 7 swim 8 watch sports on television

Activity Book, page 83

See pages TB120–132

Ending the lesson

- SA Say *We learnt about sport and hobbies*. Show the flashcards. Ask *Do you know the words?* Use the self-assessment technique (see Introduction). Learners show how they feel.
- Say *You can say the words well. Good work.*

Vocabulary 1

7

1 7.01 7.02 Listen and point. Then listen and number.

2 7.03 Say the chant.

3 7.04 Listen and say the activity.

The Friendly Farm

7.05

Learning outcomes By the end of the lesson, learners will be able to understand the present continuous tense to describe actions happening at the moment of speaking.

New language *clean, eat, paint, sing, I am …-ing, You/We/They are …-ing, He/She is …-ing, Are you/we/they …-ing? Is he/she …-ing? Yes, they are. / Yes, he/she is. What are you doing?*

Recycled language words and phrases describing sports and activities

Materials pictures from Digital photo bank of people doing activities in groups or pairs (*eating, singing, cleaning, playing tennis*), Sports and hobbies 1 flashcards, audio, video, slips of paper with activities written on them (optional)

Key Competences

Read and listen to a story; Identify the present continuous to talk about what someone is doing

Role play a story.

Warm-up

- Learners sit in two lines facing each other, with chairs touching, or feet touching if seated on the floor.
- Show each pair of learners who are facing each other a Sports and hobbies 1 flashcard, e.g. riding a bike. Go down the line and show each pair a different flashcard.
- Call out the activities. When learners hear their activity, they walk up between the other pairs. At the end of the line, they run around the back to their places. The first one back wins a point.
- **SA** Use self-assessment to check how well learners think they understand the vocabulary. See Introduction.

Presentation

- Mime eating. Say *I'm eating*. Learners mime and repeat. Act singing. Say *I'm singing*. Learners copy and repeat. Repeat the sequence with painting and playing tennis.
- Show the learners Sports and hobbies 1 flashcards, e.g. playing tennis. Ask *What is she doing?* (*She's playing tennis.*) Repeat with different flashcards.
- Point to the flashcards and ask *Is he/she playing tennis?* (*Yes, he/she is.*) Repeat with different flashcards.
- Select a learner to come to the front. They mime an activity, e.g. swimming. Ask *What's he/she doing?* (*He's/She's swimming.*) Ask *Is he/she painting?* (*No, he/she isn't.*) Repeat with different learners.
- Put up pictures of people doing activities in pairs or groups (eating / singing / cleaning / playing table tennis). Ask *What are they doing?* Point to a picture. Say *They're* (*singing*). Learners repeat.

Pupil's Book, page 84

7.05 The Friendly Farm song

- Play the introductory song at the beginning of the cartoon story. Learners listen. Repeat. Learners listen and sing. As they do, clap hands quickly twice each time the word *Friendly* appears. Repeat the song. Learners sing and clap.

Track 7.05

See The Friendly Farm song on page TB5

7.05 The Friendly Farm

- Say *Open your Pupil's Books at page 84*. Ask *Who can you see in the pictures?* Learners name the characters. Ask *What is Tom doing?* Point to Tom (*Riding a horse*). Repeat with Rocky's brother and sister (*swimming and singing*) and Gracie (*eating*).
- Ask *Who is cleaning?* Write the question on the board. Play the audio or video. Learners listen and read.

Track 7.05

The Friendly Farm song + see cartoon on Pupil's Book page 84

- Learners check answers in pairs. (*Henrietta is cleaning.*) Ask *Is she singing?* (*No – she's cleaning.*)
- Play the audio or video again. Pause after each frame and check comprehension. Frame 1: *What's Cameron doing?* (*He's watching Tom.*) Frame 2: *What are Rocky's brother and sister doing?* (*They're swimming and singing.*) Frame 3: *What's Gracie eating?* (*She's eating a sock.*) Frame 4: *Is Shelly painting her feet?* (*Yes, she is.*) Frame 5: *Is Rocky playing table tennis?* (*No, he isn't.*) Frame 6: *Who's riding a horse?* (*Rocky*)
- Play the audio or video again. Divide the class into groups and give each group a role from the cartoon. Learners repeat the speech bubbles for their character.

Fast finishers Learners can say which activities they like and don't like, e.g. *Swimming is nice. I don't like cleaning.*

Extra support Learners can read their dialogue.

Activity Book, page 84

See pages TB120–132

Ending the lesson

- **SA** Repeat the self-assessment technique used at the start of the lesson to see how well learners think they understand the vocabulary. Is there any change?
- Place flashcards of activities from this lesson on the floor like a winding river. Say *It's a river*. Show a picture of a river. Say *Let's cross the river.*
- Choose a learner to stand at the beginning of the river. The other learners watch and answer. Point to the first flashcard and ask a question, e.g. *Is he watching television?* If the learners answer correctly, the learner crossing the river can step on the first flashcard. Continue to ask questions about the flashcards, e.g. *What is he doing? Is she eating pasta?*

7 Language practice 1

Learning outcomes By the end of the lesson, learners will be able to ask and answer questions using the present continuous.

New language *What is he/she doing? What are you doing? I am …-ing. / You are …-ing.*

Recycled language family, sports

Materials pictures of people doing activities in groups or pairs (*eating, singing, cleaning, playing table tennis*), Sports and hobbies 1 flashcards, coloured pens or pencils, pictures of sports days, digital Mission poster

Key Competences

- Learn to ask and answer questions using the present continuous.
- Work together to play a guessing game.
- Reflect on their own learning.
- Interact with the digital poster.

Warm-up

- Play 'Noughts and crosses'. Put a grid on the board, three by three (nine squares). Divide learners into two groups and assign them noughts or crosses. Put a flashcard of an activity in each square. To win their square, the learners have to say what the person in the picture is doing, e.g. *He's eating*. When they get a sentence correct, replace the flashcard with their symbol. The first group to make a row, horizontally, vertically or diagonally, wins.

Presentation

- Show a selection of flashcards from the previous lesson. Encourage learners to make sentences, e.g. *He's playing basketball. They're singing.* Write them on the board
- Underline the pronoun, e.g. *He*, the auxiliary verb, e.g. *is*, and the *–ing* at the end of the verb. Write a question mark under each sentence. Say *Let's make a question*. Give the opening of the question and encourage the learners to finish it, e.g. *Is he* … (*playing basketball?*) (*Yes, he is.*) Draw a line from the *is* in the question to the *is* in the answer. Repeat with other questions.

Pupil's Book, page 85

7.06 Gracie's Grammar

- Say *Open your Pupil's Books at page 85*. Point to Gracie's Grammar box. Write the same sentences on the board.
- Play the audio. Pause for learners to repeat each sentence.

Track 7.06
See Pupil's Book page 85

- Rub out the words *are*, *'m* and *'s* in each sentence and draw a line in the space. Learners tell you what to write.

1 7.07 Listen and stick. Then look, read and write.

- Learners look at the four stickers. They do not stick them in yet. Ask them to predict what each person might be doing, e.g. *What's Grandpa doing?*
- Play the audio for learners to point to the correct sticker.

Track 7.07

1 Jim: What's Grandpa doing?
Jenny: He's listening to music.

2 Jim: What's Dad doing?
Jenny: He's reading his book.

3 Jenny: What's Mum doing?
Jim: She's playing the guitar.

4 Jenny: What's Grandma doing?
Jim: She's watching television.

- Play the audio again. Learners stick in the stickers.
- Check answers.
- Say *Look at the sentences*. Point to sentences 1–4. Show the spaces in the sentences. Say *Look, read and write*. Monitor as the learners write.

Key: 2 Dad's reading his book. 3 Mum's playing the guitar. 4 Grandma's watching television.

mission Stage 1

- Show learners the first stage of the digital Mission poster: 'Practise'. Say *Let's practise an activity*.
- Show the class pictures of sports days. Ask the names of the activities.
- Put the learners into pairs. Say *My favourite activity is (running)*. Learners work in pairs and tell their partner their favourite activity.
- Mime an activity, e.g. playing basketball. Encourage learners to say *You're playing basketball*.
- Put the learners into groups of five. Ask each learner to choose an activity. Learners take it in turns to mime their activity. The group guess what it is.
- For ideas on monitoring and assessment, see Introduction.

Activity Book, page 85

See pages TB120–132

Activity Book, page 82

- Say *Look at page 82 of your Activity Book*. Review *My unit goals*. Ask *How is your Mission?*
- Learners reflect and choose a smiley face for *My mission diary 1*. Monitor.

Ending the lesson

- **SA** Go back to Stage 1 on the digital Mission poster. Say *We practised an activity. Good work*. Add a tick to the 'Practise' stage. Use self-assessment (see Introduction).
- Give out a completion sticker.

7.06 Gracie's Grammar

What **are** you do**ing**? | I**'m** rid**ing** a horse.

What**'s** she do**ing**? | She**'s** swimm**ing**.

Are they clean**ing** the car? | Yes, they **are**. / No, they **aren't**.

1 7.07 Listen and stick. Then look, read and write.

1 Grandpa 's listening to music.

2 Dad ______________________.

3 Mum ______________________.

4 Grandma ______________________.

mission STAGE 1

Practise some activities for your sports day.

- Play the game. Act out an activity.
- Your friends say what you're doing.

What am I doing?

You're swimming.

My mission diary
Activity Book page 82

Vocabulary 2 and song

1 7.08 Listen and number. Then sing the song.

They're playing basketball, basketball.
He is [1]throwing.
She is [2]catching.
They're playing baseball with a small white ball.
They're playing baseball. They're playing baseball.

They're playing [3]badminton.
He's [4]riding his skateboard.
He's playing [5]hockey.
He's [6]hitting a small ball.

She's running. She's [7]running.
She's running in the park. ...

They're playing football with a big football.
Are they kicking? Yes, they're [8]kicking.
We're playing basketball, basketball.
We are throwing. We are catching.

We're playing basketball. ...

2 7.10 Listen and say what they're doing.

Learning outcomes By the end of the lesson, learners will have practised the language through song.

New language *badminton, catching, hitting, hockey, riding (his) skateboard, running, throwing*

Recycled language adjectives (*big/small*), colours, present continuous

Materials flashcards of badminton, skateboarding and hockey, audio, video, a simple drawing of, e.g. an apple, paper, coloured pens or pencils, card with frowning face on it, blank cards (20 per group of three learners)

Key Competences

- Learn new sports vocabulary through a song.
- Sing and act out a song.
- Colour a picture based on verbal information.

Warm-up

- Show flashcards of badminton, skateboarding and hockey. Point to the first flashcard. Say, e.g. *Badminton*. Learners repeat. Continue with the other flashcards.
- Stick the three flashcards on different sides of the classroom. Choose five learners to come to the front. Say *Jump to the picture of badminton*. Learners jump to the correct picture.
- Say *Run to the picture of skateboarding*. Learners run.
- Say *Walk to the picture of hockey*. Learners walk.
- Repeat with a new group of learners and verbs.
- SA Use self-assessment to check how well learners think they understand the vocabulary. See Introduction.

Pupil's Book, page 86

1 7.08 Listen and number. Then sing the song.

- Say *Open your Pupil's Books at page 86*. Say *Find someone playing hockey*. Learners point. Repeat with *basketball, baseball, skateboarding* and *football*.
- Say *Find someone kicking*. Learners point. Mime kicking. Ask *What am I doing?* (*Kicking*) Repeat with *hitting* and *throwing*.
- Say *He's throwing. Point to the picture.* Learners point. Say *Look*. Point and show learners number 1 is written by the boy throwing the ball. Say *Let's listen and write the numbers.*
- Play the audio or video. Learners listen and write numbers in the boxes.

Track 7.08

Rocky: I'm Rocky-Doodle-Doo and … here's our song for today: *Doing our favourite sports.*

See song on Pupil's Book page 86

- Check answers.
- Learners stand up. Say each activity that appears in the song and mime the activity, e.g. mime throwing a ball into a basketball, throwing a ball, catching one, swinging a bat for a baseball. Learners repeat and mime.
- Play the audio or video again. Learners listen and sing.
- Repeat the audio. Learners sing and mime.
- Divide the class into three groups. Give each group a different part of the song. They sing and mime again, but only their part.

7.09 **Extension** Once learners are confidently singing along to the song, try singing the karaoke version as a class.

2 7.10 Listen and say what they're doing.

- Say *Let's listen*. Play the first item on the audio. Pause and ask *What's he doing?* Learners say *He's running*. Say *Yes. He's running. Let's listen again.*

Track 7.10

1 [running]
2 [playing basketball]
3 [playing hockey]
4 [playing baseball]
5 [riding a skateboard]
6 [playing football]
7 [playing badminton]

- Play the rest of the audio.

Key: 1 running 2 playing basketball 3 playing hockey 4 playing baseball 5 riding a skateboard 6 playing football 7 playing badminton

Activity Book, page 86

See pages TB120–132

Ending the lesson

- SA Repeat the self-assessment technique used at the start of the lesson to see how well learners think they understand the vocabulary. Is there any change?
- Learners stand in a circle. Hold up a card with a frowning face on it. Look at the picture and make a disgusted face. Pretend to give it away. The aim is to give away the frowning face. Say *Throw a ball*. Mime throwing a ball. Ask *OK?* Learners say *Yes, OK*. Say *My sentence is good. I can give this away.* Give the card to a learner.
- Say an activity. If the learner mimes correctly, they can pass on the frowning face picture. Keep going around the circle until all the learners have mimed an activity. (Example instructions: *kick a ball, hit a ball, catch a ball, run to the middle, jump up and down, put your hands up.*)
- Put learners into groups of three. Give them blank cards – 20 per group. Slowly read out activity verbs: *kick, jump, run, play, catch*. As you say each word, the learners write them down, one letter per card (e.g. *R – U – N* would be on three cards). Check their cards and correct.
- Now ask the learners to mix up the cards. Tell them to remember and reassemble the words. The first group to rebuild the five words is the winner.

Learning outcomes By the end of the lesson, learners will be able to ask permission and understand if they can or can't do something.

New language *Can we play tennis? Yes, you can. No, you can't. bat, tennis racket*

Recycled language activities, places

Materials skateboard flashcard, a toy car or ball (optional), four pictures from Digital photo bank: a flat road with low hills, a cliff, the edge of a river, a skate park, Sports and hobbies 2 flashcards, audio, video, coloured pens or pencils, sports caps or flags (optional), digital Mission poster

Key Competences

- Learn and practise *can* for permission.
- Act out a dialogue.
- Work in groups to choose the activities for their sports day.
- Interact with the digital poster.

Warm-up

- Learners draw three things they like doing. In pairs, they look at the pictures and guess what their partner likes.

Presentation

- Put up the pictures of a flat road with low hills, a cliff, the edge of a river, and a skate park. Show the flashcard of the skateboard. Point to each picture and ask *Can I skateboard here? (Yes, you can. / No, you can't.)*

Pupil's Book, page 87

1 (7.11) Which sport do they play? Listen and tick ✓.

- Say *Open your Pupil's Books at page 87. Let's listen and tick.*
- Use the artwork to teach *bat* and *tennis racket*.
- Play the audio or video. Learners listen and tick the correct sport. Check answers.

Track 7.11

Jenny:	Dad! Can we play baseball?
Mr Friendly:	No, sorry. We haven't got a baseball bat.
Jenny:	We've got tennis rackets. Can we play tennis?
Mr Friendly:	Yes, you can. But you can't play here. The garden's too small.
Jim:	Can we go to the sports centre, please?
Mr Friendly:	That's a good idea, Jim. Let's go to the sports centre.
Jenny:	Great! We can all play tennis at the sports centre.

Key: Picture 3 (tennis)

(7.12) Gracie's Grammar

- Say *Look at Gracie's Grammar*. Play the audio. Learners repeat the two sentences in the grammar box.
- Write the sentences on the board, but leave out the words *can* and *can't*. Play the audio again. Ask learners which words go into the spaces and write them in.

Track 7.12
See Pupil's Book page 87

2 Read and say the dialogue. Act it out.

- Say *Look at Activity 2.*
- Act out the sentences. Learners repeat.
- Divide the class into two: A and B. Play the audio, pausing so learners can repeat the lines of their character.
- Put the learners into pairs.
- Each pair reads the dialogue a few times. Correct pronunciation.
- Pairs cover the dialogue and act it out.

mission Stage 2

- Show learners the second stage of the digital Mission poster: 'Choose an activity'.
- Show learners Sports and hobbies 2 flashcards and ask them the names.
- Put learners into groups of four. They write four activities. Choose one learner from each group to be the 'sports captain'. If you have sports caps or flags, give them out to each captain. Spread the captains around the room.
- Ask the other learners to think of two activities or sports they would like to do on a sports day. Demonstrate going around the room and asking the captains questions, e.g. *Can I play football at your sports day?* The captains say *Yes, you can* or *No, you can't*. The captain can only say *Yes* if the sport is one of the four activities the group wrote. They note who liked their activities and report back at the end, e.g. *Paolo can play tennis and swim in our sports day*.
- Learners mingle and ask about sports.
- For ideas on monitoring and assessment, see Introduction.

Activity Book, page 87

See pages TB120–132

Activity Book, page 82

- Say *Look at page 82 of your Activity Book*. Review *My unit goals*. Ask *How is your Mission?*
- Learners reflect and choose a smiley face for *My mission diary 2*. Monitor.

Ending the lesson

- **SA** Go back to Stage 2 on the digital Mission poster. Add a tick to the 'Choose?' stage. Use self-assessment (see Introduction).
- Give out a completion sticker.

1 7.11 Which sport do they play? Listen and tick ✓.

1

☐

2

☐

3

☐

7.12 Gracie's Grammar

Can we **play** tennis? Yes, you **can**, but you **can't play** here.

2 Read and say the dialogue. Act it out.

A Mum! Can we play **football**?

B Yes, you can, but you can't play in the **garden**.

A Can we go to the **park**, please?

B That's a good idea. Let's go to the **park**.

A Great. We can all play **football** in the **park**.

mission STAGE 2

Choose activities for your sports day.

Can I play hockey?

Yes, you can.

My mission diary
Activity Book page 82

Cross-curricular

Look after your body!

1 **Watch the video.**

2 **Look and write.**

stretch your arms stretch your legs ~~stretch your body~~ run jump

a

stretch your body

b

____

c

____

d

____

e

1
____

3 7.13 **Listen and number the pictures. Listen again and do the warm-up.**

Learning outcomes By the end of the lesson, learners will be able to understand more about the body and use words to describe it.

New language *stretch*

Recycled language verbs of movement

Materials flashcards of classroom, living room and park, video, some phrases on slips of paper (e.g. *eating an apple*, *playing football*, *riding a horse*), blank slips of paper, a soft ball or screwed up ball of paper, a waste paper bin, audio

Key Competences

- Learn and use expressions to talk about physical exercises.
- Do a matching activity based on verbal clues.
- Play a miming game.

Warm-up

- Put up three flashcards of places: a classroom, a living room and a park.
- Ask the learners to work in pairs and think of things they can do in the different places. Give them an example, e.g. *I can ride my bike in the park*.
- Give them three minutes to think of at least two things they can do in each place.
- Check their ideas.
- Point to different parts of your body (arms, legs, head, hands, eyes, nose, ears). Learners say the correct words.
- Say *Let's stretch our arms*. Stretch up to the ceiling. Say *Stretch*. Learners copy and repeat.
- Say *Now let's jump*. Jump up and down. Say *Jump*. Learners copy and repeat.

Pupil's Book, page 88

1 Watch the video.

- Say *Let's watch the video*. Learners watch the video about looking after your body and answer the questions at the end of the video.

2 Look and write.

- Look at the pictures. Say *Look at picture a*. Point to the phrases. Encourage learners to say *Stretch your body*. Point out the example phrase under the picture.
- Learners continue to match the phrases with the pictures. Monitor and check.
- Put learners into pairs to compare answers.
- Check answers with the whole group. When you say the phrases, learners repeat.
- Ask the learners to stand up. Say *Stretch your body* and stretch on the spot. Learners copy and repeat.
- Say the other phrases from the activity. Learners repeat and do the action.

Key: b stretch your legs c jump d stretch your arms e run

3 7.13 Listen and number the pictures. Listen again and do the warm-up.

- Play the audio. Learners work in pairs and match the pictures to the exercises.

Track 7.13

OK, everybody, it's time to warm up! Let's run in a big circle. Now let's jump.
OK, now it's time to stretch. Stretch one arm … Stretch the other arm … Stretch two arms … Good.
OK, now we stretch our legs. Can you touch your toes? Good, we're stretching our legs.
Now let's stretch our bodies. Yes, that's right, a nice big stretch. Well done, everybody. Now we're ready to do some sport!

- Check answers.
- Play the audio again. Learners do the actions.

Key: a 5 b 4 c 2 d 3 e (1)

Activity Book, page 88

See pages TB120–132

Ending the lesson

- Use a soft ball or a piece of paper screwed up into a ball. Take out your phrases written on slips of paper, e.g. *eating an apple*, *playing football*, *riding a horse*.
- Divide the learners into two groups: A and B.
- Invite a learner from group A to the front. Show him/her a slip of paper. The learner mimes the action. Other learners from group A call out what the learner is miming, e.g. *You're eating an apple*.
- Give the ball to group A and see if they can throw it into the waste paper basket. If they do, give them one point. They must give the correct sentence and get the ball into the bin to get a point.
- Repeat with group B.
- Continue to play until the phrases have all been used.

Learning outcomes By the end of the lesson, learners will be able to read and understand about being healthy.

New language *bones, diet, exercise, healthy, muscles, strong, sun cream, vitamin*

Recycled language verbs of movement

Materials picture from Digital photo bank of a skeleton, Food flashcards, large copies of the reading text or cut up copies of the text (optional)

Key Competences

- Read a text.
- Learn about healthy habits.
- Work in groups to prepare a warm-up routine.
- Reflect on their own learning.
- Interact with the digital poster.

Warm-up

- Choose four learners to come to the front. Say *Let's exercise*. Act out moving and jumping. Say *I'm doing exercise*. Check understanding. Learners repeat.
- Give the four learners at the front an instruction, e.g. *Touch the board*. They run to touch the board.
- Choose four more learners. Repeat the activity, but ask them to use a different part of their body, e.g. *Touch the window with your nose*.
- Continue the game using different parts of the body.

Presentation

- Show a picture of a skeleton. Point to the bones. Ask *What are these?* Say *Bones*. Learners repeat.
- Flex your arm and show where the muscles are. Ask *What is this?* Say *Muscles*. Learners repeat.
- Flex your arms in an exaggerated way and say *Look – I'm strong*. Learners copy and repeat. Jump around and say *I'm healthy*. Learners copy and repeat.
- Act out being weak and unhealthy. Say *I'm not strong. I'm not healthy. What can I do?*
- Encourage the learners to give you ideas, miming to help as necessary, e.g. *You can eat fruit*. Say *Yes – fruit is good for us. It gives us vitamins.* Check understanding. Encourage the learners to think about exercise and offer ideas, e.g. *You can run*.

Pupil's Book, page 89

4 What makes our bodies strong? Read and tick ✓.

- Say *Open your Pupil's Books at page 89*. Focus on the pictures. Ask *What can you see? (A child jumping/dancing, the sun, people riding bikes, a girl watching TV, a glass of water)*
- Learners work in pairs and guess which pictures show things that make our bodies strong.
- Learners read the text and check their ideas.
- Put learners into pairs and ask them to tick the correct pictures.
- Check with the whole class and see if the guesses were correct.

  Alternative Copy and cut up the text into three sections. Give one part to each group of three learners. Get them to read their own part. They work together to tick the correct pictures by sharing information.

Key: 1 dancing 2 the sun 3 riding bikes 5 drinking water

mission Stage 3

- Show the class the third stage of the Mission poster: 'Warm-up'. Bend and stretch your arms out as if limbering up for an activity. Learners copy and repeat.
- Put the learners into groups of four. Learners plan their own warm-up routine. They practise giving instructions as they plan it, e.g. *Stretch your arms*, *Kick your legs*.

  Stronger learners Learners can write a set of instructions.

  Extra support Learners can do the movements and repeat the words. Monitor and guide.
- Once the groups are ready, invite them to the front of the class, group by group. Each group leads a warm-up routine for the rest of the class to follow.
- For ideas on monitoring and assessment, see Introduction.

Activity Book, page 89

See pages TB120–132

Activity Book, page 82

- Say *Look at page 82 of your Activity Book*. Review *My unit goals*. Ask *How is your Mission?*
- Learners reflect and choose a smiley face for *My mission diary 3*. Monitor.

Ending the lesson

- Go back to Stage 3 on the digital Mission poster. Add a tick to the 'Warm-up' stage or invite a learner to do it. Use self-assessment (see Introduction).
- Give out a completion sticker.

4 What makes our bodies strong? Read and tick ✓.

Body Power

- **Exercise**
  Children need to exercise every day. Running, playing football, riding a bike and dancing help make your bones and muscles strong.
- **Play outside**
  Vitamin D is important for your bones. Vitamin D comes from the sun. It's good to play outside, but remember to use sun cream when you are in the sun!
- **Drink water**
  It's important to drink a lot of water. Drink more water when you do exercise and when it's hot.

Are you looking after your bones and muscles?

1 

2 

3 

4 

5 

mission STAGE 3

Prepare a warm-up routine.

Let's stretch our legs.

Now let's stretch our arms.

STAGE 3

My mission diary
Activity Book page 82

Literature

1 What can you see in the pictures? Talk about what you think is happening.

7.14

A good friend

'Can we go and play in the park, Mum?' Oliver asks.

'OK,' says Mum.

'Come on, Amelia. Let's go!' Oliver says to his sister. He's holding his skateboard, and Amelia's taking her bike to the park.

'Goodbye, Dad!' they shout.

'See you!' Dad says. 'Have fun!'

Now they're in the park. Amelia's riding her bike around the duck pond and Oliver's skateboarding with two boys. They're ten. Oliver's only seven, but he's tall. There's a boy called Alfie in the park too. His mum is a friend of the children's mother.

'Can I play with you, Oliver?' Alfie asks, but Oliver isn't listening. He's skateboarding with the other boys. 'Can I play with you, Oliver?' Alfie asks again.

'I'm skateboarding, Alfie,' Oliver says. 'And you haven't got a skateboard!'

Learning outcomes By the end of the lesson, learners will have read about a picnic, learnt about a balanced diet and learnt about helping a friend.

New language *duck pond, fall, have fun, help, hill, smile*

Recycled language numbers, present continuous, words and phrases describing activities

Materials pictures from Digital photo bank of a park with a duck pond and a hill, paper for each learner, coloured pens or pencils

Key Competences

- Read a story about friendship.
- Work together to predict what happens in a story based on visual clues.
- Draw what they think will happen next in a story.

Warm-up

- Show learners a smiley face emoticon. Say *Look – it's smiling*. Make an exaggerated smile. Learners repeat. Show learners a frowning emoticon. Say *Oh dear. It's not smiling.* Make an exaggerated frown. Learners repeat.
- Put learners into pairs. They tell their partner one thing that makes them smile and one thing that doesn't.

Presentation

- Say *We're going to read about a good friend*. Show a picture of a park with a duck pond. Say *In the story they go to the park and in the park there is …* Point to the duck pond. Say *A duck pond*. Learners repeat.
- Show a picture of a hill. Say *In the story there is …* Point to the hill. Say *A hill*. Check understanding. Learners repeat the word.
- Say *Be careful on the hill and at the duck pond. I don't want to …* mime falling. Say *Fall*. Learners repeat. Ask *Can you help if I fall?* Check understanding of *help*. Learners repeat *Help*. Encourage them to say *Yes, I can help*.

Pupil's Book, page 90

1 What can you see in the pictures? Talk about what you think is happening.

- Put the class into groups of four. Say *Open your Pupil's Books at pages 90 and 91. What can you see in the pictures?* Give an example by pointing to the first picture. Ask *What are they doing? Where are they? What's happening?* Learners talk about what they see, e.g. *The boy is talking to his mum. The cat is watching. They are in the house.* Monitor.
- Check their ideas.
- Write the same questions on the board: *What are they doing? Where are they? What's happening?*
- Learners look at the rest of the pictures and answer the questions for each one. Don't worry if they are correct at this stage. Ask for some of their ideas.
- Say *Who is a good friend? Point.* Learners indicate their ideas. Ask *Why?* Learners give their ideas. Don't say if they are correct or not.

7.14 A good friend

- Ask learners to guess what happens in the story. Write some key words from their ideas on the board.
- Say *Read and listen to the first part.* Show them the paragraphs on page 90. Play the audio. Learners listen and read.

Track 7.14
See story on Pupil's Book pages 90–91

- Pause the audio. Ask *Where are they going?* (*The park*) *What is Oliver taking?* (*His skateboard*) *What is Amelia taking?* (*Her bike*) *Who is Oliver playing with?* (*Two boys*) *Who else is in the park?* (*Alfie*)
- Ask *Is Oliver being a good friend?* (*No*) Ask *Why?* (*Because he isn't playing with Alfie.*) Ask *Is Alfie a good friend? Why?* Learners suggest ideas. Don't give answers yet.
- Say *Read the next part.* Show learners the paragraphs on page 91. Play the audio. Check if their guesses about Alfie were correct.
- Point to the fourth picture. Ask *What are the boys doing?* (*Jumping*) *What is Oliver doing?* (*Jumping too*)
- Ask *Where is the skateboard?* (*Going down the hill*) *Is Oliver happy?* (*No*) *Who helps Oliver?* (*Alfie*)

Activity Book, page 90

See pages TB120–132

Ending the lesson

- Draw a skateboard on the board. Write the numbers *1* to *3* along the skateboard.
- Tell learners to think of three things they can do on a skateboard. Encourage them to use their imaginations, e.g. *Have fun, Go to school.*
- Put learners in groups of four to think of ideas.
- Share ideas.

Learning outcomes By the end of the lesson, learners will have summarised a story, recognised and written the spelling of food words and listened to identify people.

Recycled language verbs of movement, present continuous

Materials audio, coloured pens or pencils

Social and Emotional Skill: Identifying ways of being a good friend

- After reading the story, ask *Where are Oliver and Amelia? (In the park) Can Alfie play with Oliver?* (No) *Is Oliver a good friend?* (No) *Is Alfie a good friend?* (Yes) Say *Yes, Alfie is a very good friend because he helps Oliver. He's kind.*
- Invite pairs of learners to role play one of the following:

  1 Alfie: *Can I play with you, Oliver?*
  Oliver: *I'm skateboarding and you haven't got a skateboard.*
- Then say to the class *Imagine you are Alfie. How do you feel? (Sad) Is Oliver being a good friend? (No)*

  2 Amelia: *Hey! Alfie wants to play with you, Oliver.*
  Oliver: *Alfie's only six and he hasn't got a skateboard. I'm playing with those boys.*
- Then say to the class *Imagine you are Amelia. How do you feel? (Angry) Is Amelia being a good friend? (Yes) Is Oliver being a good friend? (No)*

  3 Oliver: *Stop my skateboard!*
  Alfie: *Here's your skateboard.*
  Oliver: *Thank you, Alfie.*
- Then say to the class *Imagine you are Alfie. How do you feel? (Happy) Is Alfie being a good friend? (Yes) Imagine you are Oliver. How do you feel? (Happy) Is Oliver being a good friend? (Yes)*
- Point out that being a good friend makes you feel happy.
- Write on the board: *A good friend …*
  plays with me. is kind. helps me and other people. helps when I feel sad. makes me feel happy. doesn't get angry with me.

Key Competences

Read and talk about friendship.

Think about the importance of helping a friend.

Give their opinion on the story.

Warm-up

- Say *Act out the story*. Summarise the story, sentence by sentence, and mime, e.g. *Oliver and Amelia are going to the park*. Mime walking. *Oliver is playing with the big boys*. Mime skateboarding. Say *He isn't playing with Alfie*. Make a sad face. Say *The boys are jumping and Oliver is jumping*. Mime jumping. Say *His skateboard is going down the hill*. Mime shock. Say *But Alfie is running after it*. Mime running. Say *Alfie is a good friend*. Mime smiling.
- Repeat and encourage the learners to act the story with you.
- Repeat and this time encourage the learners to say the sentences to you. Only step in if they get stuck.
- As they say the sentences, write them onto the board.
- Put the learners into groups of five. Give each one a role: Alfie, Amelia, Oliver and the two older boys. Tell them to act the story in their groups using the sentences on the board to help them.
- **SA** Use self-assessment to check how well learners think they understand the vocabulary. See Introduction.

Pupil's Book, page 91

2 Answer the questions.

- Say *Open your Pupil's Books at page 91.*
- Learners work in pairs and answer the first question.
- Check answers.
- Ask learners to think about a friend. Show them some pictures of your own or use pictures from the internet if you prefer. Give an example, e.g. *This is my friend Jane. We play tennis. We talk. We have fun.* Check understanding of *fun*. Say, e.g. *Jane is nice. She helps me.* Check understanding of *help*.
- Put learners into small groups of three or four. Each learner tells the group about his/her friend and what they do.

Key: 1 Alfie is a good friend. He helps Oliver.

3 Ask and answer.

- Learners stay in their groups. Ask *Do you like skateboarding?* Learners discuss.
- Ask questions to some of the learners who say they like it, e.g. *Who do you skateboard with? Where do you skateboard?*
- Now ask *What's your favourite hobby?* Learners discuss in their groups, e.g. *I like cooking. I make eggs for breakfast.*

Activity Book, page 91

See pages TB120–132

Ending the lesson

- **SA** Repeat the self-assessment technique used at the start of the lesson to see how well learners think they understand the vocabulary. Is there any change?
- Learners draw a picture of a sports activity and write the word. Monitor and check.
- Learners stand in a circle.
- Say *Find someone with the same activity*. Learners run and find a partner. They hold up their activity and say what it is.

Amelia's riding her bike nearby. 'Hey! Alfie wants to play with you, Oliver,' she says.

'Alfie's only six and he hasn't got a skateboard!' says Oliver. 'I'm playing with those boys. They're my new friends. Wow! They're doing jumps.'

Oliver's jumping too, but it's very difficult! WHAM! He falls on the ground. 'Oh, no! Stop!' Oliver's skateboard's moving fast down the hill to the duck pond.

Little Alfie's running down the hill after the skateboard. He's got it! He's giving it back to Oliver. 'Thank you, Alfie,' says Oliver. Alfie's smiling. He's only six, but he runs fast! He's a nice boy. It's good to help your friends.

2 Answer the questions.

1 Who is the good friend in the story?

2 Have you got a good friend? Talk about your friend.

3 Ask and answer.

Do you like skateboarding?

No, I don't.

What's your favourite hobby?

It's swimming.

Pre A1 Starters

1 Write the names in the diagram.

Ben Alex Sue Sam Bill Jill Pat Hugo May

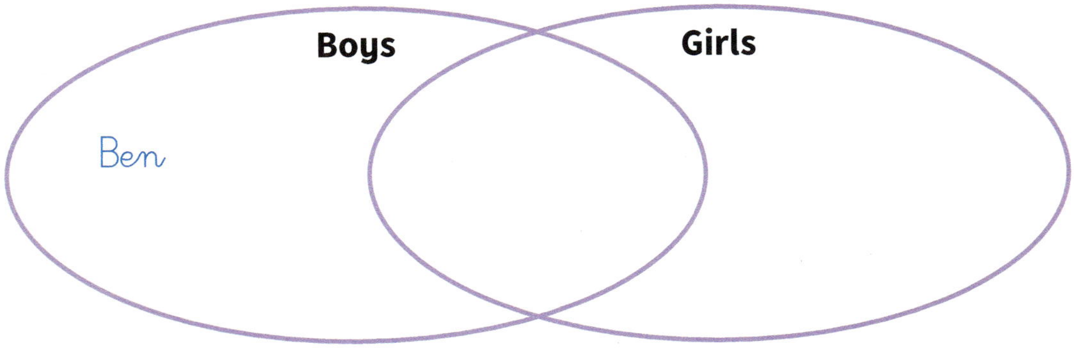

2 Look at the picture in Activity 3. Point and say what the people are doing.

These girls are playing football.

3 7.15 Listen and draw lines. There is one example.

Tom Bill Anna

Hugo Sue May

Draw one line for each name you hear.

Learning outcomes By the end of the lesson, learners will have listened and labelled a picture accurately by listening to what people are doing.

Recycled language activities, colours

Materials Sports and hobbies 1 and 2 flashcards, audio, paper, coloured pens or pencils

Key Competences

- Listen for specific information.
- Complete and interpret a Venn diagram.
- Practise activity types found in *Pre A1 Starters* exams.

Warm-up

- Put Sports and hobbies 1 and 2 flashcards on a table or the floor, picture side up. Call out one of the phrases.
- Learners run to grab or touch the card. The first person to grab or touch the card wins it.
- **SA** Use self-assessment techniques to check how well learners think they understand the vocabulary. See Introduction.

Presentation

- Say *Let's do a listening exam*. Write *Listening Exam* on the board.
- Say *We can use pictures and words to help us.*

Pupil's Book, page 92

1 Write the names in the diagram.

- Ask learners to stand up. Say *Girls, stretch your arms in the air*. Demonstrate. Repeat with the boys.
- Point to a girl. Ask *What's your name?* (e.g. *Eliza*) Repeat with a few girls. Point to a boy and repeat the sequence. Tell the learners to sit down.
- Say the names of the girls again. Ask *Are they girls' names or boys' names?* (*Girls'*)
- Say *Open your Pupil's Books at page 92. Look at number 1.* Read the first name *Ben*. Ask *Boy or girl?* (*Boy*) Show the learners where to write the name on the diagram.
- Learners continue to add the names to the diagram.

Key: Boys: Bill, Hugo Boys and Girls: Alex, Sam, Pat
Girls: Sue, Jill, May

2 Look at the picture in Activity 3. Point and say what the people are doing.

- Point to different people in the picture. Ask *What is he/she doing? What colour is he/she wearing?* Learners ask and answer in pairs.

3 7.15 Listen and draw lines. There is one example.

- Point out the exam tip at the bottom of Pupil's Book page 92. Say *Draw one line for each name you hear*. Show the first example. Play the audio to the end of the example. Pause the audio.
- Ask learners *Where's Tom?* (*In the park*) Ask *What's he doing?* (*Eating an apple*)
- Say *Now listen and draw*. Play the audio. Learners listen and draw lines. Check answers.

Track 7.15

Man: That's a nice photo, Tom.
Tom: Yes, I'm in the park with my friends. Look, that's me. I'm eating an apple.

Can you see the line? This is an example. Now you listen and draw lines.

1 Tom: Look at the funny dog! That's Bill's dog.
Man: Who is Bill?
Tom: He's the boy with the blue T-shirt.
Man: Is he under the tree?
Tom: Yes.

2 Tom: That boy is very happy!
Man: Which boy? The boy riding a bike?
Tom: Yes.
Man: What's his name?
Tom: It's Hugo.
Man: Oh, OK!

3 Man: Can you see Sue?
Tom: No. Where is she?
Man: She's playing football.
Tom: Oh, yes. There's Sue. She's got a big seven on her T-shirt.

Now listen again.
[Repeat track]

- Say *Well done. When you listened, you used the picture and the words about what people are doing. Good job!*

Activity Book, page 92

See pages TB120–132

Ending the lesson

- **SA** Repeat the self-assessment technique used at the start of the lesson to see how well learners think they understand the vocabulary. Is there any change?

Learning outcomes By the end of the lesson, learners will have revised the language in the unit, acted out a sports day and done a warm-up routine.

Recycled language unit language

Materials soft balls (one per six to eight learners)

Key Competences

- Revise vocabulary and language learnt in the unit.
- Complete self-assessment tasks and reflect on their own learning.
- Work in groups to act out their sports day.

Warm-up

- Put learners into groups. Give each group a ball. Learners throw the ball to each other. Every time they catch the ball, they say the name of a part of the body. Once they have done this, they can throw the ball to someone else. They can't say the words again.

Presentation

- Write on the board: *Sports Day*.
- Say *Write the name of a sport you like*. Monitor and support.

  Extra support You can give out a list of words. Learners choose one to copy.

  Fast finishers Learners can add extra activities.
- Put the learners into pairs. Say *Show your partner the sport*. Learners mime and their partner guesses the sport.

Pupil's Book, page 93

mission in action!

Act out your sports day.

- Learners work in groups of five. Demonstrate asking about sports. Ask *Can we play tennis?* (*Yes, that's a great idea.*) Learners choose three sports to act out together.
- Learners choose a presenter. They act out the sports and the presenter practises saying what they are doing.
- Learners practise a warm-up routine. The presenter practises describing it. Monitor as they prepare.
- Bring all the learners back together. Ask a confident group to do their warm-up with the class. The members of the group stand at the front and demonstrate. The presenter describes. All the class copy. Then the group acts out different sports and the presenter describes, e.g. *Laura and David are playing tennis*.
- Repeat with other groups.
- As each group finishes, encourage the learners to say *Well done!* and for the group to reply *Thank you*.

  Extra support Learners can act out the sports.

  Stronger learners Learners can ask additional questions, e.g. *Which sport is your favourite?*
- Say *Open your Pupil's Books at page 82*. Show the picture from the unit opener and point to the girl with the guitar. Say *Tell me about the girl*. (e.g. *She has black hair. She's skateboarding.*) Point to the boy with the football. Ask *What is he doing?* (*He's playing football.*) Point to the ball.

  Say *Tell me about the ball*. (e.g. *It's a football. We can play football in the park. It's a big black and white ball.*) Repeat with other pictures on the page and in the unit. Say, e.g. *Tell me about the picnic*. (e.g. *There are apples.*) Learners repeat the activity in pairs.
- For ideas on monitoring and assessment, see Introduction.

Self-assessment

- **SA** Say *Did you like our 'Have a sports day' Mission?* Put a picture of a smiley face on the wall at one end of the class and a picture of a frowning face on the opposite wall. Demonstrate that if learners loved the Mission they stand near the smiley face and if they didn't they stand near the frowning face.
- Say *Did you do better than the last Mission – Act out a wildlife tour? Better? Or not?* Ask them to stand near the smiley or frowning face.
- Choose learners near the smiley face and ask *What was good?* Learners answer.
- Say *Our next Mission is 'Have a friend to visit'*. Choose learners near the frowning face and say *What wasn't so good this time? How can we do better?* Learners suggest ideas, e.g. *We can read the words at home*.

Activity Book, page 93

See pages TB120–132

Activity Book, page 82

- Say *Look at page 82 of your Activity Book*. Review *My unit goals*. Ask *How is your Mission?*
- Learners reflect and choose a smiley face for *My mission diary* the final stage. Monitor.
- Point to the sunflower. Learners read the 'can do' statements and tick them if they agree they have achieved them. They colour each leaf green if they are very confident or orange if they think they need more practice.
- Point to the word stack sign. Ask learners to spend a few minutes looking back at the unit and find a minimum of five new words they have learnt. They write the new words into their word stack. See Introduction for techniques and activities.

Ending the lesson

- Go back to the completion stage on the digital Mission poster. Add a tick or invite a learner to do it. Use self-assessment (see Introduction).
- Give out a completion sticker.
- Tell the learners *You have finished your Mission! Well done!*

mission in action!

Act out your sports day.

My mission diary
Activity Book page 82

Do your warm-up routine with the class.

Now we stretch our arms.

Choose presenters for your sports day.

Can I be a presenter?

OK!

Act out your sports. The presenters say what everyone is doing.

They're running.

David is the winner!

Say 'well done' to everyone.

Well done!

Thank you.

8 At home

1 **Watch the video. Write about your house.**

My house number/name is

____

My house is

____

In my house there is

____
____
____

mission Invite a friend to my house

In this unit I will:

1. Ask when my friend can come.
2. Tidy my bedroom.
3. Make a list of things to do.
4. ★ Have my friend to visit.

Unit 8 learning outcomes

In Unit 8, learners learn to:

- talk about homes, rooms and things in them
- talk about ability using *can/can't*
- describe where things are in a house using prepositions
- read and understand about different types of home
- learn about the consequences of actions

Materials video, pictures from Digital photo bank of different types of homes (a large detached house, a small cottage, a flat, a terraced house), white sticky labels, sticky tack, digital Mission poster

Key Competences

Become familiar with different types of homes.

Reflect on their own learning by going through the unit goals.

Write about their houses.

Self-assessment

- **SA** Say *Open your Pupil's Books at page 94*. Say *Look at the picture*. Indicate items on the page and ask questions using the language from the unit, e.g. *What is it? What colour is this?* Use self-assessment (see Introduction). Say *OK. Let's learn*.

Warm-up

- Show some pictures of different types of homes, e.g. a large detached house, a small cottage, a flat, a terraced house. Say *Look at the houses*. Say *House*. Learners repeat.
- Point to each one. Ask *Is it big or small? What colour is the door? Show me the garden* (if relevant). *Do you like it?*
- Put learners into pairs. Ask *Which home is your favourite?* Learners tell their partner which house they like best. (e.g. *This is my favourite house. It's big and it's got a garden.*)

  Extension Divide the learners into groups – if you have four pictures, divide them into four groups. Give each group a picture and some white sticky labels. Ask the group to choose a captain. Give each group three minutes to label as many things in the picture as they can. The captain writes the labels and other learners suggest words and spellings. Ask the captain to report back, showing the class the picture and labels. The rest of the learners can add suggestions for additional labels.

Pupil's Book, page 94

1 Watch the video. Write about your house.

- Say *In this unit we're talking about homes*. Say *Let's watch the video*. To introduce the topic of the unit, play the video.
- Say *Look at page 94*. Show the spaces at the end of the sentences. Say *Let's write about your house*. Write the sentence stems on the board and fill them in with your own details. Make these up if you prefer, e.g. *My house number is 10. My house is small. In my house there is a table and four chairs. There is a television.*
- Learners write sentences about their own house. Monitor and check.

  Fast finishers Learners can add extra detail, e.g. *There is a red door. There are four windows.*

  Extra support Learners can complete the sentences by copying and changing your examples.

  Extension Learners can draw a picture of their own house and label it.

mission Invite a friend to my house

- Show the digital Mission poster. Say *Here's my house*, making a welcoming gesture. Learners repeat and copy.
- Say *Point to number 1*. Show them the clock. Say *Let's ask when my friend can come*. Say *Tick tock, tick tock … When?* Learners repeat.
- Say *Point to number 2*. Show them the bedroom. Say *I'm tidying my bedroom*. Mime tidying and putting things away. Learners copy. Say *Number 2* and gesture for them to copy. Say *One. Tick tock, tick tock … When?* Repeat.
- Say *Point to number 3*. Say *I'm making a list*. Mime writing. Learners copy and repeat. Say *Three* and repeat. Go through mimes 1–3, calling out the numbers for learners to mime and chant.
- Say *Point to number 4*. Say with excitement *My friend is visiting!* Mime opening the door and welcoming someone in. Encourage learners to copy. Say *Four* and learners mime and chant. Repeat the whole sequence, getting the learners to mime and chant as you call out the numbers. Say *This is our Mission*.

Activity Book, page 94

My unit goals

- Go through the unit goals with the learners. You can read these or if you prefer you can put them onto the board or a poster.
- You can go back to these unit goals at the end of each Mission stage during the unit and review them.
- Say *This is our Mission page*.

Ending the lesson

- Ask learners to stand up. Put the pictures of the homes on the walls in different parts of the classroom.
- Describe each home, but don't say which one it is, e.g. *This house is big and white. It's got five windows and a big garden*. Learners should run to the correct picture. (If you prefer, learners can just point to the correct picture.)

Learning outcomes By the end of the lesson, learners will be able to recognise and use words to describe rooms and things in a house.

New language *bath, bathroom, bed, bedroom, dining room, kitchen, living room, mirror, radio*

Recycled language *doors, home, house, windows*

Materials Rooms and objects in the house flashcards, audio, video

Key Competences

- Learn and use words related to rooms and objects in the house.
- Chant together as a class.
- Identify and say words with the letter 'i'

Presentation

- Put up flashcards and teach the rooms.
- Mime actions for rooms. Ask *Where am I?* Learners answer.

Pupil's Book, page 95

1 8.01 8.02 Listen and point. Then listen and number.

- Say *Open your Pupil's Books at page 95.*
- Ask *Where's Cameron?* (*He's in the tree.*) *What's he doing?* (*He's looking at the house.*) *Where are Jenny and Eva?* (*They're in the bedroom.*) *What are they doing?* (*Jenny's listening to the radio and Eva's reading a book.*) Continue with the other characters.
- Play Track 8.01. Learners point to the rooms and items.

Tracks 8.01 and 8.02

This evening Cameron is watching the Friendly family at home.

(1) Cameron: OK, that's nice. Yes … I'm looking in the house now.
Rocky: Good, good. What are they doing? What are they doing?
Cameron: Well, Jenny's in the bedroom with Eva.
(2) Cameron: They're sitting on the bed.
(3) Cameron: Jenny's listening to the radio and Eva's reading a blue book.
(4) Gracie: What's Grandpa Friendly doing?
Cameron: Grandpa Friendly's in the dining room and he's eating an apple.
(5) Gracie: Where's Grandma Friendly?
Cameron: She's in the kitchen.
(6) Rocky: Where is Jim? What's he doing?
Cameron: Jim's in the living room. He's playing the piano.
(7) Gracie: Oh, and where are Mr and Mrs Friendly? What are they doing?
Cameron: Hmm, let's see. Ah, yes. Here he is. Mr Friendly's in the bathroom.
(8) Cameron: I can see the bath.
(9) Cameron: He's looking at his face in the mirror.
Rocky: What's Mrs Friendly doing?
Cameron: I don't know.
Henrietta: Cameron! What are you doing?
Cameron: Ugh! I'm, er … watching the Friendlys.
Henrietta: Hmm.

- Ask *Who is Cameron talking to?* Play Track 8.01 again. (*He's talking to the other animals.*)
- Say *Listen and number.* Play Track 8.02. Learners number the rooms and objects.
- Ask *Number 1?* (*Bedroom*) Put the flashcard up. Write 1. Continue until the sequence is complete.

Key: 1 bedroom 2 bed 3 radio 4 dining room 5 kitchen 6 living room 7 bathroom 8 bath 9 mirror

2 8.03 Say the chant.

- Say *Say the chant and copy*. Play the audio or video and do actions. Learners copy.
- Repeat the audio or video. Learners chant and mime.
- Put the class into pairs: As chant and Bs do the actions. Play the audio or video. Swap and repeat.

Track 8.03

House house, in our house (x2)
Bedroom bed, bedroom bed, ra-di-o and kit-chen (x2)
Dining room, living room (x2)
Bathroom, bath and mirror (x2)

3 8.04 Listen and say the room.

- Say *Listen and say the room.*

Track 8.04

1 Jenny's listening to the radio.
2 I can see Mr Friendly. I can see a bath too.
3 Jim's playing the piano.
4 Eva's reading a blue book.
5 Grandma Friendly's washing her hands.
6 Mr Friendly's looking at his face in the mirror.
7 Grandpa Friendly's eating an apple.
8 They're sitting on the bed.

Key: 1 bedroom 2 bathroom 3 living room 4 bedroom 5 kitchen 6 bathroom 7 dining room 8 bedroom

Activity Book, page 95

See pages TB120–132

Ending the lesson

- SA Say *We learnt about homes, rooms and things in them.* Show the flashcards. Ask *Do you know the words?* Use self-assessment (see Introduction). Learners show how they feel.
- Say *You can say the words well. Good work.*

1 8.01 8.02 **Listen and point. Then listen and number.**

2 8.03 **Say the chant.**

3 8.04 **Listen and say the room.**

The Friendly Farm

8.05

Learning outcomes By the end of the lesson, learners will be able to understand *can* to talk about ability.

New language *I can … Can you … ? dance, look at*

Recycled language *ride (a horse), sing, swim*

Materials sticky notes, flashcards of swimming and skateboarding, pictures from Digital photo bank of singing and playing table tennis, slips of paper with activities written on them (optional), audio, video

Key Competences

Read and listen to a story; Understand *can / can't* for ability.

Role play a story in groups.

Warm-up

- Draw a sketch of a toothbrush on the board. Ask learners *Where am I? (In the bathroom)*
- Give out sticky notes. Learners draw something you can find in a home on the sticky note. Tell learners the name of the item. They write it on the back.
- Learners attach their sticky note to the front of their clothes. They stand in two lines facing each other. They look at the drawing of the learner opposite and say where they are, e.g. (Picture of bed) *You're in the bedroom*.
- Learners in one line move along one so all the learners are talking to a new partner. Repeat the task.
  Stronger learners Learners try to name the object in the picture.
- **SA** Use self-assessment to check how well learners think they understand the vocabulary. See Introduction.

Presentation

- Mime cutting food. Ask *What am I doing? (Cutting food)* Ask *Where am I? (In the kitchen)* Say *Yes. I'm cooking food.* Say *Yum yum. My food is good.* Look happy. Say *I can cook*. Learners mime and repeat.
- Mime playing the piano. Ask *What am I doing? (Playing the piano)* Say *Yes. But it sounds very bad*. Make a disgusted face and put your fingers in your ears. Say *I can't play the piano*. Learners repeat.
- Put up pictures of activities (*swimming, singing, playing table tennis, skateboarding*). Point to a flashcard. Say *I can (swim)*. Learners repeat. Continue with different flashcards, using *can/can't*, e.g. *I can't skateboard*.
- Ask a learner *Can you swim? (Yes, I can* or *No, I can't.)*
- Point to each flashcard. Learners chant *Can you (skateboard)?*

Pupil's Book, page 96

8.05 The Friendly Farm song

- Play the introductory song at the beginning of the Friendly Farm cartoon story. Learners listen and sing. Learners choose an animal to mime. Repeat with the mimes.

Track 8.05
See The Friendly Farm song on page TB5

8.05 The Friendly Farm

- Say *Open your Pupil's Books at page 96.* Ask *Who can you see in the pictures?* Learners name the characters. Ask *What can Rocky do? (Ride a horse) What can Rocky's brother and sister do? (Swim)*
- Say *What can Gracie do?* Write the question on the board. Say *Listen*. Play the audio or video. Learners listen and read.

Track 8.05
The Friendly Farm song + see cartoon on Pupil's Book page 96

- Learners check answers in pairs. (*Gracie can eat socks.*)
- Play the audio or video again. Pause after each frame and check comprehension: Frame 1: *What's Rocky doing? (He's riding a horse.)* Frame 2: *Can Shelly ride a horse? (No, she can't.) What can Shelly do? (She can look in a mirror and she can sing.)* Frame 3: *Can Cameron swim? (No, he can't.)* Frame 4: *Can Harry swim? (No, he can't.) What can he do? (He can dance.)* Frame 5: *What can Rocky do? (He can ride a horse and dance.)* Frame 6: *Can Rocky eat socks? (No, he can't.) Can he eat books? (No, he can't.)*
- Play the audio or video again. Divide the class into groups and give each group a role from the cartoon, e.g. some are Gracie, some are Cameron. Learners repeat the speech bubbles for their character.

Activity Book, page 96

See pages TB120–132

Ending the lesson

- **SA** Repeat the self-assessment technique used at the start of the lesson to see how well learners think they understand the vocabulary. Is there any change?
- Stand on one leg. Ask the learners *Can you stand on one leg?* Learners answer. Choose a learner who answered *Yes, I can*. Invite him/her to stand up and show everyone. Repeat with a different learner and different example, e.g. *Can you write your name on the board?*
- Put learners into groups of three or four and give them a minute to think of a challenge.
  Extra support Give learners notes with ready-made ideas, e.g. *Throw a paper ball into the bin. Find three red things in the classroom.*
- Each group chooses another to do their challenge.

Learning outcomes By the end of the lesson, learners will be able to ask and answer questions using *can/can't*.

New language days of the week, *morning*, *afternoon*, *evening*

Materials Sports and hobbies 1 flashcards, pictures from Digital photo bank of table tennis, sing, clean and eat, digital Mission poster

Key Competences

- Learn to ask and answer questions using *can / can't*.
- Work together to play a game.
- Reflect on their own learning.
- Interact with the digital poster.

Warm-up

- In groups, learners ask *Can you spell (a word they choose)?* The group write the word.

Presentation

- Learners stand in a circle. Show a Sports and hobbies 1 flashcard and say, e.g. *I can play tennis*. Learners repeat. Repeat with another flashcard, using *can't*.
- Give the first flashcard to a learner, who says *I can/can't play tennis*. He/She passes on the flashcard and the next learner makes a sentence. Continue.
- Ask, e.g. *Can you play tennis?* (*Yes, I can. / No, I can't.*)

Pupil's Book, page 97

8.06 Gracie's Grammar

- Say *Open your Pupil's Books at page 97*. Point to Gracie's Grammar box. Write the same sentences on the board.
- Play the audio. Pause for learners to repeat.

Track 8.06
See Pupil's Book page 97

1 8.07 Listen and stick. Then look, read and write.

- Play the audio for learners to point to the correct sticker.

Track 8.07

1 Jim: Can you swim, Grandpa?
Grandpa: No, I can't, but I can play badminton.

2 Jim: Can you sing, Dad?
Mr Friendly: Yes, I can.

3 Jenny: Can you use a computer, Grandma?
Grandma: Yes, I can.

4 Jenny: Can you ride a horse, Mum?
Mrs Friendly: No, I can't, but I can play the piano.

- Play the audio again. Learners stick in the stickers.
- Say *Look, read and write*. Learners write.

Key: 2 sing 3 use a computer 4 play the piano

mission Stage 1

- Show learners the first stage of the digital Mission poster: 'When?' Say *Let's find out when your friend can come to your house.*
- Learners complete the worksheet task in the Teacher's Resource Book page 84 (see teaching notes on TRB page 77).
- Alternatively if you do not have the Teacher's Resource Book, draw a table on the board:

Saturday morning	*Saturday afternoon*	*Saturday evening*	*Sunday morning*	*Sunday afternoon*	*Sunday evening*

- Learners copy the table. Divide them into two groups. Group A add three activities on Saturday morning, evening and Sunday afternoon, e.g. *cinema*, *birthday party*, *dinner with Grandpa*. Group B add three activities to Saturday afternoon, Sunday morning and evening.
- Whisper to a confident learner a question to ask you: *Can you come to my house on Sunday afternoon?* Say *Sorry – no. I'm playing tennis on Sunday afternoon.* Learners repeat.
- Another learner asks *Can you come to my house on Sunday morning?* Say *Yes, I can!* Write, e.g. *Sam's house* in the correct space. Ask the same learner *Can you come to my house on Saturday afternoon?* The learner checks their diary. If they say *Yes, I can*, write, e.g. *Sam coming* in the space. If they say *No*, find another time.
- Tell learners *Find three friends to come to your house*.
- Learners mingle, asking and answering, and writing in the name of their friend when they find an available time.
- For ideas on monitoring and assessment, see Introduction.

Activity Book, page 97

See pages TB120–132

Activity Book, page 94

- Say *Look at page 94 of your Activity Book*. Review *My unit goals*. Ask *How is your Mission?*
- Learners reflect and choose a smiley face for *My mission diary 1*. Monitor.

Ending the lesson

- Go back to Stage 1 on the digital Mission poster. Say *We found a time for our friend to come. Good work.* Add a tick to the 'When?' stage or invite a learner to do it. Use self-assessment (see Introduction).
- Give out a completion sticker.

8.06 Gracie's Grammar

I **can swim**.

She **can play** the piano.

Can you **ride** a horse?

I **can't play** the guitar.

He **can't sing**.

Yes, I **can**. / No, I **can't**.

1 8.07 **Listen and stick. Then look, read and write.**

1 Grandpa Friendly can play badminton.

2 Mr Friendly can ______.

3 Grandma Friendly can ______.

4 Mrs Friendly can ______.

mission STAGE 1

Ask when your friend can come to your house.

Can you come on Saturday morning?

No. I've got swimming on Saturday morning.

My mission diary

Activity Book page 94

Vocabulary 2 and song

1 8.08 Listen and circle. Then sing the song.

There's a pink armchair
in the (living) / **dining** room
and a red **sofa / lamp**
under the window ...

There's a yellow lamp
in the **living / dining** room
and an old **armchair / painting**
next to the phone ...

In the hall,
there's a **lamp / clock**
on the wall.
There's a rug on the **floor / sofa**
next to the door.

2 Choose a picture and tick ✓. Then play a guessing game.

1  ☐

2  ☐

3  ☐

4  ☐

What's in your living room?

Is the phone under the lamp?

No, it isn't.

Learning outcomes By the end of the lesson, learners will have practised the language through song.

New language *armchair, clock, floor, hall, lamp, painting, phone, rug, sofa*

Recycled language colours, prepositions of place, *There is/are*

Materials Furniture and household items flashcards, Rooms and objects in the house flashcards, audio, video, large cards with words on them (*a mirror, a TV, a dining table, a bed, food*), sticky tack, picture of a rug, toy phone (or flashcard of phone)

Key Competences

- Learn and practise new house vocabulary.
- Sing a song.
- Play a guessing game in pairs.

Warm-up

- Show flashcards of rooms: bathroom, kitchen, living room, bedroom and dining room. Learners say the names as you show them. Show the flashcard of a hall. Say *And this is a hall. Hall.* Learners repeat.
- Stick the flashcards on the board. Now show large cards with words on them: *a mirror, a TV, a dining table, a bed, food*.
- Choose learners to come and stick the words next to the correct rooms. Some could be in more than one room, e.g. *food*. Accept whichever the learner chooses, but show the alternative, e.g. say *We can make food in the kitchen. And we can eat food in the dining room.*
- **SA** Use self-assessment to check how well learners think they understand the vocabulary. See Introduction.

Presentation

- Show the picture of the rug. Say *Rug*. Learners repeat. Ask *Where can we find a rug?* (*The living room, the dining room, the bedroom*) Show it can be in more than one place. Say *We put it on the floor*. Show the floor of the room you are in. Say *Floor*. Learners repeat.
- Put the room flashcards on the board. Choose a learner to come up. Say *Put the rug in the bedroom*. The learner puts the picture on or under the correct room flashcard. Repeat, using flashcards of the other household items.

Pupil's Book, page 98

1 8.08 Listen and circle. Then sing the song.

- Say *Open your Pupil's Books at page 98*. Say *Point to the hall*. Learners point. Repeat with *armchair, rug, phone, clock, painting, lamp, sofa*. For each one, ask *What colour is it?*
- Write up on the board *The rug is next to the window/door*. Ask a confident learner to come to the board. Say *The rug is next to the door*. The learner circles the word *door*.
- Play the audio or video. Learners listen and circle the words.

Track 8.08

Rocky: I'm Rocky-Doodle-Doo and … here's our song for today: *In the house*.

See song on Pupil's Book page 86 and Key below

- Check answers.
- Play the audio or video again. Learners listen and sing. Monitor.

Key: sofa, living, painting, clock, floor

8.09 **Extension** Once learners are confidently singing along to the song, try singing the karaoke version as a class.

2 Choose a picture and tick ✓. Then play a guessing game.

- Say *Look at the first picture*. Ask *Where is the phone?* (*It's on the sofa.*) Repeat for pictures 2–4. (*next to the lamp, next to the clock, under the armchair*)
- Ask a confident learner to choose a picture. Say *Don't tell me the picture!* Ask questions, e.g. *Is the phone on the sofa? Is it next to the clock?* Continue until the learner says *Yes, it is*. Repeat with another learner.
- Put the learners into pairs to play the same game.
- Read the speech bubble from Rocky. Learners call out their ideas.

Activity Book, page 98

See pages TB120–132

Ending the lesson

- **SA** Repeat the self-assessment technique used at the start of the lesson to see how well learners think they understand the vocabulary. Is there any change?
- Check learners understand *hot* and *cold*. Teach *warm*.
- Show a toy phone or the flashcard of a phone.
- Ask two or three learners to wait just outside the door. While they are outside, the other learners hide the phone or flashcard somewhere in the classroom.
- Bring the learners back into the classroom. Say *Can you find the phone?* The learners look. As they search, tell them *No, you are cold* if they aren't near the phone. Tell them *Oh, you are getting warm* as they get closer. Say *Hot!* if they have nearly reached it.
- Once they have found the phone, send out two or three different learners and repeat, encouraging the other learners to call out *Cold*, *Warm* and *Hot*.

  Extra support Learners can be selected to search.

  Stronger learners Learners can describe where the phone is hidden after it has been found.

8 Language practice 2

Learning outcomes By the end of the lesson, learners will be able to describe where things or people are.

New language *behind, between, in front of*

Recycled language *next to*, rooms and furniture in a house

Materials large picture of a living room, A3 paper with a bedroom map (one per group of three learners), small pieces of paper, coloured pens or pencils, cocktail sticks, audio, video, digital Mission poster

Key Competences

- Learn and practise prepositions to describe where people or things are.
- Work in groups to decide how to tidy up their room.
- Reflect on their own learning.
- Interact with the digital poster.

Warm-up

- Show learners a large picture of a living room. Learners remember as much as they can in one minute.
- Turn the picture over. Learners work in groups of three and make as many sentences as they can about the picture, e.g. *There is a blue sofa. There is a lamp next to the sofa.*
- Ask learners to say what they remember. The group with the most sentences are the winners.

Presentation

- Ask three learners to come to the front and stand in a line. Say *Look, (Paola), (José) and (Sonya) are next to each other*.
- Point to the learner in the middle. Say, e.g. *José is between Paola and Sonya*. Learners repeat. Move the learners so that a different one is in the middle. Ask, e.g. *Where is Sonya? (She's between José and Paola.)*
- Bring one learner forward to stand in front of another. Say, e.g. *Paola is in front of José*. Learners repeat. Say, e.g. *And José is behind Paola*. Learners repeat.

Pupil's Book, page 99

1 (8.10) Who is Sam? Listen and circle.

- Say *Open your Pupil's Books at page 99. Listen and circle*.
- Play the audio or video. Learners listen and circle Sam in the picture. Check answers.

Track 8.10

Alice: Look at this. It's a photo of my family in our living room.
Boy: Hmm. You've got a nice living room, Alice. Who are the boys sitting on the rug on the floor?
Alice: They're my brothers, Sam and Ben. I'm sitting between them, and my grandparents are sitting on the sofa behind us. Sam is in front of my grandpa and Ben is in front of my grandma. My young sister Lucy is on the floor next to us.
Boy: Who's standing behind your grandparents?
Alice: My mum and dad are standing behind them.
Boy: Hmm, it's a beautiful photo. You're all very happy.

Key: Sam is the boy in front of the grandpa.

(8.11) Gracie's Grammar

- Say *Look at Gracie's Grammar*. Play the audio. Learners repeat the sentences in the grammar box.
- Write the sentences on the board, but leave out the prepositions. Play the audio again. Ask learners which words go into the spaces and write them in.

Track 8.11
See Pupil's Book page 99

2 Sit in groups. Talk about where you're sitting.

- Say *Look at Activity 2*.
- Act out the sentences, demonstrating the request and response. Learners repeat.
- Put the learners into groups of five and get them to sit in different positions, e.g. a line of three with a learner in front of the line and another behind. Learners work together and describe where they are in relation to the group. Learners change places and repeat.

mission Stage 2

- Show learners the second stage of the digital Mission poster: 'Tidying'.
- Learners complete the worksheet task in the Teacher's Resource Book page 84 (see teaching notes on TRB page 77).
- Alternatively if you do not have the Teacher's Resource Book, show a picture of a messy bedroom. Put learners into groups of three. Learners decide where to put things to make the room tidy.
- Each group reports back what they have planned.

Activity Book, page 99

See pages TB120–132

Activity Book, page 94

- Say *Look at page 94 of your Activity Book*. Review *My unit goals*. Ask *How is your Mission?*
- Learners reflect and choose a smiley face for *My mission diary 2*. Monitor.

Ending the lesson

- SA Go back to Stage 2 on the digital Mission poster. Add a tick to the 'Tidying' stage. Use self-assessment (see Introduction).
- Give out a completion sticker.

1 8.10 **Who is Sam? Listen and circle.**

Gracie's Grammar

8.11

There's a small rug **in front of** the armchair.
There's a lamp **between** the armchair and the sofa.
There's a clock on the wall **behind** the sofa.

2 **Sit in groups. Talk about where you're sitting.**

I'm sitting between Juan and Maria.

Who's sitting in front of you?

Alex and Kim.

Who's behind you?

Paula and Anna.

mission STAGE 2

Tidy your bedroom.

Let's put the lamp between the cupboard and the bed.

Good idea!

STAGE 2

My mission diary
Activity Book page 94

Cross-curricular

Houses around the world

1 **Watch the video.**

2 8.12 **Listen and say. Which houses can you see in your town? Which house is your favourite?**

a

hut

b

stilt-house

c

detached house

d

ranch

e

houseboat

f

flats

3 8.13 **Where do the children want to live? Listen and number the pictures.**

Learning outcomes By the end of the lesson, learners will be able to understand more about different places where people live.

New language *detached house, flats, houseboat, hut, ranch, stilt-house*

Recycled language adjectives

Materials pictures from the Internet of houses from your local town, four pictures from Digital photo bank of people who look very different (an old man, a young couple, a family with a young child, a group of university students), video

Key Competences

Learn to talk about different types of houses.

Learn about houses around the world.

Complete a crossword puzzle.

Warm-up

- Write a sentence stem on the board: *I like my bedroom because …* Give an example of how to finish the sentence: *… it is big. It's got a nice bed and a lamp. There is a white table and a nice painting. It is warm and I can sleep there.*
- Ask the learners to work in pairs and finish the sentence.
- Monitor and check.
- Learners share their ideas.

Pupil's Book, page 100

1 Watch the video.

- Say *Let's watch the video.* Learners watch the video about houses around the world and answer the questions at the end of the video.

2 8.12 Listen and say. Which houses can you see in your town? Which house is your favourite?

- Play the audio. Pause for learners to repeat. Correct pronunciation.

  Track 8.12
  See Pupil's Book page 100
- Say, e.g. *I can see detached houses and flats in my town. I can't see houseboats or stilt-houses. The hut is my favourite house because it is small and it is in a field.*
- Put learners into groups of four. They say which houses they can see in their town and what their favourite house is.
- Show pictures from the Internet of houses in your local town. Learners say what types of houses they are.
- Show four pictures of people who look very different: an old man, a young couple, a family with a young child, and a group of university students.
- Put the learners into pairs. Learners talk together and decide which person should live in which house.
- Monitor and check.
- Point to each picture and ask pairs which person they think lives in each house.

3 8.13 Where do the children want to live? Listen and number the pictures.

- Say *Where do the children want to live? Listen and number.*
- Play the audio. Learners listen and number the pictures.

Track 8.13

1	Boy:	Look at these cool houses! There's a hut, a stilt-house, a detached house, a ranch, a houseboat and some flats. Wow! I want to live on a ranch!
2	Boy:	Where do you want to live, Grace?
	Grace:	Hmm … I want to live in a hut. A small hut.
3	Girl:	I don't want to live in a hut. I want to live in a big detached house.
4	Girl:	Where do you want to live, Nick?
	Nick:	I want to live on the water … in a houseboat!
5	Boy:	I like water too, but I want to live in a stilt-house.
	Boy:	A stilt-house? Yes, that's cool too.
6	Boy:	And you, Jill? Where would you like to live?
	Jill:	I like my flat. I want to live here.

Key: 2 hut 3 detached house 4 houseboat 5 stilt-house 6 flats

Activity Book, page 100

See pages TB120–132

Ending the lesson

- Tell the learners to listen. Say three sentences about your house. Two should be true and one false, e.g. *My house has got three bedrooms. There is a big garden. I have got a piano in the living room.* Ask *Which one isn't true?* The learners guess, e.g. *You haven't got a piano. (Yes, I have – it's true.) You haven't got a big garden. (You're right! I've got a very small garden.)*
- Put learners into pairs. They think of three sentences about their house – two true and one false. Their partner guesses which is false.
- Re-pair students with a new partner and repeat.

Learning outcomes By the end of the lesson, learners will be able to read and understand about places to live.

New language *different, same*

Recycled language *can/can't, have got*, numbers, rooms, things found in houses

Materials pictures of food, paired pictures from Digital photo bank of the same object (some the same item and some different, e.g. two armchairs, a sofa and a chair, two clocks, two lamps, a bedroom and a bathroom, two mirrors, a rug and a painting, two beds, a table and a chair, two kitchens, two halls), large copies of the reading text or cut up copies of the text (optional)

Key Competences

- Read a description of a houseboat.
- Write about their houses.
- Work together to make a list of things they can do or can't do at home.
- Reflect on their own learning.
- Interact with the digital poster.

Warm-up

- Write a room on the board, e.g. *bathroom*. Tell learners they have 30 seconds to think of three things you can see in that room. Check ideas. Repeat with more rooms.

Presentation

- Put the prepared set of paired pictures face down in two piles. One of each pair goes onto each pile in the same order (so if you turn over the top two of each pile they are from the same pair).
- Show the game. Display a picture of a bedroom and a bathroom. Ask *Are they the same thing or different?* (*Different*) Ask *Why? What are they?* (*A bedroom and a bathroom*) Say *They're different*. Learners repeat. Show a picture of two chairs (slightly different design). Ask *Are they the same thing or different?* (*Same – they are chairs*) Say *They're the same*. Learners repeat.
- Divide the class into two groups. Choose one learner from each group to come to the front. Ask each group to choose a team noise, e.g. beep or ring. Tell them to look at the pictures and decide if they are the same or different.
- The learners at the front hold up the top flashcards from each pile when you say *Now*. Each group makes their team noise if they know the answer. The first team to make the noise can answer. They say if the objects are the same or different and what the objects are.
- Each team gets a point for the correct answer. The team with the most points wins.

Pupil's Book, page 101

4 Read about David's house and think about your house. What's the same? What's different?

- Say *Open your Pupil's Books at page 101*. Focus on the photos. Ask *What can you see?* (*A boy – David. A houseboat.*)
- Learners read the text and check if they were correct.
- Learners read again, think about their house and David's house and find out what is the same and different, e.g. *David's house has got two bedrooms and my house has got two bedrooms.*

5 Write about your house.

- Say *Look at Activity 5*. Read out the first sentence: *Hi, I'm …* Show learners the first sentence in the reading text in Activity 4 (*Hi, I'm David.*) Show that they write their own name.
- Learners continue to work on their own and complete the writing. Monitor and support.

mission Stage 3

- Show the class the third stage of the Mission poster: 'List'. Get out a pen and paper. Say *At my house we can throw a ball in the garden. We can't play football because the garden is small.* Act out writing phrases onto the paper saying *Throw a ball …* (note this down) *Yes* (put a tick). *Play football … No* (put a cross).
- Learners write a list of what they can do or can't do at their house.

  Stronger learners These learners should write a minimum of three *can* sentences and three *can't* sentences.

  Extra support Learners can copy the sentences from the reading text, but change the activity.
- In pairs, learners find out if they can do the same or different things in their houses.
- Keep the lists for the final lesson of the unit.

Activity Book, page 101

See pages TB120–132

Activity Book, page 94

- Say *Look at page 94 of your Activity Book*. Review *My unit goals*. Ask *How is your Mission?* Learners reflect and choose a smiley face for *My mission diary 3*. Monitor.

Ending the lesson

- Go back to Stage 3 on the digital Mission poster. Add a tick to the 'List' stage or invite a learner to do it. Use self-assessment (see Introduction).
- Give out a completion sticker.

4 Read about David's house and think about your house. What's the same? What's different?

Hi, I'm David. I live in a houseboat with my mum, dad and sister. It's got five rooms – a living room, a kitchen, a bathroom and two bedrooms. It hasn't got a garden. We can play board games at my house, but we can't skateboard or play football! I like my house because at night I can hear the water and the ducks.

My house has got two bedrooms too.

I can't hear ducks at my house. I can hear birds.

5 Write about your house.

Hi, I'm ____________________. I live in a ____________________ with my ______________________________. It's got ____________________ rooms – ________________________________. It hasn't got ____________________. We can ____________________ at my house, but we can't ____________________. I like my house because ______________________________.

mission STAGE 3

Make a list of things you can do with your friend.

My mission diary
Activity Book page 94

Literature

1 **Look at the pictures. Which rooms can you see? What's your favourite room in your house?**

8.14

The clock on the wall

At Sue's home today,
Rob says, 'Sue, can we play,
In the bedroom, the garden, the kitchen, the hall,
On the sofa and mat with this ugly old ball?'

'Yes, we can,' replies Sue. 'That's a nice thing to do.
You can throw it to me, I can throw it to you.
We can catch it and bounce it and kick it and run,
Then catch it, and kick it, and throw it for fun.'

In the bath, on the sofa, on the table and the chair,
Rob throws the ball here, Sue runs for it there.

Learning outcomes By the end of the lesson, learners will have read about playing in a house, and learnt about being careful.

New language *bounce, hit, mat, ugly*

Recycled language *can/can't*, furniture, rooms, verbs (*catch, kick, play, throw*)

Materials soft ball, flashcards of activities (football, board game, computer, swim, horse) and places (park, living room, bedroom), pictures of a swimming pool and a farm, picture of a mat, pictures of a new ball and an old ugly ball, coloured pens or pencils

Key Competences

Work in pairs to predict what happens in a story.

Talk about their favourite room.

Read and listen to a story.

Warm-up

- Show some flashcards of activities (football for *playing football*, board game for *playing a game*, computer for *computer game*, swim for *swimming*, horse for *horse-riding*). Learners say the names. Display on the board some flashcards and pictures of places (flashcards: park, living room, bedroom; pictures: swimming pool, farm).
- Ask the learners which place is good for each activity. Hold up the activities one by one and ask the learners to point to the best place (e.g. playing football – *park*, computer game – *living room*, board game – *bedroom*, swimming – *swimming pool*, horse-riding – *farm*).

Presentation

- Say *We are going to read about playing*.
- Get out a soft ball. Say *We can play with a ball. We can throw it.* Throw the ball in the air. Say *But be careful! Or the ball can hit the window.* Hold the ball in your hand and demonstrate hitting it, e.g. against your hand. Say *Hit*. Learners repeat. Say *The ball can hit the window*. Learners repeat.
- Say *We can kick it*. Kick it (very gently) to a learner and they kick it back. Say *Be careful!* Say *We can catch it*. Throw it to a learner and call out *Catch!* The learner throws it back to you. Say *Be careful!* Say *We can bounce it*. Bounce the ball on the ground. Say *Bounce*. Learners repeat.
- Show pictures of a new ball and an old ball. Point to the new ball. Ask *Is it new?* (*Yes*) *Is it nice?* (*Yes*) Point to the old ball. Ask *Is it new?* (*No*) *Is it nice?* (*No*) Say *It looks bad. It's ugly.* Learners repeat.
- Show a picture of a mat. Ask *What's this?* (*A mat*) Learners repeat.

Pupil's Book, page 102

1 Look at the pictures. Which rooms can you see? What's your favourite room in your house?

- Put the class into groups of four. Say *Open your Pupil's Books at pages 102 and 103. Which rooms can you see in the pictures?*
- Check ideas.
- Ask *Which is your favourite room in your house?* Learners discuss in pairs. A few learners report back.
- Say *Look at the children. Can you find their names?* (*Rob and Sue*) Say *Point to Rob. Point to Sue.* Learners point.
- Say *Look at the name of the story*. Read: *The clock on the wall*. Ask *What happens with the ball?* Learners look at the pictures and guess. Don't worry if they are correct or not at this stage.

8.14 The clock on the wall

- Say *Read and listen to the first part*. Show learners paragraphs 1–3 on page 102. Play the audio. Learners listen and read. Pause the audio to check understanding. First picture: *What does Rob want to play with?* (*The ball*) Second picture: *Is Sue playing too?* (*Yes*) *What can they do with the ball?* (*Throw it, catch it, bounce it, kick it*) Third picture: *Where are they throwing the ball?* (*In the bath and on the sofa, table and chair*)
- Ask *Is it a good idea to play with the ball in the house?* Ask *Why?* Learners suggest ideas. Don't give answers yet.

Track 8.14

See story on Pupil's Book pages 102–103

- Say *Read the next part*. Show them the paragraphs on page 103. Play the audio. Pause to check understanding. Fourth picture: *Does the ball hit the door?* (*No. It hits the clock.*) Ask *Where is the clock now? Is it on the wall?* (*No. It's on the mat on the floor.*) Fifth picture: *Is the clock OK?* (*Yes, it is OK.*)
- Ask *Are Rob and Sue happy?* (*Yes, because the clock is OK.*) *Is it a good idea to play ball in the house?* (*No*)

Activity Book, page 102

See pages TB120–132

Ending the lesson

- Divide the board into two by drawing a line in the middle. Divide the class into two: group A and group B. One learner from each group comes to the front.
- Say to group A *Think of games you can play outside in the garden or park*. Say to group B *Think of games you can play in the house*. The two learners at the front write down the ideas. The groups give ideas to the writer, but say *You can't speak. You can show.*
- Learners mime game ideas to the learners at the front, who write them in a list.
- See which group has the most answers.

Learning outcomes By the end of the lesson, learners will have summarised a story, and recognised and thought about the consequences of actions.

New language *come down, shocked*

Recycled language *angry, happy, sad, sorry*, rooms and furniture, verbs (*bounce, catch, kick, throw*), *can/can't*

Materials audio, coloured pens or pencils

Social and Emotional Skill: Comforting others

- After reading the story, ask *Who hits the clock?* (Rob) *What does he say?* (*I'm sorry.*) *Is Sue angry?* (No) *What does she say?* (*Don't worry. Rob, it's OK!*) Explain what happens: *Rob is sorry for hitting the clock. It's important to show respect for other people's things. Sue can see Rob is sad and shocked. She tells him not to worry and the clock's OK. She helps Rob feel happy again.*
- Ask *Do you break things when you play ball? What happens when you do? Do you say sorry?*
- Remind learners that it's important to play in the playground and not in the classroom.
- Talk about situations when learners can help someone to feel better. For example, if someone falls over in the playground or breaks a toy or loses their crayons or books, they can say *It's OK* or *Are you OK?*
- Hand out paper to each learner. They draw a situation with two or more people. Then they write *Don't worry* and *It's OK* in speech bubbles on the paper.
- Ask some learners to come to the front and act out the situation they have drawn. They can choose who to act it out with.

Key Competences

- Talk about where they play games.
- Act out a story.
- Think about how other people feel; Think about the consequences of their actions.

Warm-up

- Call out *Throw a ball. Kick a ball. Catch a ball. Bounce a ball.* Learners mime.
- **SA** Use self-assessment to check how well learners think they understand the vocabulary. See Introduction.

Presentation

- Say *Open your Pupil's Books at pages 102 and 103. Look at the pictures in the story.* Summarise the story and mime. Learners copy the mimes as you go. Say *Rob and Sue are playing. Rob wants to play with the ball. He's excited.* Mime excitement. Say *Sue likes the game. She says they can throw the ball* Mime throwing. *Kick the ball.* Mime kicking. *And bounce the ball.* Mime bouncing. Say *They play on the sofa, on the table and on the chair.* Mime throwing, catching and running. Say *Oh no!* Mime shock. *The ball hits the clock …* Gesture as if something has fallen down. Say *The clock comes down on the mat. Sue and Rob are shocked.* Mime shock. Say *But it's OK! The clock is OK!* Mime being relieved.

Pupil's Book, page 103

2 How do they feel? Read and circle.

- Say *excited* and mime the meaning. Learners copy. Repeat with *shocked, happy, sad* and *angry*.
- Write the words *excited, shocked, happy* on the board.
- Say *I am playing a game*. Mime playing a game, e.g. throwing a ball. Ask *How do I feel?* Point to the three words. Choose a confident learner to come up and circle the correct word on the board (*happy*).
- Say *My friend is here to play*. Clap your hands and jump and look excited. Ask *How do I feel?* Choose a learner to come and circle the correct word (*excited*).
- Point to the remaining word (*shocked*). Say to learners *Show me 'shocked'*. Learners mime shock.
- Say *Well done. Now look at Activity 2. Let's try again.*
- Check answers.

Key: 2 happy 3 surprised 4 happy

3 Ask and answer.

- Put learners into groups of three or four. Tell them to choose a reporter.
- Ask *Has your house got a garden?* Tell the reporter to note the answers. The groups discuss if they have gardens at home.
- Ask the reporter to summarise what the group said.
- Say *In my house we play board games in the living room. We play football in the garden.*
- Ask *Where do you play in your house?* Tell reporters to remember two things to report back at the end of the activity. Learners discuss in their groups.
- Ask the reporters to tell the class two things their group discussed.

Activity Book, page 103

See pages TB120–132

Ending the lesson

- **SA** Repeat the self-assessment technique used at the start of the lesson to see how well learners think they understand the vocabulary. Is there any change?
- Write *happy, sad, angry, excited, shocked* on the board. Put learners into pairs. They take turns miming the emotion and their partner guesses which feeling it is.

But the ball hits the clock on the wall by the door,

And down comes the clock, hits the mat on the floor.

And Rob says, 'I'm sorry, so sorry for that.'

But Sue says 'Don't worry,' and looks at the mat.

She picks up the clock, and says, 'Today's a good day.'

And she points to the clock and says, 'Rob, it's OK!'

2 How do they feel? Read and circle.

1 When Rob finds a ball, he feels:

2 When Rob and Sue play a game with the ball, they feel:

3 When the clock falls on the floor, Rob feels:

4 When Sue says the clock is OK, Rob feels:

3 Ask and answer.

Has your house got a garden?

Yes, it has.

Where do you play in your house?

In my bedroom.

Pre A1 Starters

1 Look at the picture in Activity 3. Read and find.

pineapple table clock bookcase milk bread phone cake

2 8.15 Listen and point to the correct pineapple. Then practise with a friend.

It's in front of the boy.

3 8.16 Listen and colour. There is one example.

You can use coloured pencils, pens or crayons.

Learning outcomes By the end of the lesson, learners will have listened and found the correct object by listening for detail.

Test skills Effective listening for detail (see Introduction)

New language *milk, pineapple*

Recycled language colours, prepositions, words and phrases describing furniture and things in a house

Materials Rooms and objects in the house flashcards, Furniture and household items flashcards, picture of a pineapple, audio, coloured pens or pencils

Key Competences

- Practise listening for detail.
- Practise activity types found in *Pre A1 Starters* exams.
- Colour a picture based on verbal information.

Warm-up

- Hide flashcards from the unit around the classroom before the learners come in.
- Choose learners to come up to the front in pairs. Tell them where to find the flashcards, e.g. *The sofa is between the bookcase and the door.* They run to get them.
- SA Use self-assessment to check how well learners think they understand the vocabulary. See Introduction.

Presentation

- Say *Let's do a listening exam*. Write *Listening Exam* on the board.
- Say *We can listen for names of things. And we can listen for where things are. This can help us. Let's see how.*
- Show a picture of a pineapple. Say *We are finding pineapples*. Say *Pineapple*. Learners repeat.

Pupil's Book, page 104

1 Look at the picture in Activity 3. Read and find.

- Say *Open your Pupil's Books at page 104*. Look at the picture. Ask *How many pineapples can you see?* (*Five*)
- Ask *What can you see in the picture?* Learners call out ideas. Say *Look at the words in the box. Can you find them?* Learners read and find the objects. They write the words onto the objects.

2 8.15 Listen and point to the correct pineapple. Then practise with a friend.

- Use the artwork to teach *milk*.
- Say *Let's listen and point*.

Track 8.15

It's in front of the boy.
It's on the bookcase.
It's in the mother's hands.
It's under the table.
It's between the milk and the father's phone.

3 8.16 Listen and colour. There is one example.

- Say *Very good. Now let's listen and colour. Listen to the example*. Play the first part of the audio. Say *Point to the yellow pineapple*. Learners point. Show learners the monkey picture and read his speech bubble. Learners get out coloured pens or pencils. Say *Show me purple*. They hold up purple. Repeat with *pink* and *blue*.
- Play the rest of the audio. Learners listen and colour.

Track 8.16

Girl: There are lots of pineapples in this dining room. Can I colour one of them?
Man: Yes. There's a pineapple in front of the boy. Can you see it?
Girl: In front of the boy?
Man: That's right. Colour it yellow.
Girl: OK. I'm doing that now.
Can you see the yellow pineapple in front of the boy? This is an example. Now you listen and colour.

1
Girl: Can you see the children's mother?
Man: Yes. She's in front of the door … and she's got a pineapple in her hands.
Girl: Can I colour that one purple?
Man: That's a funny colour for a pineapple! But OK – do that.
Girl: This is fun!

2
Man: Now, can you colour the pineapple on the table?
Girl: The one between the milk and the phone?
Man: Yes. Can you colour it pink?
Girl: Pink! Really? OK then.

3
Man: Can you see the bookcase? There's a pineapple on it.
Girl: Where?
Man: Look … There – next to the clock. Colour it blue, please.
Girl: All right.
Man: Great. Well done!
Now listen again.
[Repeat track]

Key: Learners colour: 1 pineapple in mother's hands – purple, 2 pineapple on table, between milk and phone – pink, 3 pineapple on bookcase, next to clock – blue

Activity Book, page 104

See pages TB120–132

Ending the lesson

- SA Repeat the self-assessment technique used at the start of the lesson to see how well learners think they understand the vocabulary. Is there any change?

Learning outcomes By the end of the lesson, learners will have revised the language in the unit and acted out having a friend to visit their house.

Recycled language unit language

Materials Rooms and objects in the house flashcards, Furniture and household items flashcards, paper, coloured pens or pencils

Key Competences

- Revise vocabulary and language learnt in the unit.
- Complete self-assessment tasks and reflect on their own learning.
- Work together to act out having a friend to visit.

Warm-up

- Put learners into pairs. Say *I like my friends visiting my house. We eat nice food. We play board games.*
- Ask *Do you like friends visiting your house? What do you eat and play?* Learners talk in pairs.

Presentation

- Write on the board: *My friend is visiting my house.*
- Say *Let's get ready.* Put the learners into pairs. Ask *Where can we play?* Learners talk about rooms and places to play.
- Ask *Which food and drink have you got?* Learners talk in pairs. Monitor and check.
- Ask *What can you play?* Give back the lists of games and activities to do in the house or garden that learners wrote in Mission 3.

  Extra support Give out a list of words at each stage. Learners can choose and copy.
- Choose a learner to come to the front and tell them they are visiting you. Encourage them to mime ringing a doorbell and make a ringing sound. Mime opening the door and saying *Hello!* Encourage the learner to reply.
- Encourage them to mime going into your house and follow you as you show them around. Say *This is my living room. Look – here is my television and this is my sofa.* Continue with another few rooms, e.g. mime going upstairs or showing the bathroom.
- Offer the learner some food, e.g. *Would you like some cheese sandwiches and some orange juice?* (*Yes, please!*) Mime eating and drinking.
- Suggest playing a game, e.g. *Let's play tennis in the garden.* (*OK – that's a good idea.*) Mime playing tennis.
- Put the learners into pairs to practise.
- Learners work in pairs and show their house to their partner. Monitor and check. Their partner should respond by saying what they like.
- Tell the 'host' learner to offer food and drink. Monitor.
- Finally ask them to suggest games and activities. Learners mime playing the game. Monitor and check.

Pupil's Book, page 105

mission in action!

Have your friend to visit.

- Divide the class into two groups: A and B.
- Tell the group A learners that they will have a friend to visit. They must show their house and then offer food and drink and some games or activities. Assign each Learner B to a Learner A. Learner A shows their house, offers food and drink and then suggests games.
- When they have finished, swap roles so that Learner Bs are the hosts and Learner As visit.

  Extra support Write some of the phrases on the board and encourage learners to read, e.g. *This is the bedroom/ living room/kitchen. Would you like some … ? We can play …*

  Stronger learners Learners can ask additional questions, e.g. *Where is the bathroom? Is there a clock in the hall? Can I have some cake, please?*

Self-assessment

- **SA** Say *Did you like our 'Have a friend to visit' Mission?* Ask them to show you a thumbs up, thumbs down or thumbs in the middle.
- Say *Our next Mission is 'Let's have a holiday'. Say one thing you can do and one thing you want to learn.* Learners talk in pairs, e.g. *I can write the words. I want to answer all the questions for the story.*

Activity Book, page 105

See pages TB120–132

Activity Book, page 94

- Say *Look at page 94 of your Activity Book.* Review *My unit goals*. Ask *How is your Mission?*
- Learners reflect and choose a smiley face for *My mission diary* the final stage. Monitor.
- Point to the sunflower. Learners read the 'can do' statements and tick them if they agree they have achieved them. They colour each leaf green if they are very confident or orange if they think they need more practice.
- Point to the word stack sign. Ask learners to spend a few minutes looking back at the unit and find a minimum of five new words they have learnt. They write the new words into their word stack. See Introduction for activities.

Ending the lesson

- Go back to the completion stage on the digital Mission poster. Add a tick or invite a learner to do it. Use self-assessment (see Introduction).
- Give out a completion sticker.
- Tell the learners *You have finished your Mission! Well done!*

Review

mission in action!

Have your friend to visit.

My mission diary
Activity Book page 94

★ Show your friend your house.

This is the living room.

Where's the bathroom?

★ Offer your friend some food and drink.

Would you like a drink?

Yes, please. Can I have some water?

★ Choose things you and your friend can do together.

We can play a game.

Let's play 'Hide and seek'.

9 Happy holidays

1 **Watch the video. Draw something at the beach.**

mission Go on holiday

In this unit I will:

1. Prepare for my holiday.
2. Make a friend.
3. Write a postcard.
- ★ Make a holiday photo album.

Unit 9 learning outcomes

In Unit 9, learners learn to:

- talk about clothes and what people are wearing
- give instructions using imperatives
- talk about hobbies and things you enjoy doing
- read and understand about things we see on holiday
- learn about honesty and friendship

Materials video, pictures from Digital photo bank of different holiday destinations (a skiing holiday, a beach holiday, museums in a city, the countryside), sticky tack, digital Mission poster

Key Competences

Become familiar with language related to holidays.

Reflect on their own learning by going through the unit goals.

Draw a picture of something at the beach.

Self-assessment

- SA Say *Open your Pupil's Books at page 106*. Say *Look at the picture*. Indicate items on the page and ask questions using the language from the unit, e.g. *What is it? What is he doing? What colour is this?* Use self-assessment (see Introduction). Say *OK. Let's learn*.

Warm-up

- Show pictures of different holiday destinations, e.g. a skiing holiday, a beach holiday, museums in a city, the countryside.
- Say *Let's have a holiday*. Check learners understand the word *holiday*. Ask *Which place is your favourite? What can you do?*
- Put learners into pairs. Learners tell their partner which place they like best and what they can do there.

Pupil's Book, page 106

1 Watch the video. Draw something at the beach.

- Say *In this unit we're talking about holidays*. Say *Let's watch the video*. To introduce the topic of the unit, play the video.
- Ask *What kind of holiday do you have? Do you play on holiday?* Different learners answer.
- Learners draw a picture of something at the beach.

  Fast finishers Learners can label their pictures. Monitor and, as they finish, give them additional words.

mission Go on holiday

- Show the digital Mission poster. Say *Let's go on holiday*. Learners repeat.
- Say *Point to number 1*. Show them the bag. Say *Let's prepare for your holiday*. Mime packing. Learners copy and repeat. Say *Number 1* and get the learners to repeat the mime and words again.
- Say *Point to number 2*. Show them the children talking. Say *Let's make a new friend*. Mime waving and smile. Learners copy and repeat. Say *Number 2* and gesture for them to copy and repeat again. Say *One* and learners repeat the packing mime.
- Say *Point to number 3*. Say *Let's write a postcard*. Mime writing, and posting a postcard into a letterbox. Learners copy and repeat. Say *Three* and repeat. Go through mimes 1–3, calling out the numbers for learners to mime and chant.
- Say *Point to number 4*. Say *Let's make a photo album!* Mime taking photos. Encourage them to copy. Say *Four* and learners mime and chant. Repeat the whole sequence, getting the learners to mime and chant as you call out the numbers. Say with excitement *Let's go on holiday! This is our Mission*.

Activity Book, page 106

My unit goals

- Go through the unit goals with the learners. You can read these or if you prefer you can put them onto the board or a poster.
- You can go back to these unit goals at the end of each Mission stage during the unit and review them.
- Say *This is our Mission page*.
- For ideas on monitoring and assessment, see Introduction.

Ending the lesson

- Play 'The photo game'. Choose a confident learner to come to the front. Ask him/her to mime an activity. If he/she can't think of one, whisper an idea, e.g. *Play football*. Explain that when you take the photo, he/she should freeze. Let the learner begin their mime and then, as he/she moves, act taking a photo, aiming and clicking your camera.
- The learner should freeze. Ask the other learners *What is he/she doing?* The learners answer, e.g. *He's/She's playing football*.
- Repeat with other learners.

  Stronger learners These learners can think of activities.

  Extra support Learners can be given activities to mime. You can whisper this to them.

Learning outcomes Learners will be able to recognise and use words to describe clothes.

New language *baseball cap, boots, dress, hat, jacket, jeans, shirt, shoes, shorts, skirt, sunglasses, trousers, T-shirt*

Recycled language *doors, home, house, windows*

Materials Clothes flashcards, a picture from Africa and a picture from Alaska, audio, video

Key Competences

- Identify and name clothes.
- Chant together as a class.
- Identify and say words with the letters 'j' and 'h'.

Warm-up

- Stick some Clothes flashcards on the board.
- Say *I'm going to Africa. It's hot.* Put up a picture of Africa.
- Ask *What can I pack for Africa?* Learners point to the clothes.

Presentation

- Draw stick figures of a boy and a girl on the board.
- Draw items of clothing on the figures, saying, e.g. *He's wearing jeans.* Learners repeat.

Pupil's Book, page 107

1 9.01 Listen and point. Then listen again and draw. What does Jenny like?

- Say *Open your Pupil's Books at page 107.*
- Ask *Who can you see? Who's wearing a baseball cap? (Jenny) What colour is it? (Pink) Who's wearing shorts? (Grandpa) Who's wearing orange shoes? (Jim)*
- Play the audio. Learners point to the clothes in the picture.

Track 9.01

The children and their grandparents are shopping for their holiday.

Grandpa: Look at these big, black sunglasses, Jenny!
Jenny: Ooh, they're nice, Grandpa, and the hat's good for our holiday.
Grandpa: Yes, it is. Green's my favourite colour, and I'm wearing green boots too.
Grandma: Oh, Grandpa! What are you wearing? You can't wear boots and shorts!
Grandpa: Tee hee. Do you like my shirt?
Jenny: It's great! Very colourful! I'm wearing a blue skirt. I love it! My favourite colour's blue.
Grandma: Yes, it's nice. The red T-shirt's nice too. Do you like this pink dress, Jenny?
Jenny: Huh! Hmm … no. Pink isn't my favourite colour.
Grandpa: I like that T-shirt, Jenny.
Jenny: Thanks. I like it too.
Grandpa: But the baseball cap … hmm … I don't know about the pink baseball cap. Oh, Jim! Those jeans are small for you.
Jenny: And that grey jacket's very big.
Grandma: Look at these brown trousers, Jim. Do you want them?
Jim: Oh, yes please, Grandma. They're nice … and are these shoes OK?
Grandma: Er, well, the shoes, er, they're very … orange, Jim.
Jenny: Er, I don't know … No, Jim, those shoes are ugly.
Grandma: But that yellow T-shirt's nice.
Jim: Humph! This yellow T-shirt? This is my old T-shirt.
Grandma: Whoops! Sorry!

- Say *Listen again and draw. What does Jenny like?* Play the audio. Learners add smiles or frowns.

Key: ☺ sunglasses, hat, shirt, skirt, T-shirt
☹ dress, shoes

2 9.02 Say the chant.

- Play the audio or video. For each item of clothing, learners point to it in the picture.
- Repeat the audio or video. Learners chant and point.

Track 9.02

Sunglasses, hat, boots and shorts (x2)
Shirt, skirt, T-shirt, dress (x2)
Baseball cap and jeans (x2)
Jacket, trousers, shoes (x2)

3 9.03 Listen, point and answer.

- Play the audio and pause. Learners point and call out answers.

Track 9.03

1 Where is Grandpa's hat? What colour is it?
2 Where is Jenny's baseball cap? What colour is it?
3 Where is Jenny's T-shirt? What colour is it?
4 Where are Jim's jeans? What colour are they?
5 Where is Jenny's skirt? What colour is it?
6 Where is Jim's jacket? What colour is it?
7 Where are Jim's shoes? What colour are they?
8 Where is Grandpa's shirt? What colour is it?
9 Where are Grandpa's sunglasses? What colour are they?
10 Where are Grandpa's boots? What colour are they?

Key: 1 green 2 pink 3 red 4 blue 5 blue 6 grey 7 orange 8 red and yellow 9 blue and black 10 green

Activity Book, page 107

See pages TB120–132

Ending the lesson

- SA Say *We learnt about clothes.* Show the flashcards. Ask *Do you know the words?* Use the self-assessment technique (see Introduction). Learners show how they feel.
- Say *You can say the words well. Good work.*

Vocabulary 1

9

1 9.01 **Listen and point. Then listen again and draw. What does Jenny like?**

2 9.02 **Say the chant.**

3 9.03 **Listen, point and answer.**

9

The Friendly Farm
9.04
1
I've got four oranges here. Nice!
Do you like the green hat or the red one?
Shelly! That's Grandpa's new hat!
2
Let's go and play in the barn.
It's Jim and Jenny.
3
Gracie! Eat your oranges … now!
OK.
Shelly! Come here and pick up these clothes, please!
4
Now clean the table, Gracie. It's dirty. And clean your face, please!
5
Harry! Put that hat on the table, now! Rocky! Take those pencils and put them in the bag.
OK, Mum.
6
Look at the barn. It's nice and clean.
Look! Grandpa's hat's there on the table, in the barn!

Learning outcomes By the end of the lesson, learners will be able to understand instructions.

New language imperatives (e.g. *eat the oranges, clean the table*), *clean, dirty, pick up, put on*

Recycled language clothes, colours, fruit, possessives

Materials pictures from Digital photo bank of a dirty, messy bedroom, and of a clean, tidy bedroom, audio, video, coloured pens or pencils

Key Competences

Read and listen to a story; Understand the use of imperatives.

Role play a story.

Warm-up

- Divide the class into four groups. Choose a team leader for each group. Each group should sit in a circle.
- Tell the learners to listen and do what you say. The last learner in each group to do the action will be 'out'. The team leader's job is to watch and check who is out. Give an example: *Ride a horse*. Learners mime.
- Give the instructions: *Stand up. Catch a ball. Put your hands on your head. Find something blue. Sit down. Play tennis. Throw a ball. Find something with a circle. Swim. Wave goodbye.* Add more instructions if necessary or repeat them faster until only one learner is left in each group.
- **SA** Use self-assessment to check how well learners think they understand the vocabulary. See Introduction.

Presentation

- Show a picture of a messy, dirty bedroom. Ask *What is it? (A bedroom)* Say *Oh no! It's dirty.* Make a disgusted face.
- Mime cleaning (sweeping and dusting). Ask *What am I doing?* (*Cleaning*) Say *I'm cleaning the room*. Learners repeat several times.
- Go to a table and clean it. Say *I'm cleaning the table*. Learners repeat.
- Mime picking up clothes. Say *I'm picking up clothes*. Learners repeat several times.
- Mime putting books on shelves. Say *I'm putting the books on the bookshelf.* Learners repeat several times.
- Show a picture of a clean, tidy bedroom. Say *Now it's clean*. Learners repeat.

Pupil's Book, page 108

9.04 The Friendly Farm song

- Play the introductory song at the beginning of the cartoon story. Learners listen and sing. Ask *Can you remember?* Encourage the learners to sing the song from memory.

Track 9.04
See The Friendly Farm song on page TB5

9.04 The Friendly Farm

- Say *Open your Pupil's Books at page 108*. Ask *Who can you see in the pictures?* Learners name the characters. Say *Point to picture 1*. Learners point. Ask *Is the barn clean or dirty? (Dirty)* Ask *Who's coming to the barn? (Jim and Jenny)*
- Ask *What are the animals doing?* Write the question on the board. Say *Listen*. Play the audio or video. Learners listen and read.

Track 9.04
The Friendly Farm song + see cartoon on Pupil's Book page 108

- Learners check answers in pairs. (*They are cleaning the barn.*) Check with the whole group.
- Play the audio or video again. Pause after each frame and check comprehension by asking learners questions. Frame 1: *What's Shelly doing? (She's putting on Grandpa's new hat.)* Frame 2: *Who can see Jim and Jenny coming? (Cameron)* Frame 3: *What is Gracie doing? (She's eating her oranges.) What is Henrietta saying to Shelly? (Come and pick up the clothes.)* Frame 4: *What is Henrietta saying to Gracie? (Clean the table and clean your face.)* Frame 5: *What is Harry doing with the hat? (He's putting it on the table.)* Frame 6: *Is the barn clean? (Yes, it is.)*
- Play the audio or video again. Divide the class into groups and give each group a role from the cartoon, e.g. some are Gracie and some are Cameron. Learners repeat the speech bubbles for their character.

Activity Book, page 108

See pages TB120–132

Ending the lesson

- **SA** Repeat the self-assessment technique used at the start of the lesson to see how well learners think they understand the vocabulary. Is there any change?
- Tell learners about your favourite outfit, e.g. *My favourite clothes are my black trousers, a green shirt and black boots. I like wearing green sunglasses too.*
- Check learners have coloured pens and pencils. Tell them to draw their favourite clothes.

  Fast finishers Learners can write sentences describing the outfit, e.g. *My favourite clothes are my jeans, a blue and red T-shirt and a red baseball cap.*

  Extra support Learners copy words in the Pupil's Book.
- Collect up all the pictures and give them out randomly. Learners need to find the owner of the outfit. They should speak to the learner they think it belongs to and ask questions: *Do you like jeans? Do you like red shoes? Are these your clothes?*
- Once they have found the person who owns the drawing, they should give it back.

9 Language practice 1

Learning outcomes By the end of the lesson, learners will be able to use imperatives to give directions or instructions.

New language *look at, pack, put in*

Recycled language clothes, colours, verbs

Materials a rucksack, coloured pens or pencils, sticky tack, audio, pictures of holiday destinations (a beach, a city, a snowy mountain), digital Mission poster

Key Competences

- Learn to use imperatives to give directions or instructions.
- Work in pairs to make a holiday list.
- Reflect on their own learning.
- Interact with the digital poster.

Warm-up

- Say *I'm going on holiday.* Put a rucksack on the desk. Say *I'm packing my bag.* Show some things to go in your bag, e.g. *Here are my shorts, sunglasses, T-shirts, trousers.*
- Ask *Can you write the list? What's in my bag?*
- In pairs, learners write as many items as they can remember. They get a point for each item.

Presentation

- A confident learner comes to the front to carry out instructions. Say *Put the bag on the table. Put it in the cupboard. Look at the clock. Write on the board.*

Pupil's Book, page 109

9.05 Gracie's Grammar

- Say *Open your Pupil's Books at page 109.* Point to Gracie's Grammar box. Write the same sentences on the board.
- Play the audio. Pause for learners to repeat each sentence.

Track 9.05

See Pupil's Book page 109

1 9.06 Listen and stick. Then look, read and write.

- Play the audio for learners to point to the correct sticker.

Track 9.06

1 Mr Friendly: Clean those shoes, please, Jenny.
Jenny: What? These shoes?
Mr Friendly: Yes, the black ones. They're very dirty.
Jenny: OK.

2 Grandpa: Can you see my glasses, Grandma? They're over there, in front of the phone.
Grandma: Ah, yes.
Grandpa: Pass those glasses to me, please.
Grandma: OK, here you are.

3 Mrs Friendly: Put that T-shirt in the cupboard!
Mr Friendly: This red one?
Mrs Friendly: Yes, that's right.
Mr Friendly: OK.

4 Mrs Friendly: Pick up those shoes, please, Jim.
Jim: Which ones?
Mrs Friendly: Those brown ones.
Jim: OK.

- Play the audio again. Learners stick in the stickers.
- Say *Look, read and write.* Learners write.

Key: 2 Pass 3 Put 4 Pick up

mission Stage 1

- Show learners the first stage of the digital Mission poster: 'List for packing'. Say *Let's make a list for packing.*
- Put up some pictures of holiday destinations: a beach, a city with museums, a snowy mountain.
- Put the learners into pairs. Ask *Which is your favourite holiday? Tell your partner.*
- Learners complete the worksheet task in the Teacher's Resource Book page 94 (see notes on TRB page 87).
- Alternatively, if you do not have the Teacher's Resource Book, learners make a list of the clothes they need for their holiday.
- Ask learners to get out their bags. They can use a real bag or draw a case.
- Tell learners to pack. Each learner gives their list to their partner. Their partner checks: e.g. *Have you got jeans?* (*Yes, here they are.*) *OK. Put them in the bag.* Learners mime or put their clothes into their bags.

  Fast finishers These learners repeat with a new partner.

  Extra support Learners look at their partner's list and tell them, e.g. *Put the T-shirt in the bag.*
- For ideas on monitoring and assessment, see Introduction.

Activity Book, page 109

See pages TB120–132

Activity Book, page 106

- Say *Look at page 106 of your Activity Book.* Review *My unit goals.* Ask *How is your Mission?*
- Learners reflect and choose a smiley face for *My mission diary 1.* Monitor.

Ending the lesson

- **SA** Go back to Stage 1 on the digital Mission poster. Say *We made a holiday list. Good work.* Add a tick to the 'List for packing' stage. Use self-assessment (see Introduction).
- Give out a completion sticker.

Language practice 1

9

9.05 Gracie's Grammar

Look at this T-shirt. **Point to** that dress there.

Pick up these socks. **Clean** those shoes.

1 9.06 Listen and stick. Then look, read and write.

1 Clean those shoes, please.

2 ______ those glasses to me, please.

3 ______ that T-shirt in the cupboard, please.

4 ______ those shoes, please.

mission STAGE 1

Make a holiday list. Then help your friend to pack a bag.

Have you got a hat?

Yes. Here it is.

OK. Put it in the bag.

My mission diary

Activity Book page 106

9

Vocabulary 2 and song

1 9.07 Listen and write. Then sing the song.

We're at the beach,
next to the sea.
I've got my camera, here
with ___me___.
I'm on the sand.
I'm having fun.
I'm taking photos in the
________.

Oh, we can play. We can play
at the beach in the sun.
We can play. We can play
at the beach in the sun,
the beach in the sun.

In a ________ on the sea,
Dad's fishing, next to me.
We've got two ________,
and seven fish,
and a purple ________.

Chorus

2 Read, think and say. Compare with your classmates.

Think of ...

- three things you can do at the beach.
- four things you can wear at the beach.
- five things you can see at the beach.

Learning outcomes By the end of the lesson, learners will have practised the language through song.

New language *beach, boat, fish, fishing, jellyfish, photos, sand, sea, shells, sun, take photos*

Recycled language *can, have got*, prepositions of place, present continuous

Materials pictures of different shaped and coloured shells (e.g. a round one, a long triangular one, pink, white and brown ones), large picture of a beach with sea and sand, At the beach flashcards, audio, video, a long rope or ribbon, a box for flashcards

Key Competences

- Learn vocabulary related to the beach.
- Listen to a song and do the actions.
- Work together to make a list of things related to the beach.
- Complete a crossword puzzle.

Warm-up

- Stick some pictures of different shaped and coloured shells on the board. Say *Shells*. Learners repeat.
- **SA** Use self-assessment to check how well learners think they understand the vocabulary. See Introduction.

Presentation

- Show the large picture of the beach. Point to the beach. Say *Beach*. Learners repeat. Do the same with *Sea* and *Sand*.
- Give out the flashcards. Ask the learner with the fish to come up, and ask him/her *Where can you put the fish?* The learner places it in the sea. Say *It's a fish*. Learners repeat. Say *We can see fish in the sea.* Learners repeat. (Jellyfish – in the sea, shells – on the beach/sand, boat – on the sea, sun – in the sky.)
- Stand back and mime taking a photo. Say *Let's take a photo.* Learners copy and repeat.

Pupil's Book, page 110

1 9.07 Listen and write. Then sing the song.

- Say *Open your Pupil's Books at page 110*. Say *Point to the sea*. Learners point. Repeat with *beach, sand, sun, fish, jellyfish, boat, shells*. Ask *Where's the shell?* (*Next to Grandpa's foot*) *What is Mr Friendly doing?* (*He's fishing.*)
- Write on the board *The Friendly Family are at the* ________. Ask *What can we write here?* and point to the space in the sentence. Learners suggest ideas. Say *Listen. The Friendly Family are at the beach.*
- Say *Listen and write*. Play the audio or video. Learners listen and write the missing words into the spaces.

Track 9.07

Rocky: I'm Rocky-Doodle-Doo and … here's our song for today: *At the beach.*

See song on Pupil's Book page 110

Key: sun, boat, shells, jellyfish

- Play the audio or video again. Learners sing along and mime with you (*I'm taking photos*: mime clicking a camera; *At the beach in the sun*: mime sunbathing and throwing a ball; *In a boat on the sea. Dad's fishing*: mime throwing out a fishing line; *seven fish*: make a wiggling movement with your hand like a fish).

9.08 **Extension** Once learners are confidently singing the song, try singing the karaoke version as a class.

2 Read, think and say. Compare with your classmates.

- Put learners into groups of three or four. Say *Look at Activity 2. Let's read, think and say.* Read the instructions.
- Learners work together and think of three things they can do at the beach, four things they can wear at the beach and five things they can see. If learners don't know the word for something, they can draw a picture or tell you in their first language. Tell them the correct word. Learners repeat.
- Read Rocky's speech bubble. Learners call out ideas.

Activity Book, page 110

See pages TB120–132

Ending the lesson

- **SA** Repeat the self-assessment technique used at the start of the lesson to see how well learners think they understand the vocabulary. Is there any change?
- Use a long rope or ribbon and ask two learners to hold the rope out low. Put a box on one side of the rope and At the beach flashcards on the other side.
- Divide the learners into two groups (A and B) with a maximum of 10 or 11 learners in each group. Learners stand on the same side as the box.

  Large class You can play twice or have two ropes.
- Learners from group A choose a learner from group B and call out a word. The learner they select must crawl under the rope, grab the correct flashcard, jump back over the rope and drop it into the box.
- Once all the words are in the box, repeat, but groups swap roles.

  Extra support Learners can be given words on pieces of paper or you can whisper the word to them before they call out.

  Stronger learners Learners can be asked to spell the word as they drop it into the box.

9 Language practice 2

Learning outcomes By the end of the lesson, learners will be able to describe things they like doing.

New language *collect shells, fly a kite, I enjoy ...-ing, I like ...-ing, Me too, So do I*

Recycled language *can/can't, Good idea*, words describing the beach and what you can see around it

Key Competences

- Learn and practise *like / enjoy + ing* to describe things they like doing.
- Practise a dialogue in pairs.
- Work in groups to role play talking to a new friend at the beach.
- Reflect on their own learning.
- Interact with the digital poster.

Warm-up

- Mime studying. Ask *What am I doing?* (*You're reading and writing.*)
- In groups of three, learners take it in turns to mime. Other learners guess what they are doing.

Presentation

- Say *I'm going to the beach*. Mime walking. Learners copy. Say *I like going to the beach*. Mime sunbathing and looking happy. Learners copy. Say *I'm walking on the beach. I'm collecting shells.* Mime collecting shells. Say *I like collecting shells*. Learners copy and repeat. Say *And I enjoy flying my kite*. Mime flying a kite. Draw a picture of a kite on the board. Learners copy and repeat. Say *I enjoy playing on the sand*. Mime building sandcastles. Learners copy and repeat.
- Write *like* and *enjoy* on the board with a heart next to them.
- Mime collecting shells. Ask *What am I doing?* (*You're collecting shells.*) Learners copy. Say *I like collecting shells*. Learners say *So do I*.
- Do another mime, e.g. flying a kite. Say *I enjoy flying a kite*. Learners copy and say *So do I*.
- Say *So do I* and *Me too* are the same.

Pupil's Book, page 111

1 (9.09) What is the girl doing now? Listen and tick ✓.

- Say *Open your Pupil's Books at page 111*. Ask *What can you see in picture one/two/three?* (*Fishing, shells, camera*)
- Say *I like collecting shells, but I can't see shells today. So I'm going fishing*. Learners point to picture 1.
- Play the audio or video. Learners listen and tick.

Track 9.09

Girl: What do you like doing at the beach?
Boy: I like picking up shells.
Girl: So do I.
Boy: Look! I've got seven shells.
Girl: Yes, they're beautiful, but today I'm not picking up shells. I've got my camera and I'm taking photos.
Boy: I enjoy taking photos.
Girl: Me too. Look, I'm taking a photo of that boat on the sea.
Boy: Ooh, yes. That's a nice photo.

Key: Picture 3 (taking photos)

(9.10) Gracie's Grammar

- Say *Look at Gracie's Grammar.* Play the audio. Learners repeat the sentences in the grammar box.
- Write the sentences on the board, but delete *kite* and *photos* and draw a line for the blank. Learners say the sentences but fill in the missing words. Rub out *So do* and *Me*. Learners say the sentences again, filling in the spaces. Rub out *like* and *enjoy*. Repeat. Continue until all the words are replaced by lines.

Track 9.10
See Pupil's Book page 111

2 Read and say the dialogue. Act it out.

- Put the learners in pairs to role play.

mission Stage 2

- Show learners the second stage of the digital Mission poster: 'Make a new friend'.
- Learners write down five things they like doing at the beach.
- Say to a learner *I like flying kites*. The learner says *So do I* and then something they enjoy doing.
- Say *Speak to three other new friends*. Learners mingle and talk.
- For ideas on monitoring and assessment, see Introduction.

Activity Book, page 111

See pages TB120–132

Activity Book, page 106

- Say *Look at page 106 of your Activity Book.* Review *My unit goals*. Ask *How is your Mission?*
- Learners reflect and choose a smiley face for *My mission diary 2*. Monitor.

Ending the lesson

- **SA** Go back to Stage 2 on the digital Mission poster. Add a tick to the 'Make a new friend' stage. Use self-assessment (see Introduction).
- Give out a completion sticker.

1 What is the girl doing now? Listen and tick ✓.

9.09

1

2

3

Gracie's Grammar

9.10

I **like** fly**ing** my kite.	**So do I.**
I **enjoy** tak**ing** photos.	**Me too.**

2 Read and say the dialogue. Act it out.

A What do you like doing at the beach?
B I like swimming in the sea.
A So do I, but we can't swim today. Let's play on the sand.
B Good idea. I enjoy playing on the sand.
A Me too.

mission STAGE 2

Talk to a new friend at the beach.

Hello. I'm Sam.

Hi, Sam. I'm Nina. Do you like collecting shells?

My mission diary
Activity Book page 106

Cross-curricular

What can we see on holiday?

1 **Watch the video.**

2 **Where can we see these things? Look and say.**

a 
shells

b 
snow

1 

forest

2 
mountain

e 
waterfall

f 
frog

c 
flowers

d 
tree

3 
river

4 
beach

g 
rocks

h 
jellyfish

We can see shells at the beach.

3 9.11 **Listen to the children talking about their holidays. Match the places with the things they see.**

Learning outcomes By the end of the lesson, learners will be able to understand and talk about the environment, what we can see on holiday and in nature.

New language *forest, mountain, river, rocks, snow, waterfall*

Recycled language *can*, imperatives, *beach, flowers, frog, jellyfish, shells, trees*

Materials a set of words per group of five learners on slips of paper (all words from the unit so far), coloured pens and pencils, video, audio

Key Competences

- Talk about things we can see on holiday.
- Learn about natural features.
- Draw a landscape and label things they can see there.

Warm-up

- Give out coloured pens or pencils, and paper.
- Say *Listen and draw*. Give instructions. Pause between instructions so they have time to draw.
- Say *Draw a beach. Draw a sun in the sky. Draw a boat on the sea. Draw a fish next to the boat. Draw a ball on the beach. Draw a shell in front of the ball. Draw some sunglasses next to the ball.*
- Check the drawings. Now ask learners to write the names of each item.

Presentation

- Say *Open your Pupil's Books at page 112*. Ask learners to look at the four big pictures. Say *Point to the forest*. Learners point and repeat. Follow the same sequence with *mountain* and *river*.
- Point to the pictures the learners know and ask *What is it?* (*Shells, flowers, tree, frog, jellyfish*)
- Say *Point to the waterfall*. Learners point and repeat. Follow the same sequence with *snow* and *rocks*.

Pupil's Book, page 112

1 Watch the video.

- Say *Let's watch the video*. Learners watch the video about what we can see on holiday and answer the questions at the end of the video.

2 Where can we see these things? Look and say.

- Put learners into pairs. Say *We can see shells on the …* Learners say *beach*. Say *Well done. What about the other pictures?* Tell them some of the pictures can be found in more than one place.
- Learners work in pairs and guess where each thing can be found. Check answers.

Key: (possible answers) 1 forest – flowers, tree, frog 2 mountain – snow, flowers, rocks 3 river – waterfall, frog, rocks 4 beach – shells, rocks, jellyfish

3 9.11 Listen to the children talking about their holidays. Match the places with the things they see.

- Play the audio. Learners listen and match.

Track 9.11

1 Matt: Hi, Grandma.
Grandma: Hello, Matt. How's your holiday?
Matt: It's fantastic! We're in the forest.
Grandma: Oh, that's nice. What can you see?
Matt: I can see lots of big trees and beautiful flowers.
Grandma: Ooh.

2 Woman: Do you like it here in the mountains, Sam?
Sam: Yes, it's beautiful. The mountains are very white!
Woman: Yes, there's a lot of snow.
Sam: Yes, there is. There are a lot of rocks too. Look at that big rock over there!

3 Girl 1: I love holidays at the river!
Girl 2: So do I. Look at those frogs!
Girl 1: Oh yes … One, two, three, four little frogs.
Girl 2: Let's go and look at the waterfall.
Both girls: Wow!

4 Dad: What are you doing?
Girl: I'm picking up shells, Dad. Look, there are lots of shells on this beach.
Dad: Oh, yes, there are.
Girl: What's that?
Dad: I don't know … Oh! It's a jellyfish!

- Check answers and see if the learners' guesses were correct.

Key: 1 d, c 2 b, g 3 f, e 4 a, h

Activity Book, page 112

See pages TB120–132

Ending the lesson

- Divide the learners into groups of five. Give each group a pile of words on slips of paper face down. Choose a group monitor for each group.
- Demonstrate how to play. Each learner picks up a word in turn and gives clues to the group until they say the word. They can mime, draw or give verbal clues, e.g. *This is on the beach. We can walk on it. It is yellow.* (*Sand*)
- Once the learners say the word, the next person takes a new word. The group monitor checks that no one looks at the words, spells out or tells the group the word.

Learning outcomes By the end of the lesson, learners will be able to read and understand about places to go on holiday.

New language *hotel, stay in, volcano*

Recycled language *can/can't, postcard*, present continuous, things found on the beach

Materials picture from Digital photo bank of a volcano, postcards (if possible) or card cut up to look like postcards, coloured pens and pencils

Key Competences

- Read and write a postcard about a holiday.
- Learn facts about places around the world.
- Reflect on their own learning.
- Interact with the digital poster.

Warm-up

- Write on the board:
  1 Where … ? 2 Is it … ? 3 What can you … ?
- Pretend to make a call on your mobile. Say *Hello!* Learners say *Hello*. Say *I'm on holiday.*
- Point to *1* on the board. Learners say *Where are you?* Say *I'm on the beach in Spain.*
- Point to *2* and mime being hot. Learners ask *Is it hot?* Say *Yes, it's very sunny.*
- Point to *3* and mime looking at things. Learners ask *What can you see?* Say *I can see sand and rocks. I can see fish in the sea. I can see a mountain near the beach.*
- Put learners into pairs. They act out a phone call.

Presentation

- Show a picture of a volcano. Ask what a volcano can do. Learners act out an eruption. Say *It's a volcano*. Learners repeat.
- Say *On holiday, I stay in a hotel or a house*. Check understanding. Ask *Can I stay in a volcano?* (*No*)

Pupil's Book, page 113

4 Read the postcard and say the missing words.

- Say *Open your Pupil's Books at page 113*. Focus on the picture. Ask *What can you see?* (*A beach*) *What colour is the sand?* (*Black*) *Why is it black?* Learners give their ideas.
- Point to the writing. Say *It's a postcard. We send postcards when we are on holiday.*
- Say *Look at the name at the top: Paula. Look at the name at the bottom: Laura. Who is on holiday?* (*Laura*)
- Read the beginning of the postcard: *Dear Paula, I'm on holiday with my family in the Canary Islands. We are staying in a hotel next to a …* Point to the picture. Learners say *beach*.
- Learners read the postcard in pairs and fill in the missing words, using the pictures as clues.

Key: beach, black, animals, love, shells

5 Answer the questions.

- Say *Look at Activity 5*. Read out the first question. Learners suggest answers. (*In the Canary Islands*)
- Learners work on their own and answer the questions.

Key: 1 In the Canary Islands. 2 Next to the beach. 3 Because there's a volcano on the island. 4 She likes the lizards. 5 She can see lots of shells.

mission Stage 3

- Show the class the third stage of the Mission poster: 'Postcard'.
- Give out blank postcards to the learners.
- Ask learners to think of the place they are on holiday and to draw a picture on one side of the postcard.
- When they have finished, tell them someone in the class to write a postcard to.
- Tell learners to write a list. Give some prompts: *Place I am staying, What I can see, Weather, What I can do.*
- Show learners the example with words and pictures. Learners write and draw their postcard.

  Stronger learners Learners can write on their own.

  Extra support Learners can use the postcard in the book as a writing frame, but they change the details. They can work in pairs and write the same thing.
- Once the learners have finished, get them to 'post' their card to the person they chose. They each read a postcard they have received.
- For ideas on monitoring and assessment, see Introduction.

Activity Book, page 113

See pages TB120–132

Activity Book, page 106

- Say *Look at page 106 of your Activity Book*. Review *My unit goals*. Ask *How is your Mission?*
- Learners reflect and choose a smiley face for *My mission diary 3*. Monitor.

Ending the lesson

- Go back to Stage 3 on the digital Mission poster. Add a tick to the 'Postcard' stage or invite a learner to do it. Use self-assessment (see Introduction).
- Give out a completion sticker.

4 Read the postcard and say the missing words.

Dear Paula,

I'm on holiday with my family in the Canary Islands. We are staying in a hotel next to a . The sand is ! It's black because there's a volcano on the island. There are lots of interesting  on Tenerife. I  the lizards. There are lots of  on the beach.

See you soon,

Laura

5 Answer the questions.

1 Where is Laura on holiday?
2 Where is the hotel?
3 Why is the sand black?
4 What animal does Laura like?
5 What can Laura see on the beach?

mission STAGE 3

Write a postcard about your holiday. Use words and pictures.

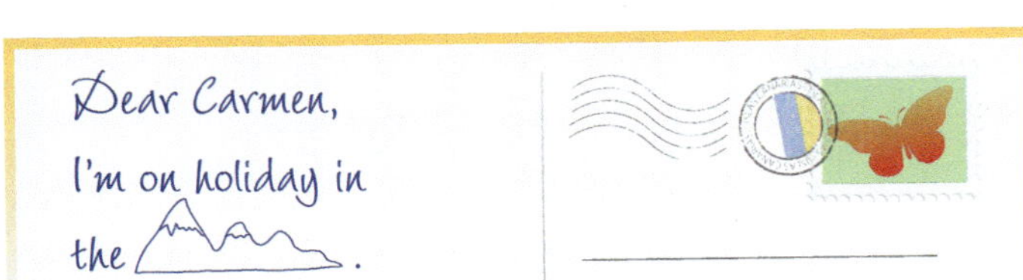

My mission diary
Activity Book page 106

Literature

1 **Find these things in the pictures. Talk about what you think is happening.**

heart shark tree king monkey

The monkey and the shark

9.12

In Africa there is a big coconut tree. It is next to the sea and a town. Every day a monkey goes and eats its delicious coconuts. Every day he gives some to a shark. One day, the shark says, 'You are very nice to me. I would like to invite you to my house.'

'But I don't go in the sea,' says the monkey.

'No problem,' says the shark. 'Jump on my back!' The shark swims away with the monkey.

'At home our king is very ill,' the shark says. 'He needs a monkey's heart to make him well.' The monkey thinks for a moment.

'Oh, no!' he says. 'I haven't got my heart with me. When I go out I put my heart in the tree.'

'No problem,' says the shark. 'Let's go back and get it!'

Learning outcomes By the end of the lesson, learners will have read about a trick and thought about a problem.

New language *coconut tree, delicious, heart, ill, king, monkey, shark, trick*

Recycled language imperatives, present continuous, the beach

Materials a list of words (*sand, houses, jellyfish, waterfall, rocks, fish, frogs, trees, shells, flowers, animals, cars, buses*) for each group of learners, flashcard of monkey, picture of a shark, a soft ball

Key Competences

- Work in groups to predict what happens in a story.
- Read and listen to a story.
- Order the events of a story using visual clues.

Warm-up

- Put learners into pairs. Give out to learners a list of words (*sand, houses, jellyfish, waterfall, rocks, fish, frogs, trees, shells, flowers, animals, cars, buses*).
- Write *Beach, River, City, Forest* on the board. Learners look at the words and write *B* for beach, *R* for river, *C* for city or *F* for forest next to each word, depending on where it is found. Some words have more than one answer.

Presentation

- Say *We are going to read a story about a monkey and a shark.* Say *Open your Pupil's Books at page 114. Which is the monkey?* Learners point. Say *Monkey*. Learners repeat. Point to the shark. Say *Shark*. Learners repeat. Say *Point to the coconut tree. Point to the sea.* Learners point and repeat.
- Ask *Who lives in the sea?* (*Shark*) *Where does the monkey live?* (*In the coconut tree*) Say *Yes, because the coconuts are delicious.* Mime enjoyment. Say *I love eating coconuts. They're delicious.* Mime enjoyment of delicious food. Learners mime and repeat. Say *I love eating coconuts because they are delicious*. Draw a heart on the board. Point to the heart. Say *This is a heart*. Learners repeat. Say *Show me your heart*. Learners point to where their heart is. Ask *What sound does a heart make?* Learners make a *boom-boom* heartbeat sound. Say *Heart*. Learners repeat.
- Say *I love eating coconuts. But if I eat a lot of coconuts* (mime *a lot* by holding out your hands), *I'm ill*. Mime being ill, groaning and rubbing your stomach. Say *I'm ill*. Learners mime and repeat.
- Show the picture of the shark king in the thought bubble on page 114. Say *He's a king*. Learners repeat. Say *There is a shark king in the story. And there is a trick.*

Check understanding of *trick*. Say *Let's find out why*.

Pupil's Book, page 114

1 Find these things in the pictures. Talk about what you think is happening.

- Say *Look at Pupil's Books pages 114 and 115*. Show learners the words at the top of the page. Ask *Where is the heart?* Learners point to the word and the picture. Go through the other words, encouraging learners to point.
- Put the class into groups of three. Say *Look at the name of the story*. Read it aloud. Learners look at the pictures and talk about what they think happens in the story. Check ideas.

9.12 The monkey and the shark

- Say *Read and listen to the first part*. Show them the paragraphs next to pictures 1 and 2 on page 114. Play the audio. Learners listen and read. Pause the audio after the first section to check understanding. Frame 1: *Where does the monkey live?* (*In Africa*) *Who does he give the coconut to?* (*The shark*) *Is the monkey nice to the shark?* (*Yes*) *Where does the shark want to go?* (*To his house in the sea*) *How is the monkey going?* (*He jumps on the shark's back and the shark swims.*)
- Say *Read and listen to the next part*. Play the audio for the paragraphs next to picture 3. Pause to check understanding. Ask *Who is ill?* (*The shark king*) *What does he need?* (*A monkey's heart*) *Is the monkey happy?* (*No*) *Where is his heart, he says?* (*In the tree*)
- Say *Read and listen to the next part*. Play the rest of the audio. Ask *Where are they going?* (*Back to the tree*) *What is the shark doing?* (*He's waiting.*) *Does the shark want to go?* (*Yes*) *Does the monkey want to go?* (*No*)

  Track 9.12
  See story on Pupil's Book pages 114–115
- Ask *Is the shark a good friend?* (*No*) *Why?* Learners suggest ideas. *Which trick was good – the monkey's or the shark's?* (*The monkey's*)

Activity Book, page 114

See pages TB120–132

Ending the lesson

- Divide the class into two: one group are monkeys and one group are sharks. Get them to stand on different sides of the room.
- Throw a ball to a monkey. Tell the monkey to throw the ball to a shark. As you throw it, say a word from the unit. Show learners they can only throw the ball to someone who is in the opposite group and they should say a word they remember from the unit.
- Learners throw the ball back and forwards until they run out of words.

Learning outcomes By the end of the lesson, learners will have summarised a story and thought about real friendship.

New language *at the beginning, at the end*

Recycled language animals, imperatives, present continuous

Materials a set of word cards for each group of eight learners (each set in a different colour, e.g. red, blue and green, cards cut into half sentences: *be / nice*; *help / your friends*; *tell them / your problems*; *don't / be unkind*), audio, coloured pens or pencils

Social and Emotional Skill: Identifying friends

- After reading the story, ask *What trick does the shark play? (He says the king is ill.) Why? (Because he wants to eat the monkey) What trick does the monkey play? (He says his heart is in the tree.) Why? (Because he's scared/ worried and wants to escape)* Say *Friends don't make friends feel scared. Do friends play bad tricks on other friends?* (No) Say *No, they don't. A good friend is someone you can trust.*
- Write a list of imperatives on the board:
  - *Be nice.*
  - *Help.*
  - *Don't play with them.*
  - *Tell them your problems.*
  - *Don't listen to them.*
  - *Share.*
- Put learners into pairs. Ask *How can you be a good friend?* Learners choose from the list. Read them out and the learners put up their hands if it refers to a good friend and they look down if it refers to 'not a good' friend. Point out that a 'friend' who does the 'bad' things maybe isn't a friend at all.

Key Competences

- Read a story about a trick.
- Learn and think about real friendship.
- Retell a story and create their own mimes.

Warm-up

- **SA** Use self-assessment to check how well learners think they understand the vocabulary. See Introduction.

Presentation

- Say *Open your Pupil's Books at pages 114 and 115. Show me the picture at the beginning. Show me the picture at the end.* Learners point.
- Put learners into groups of eight. Give out a set of word cards randomly: give a single card to each member of the group. (Use different colours to keep each set separate, e.g. a red group, a blue group, a green group.)
- Tell the learners that they have half a sentence and need to find their other half.
- Learners mingle in their group and find their partner to create a sentence: *be / nice*; *help / your friends*; *tell them / your problems*; *don't / be unkind*. Check answers.
- Standing in their group, each pair says their sentence.

Pupil's Book, page 115

- Put the learners into pairs. Say *Look at the pictures in the story. Tell the story again and make up mimes.* Learners work together, creating their own mimes.
- Choose two confident learners to tell the story and show their mimes to the class. As they do their mimes, ask the other learners to tell the story.

2 Answer the questions.

- Learners work in threes and answer the questions.

Key: 1 Yes, they are friends at the beginning of the story. 2 No, the monkey says his heart is in the tree, but it isn't really – he is playing a trick. 3 No, they aren't friends at the end – the shark is angry because the monkey played a trick on him.

- Ask *Do your friends play tricks on you?* Learners answer. Say *Our friends play with us. They don't play bad tricks.*

3 Ask and answer.

- Ask learners *Do you go to the beach?*
- Put learners into pairs. Ask them to share answers.
- Ask *What do you like doing on holiday?*
- Give each learner a slip of paper. Ask the learners to write a sentence about what they like doing on holiday.
- In groups of five or six, each learner mimes what they like doing on holiday. The rest of the group guesses.
- Tell learners to put their sentences face down in a random pile on the table and mix them up. They each take one paper back. If someone picks up their own paper tell them to start again.
- Each learner reads the sentence and chooses the learner who wrote it by remembering what they mimed, e.g. *Jo likes playing on the beach.*

Activity Book, page 115

See pages TB120–132

Ending the lesson

- **SA** Repeat the self-assessment technique used at the start of the lesson to see how well learners think they understand the vocabulary. Is there any change?
- Each learner draws a few sketches of their holiday.
- In pairs, they talk about their drawings.

9

They go back to the tree and the monkey jumps off the shark's back. 'Wait here,' says the monkey.

The shark waits and waits … and waits … and waits. 'What are you doing?' the shark shouts. 'Let's go!'

'No way!' the monkey shouts back. 'You're not tricking me again! I need my heart!' and he runs away laughing.

2 Answer the questions.

1 Are the monkey and the shark friends at the beginning of the story?

2 Is the monkey's heart in the tree?

3 Are the monkey and the shark friends at the end of the story?

3 Ask and answer.

Do you go to the beach?

Yes, I do.

What do you like doing on holiday?

I like taking photos.

1 Complete the questions. Then look at the first picture in Activity 2 and match.

how many what ~~where~~ which who

1 Where are the sunglasses?
2 ______________ colour is the ball?
3 ______________ is wearing a dress?
4 ______________ people are there?
5 ______________ child is taking photos?

a four
b on the sand
c the boy
d black and white
e the girl with the brown hair

2 Look at the pictures and read the questions. Write one-word answers.

Example

Where are the children?

at the beach

Questions

1 What is the man doing?

____

2 What has the man got?

a ______________

Learning outcomes By the end of the lesson, learners will have written questions about a text accurately and found the correct answers by reading carefully.

Recycled language colours, present continuous, things we see on holiday

Materials card/paper with a word from the unit for each pair of learners (e.g. *holiday*, *trousers*, *shells*), audio, coloured pens or pencils

Key Competences

- Complete and write questions.
- Work in groups to write one-word answers to questions.
- Practise activity types found in *Pre A1 Starters* exams.

Warm-up

- Put learners into pairs. Give each learner a word from the unit and tell them not to show it, e.g. *holiday*, *trousers*, *shells*.
- Each learner spells the word out to their partner. Their partner writes it down and tells them the word.

  Fast finishers Learners say and write sentences using their word.
- **SA** Use self-assessment techniques to check how well learners think they understand the vocabulary. See Introduction.

Presentation

- Say *Let's do a reading exam*. Write *Reading Exam* on the board.
- Say *Let's think about the questions we read. This can help us answer better. Let's see how.*
- Write on the left of the board a list of question words: *Where? Who? What? How many?* Say *Think about your answers.*
- Write on the right of the board: *A person*, *A number*, *A colour*, *A place*. Say *Let's match them*. Invite a learner to the board and encourage the group to say which words match. The learner draws lines between them (*Where? – A place, Who? – A person, What? – A colour, How many? – A number*).

Pupil's Book, page 116

1 Complete the questions. Then look at the first picture in Activity 2 and match.

- Say *Open your Pupil's Books at page 116. Look at the sentences.* Show learners the question word *Where* and how it has been added to sentence 1.
- In pairs, learners complete the sentences.
- Tell them to look at the first picture and match the questions to their answers. Point to the linked words on the board. Learners work in pairs again.

Key: 1 Where – b 2 What – d 3 Who – e 4 How many – a 5 Which – c

2 Look at the pictures and read the questions. Write one-word answers.

- Put learners into groups of three. Look at the first picture and read the answers. Tell them to look at the other questions and decide if the answer is an activity, a place, a thing or a person.
- Say *Now look and answer. Use one word.*
- Learners complete the task.
- Point out the text in the speech bubble.
- Monitor and check.
- Say *Well done. We are thinking about the question words and how we can answer. Good job!*

Key: 1 fishing 2 boot

Activity Book, page 116

See pages TB120–132

Ending the lesson

- **SA** Repeat the self-assessment technique used at the start of the lesson to see how well learners think they understand the vocabulary. Is there any change?
- Learners work in pairs. Write question words on the board: *Who? What? How many? What colour? Where?*
- Tell each pair to create a minimum of three questions that other learners can answer, e.g. *What colour is the classroom door?* (not *What colour is my bedroom?*)
- Put each pair with another pair to make a group of four. They ask and answer their questions.
- Ask learners to bring at least two photos from their family holiday or a day out to the next lesson.

Learning outcomes By the end of the lesson, learners will have revised the language in the unit and made a holiday album.

Recycled language unit language

Materials a photo album containing holiday photos (optional), paper, coloured pens or pencils, real photos of holidays brought in by learners (optional), glue sticks, paper folded into booklets

Key Competences

- Revise vocabulary and language learnt in the unit.
- Complete self-assessment tasks and reflect on their own learning.
- Work in groups to make a holiday photo album.
- Create an online photo album using digital photos.

Warm-up

- Say some simple words, e.g. *sun, sea, shell, kite*. Learners spell out the words using their bodies to create the shapes of the letters.
- Pretend to take a photo each time and say *I'm putting this in my photo album*. Mime sticking a photo into an album.

Presentation

- Write on the board: *Make a holiday photo album*. Show a real photo album. Say *Photo album*. Learners repeat.
- Show the inside of the photo album and tell the learners about it, e.g. *This is a picture of my holiday. This is a river. This is me and my friend on a boat. We are having fun.*

Pupil's Book, page 117

mission in action!

Make a holiday photo album.

- Say *Let's make a holiday photo album*. Put learners into pairs. They show their partner the photos they brought in. Say *Talk about the place: This is my hotel. It is near the beach. There are mountains behind the hotel. It is nice.* They describe the place they went to on holiday to their partner.
  Alternative Learners can draw if they don't have photos.
- Ask *What can you do? You can walk on the beach and play games. You can see the mountains. You can swim.* Learners talk in pairs and describe their activities.
- Say *Let's work together*. Put learners into groups of four.
- Say *First let's look at our photos*. Demonstrate again showing your photos. Say, e.g. *This is the beach. You can see the sand and the sea. You can see some shells.* Learners say *I like this photo. Let's put this in the album.*
- Give out glue sticks and paper booklets. Say *Let's create a photo album together.*
- Say *Let's use this photo.* Hold up an example photo, e.g. one from a confident learner. Give the photo back and encourage the learner to repeat this to you. Say *That's a good idea*. Draw a tick on the board.
- Hold up another example photo from a confident learner. Say *I like this photo. Let's put this photo in the album*. Give the photo back and encourage the learner to repeat to you. Say *It's a nice photo, but it's the same – there are two photos of a beach. Let's choose a different picture.* Rub out the tick.
- Ask learners to hold up the photos they brought in. Ask *How many photos have you got? (A lot)* Say *OK – choose the photos in your group. But only six!*
- Learners work in their groups and create their photo albums. They write *Our holiday photo album* and draw a design on the front. They choose and stick in pictures.
- Put each group of learners with a new group. Learners show their photo albums to each other and describe them, e.g. *This is my mum and dad. They are swimming in the sea.*
- Ask some confident learners to show their photo albums to the class and describe the photos.

Self-assessment

- **SA** Ask *Did you like all the Missions? Which did you like best?* Learners say their favourite Mission.
- Ask *How can you learn more?* (e.g. *I can read an English story. I can watch a cartoon on the internet in English.*)

Activity Book, page 117

See pages TB120–132

Activity Book, page 106

- Say *Look at page 106 of your Activity Book*. Review *My unit goals*. Ask *How is your Mission?*
- Learners reflect and choose a smiley face for *My mission diary* the final stage. Monitor.
- Point to the sunflower. Learners read the 'can do' statements and tick them if they agree they have achieved them. They colour each leaf green if they are very confident or orange if they think they need more practice.
- Point to the word stack sign. Ask learners to spend a few minutes looking back at the unit and find a minimum of five new words they have learnt. They write the new words into their word stack. See Introduction for techniques and activities.

Ending the lesson

- Go back to the completion stage on the digital Mission poster. Add a tick or invite a learner to do it. Use self-assessment (see Introduction).
- Give out a completion sticker.
- Tell the learners *You have finished your Mission! Well done!*

Review

mission in action!

My mission diary
Activity Book page 106

Make a holiday photo album.

In groups, show your photos.

This is me and my family. We're at the beach.

Look at your friends' photos. Say which ones you like.

I love this photo!

That photo is beautiful.

Choose photos for your album.

I like this photo because I like swimming.

Let's put this photo in the album.

Review • • • Units 7–9

1 Watch the video and do the quiz.

2 9.13 Listen and follow. Draw lines.

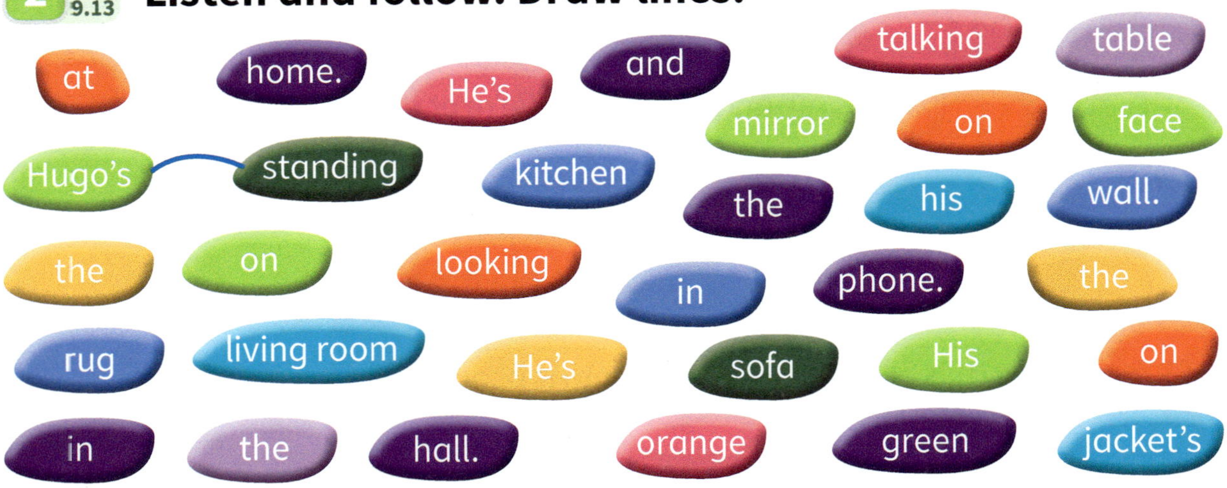

3 Look at the picture and remember. Ask and answer.

Learning outcomes By the end of the lesson, learners will have consolidated language from Units 7–9.

Recycled language houses and rooms, prepositions, present continuous

Materials flashcards from Units 7–9, cards with actions written on them (e.g. *You're playing tennis. You're eating ice cream.*), audio

Warm-up

- Learners stand in two lines facing you. Take out flashcards from Units 7–9 and divide them into two equal piles.
- Demonstrate how to play the game with an example flashcard. Give the flashcard to the learner at the front of the line. This learner says the word for the flashcard picture and passes it over his/her head to the next learner. The second learner says the word and passes the flashcard under their legs to the next learner. The next learner passes the card over their head, the next under their legs and so on, saying the word each time. When the flashcard reaches the last learner, he/she runs to the front and gives you the flashcard, saying the word. The first group to do this gets a point.
- Begin the game. Give a flashcard to each learner at the front of the two lines. Once the flashcard has moved down the line, pass out the next flashcard.

Pupil's Book, page 118

1 Watch the video and do the quiz.

- Show the video to learners.
- Ask learners to do the quiz. Check their answers to see how much the learners can remember.
- Repeat this at the end of the Review unit and compare the results to measure progress.

2 9.13 Listen and follow. Draw lines.

- Say *Open your Pupil's Books at page 118*. Point to the words in Activity 2. Ask *Which room words can you see?* (*Kitchen, living room, hall*) Ask *Which things from the house can you see?* (*Table, mirror, phone, rug, sofa*)
- Say to the learners *Listen and point. He's standing in the kitchen*. Learners point.
- Say *Now listen and draw lines*. Play the audio.

  Fast finishers Learners draw the scene in the sentence. They add labels to the objects in their drawing.

  Extra support Learners listen again to finish the lines.

  Track 9.13

  Hugo's standing on the rug in the hall. He's looking in the mirror and talking on his phone. His green jacket's on the wall. (x3)
- Ask the learners for each word in order and write the sentences onto the board so learners can check their lines.

3 Look at the picture and remember. Ask and answer.

- Say *Look at Activity 3*. Point to the picture. Put learners into pairs and ask them to write labels for the picture, e.g. *sunglasses, rug, boat*.
- Learners ask questions about the picture and others answer, e.g. *What are the two boys doing?* (*They're playing football.*)
- Put the learners into pairs – A and B. Tell all the learners to look and try to remember the picture. Tell the learners who are 'A' to close their Pupil's Books. Tell the learners who are 'B' to look at the picture and ask their partner questions.
- After a few minutes, ask them to swap roles and repeat.

Key (example questions and answers): What is the girl in the sunglasses doing? (She's reading a book.) What is the man in the boat doing? (He's fishing.) Where is the bike? (It's next to the car.) What is the small boy making? (He's making a sandcastle.) Who is taking a photo? (The man sitting in the chair.)

- Put learners into pairs. Ask them to draw a picture of a beach, classroom or room in the house, e.g. bedroom or living room. Write the names of the places on the board. Say *Choose one and draw a picture*. Tell them to include five of their classmates in the picture. Each person should be doing something. Write *5 friends* on the board.
- Give an example, e.g. draw a rough outline of a classroom with two stick figures – one reading a book and the other drawing. Choose two learners and label the stick figures with their names. Say *In my picture (Camila) is reading a book and (Matias) is drawing a picture.*
- Learners draw and label their own pictures.
- Put the learners into pairs and ask them to describe their drawing to their partner. Their partner tries to draw what they hear.

Activity Book, page 118

See pages TB120–132

Ending the lesson

- Put learners into groups. Ask them to mime actions. The other learners guess what they are doing, e.g. *You're reading a book*.

  Fast finishers Learners can mime a few different actions.

  Extra support Learners can be given cards with sentences and little sketches to copy, e.g. *You're playing tennis. You're eating ice cream.*

Learning outcomes By the end of the lesson, learners will have consolidated language from Units 7–9.

Recycled language *can/can't*, clothes, hobbies and activities, prepositions

Materials flashcards from Units 7–9, coloured pens or pencils, audio

Warm-up

- Draw on the board two stick figures doing different activities, e.g. one with a speech bubble saying hello and one kicking a football. Ask the learners to tell you the activity, e.g. point and say *In this picture I'm …* (*speaking English*). *In this picture I'm …* (*playing football*).
- Draw a tick under the first picture and a cross under the second. Point to the first. Say *I like speaking English. I can …* (*speak English*). Point to the second. Say *But I don't like playing football. I am very bad. I can't …* (*play football*).
- Say *What can I do?* (*You can speak English.*) *What can't I do?* (*You can't play football.*)
- Learners draw two stick figures showing something they can do and something they can't do, but do not put a tick or cross. Remind them they can change the order.
- Learners draw. They mingle and talk to at least three other learners. They show their pictures to each other. Their partner guesses which activity they can do and which they can't do, e.g. *You can play the piano. You can't draw.*

Pupil's Book, page 119

4 9.14 Listen and number.

- Say *Open your Pupil's Books at page 119*. Say *Show me Sam*. Learners point. Say *Show me May*. Learners point. Continue going through the different characters.
- Ask *What is Sam doing?* (*He's playing the piano.*)
- Say to the learners *Now listen and number*.
- Play the audio for number 1. Pause the audio. Indicate the example *1* in the box next to Sam.
- Continue playing the rest of the activity. Learners complete the task.

Track 9.14

1 He's wearing glasses. He's got short black hair and he's playing the piano.
2 She's wearing purple shorts and a green baseball cap. She's got a skateboard under her arm.
3 He's wearing black trousers and a blue shirt. He's putting a jacket on a chair.
4 She's playing table tennis. She's wearing jeans and a red T-shirt.
5 He's drinking lemonade. He's wearing an old hat.
6 She's wearing jeans and a green T-shirt. She's picking up a guitar.
7 He's wearing black trousers. He isn't wearing glasses.
8 She's dancing to the music on the radio. She's wearing a red dress.

Key: 2 Pat 3 Dan 4 Anna 5 Ben 6 Lucy 7 Bill 8 Sue

5 Write about you.

- Show the picture in Activity 4 again. Pick out a few of the activities, e.g. *play the piano*, *skateboarding*, *play the guitar*, *dancing*. Ask learners, e.g. *Can you play the piano?* Learners say *Yes, I can. / No, I can't.* If they answer *Yes, I can*, ask a follow-up question: *Do you like playing the piano?* Learners say *Yes, I do. / No, I don't.*
- Point to some of the characters in Activity 4. Ask *What is he/she wearing?* Learners answer. Put learners into pairs and ask them to describe each other's clothes.
- Tell learners to look at Activity 5 in the Pupil's Book. Choose different learners to read out each question. Choose other learners to answer each question.
- Learners write their answers to the questions.
- Once all the learners have finished, they should interview each other, using the questions.

Activity Book, page 119

See pages TB120–132

Ending the lesson

- Repeat the video and quiz.
- Say *We've finished the book. But let's sing one of the songs. Let's choose.* Ask *Which song is your favourite?* If possible, play short snippets of the songs from the audio. Say *Let's listen again. Put your hand up for your favourite.* Demonstrate putting up your hand.
- Play the song snippets again while learners vote. (If you can't play snippets, the learners can call out the songs they remember and vote that way.)
- Replay the song and sing it again using the same actions as before.
- Encourage the learners to give each other a round of applause.
- Ask learners to look at their Pupil's Books. Tell them to find five things they can do in English really well, e.g. *I can say things I like doing. I can name different foods.*
- Ask them to think of one thing they want to do more, e.g. *I can't remember the names of rooms. I want to read these more.*
- Put learners into groups of four and ask them to tell their group what they can do well and what they want to learn better.
- When they have finished, invite a few learners to share with the whole group. Ensure you choose a mix of learners (not just fast finishers).
- Say *Well done, everyone! You have learnt a lot!*
- Encourage the learners to stand up, mingle and shake hands, saying *Well done* to each other.

4 9.14 Listen and number.

5 Write about you.

Can you ride a bike?

___

Can you play the guitar?

___

What instrument can you play?

___

Have you got a skateboard?

___

What are you wearing?

___

Do you like going to the beach?

___

Do you like fishing?

___

Activity Book answer key and audioscript

Hello Unit

1 0.07 Listen and number. Then colour. page 4

1 red
2 yellow
3 white
4 pink
5 orange
6 blue
7 purple
8 green
9 black
10 grey

Key: green 8 yellow 2 black 9 white 3 pink 4 purple 7 orange 5 grey 10 blue 6

2 Answer and draw.

Key: Learners' own answers and drawings

1 0.08 Listen and circle the number. page 5

1 Shelly: I'm Shelly. I'm four.
2 Cameron: I'm Cameron. I'm three.
3 Rocky: I'm Rocky. I'm two.
4 Harry: I'm Harry. I'm eight.
5 Henrietta: I'm Henrietta. I'm five.
6 Gracie: I'm Gracie. I'm ten.

Key: 2 3 3 2 4 8 5 5 6 10

2 Write the words.

Key: 2 seven 3 nine 4 two 5 one 6 four 7 eight 8 five 9 ten 10 six

Unit 1

1 Look and read. Write *yes* or *no*. page 7

Key: 2 no 3 no 4 yes 5 no 6 yes 7 no 8 yes

2 1.14 Listen and point to the letter. Then say and match.

p p bag pen boy
b b book pencil

Key: 1 bag – b 2 book – b 3 pen – p 4 pencil – p 5 boy – b

1 1.15 Listen and read. Who says it? Circle the name. page 8

See Pupil's Book page 8

Key: 2 Rocky 3 Shelly 4 Gracie 5 Jenny 6 Henrietta

1 1.16 Listen and tick ✓ or cross ✗. page 9

1 Woman: Where's the teacher?
Man: The teacher's in the classroom.
2 Woman: Where's the bag?
Man: It's next to the table.
3 Woman: Where's the rubber?
Man: It's on the chair.
4 Woman: Where's the book?
Man: It's in the bag.
5 Woman: Where's the pencil?
Man: It's under the book.
6 Woman: Where's the pen?
Man: It's under the chair.

Key: 2 ✗ 3 ✓ 4 ✗ 5 ✗ 6 ✓

2 Look at the picture. Complete the sentences.

Key: 2 under 3 in 4 next to 5 under 6 on

1 Write the words. Find the secret word. page 10

Key: 2 wall 3 cupboard 4 boy 5 bag 6 board 7 bookcase 8 ruler 9 window 10 door
Secret word: playground

2 1.17 Listen and draw lines.

1 Boy: Hello, Anna.
Girl: Hello, Mark. Look! This is my classroom.
Boy: Hmm.
Girl: Look! My teacher's next to the door.
2 Boy: Oh, yes! Where's your bag?
Girl: It's on the green wall, next to the window.
Boy: Ah, yes, on the green wall, next to the blue window.
3 Girl: And the cupboard's under the window.
Boy: Under the window? Oh, yes. The grey cupboard's under the window.
4 Boy: Where's your rubber? Is it in your bag?
Girl: Oops, no. It's under my desk.
Boy: Hmm, yes. It's under your brown desk.
5 Boy: What's on the bookcase?
Girl: It's paper. It's next to the red crayon.
Boy: Oh yes. The paper's on the bookcase.

Key: 2 line to green wall next to window 3 line to under window 4 line to under desk 5 line to on bookcase

1 1.18 Listen and number. page 11

1 Man: What's this?
Girl: It's a wall.
2 Man: What's this?
Girl: It's a bookcase.
3 Man: What are these?
Girl: They're doors.
4 Man: What are these?
Girl: They're rulers.
5 Man: What's this?
Girl: It's a window.
6 Man: What's this?
Girl: It's the playground.
7 Man: What are these?
Girl: They're rubbers.
8 Man: What's this?
Girl: It's a cupboard.

Key: a 6 b 8 c 7 d 4 e 2 (f 1) g 3 h 5

2 Look and draw. Then write the words.

Key: 1 crayon 2 this / cupboard 3 these / rulers 4 It's / window

1 Who is kind? Look and circle. page 12

Key: the girl holding the apple the boy offering help to the boy who has fallen the boy inviting the girl to play football the boy and girl helping another boy pick up his things the girl helping a boy to climb

2 **Look and write the words.**

Key: 1 Yes, thank you. 2 Here you are. / Thank you.

3 **How are you kind at school? Write the words.** page 13

Key: 2 listen 3 help 4 work

4 **How are you kind at home? Think and draw.**

Key: Learners' own pictures

1 1.19 **Listen and draw.** page 14

1 Mum: It's time to pack your bag.
Max: My bag …
Mum: It's in the cupboard.
2 Max: Where's my pencil?
Lucy: It's under the chair.
Max: Oh, yes.
3 Max: Where's my pen?
Lucy: It's on the table.
Max: Oh, yes.
4 Max: And where's my ruler?
Lucy: It's next to your pen.
Max: Oh, yes.
5 Max: Where are my books?
Lucy: They're on the bookcase.
Max: Oh, yes.

Key: Learners draw bag in cupboard, pencil under chair, pen on table, ruler next to pen, books on bookcase

2 **What do you take to school? Complete the rhyme.**

Key: Learners' own answers, e.g. a rubber / crayons / a pen

3 1.20 **Listen, point and draw lines.** page 15

Look at the pictures.
Which is the pen? I'm putting the pen on the desk.
Which is the rubber? Put the rubber under the blue chair.
Which are the crayons? Put the crayons on the bookcase.
Which is the ruler? Put the ruler next to the bag.
Which is the paper? Put the paper in the cupboard.

Key: Lines from paper to cupboard, from rubber to under chair, from ruler to next to bag, from crayons to on bookcase

4 **Look and point. Ask and answer.**

Key: Learners' own questions and answers

1 **Look and read. Put a tick (✓) or a cross (✗) in the box. There are two examples.** page 16

Key: 1 ✓ 2 ✓ 3 ✗ 4 ✗ 5 ✓

1 **Play the game.** page 17

Learners play the game in groups of three to five. They need one dice, and a different coloured counter for each learner. Learners take turns to throw the dice and move their counter round the board, counting as they go. When they land on a picture, they read the question and answer it. If they answer correctly, they stay on the square; if they answer incorrectly, they go back to their previous square. If they land on a coloured square, they follow the instruction. The learner who finishes first is the winner.

Unit 2

1 **Look and say.** page 19

Key: 1 mum/mother 2 dad/father 3 sister
4 dad/father

2 2.15 2.16 **Listen and repeat. Which words have these sounds? Listen and write *th* or *t*.**

th th
mother mother

t t
cat cat

th t
1 mother mother
2 cat cat
3 father father
4 brother brother
5 grandfather grandfather
6 sister sister
7 grandmother grandmother

Key: 2 t 3 th 4 th 5 th 6 t 7 th

1 **Read and tick ✓ or cross ✗.** page 20

Key: 2 ✗ 3 ✗ 4 ✓

2 **Who is in Rocky's family? Look and tick ✓ or cross ✗.**

Key: 2 ✓ 3 ✗ 4 ✗ 5 ✓ 6 ✓

1 2.17 **Listen and follow. Draw lines.** page 21

Boy: This is my family.
Girl: Who's she?
Boy: She's my mum.
Girl: Who's he?
Boy: He's my brother.
Girl: Who's he?
Boy: He's my dad.
Girl: Who's she?
Boy: She's my grandma.
Girl: Who's she?
Boy: She's my sister.
Girl: Who's he?
Boy: He's my grandpa.

Key: Line to mum, brother, dad, grandma, sister, grandpa

2 **Read and write.**

Key: 1 He's 2 She's / She's 3 He's / He's 4 She's / She's

1 Find and circle the words. Then write. page 22

Key: 2 ear 3 eye 4 mouth 5 nose 6 hair 7 face 8 tail 9 hand 10 arm 11 leg 12 foot 13 feet 14 body

2 Write the words.

Key: 2 tail 3 body 4 hair 5 foot 6 nose

1 Look and read. Write *yes* or *no*. page 23

Key: 2 no 3 yes 4 no 5 no 6 no 7 yes 8 yes

2 Read and draw. Colour.

Key: Learners draw and colour the robot with a yellow body, a blue head, orange arms, grey hands, green legs, black feet, a pink face, two purple eyes, a grey nose, a brown mouth and two red ears.

1 Look and write the words. page 24

Key: 2 hear 3 taste 4 see 5 smell

2 Which sense are they using? Look and colour the T-shirts.

Key: mum on phone – red T-shirt girl looking at butterfly – blue T-shirt boy smelling flowers – yellow T-shirt dad eating ice cream – green T-shirt boy putting foot in water – purple T-shirt

3 Which senses do you use when you do these things? Read, think and tick ✓. page 25

Key: eat a sandwich: I smell, I taste, I touch, I see watch TV: I see, I hear play with a pet: I see, I hear, I touch

4 Think of something you do at home. Draw it and tick ✓ the senses you use.

Key: Learners' own ideas

1 Number the sentences in order. page 26

Key: a 2 b 6 c (1) d 5 e 3 f 4

2 Draw Pablo in the picture. Play 'Where's Pablo?'

Learners draw Pablo onto their picture, but don't show it to their partner. They work in pairs. Each learner asks questions about their partner's picture until they find Pablo, e.g. *Is he under the table? No, he isn't. Is he next to the bookcase? Yes, he is.*

3 Which body part can you see? Write the words. page 27

Key: 2 head 3 eyes 4 feet 5 hair 6 mouth

4 Look and point. Ask and answer.

Learners work in pairs. They look at Activity 3 and take turns to point to a picture and ask *What's this? / What are these?* The partner answers, e.g. *It's a hand. / They're eyes.*

1 Look and read. Write *yes* or *no*. page 28

Key: 1 yes 2 no 3 no 4 yes 5 no

1 Play the game. page 29

Learners play the game in groups of three to five. They need one dice, and a different coloured counter for each learner. They also need a coloured pen or pencil in the colour of their counter. The object of the game is to make a robot by collecting all the body parts in the shopping list. Learners take turns to throw the dice and move their counter round the board. When they land on a picture, they say what it is, e.g. *It's a head*. Their partner asks *What colour is it?* and they answer, e.g. *It's grey*. If no one has already got the body part, they colour the square on their shopping list in their colour; if someone has already got it, they don't colour it. The learner who colours all / the most items on the shopping list is the winner.

Unit 3

1 Count and write. page 31

Key: 2 cows 3 donkeys 4 sheep 5 goats 6 dogs 7 cats 8 ducks 9 chickens

2 3.16 **Can you hear the /k/ sound? Listen and say *yes* or *no*.**

cat	horse
duck	spider
sheep	donkey
chicken	cow

Key: 1 yes 2 yes 3 no 4 yes 5 no 6 no 7 yes 8 yes

3 3.17 **Listen and colour the letters that make the /k/ sound.**

1 cat cat	4 donkey donkey
2 duck duck	5 cow cow
3 chicken chicken	

Key: 2 duck 3 chicken 4 donkey 5 cow

1 Read and tick ✓ or cross ✗. page 32

Key: 2 ✗ 3 ✓ 4 ✗ 5 ✗ 6 ✓

2 Talk about the animals. Use the words in the box.

Key: Learners' own answers, e.g. Rocky's small. Cameron's a long/short cat. Henrietta's old. Rocky's young. Cameron's a nice cat.

1 Read and colour. page 33

Key: Learners colour: small horse – black, long pencil – blue, young cat – orange, big duck – yellow, new book – green, short ruler – purple, old cat – grey

2 Write the words in the correct order.

Key: 2 It's a small spider. 3 They're nice ducks. 4 The horse is big. 5 They're old cats. 6 The donkeys have got big ears. 7 I'm small and young.

1 Read and circle the correct words. page 34

Key: 2 ugly 3 angry 4 sad 5 beautiful 6 funny

2 Write the words.

Key: 2 ugly 3 beautiful 4 funny 5 happy 6 angry 7 sad

1 3.18 **Listen and tick ✓.** page 35

1 Boy: That's a beautiful horse, Mum.
Woman: Which horse? The grey one with the long white tail?
Boy: No, the grey one with the long black tail.
Woman: Ah, yes. That is a beautiful horse.

2 Girl: Look, Dad. That's my friend May with her dog.
Man: Who's May? Has she got a big white dog?
Girl: No. She's the one with the small black dog.
Man: Ah, yes. It's a funny dog.

3 Woman: Have you got your ruler in your bag, Alex?
Boy: Yes, Mum. I've got a nice, long one.
Woman: OK, and have you got a pen?
Boy: No, but I've got a pencil.

4 Woman: Jill, where's your cat?
Girl: He's under my chair, Mum.
Woman: Is he angry?
Girl: No, he isn't. He's happy. Look, he's got a ball.
Woman: Oh, yes. He's very happy.

5 Girl: Look at this picture of my robot, Dad.
Man: Ooh, it's got big red eyes and a black mouth.
Girl: Yes. It's an ugly robot! It's got an angry face.
Man: Ooh! Yes, it has.

6 Girl: Is your house on a farm, Dan?
Boy: Yes, it is.
Girl: Has your dad got cows?
Boy: No, he hasn't got cows. He's got ducks.
Girl: Ooh, ducks. He's got a duck farm.

Key: 2 B 3 A 4 C 5 C 6 B

1 Which animal does it come from? Read and write. page 36

Key: 2 chickens 3 bees 4 sheep

2 Which things come from animals? Look and circle.

Key: Learners circle: egg, butter, ice cream, milk, honey, chicken, cheese, woolly scarf

3 Read the sentences. Number the pictures in order. page 37

Key: a 2 c 4 d 3

4 What things from animals have you got at home? Think and draw.

Key: Learners' own ideas, e.g. milk, honey, cheese, butter, meat, woolly jumpers and hats

1 Read the sentences. Number the pictures in order. page 38

Key: a 4 b 1 c 3 d 2

2 Read and write. Then write and draw.

Key: 1 flies 2 Learners' own answers and drawing

3 Look and read. Write *yes* or *no*. page 39

Key: 2 no 3 yes 4 no 5 yes 6 yes 7 yes

1 Look at the pictures. Look at the letters. Write the words. page 40

Key: 1 chicken 2 spider 3 dog 4 sheep 5 duck

1 Play the game. page 41

Learners play the game in groups of three to five. They need one dice, and a different coloured counter for each learner. Learners take turns to throw the dice and move their counter round the board, counting as they go. When they land on a picture, they read the word and say a sentence, e.g. *Small. The duck has got small eyes*. If they say a correct sentence, they stay on the square; if they say an incorrect sentence, they go back to their previous square. The learner who finishes first is the winner.

Review Units 1–3

1 Circle the words. page 42

Key: blue six four red five orange eight ten nine chair rubber crayon book pencil grandpa brother father sister mother head mouth eyes feet face chicken spider goat donkey horse angry beautiful funny sad ugly

2 3.19 **Listen and colour.**

This is my grandpa. Colour his balloon black.
This is my brother. Colour his balloon orange.
This is my dad. Colour his balloon red.
This is my sister. Colour her balloon blue.
This is my mum. Colour her balloon yellow.
This is my grandma. Colour her balloon green.

Key: Learners colour: brother's balloon – orange, dad's balloon – red, sister's balloon – blue, mum's balloon – yellow, grandma's balloon – green

3 Ask and answer. page 43

Learners mingle to complete the survey. They ask four people the questions, writing their names at the top of the table. They take it in turns to ask and answer. They write in the table ticks for 'yes' answers and crosses for 'no' answers.

4 Look at Activity 3. Write about your friends.

Key: Learners' own answers

Unit 4

1 Write the words. page 45

Key: 2 banana 3 bread 4 burger 5 chicken 6 chocolate 7 salad 8 water

2 4.17 4.18 Listen and say. Then listen and match.

/æ/ /æ/
mango mango

/eɪ/ /eɪ/
cake cake

/æ/ mango
/eɪ/ cake
1 salad salad
2 cat cat
3 paper paper
4 lemonade lemonade
5 bag bag

Key: 2 mango 3 cake 4 cake 5 mango

1 Read and tick ✓ the things Gracie likes. page 46

Key: bread, bananas, book, socks

2 4.19 Listen and match the animals with the things they like.

1 Gracie: Do you like chocolate, Cameron?
Cameron: Er, … Yes, I do.
2 Harry: Yuk, I don't like books.
Rocky: I like books.
3 Rocky: What do you like, Harry?
Harry: Hmm, I don't like books or chocolate. I like mangoes.
4 Rocky: What do you like, Shelly?
Shelly: I like water. I can see my face in water.

Key: 2 book 3 mango 4 water

1 Read and circle. page 47

Key: Learners' own answers

2 Read and match. Colour.

Key: Learners colour picture frames: 2 orange 3 green 4 pink 5 purple 6 yellow

1 Look and read. Put a tick ✓ or a cross ✗. page 48

Key: 2 ✓ 3 ✓ 4 ✓ 5 ✗ 6 ✗ 7 ✓ 8 ✓

2 Write the word and ask your friend. Put a tick ✓ or a cross ✗.

Key: Learners' own answers

1 Read and complete. Then draw and write. page 49

Key: 2 burger 3 Can 4 Would 5 like 6 Learners' own answers

1 Write the words. page 50

Key: 2 meat 3 onions 4 potatoes 5 cheese 6 tomatoes 7 carrots 8 rice

2 Match the ingredients with the dish.

Key: a 2 b 1 c 3

3 Read the recipe and write the words. page 51

Key: 1 tomatoes 2 onion 3 eggs 4 cheese 5 omelette

4 What would you like in your omelette? Draw and write.

Key: Learners' own answers and drawing

1 Find the words in the puzzle. Then tick ✓ the things Matt and Mia take on their picnic. page 52

Key: Across: watermelon, (lemonade), apples, grapes, chips, sandwich, biscuits, chocolate
Down: burger, bananas, cake, milk
✓ bananas, watermelon, sandwich, chocolate

2 Put the pictures in order. Then tell the story.

Key: a 3 b 4 c (1) d 2
Learners' own answers, e.g. Matt wants burgers on the picnic. Mum says 'No, but you can take sandwiches and fruit.' Mia and Matt are in the woods. They've got sandwiches, fruit, lemonade and chocolate. They put some clothes on the watermelon. The birds fly away. They take the scarecrow down. They share the picnic with the birds.

3 4.20 Listen and draw lines from the names to the children in the picture. page 53

Matt and Mia are in the garden with three friends from school. Their names are Tom, Tina and Sam. Look at their picnic. Matt has got a glass of lemonade. He likes burgers, but he doesn't like chicken. Tom has got a chocolate biscuit. Tom likes chocolate biscuits very much. Mia has got a banana and Sam has got an egg sandwich. What about Tina? Oh! Tina's got crisps. Tina likes crisps.

Key: Learners draw lines between: Mia – girl with banana, Tom – boy with chocolate biscuit, Tina – girl with crisps, Sam – boy with egg sandwich

1 4.21 **Look at the pictures. Listen and tick (✓) the box. There is one example.** page 54

Look at the pictures. Now listen and look. There is one example.
Which is Bill's sister?
Girl: Bill, is that girl your sister? Look … there … She's eating an apple.
Boy: Where? … Oh her … No. That's my friend. My sister's there. She's reading a book.
Girl: The girl with the blue T-shirt?
Boy: No, she's got a red T-shirt.
Girl: Oh, yes. There she is.
Can you see the tick? Now you listen and tick the box.

1 How old is Anna?
Woman: Hello. What are your names?
Girl: I'm Anna and this is Jill. She's eight.
Woman: How old are you, Anna? Are you seven?
Girl: I'm six. It's my birthday today!

2 Where's Matt's rubber?
Boy: I can't find my rubber, Mr Hall. It isn't on the desk.
Man: Well, is it under your book, Matt?
Boy: Ah, it's OK … I can see it. It's under the bookcase!
Man: Right! Good!

3 What are the new animals on the farm?
Boy: We've got some new animals on the farm!
Woman: Really? Have you got horses? They're cool!
Boy: Well, we've got two horses. They're big and they're old now. But we've got two donkeys – they're really cool and they're our new ones!
Woman: Oh, donkeys are funny! I like them – but I really love dogs.
Boy: Well, we have some of them too.

4 What would Sam like for lunch?
Man: Hi, Sam! Would you like some sausages?
Boy: No, thank you. Have you got some chicken, please?
Man: We've got lots of it. Here you are. And orange juice?
Boy: Er … lemonade, please.

5 Which is Lucy's brother?
Man: Is that your brother, Lucy? The boy there with red hair.
Girl: My brother's got brown hair.
Man: And brown eyes too?
Girl: No. His eyes are blue.
Man: Oh, I can see him now.

Key: 1 A 2 B 3 C 4 B 5 B

1 **Play the game.** page 55

Learners play the game in groups of four. They need one dice, and a different coloured counter for each learner. They each choose six items of food and drink and write their own shopping list. They start at 'Open'. Learners take turns to throw the dice and move their counter round the board, vertically or horizontally, but not diagonally. When they land on a picture, they look at the picture and say the word, e.g. *Lemonade.* The learner on their right asks them, e.g. *Would you like some lemonade?* The learner replies *Yes, please!* and ticks the item if it is on their shopping list, or *No, thank you* if it isn't on their shopping list. When they land on a 'Can I have … ?' square, the learner asks for an item they still need, e.g. *Can I have some oranges?* When a learner has 'bought' and ticked all of their items, they head for the 'Finish!' square. The learner who reaches 'Finish!' first is the winner.

Unit 5

1 **What is it? Look and write.** page 57

Key: 2 It's a car. 3 It's a plane. 4 It's a doll. 5 It's a kite. 6 It's a ball. 7 It's a house. 8 It's a robot.

2 5.14 **Listen and match the words with the pictures. Then listen again and say.**

1 house
2 happy
3 horse
4 hat

Key: a 4 b 3 c (1) d 2

3 5.15 **Listen and say the rhyme.**

How is the horse in his little brown house?
He's happy in his hat in his house with a mouse. (x2)

1 5.16 **Listen and read. Who says it?** page 58

See Pupil's Book page 58

Key: 2 Shelly 3 Gracie 4 Rocky 5 Harry 6 Cameron

2 **Read and correct.**

Key: 2 Jenny's car is red. 3 Jenny doesn't like dolls. 4 Jim's favourite toy is his kite. 5 Their present is a plane. 6 Cameron doesn't like planes.

1 **Read and write *his, her* or *their*.** page 59

Key: 2 his 3 her 4 their 5 her 6 his 7 her 8 her

1 **Write.** page 60

Key: 2 computer 3 radio 4 teddy 5 board game 6 helicopter 7 balloon

1 **Write *Yes, she does* or *No, she doesn't*.** page 61

Key: 2 No, she doesn't. 3 Yes, she does. 4 Yes, she does. 5 No, she doesn't. 6 No, she doesn't. 7 No, she doesn't. 8. Yes, she does.

1 **Write the words.** page 62

Key: 2 circle 3 square 4 rectangle

2 **Which shapes can you see? Look and write.**

Key: 2 rectangles and triangles 3 circles 4 a square and circles

3 **Read and draw the robot.** page 63

Key: Learners' own drawings

4 **How many shapes can you find at home? Count and write.**

Key: Learners' own answers

1 **Read and write *yes* or *no*.** page 64

Key: 2 no 3 no 4 yes 5 yes

2 **Choose Dora and Cora's toys and complete the dialogue. Act it out with a partner.**

Key: Learners' own answers

3 **Cora and Dora share their robots. What do you share?**

Key: Learners' own answers

4 **Look and read. Put a tick ✓or cross ✗.** page 65

Key: 2 ✓ 3 ✓ 4 ✓ 5 ✗ 6 ✗

1 5.17 **Read the question. Listen and write a name or a number. There are two examples.** page 66

Woman: Hello, Kim. Is this your doll?
Girl: Yes. Her name's Lucy.
Woman: Is that L-U-C-Y?
Girl: Yes, that's right.
Woman: How old is she?
Girl: She's nine.
Woman: Nine? She isn't a baby.

Can you see the answers? Now you listen and write a name or a number.

1 Woman: Does Lucy go to school?
Girl: Yes, she does. It's Green School.
Woman: Green School. Is that G-R-E-E-N?
Girl: Yes.
2 Woman: Are there lots of children in Lucy's class?
Girl: There are 18.
Woman: Pardon?
Girl: There are 18 children in the class.
3 Girl: Lucy sits next to a nice boy.
Woman: Does she? What's his name?
Girl: Matt.
Woman: Is that M-A-T-T?
Girl: Yes.
4 Girl: Lucy's got a lot of lessons today.
Woman: How many lessons has she got?
Girl: She's got 11.
Woman: 11 lessons? That is a lot.
5 Woman: Is Lucy's teacher nice?
Girl: Yes, he is.
Woman: What's his name?
Girl: Mr Fish. That's F-I-S-H.
Woman: Mr Fish? That's a funny name!

Key: 1 Green 2 18 3 Matt 4 11 5 Fish

1 **Play the game.** page 67

Learners play the game in groups of five or six. They need one dice, and a different coloured counter for each learner. Learners take turns to throw the dice and move their counter round the board, going along and up from IN to OUT. When they land on a picture, they say what they can see, e.g. *It's Grandma's eyes.* If they land on a ladder, they go up; if the land on a snake, they go down. The learner who finishes first is the winner.

Unit 6

1 6.14 **Where are they? Listen and match.** page 69

1 The cat's in the flowers.
2 Dan's in the car.
3 Alice is in the lorry.
4 Bill's on the motorbike.
5 The horse is under the tree.
6 Mark's in the bookshop.
7 Lucy's in the garden.
8 The dog's in the park.
9 Hugo's on the train.
10 Jill's on the bus.

Key: 2 f 3 j 4 h 5 c 6 e 7 b 8 a 9 g 10 i

2 6.15 **Listen and point. Then listen again and say.**

train, tail, plane, cake, table, grapes

3 6.16 **Listen again and colour the letters that make the /eɪ/ sound.**

/eɪ/ /eɪ/
train train plane plane table table
tail tail cake cake grapes grapes

Key: tail plane cake table grapes

1 6.17 **Listen, read and write the number.** page 70

See Pupil's Book page 70

Key: a 2 c 6 d 3 e 5 f 4

2 **What's in the lorry? Look and tick ✓ or cross ✗.**

Key: 2 ✓ 3 ✗ 4 ✗ 5 ✓

1 **Read and colour.** page 71

Key: Learners colour: car – purple, lorry – blue, bus stop – red, big train – green, small train – brown, three flowers – yellow, tree – green and brown

2 **Draw two more things in the picture. Listen to your friend and draw.**

Key: Learners' own answers and drawings

1 Write the words. page 72

Key: 2 monkey 3 giraffe 4 bear 5 crocodile
6 elephant 7 lizard 8 snake 9 polar bear
10 hippo 11 tiger 12 zebra

2 6.18 Listen and write a name or a number.

Man: Hello, children. My name's Mark and I'm your teacher today. What's your name?
Girl: It's May.
Man: How old are you, May?
Girl: I'm seven.

Man: Now we're at the monkey house. We've got nine monkeys.
Girl: Ooh, nine monkeys. Look at these monkeys. What's the small one's name?
Man: It's Matt.
Girl: That's a good name. 'Matt the monkey'. I like it. How old is he?
Man: He's one. He's very young.
Girl: Oh, he's only one. Is he next to his mum?
Man: No, that's his dad.
Girl: Oh, and what's his name?
Man: It's Hugo.
Girl: Ha ha ha. Hello, Hugo. Your boy's beautiful. How old is Hugo?
Man: Hugo's ten.
Girl: Ten. Ah. So he isn't an old monkey. Can we look at the snakes now, please?
Man: OK!

Key: 3 9 4 Matt 5 1 6 Hugo 7 10

1 Read and write the words. page 73

Key: 2 Let's 3 door 4 Let's 5 close 6 listen

1 Which animals live in the wild? Look and tick ✓. page 74

Key: 2 ✓ 4 ✓ 5 ✓ 7 ✓ 8 ✓ 9 ✓ 10 ✓

2 Where do the wild animals live? Write the words.

Key: jungle: chameleon grassland: zebra, giraffe
ice: penguin, polar bear ocean: whale, jellyfish

3 Read about the animals. Write the words. page 75

Key: 2 small 3 water 4 snakes 5 spiders
6 rhino 7 big 8 meat 9 trees

4 Choose an animal to learn about. Draw and write.

Key: Learners' own drawing and answers, e.g. This is an elephant. It is big and grey. It lives in grasslands. It can drink water with its trunk. It eats plants.

1 6.19 Listen and number the animals in order. page 76

See Pupil's Book pages 76–77

Key: a 8 b 3 c 2 d 7 e 4 f 9 g 5 h (1) i 6

2 Match the words that rhyme.

Key: 2 tree 3 day 4 zoo

3 Make your own zoo poem. Write the animals that you like at the zoo.

Key: Learners' own answers, e.g. I really like monkeys, I like lions too, But I really love the penguins, When I go to the zoo.

4 6.20 Listen and point. Then draw lines. page 77

Look at the big picture. This is a zoo. The boy is taking photos of the animals.
Where's the elephant?
Where's the zebra?
Where are the giraffes?
Where are the flowers?
Now look at the small pictures and draw lines.
Which is the monkey? I'm putting the monkey on the zebra.
Which is the bag? Put the bag on the girl.
Which are the bananas? Put the bananas next to the boy.
Which is the snake? Put the snake under the elephant.
Which is the balloon? Now you put the balloon on the tree.

Key: Learners draw lines: bag – on girl, bananas – next to boy, snake – under elephant, balloon – on tree

5 Ask and answer.

Key: Learners' own answers

1 Read this. Choose a word from the box. Write the correct word next to numbers 1–5. There is one example. page 78

Key: 1 tail 2 eyes 3 zoo 4 water 5 meat

1 Play the game. page 79

Learners play the game in groups of four to six. They need one dice, and a different coloured counter for each learner. They begin on the 'START' square. Learners take turns to throw the dice and move their counter round the board, counting as they go. When they land on a picture, they say what they see, e.g. *There are two trees in the park*. When they land on a square with text, they read it and follow the instruction, moving their counter forward or back to the corresponding picture. The learner who reaches the 'FINISH' square first is the winner.

Review Units 4–6

1 Find three words in a line from the same group. page 80

Key: 2 lizard, polar bear, tiger 3 motorbike, train, lorry 4 chocolate, chicken, meat

2 6.21 Listen and colour.

Look at the picture. Listen and look. There is one example.

Woman: Hello. Here's a picture of a toyshop.
Boy: Ooh. I've got my crayons.
Woman: Yes, good. Colour the balls.
Boy: OK.
Woman: Look at the ball next to the big yellow kite.
Boy: What colour is it?
Woman: It's purple. Colour the ball purple.

The ball next to the big yellow kite is purple. This is an example. Now you listen and colour.

1 Woman: Look at the ball under the blue radio. Colour it orange.
Boy: OK. The ball under the blue radio is orange.

2 Woman: Colour the ball on the computer now.
Boy: Pardon? The ball on the computer?
Woman: Yes. The ball on the computer. Have you got a yellow crayon?
Boy: Yes, I have.
Woman: Good. Colour it yellow.

3 Woman: Now, there's a ball under the board game.
Boy: Yes, it's here.
Woman: Good. Colour that ball pink, please.
Boy: A pink ball?
Woman: Yes … a pink ball under the board game.

4 Woman: Now find the ball next to the grey elephant.
Boy: The ball next to the grey elephant … OK! What colour is it?
Woman: It's blue. Have you got a blue crayon?
Boy: Yes, I have. The ball next to the grey elephant is blue.

5 Woman: There's a ball in the big red box.
Boy: In the big red box … Oh, yes. I've got it.
Woman: Good. Colour it green.
Boy: OK. A green ball in a red box. I like it.
Woman: Good. Now you've got a nice picture.

Key: Learners colour: ball under blue radio – orange, ball on computer – yellow, ball under board game – pink, ball next to grey elephant – blue, ball in big red box – green

3 Read and match. Colour. page 81

Key: Learners colour borders: 2 green 3 pink 4 red 5 purple 6 blue

4 Write.

Key: food: cake, meat transport: helicopter, lorry, plane wild animals: bear, crocodile, lizard other: dog, kite, robot

Unit 7

1 Read and match. page 83

Key: 2 d 3 g 4 c 5 b 6 a 7 f 8 h

2 7.16 Listen and say the rhyme.

My sister Sally likes salad and swimming,
but I like spiders, sausages and snakes! (x2)

1 Read and circle the correct word. page 84

Key: 2 singing 3 sock 4 feet 5 guitar 6 cleaning

2 Look and talk about the people and animals. Use the words in the box.

Key: Learners' own ideas, e.g. Tom is riding Harry. Rocky and Cameron are talking. Grandpa is walking. Rocky's brother and sister are singing. Gracie is smiling.

1 Look and read. Write *yes* or *no*. page 85

Key: 2 no 3 no 4 no 5 yes 6 no

2 Look and write the words.

Key: 1 am 2 aren't 3 isn't 4 is

1 Look and write the words. page 86

Key: 2 skateboard 3 basketball 4 badminton 5 baseball 6 running 7 hitting 8 kicking

2 7.17 Listen and colour.

1 Woman: Look at the children in the park.
Boy: Ooh, they're playing with a lot of balls.
Woman: Yes, they are. There are two boys. They're playing football. Can you see them?
Boy: Yes, I can. One's kicking the ball.
Woman: That's right. Colour their ball brown, please.
Boy: A brown football, OK.

2 Woman: Look at the girl playing hockey.
Boy: Yes, I can see her. She's running with the ball.
Woman: Yes, she is. Colour that ball green, please.
Boy: OK. She's hitting a green ball.

3 Woman: Can you see the boy playing with his small black dog?
Boy: Yes. He's throwing the ball. Can I colour that ball yellow? It's my favourite colour.
Woman: Yes, that's nice. He's throwing a yellow ball.

4 Woman: Look. There's a skateboard under that tree.
Boy: Yes, there is.
Woman: Can you colour the ball next to the skateboard, please?
Boy: Yes. What colour is it?
Woman: It's red. There's a red ball next to the skateboard.

5 Boy: There's a ball in the tree too.
Woman: Yes, there is. Can you colour it orange, please?

Boy: Oh! The small boy is sad. His orange ball's in the tree.
Woman: Yes, but the tree isn't big. His mum can get it for him.

6 Woman: Look at that happy boy. He wants to play baseball with his dad.
Boy: Yes. He's got a ball in his hand.
Woman: Yes, he has. Can you colour that ball grey, please?
Boy: OK. The boy's got a grey baseball in his hand.

Key: Learners colour: ball with girl playing hockey – green, ball with boy and dog – yellow, ball next to skateboard – red, ball in tree – orange, ball with boy and dad with baseball bat – grey

1 Write the words in the correct order. page 87

Key: 2 Can I throw the ball for your dog? 3 Can we eat some cake, please? 4 Can we go on the train, please? 5 Can I watch television, please? 6 Can we play badminton in the garden?

1 Play a mime game. Do and say. page 88

Learners play the game in pairs. One learner mimes an action and their partner says what they are doing. Then they swap roles.

2 What are they doing? Look, read and write.

Key: 2 Hugo 3 Andrea 4 running 5 jumping

3 Who is looking after their bodies? Look and tick ✓. page 89

Key: 2 ✓ 3 ✓ 4 ✓ 7 ✓ 8 ✓

4 How do you look after your body? Draw and write.

Key: Learners' own drawings and sentences, e.g. *I run and I drink water.*

1 Talk about what you think happens next in the story. page 90

Key: Learners' own ideas

2 Draw the next picture in the story.

Key: Learners' own drawings

3 Look at your drawing. Write a conversation.

Key: Learners' own ideas, e.g.
Oliver: Thank you, Alfie.
Alfie: That's OK. Let's play on the skateboard.
Oliver: OK. You go first.
Alfie: Thanks, Oliver. I like it! Now it's your turn.
Oliver: Thanks. It's fun.

4 Act out the conversation.

Learners act out their conversations from Activity 3 in pairs.

5 7.18 Listen and tick ✓. page 91

1 Woman: What's that little boy's name?
Boy: Alfie.
Woman: Has Alfie got a skateboard or a bike?
Boy: No, but he's got a football.

2 Girl: Is that your sister?
Oliver: Yes. That's Amelia.
Girl: Is she eight?
Oliver: She's nine and I'm seven.

3 Amelia: What's Oliver doing?
Man: He's playing with Alfie.
Amelia: Are they playing computer games?
Man: No, they're playing football.

4 Boy: Is Amelia sad?
Girl: She isn't sad, but she isn't happy.
Boy: Oh! Is she angry?
Girl: Yes, she is.

5 Woman: Oliver, where's your skateboard?
Oliver: I don't know. It isn't in the cupboard.
Woman: Is it under the tree?
Oliver: I can't see it there … Oh, no! It's in the water!

6 Amelia: Would you like some sweets, Alfie?
Alfie: No, thank you. I don't eat sweets, but can I have some ice cream, please?
Amelia: We haven't got any ice cream. Would you like a pear?
Alfie: No, thanks. I don't like them.

Key: 2 C 3 A 4 B 5 A 6 C

1 7.19 Listen and draw lines. There is one example. page 92

Look at the picture. Listen and look. There is one example.
Woman: Come and look at this picture of my class. The children are all doing hobbies. Can you see that girl there? Look … She's playing the piano.
Boy: Who is she?
Woman: That's Eva.
Boy: She's very good.
Woman: Yes. She loves playing the piano.
Can you see the line? This is an example. Now you listen and draw lines.

1 Boy: Where's Matt?
Woman: Can you find him? He's got a hockey lesson today.
Boy: Is that Matt, next to the door?
Woman: Yes, it is. He's got a big sports bag.
Boy: Oh, yes. I can see him.

2 Boy: And who's that girl? She's got very long hair.
Woman: Oh, that's Grace.
Boy: Is she listening to music?
Woman: Yes, she is.

3 Boy: Is Sam at home today?
Woman: No, she isn't. She's riding her horse. Can you see her photo?
Boy: Wow! Sam's on her black horse. It's beautiful!
Woman: You're right. It's very nice!

4 Boy: Who's that boy?

Woman: Which one?
Boy: The boy with red hair.
Woman: That's Nick. He loves skateboarding.
Boy: I can see that!

5 Boy: What's May doing?
Woman: May's playing the guitar.
Boy: Yes. She's got a new guitar.
Woman: Great … and that's my favourite hobby too.

Key: Learners draw lines: Matt – boy next to door with hockey kit, Nick – skateboarding, Grace – girl with very long hair listening to music, Sam – girl in photo riding horse, May – playing guitar

1 Play the game. page 93

Learners play the game in groups of three to five. They need one dice, and a different coloured counter for each learner. Learners take turns to throw the dice and move their counter round the board in the direction of the arrows. They begin on the 'START' square. When they land on a picture, the learner on their right asks *What's he/she doing?* or *What are they doing?* The learner describes the activity, e.g. *He's riding a bike*. If they say the sentence correctly, they stay on the square; if they say it incorrectly, they go back to their previous square. The learner who reaches 'FINISH' first is the winner.

Unit 8

1 (8.17) Listen and tick ✓ or cross ✗. page 95

1 Cameron: Jim's in the living room. He's watching television.
2 Cameron: Eva's reading a book in the bedroom.
3 Cameron: Grandma's in the dining room. She's eating an apple.
4 Cameron: Jenny's listening to music in the bathroom.
5 Cameron: Mr Friendly's in the bathroom. He's looking at his face in the mirror.
6 Cameron: Grandpa's in the kitchen. He's cleaning the floor.

Key: 2 ✓ 3 ✓ 4 ✗ 5 ✓ 6 ✗

2 (8.19) Listen and say. Then listen and match.

/ɪ/ living room
/aɪ/ dining room
1 lizard lizard
2 mirror mirror
3 kite kite
4 tiger tiger
5 ship ship
6 bag bag

Key: 2 living room 3 dining room 4 dining room 5 living room 6 dining room

1 (8.20) Listen, read and tick ✓ or cross ✗. page 96

See Pupil's Book page 96

Key: 2 ✓ 3 ✗ 4 ✗ 5 ✓ 6 ✗

2 What can you do? Look and say.

Key: Learners' own answers

1 (8.21) Listen and join. Then write. page 97

1 Hugo can play tennis.
2 Sam can swim.
3 Pat can play the piano.
4 May can ride a horse.
5 Tony can sing.
6 Alex can ride a bike.

Key: 2 f 3 c 4 b 5 a 6 d
2 Sam can swim. 3 Pat can play the piano.
4 May can ride a horse. 5 Tony can sing.
6 Alex can ride a bike.

3 Answer the questions. Write *Yes, I can* and *No, I can't*.

Key: Learner's own answers

1 Find and circle the words. Then say. page 98

Key: Across: phone, mirror, lamp, (photo)
Down: sofa, rug, clock, armchair, bed
Number 2 is a clock. Number 3 is a sofa. Number 4 is a lamp. Number 5 is a rug. Number 6 is a phone. Number 7 is an armchair. Number 8 is a mirror. Number 9 is a bed.

2 Look at the picture and read the questions. Write one-word answers.

Key: 2 boy 3 living 4 television 5 armchair 6 yellow 7 window

1 Read and draw lines. page 99

Key: Learners draw lines: 2 – in front of bath in bathroom
3 – between window and cupboard in kitchen
4 – on floor in front of television in living room
5 – behind armchair in living room
6 – between door and cupboard in bedroom

1 Write the words. page 100

Key: 2 hut 3 detached house 4 flat 5 ranch 6 houseboat

2 Read and match. page 101

Key: 1 c 2 b 3 a

3 Think about the house you want to live in. Draw and write.

Key: Learners' own drawings and texts, e.g. My house is a farm with 4 bedrooms. There are cows and sheep on the farm. There is a big garden and we can see the animals. I like it because I can ride horses and play football there.

1 Read and write the words. page 102

Key: 2 bounce 3 bath 4 table 5 clock 6 OK

2 Sue and Rob play with the ball in the house. That isn't a good idea! What can you do with your friends in the house? What can you do in the garden?

Key: Learners' own answers

3 Look at the pictures and read the questions. Write one-word answers. page 103

Key: 2 trains 3 table 4 car 5 sue 6 bed 7 Rob

1 8.22 Listen and colour. There is one example. page 104

Man: Look! The children are in the bathroom with their dad.
Girl: Yes! And I can see lots of cars too! Can I colour them?
Man: Yes! There's a car on the clock. Can you colour that one?
Girl: OK. What colour?
Man: Make the car on the clock red.

Can you see the red car on the clock? This is an example. Now you listen and colour.

1 Man: Colour the car in the bath now.
Girl: Sorry? The car in the bath?
Man: Yes. Have you got a blue crayon?
Girl: Yes, I have.
Man: Colour it with that crayon then, OK?

2 Man: And there's a car between the duck and the ball. Can you see it?
Girl: The car between the duck and the ball …? Yes! Can I colour it pink? I like that colour.
Man: OK – do that.
Girl: All right.

3 Man: Now, there's a car behind the dad.
Girl: Behind the dad … Oh, yes. I can see it.
Man: Would you like to colour it purple?
Girl: Yes, please! I love that colour!

4 Man: There's a car on the chair too.
Girl: I can't see it.
Man: Look – there's a toy elephant next to it.
Girl: Oh, yes.
Man: Colour that car green, please.

5 Man: Can you see the car with big windows?
Girl: Where is it?
Man: It's on the rug. Can you colour it yellow?
Girl: OK. I'm colouring it now.
Man: That's a very nice picture.

Key: Learners colour: car in bath – blue, car between duck and ball – pink, car behind dad – purple, car on chair next to elephant – green, car with big windows on rug – yellow

1 Play the game. page 105

Learners play the game in groups of four. They need one dice, and a different coloured counter for each learner (ideally purple, green, orange and yellow). They each start on a different bedroom square. The object of the game is for each player to collect items of furniture for their bedroom. They each write out the shopping list of items to collect. Learners take turns to throw the dice and move their counter clockwise round the board. When they land on a picture, the learner to their right asks *What have you got?* and the learner replies, e.g. *I've got a lamp for my bedroom*. The learner ticks the item off their shopping list. They continue until they have ticked off all the items on their list, and moved back to their bedroom square. The first learner to return to their bedroom is the winner.

Unit 9

1 Look and read. Write *yes* or *no*. page 107

Key: 2 no 3 yes 4 no 5 yes 6 yes 7 no 8 yes

2 9.15 Listen and point to the letter. Then say, match and write the letter.

j j	2 hand	5 horse
h h	3 hat	6 jacket
1 jeans	4 juice	7 hippo

Key: 2 hand 3 hat 4 juice 5 horse 6 jacket 7 hippo

1 9.16 Listen, read and correct. page 108

See Pupil's Book page 108

Key: 2 ~~eat~~ play 3 ~~toys~~ clothes 4 ~~mirror~~ table
5 ~~box~~ bag 6 ~~sofa~~ table

2 Act it out with a partner. Say and do. Use the words in the box.

Key: Learners' own answers, e.g. Clean the table. Put the pens on the table, please.

1 Look, read and write the number. page 109

Key: a 6 b 4 c (1) d 2 e 5 f 3

2 Write the words.

Key: 2 sunglasses 3 boots 4 trousers

1 Find and circle the words. Then write. page 110

Key: Across: (shell), beach, take a photo, fish, sea, sun, boat
Down: jellyfish, camera, sand
Diagonal: sunglasses
2 sea 3 beach 4 sand 5 boat 6 sun 7 camera
8 sunglasses 9 fish 10 take a photo 11 jellyfish

2 Read and colour.

Key: Learners colour: sand – yellow, camera – purple, shell – pink, sunglasses – green, boat – orange, sea – blue, fish – red

1 Read and write the words. page 111

Key: 1 T-shirt 2 radio 3 shells 4 sea 5 fish

1 Write the words. page 112

Key: 2 forest 3 beach 4 mountains

2 Draw a landscape from Activity 1. Draw and label four things you can see there.

Key: Learners' own answers, e.g. river, tree, rocks, mountain

3 Read the postcard and write the words. page 113

Key: 2 birds 3 trees 4 flowers 5 photos 6 bikes

4 Read again and write *yes* or *no*.

Key: 2 yes 3 no 4 yes 5 yes 6 yes

1 Number the pictures in order. Then tell the story. page 114

Key: a 2 b 4 c 3 d (1)
Learners' own answers, e.g. The monkey gives coconuts to the shark. The monkey jumps on the shark's back and the shark swims away. The shark says the king is ill and he needs a monkey's heart. The monkey says, 'Oh, no! I haven't got my heart!' The shark swims back to the tree. The monkey jumps off the shark's back. The shark waits. The monkey runs away.

2 Imagine you are the monkey or the shark in the story. What do you do next? Draw a picture. Write about your picture.

Key: Learners' own drawings and text

3 9.17 **Listen and colour.** page 115

1 Woman: Can you see the shark in the sea?
Boy: Yes, I can.
Woman: Right. Now colour it grey.
Boy: Pardon?
Woman: Colour the shark in the sea grey.

2 Woman: Now find the monkey in the tree.
Boy: It's giving fruit to the shark!
Woman: Yes, it is. What a funny monkey! Can you colour it brown?
Boy: Brown?
Woman: That's right.

3 Woman: Look at the girl on the beach.
Boy: OK. I can see her. Can I colour her dress?
Woman: Yes. Colour it blue.
Boy: OK. I really like her blue dress.

4 Woman: Can you see the bird on the boy's arm?
Boy: Pardon? Which bird?
Woman: The bird on the boy's arm. It's got a very long tail.
Boy: Oh, yes. I can see it.
Woman: Colour it green.
Boy: Right. I'm colouring it green now.

5 Woman: Look at the boy's clothes.
Boy: OK. He's wearing a T-shirt and shorts.
Woman: Yes. That's right. Colour his shorts yellow.
Boy: OK. Yellow shorts. I'm doing that now.

6 Woman: Can you see the bird under the monkey?
Boy: Yes. It's eating fruit.
Woman: Colour it red.
Boy: A red bird under the monkey?
Woman: That's right. Well done! The picture looks good now.

Key: Learners colour: monkey – brown, girl's dress – blue, bird on boy's arm – green, boy's shorts – yellow, bird under monkey – red

4 Ask and answer.

Key: It's a fish. It's a monkey. It's the sea.
Learner's own answers

1 Look at the pictures and read the questions. Write one-word answers. page 116

Key: 1 music 2 bird 3 apple 4 sleeping 5 cake

1 Play the game. page 117

Learners play the game in groups of four or five. They need one dice, and a different coloured counter for each learner. They begin on the START square. Learners take turns to throw the dice and move their counter round the board, following the arrows and counting as they go. When they land on a picture, the learner says if the people in the picture like or don't like the activity or object, e.g. *They like playing at the beach*. If they say the sentence correctly, they stay on the square; if they say it incorrectly, they go back to their previous square. If they land on a text square, they follow the instruction. The learner who reaches the FINISH square first is the winner.

Review Units 7–9

1 Write the words. page 118

Key: 1 bed 2 shoes, shell 3 jeans, jellyfish
4 photo, phone 5 boots, boat 6 sun, sand

2 Read and colour.

Key: Learners colour: skirt – red, jacket – blue, horse – black, shoes – purple, hat – orange, handbag – yellow

3 Read and complete. page 119

Key: 2 dress 3 camera 4 sand 5 bathroom
6 photo 7 sea 8 phone 9 ball 10 shell

4 Read and correct.

Key: 2 ~~like~~ don't like 3 ~~dancing~~ swimming 4 ~~enjoys~~ doesn't enjoy 5 ~~shoes~~ socks 6 ~~catching~~ throwing